Saves time and improves results!

Over 200,000 students use the award-winning MyLanguageLabs online learning and assessment system to succeed in their basic language courses. If your instructor has required use of MyChineseLab, you will have online access to an eText, an interactive Student Activities Manual, audio and video materials, and many more resources to help you succeed. For more information or to purchase access, visit www.mylanguagelabs.com.

A GUIDE TO *CHINESE LINK* ICON

 Text Audio Program

This icon indicates that recorded material to accompany *Chinese Link* is available in MyChineseLab, on audio CD, or the Companion Website.

Chinese Link

中 文 天 地

Zhōng　　Wén　　Tiān　　Dì

Intermediate Chinese

Second Edition

Level 2	Part 2

吴 素 美

Sue-mei Wu

于 月 明

Yueming Yu

Prentice Hall

Boston　Columbus　Indianapolis　New York　San Francisco　Upper Saddle River
Amsterdam　Cape Town　Dubai　London　Madrid　Milan　Munich　Paris　Montréal　Toronto
Delhi　Mexico City　São Paulo　Sydney　Hong Kong　Seoul　Singapore　Taipei　Tokyo

Executive Acquisitions Editor: Rachel McCoy
Editorial Assistant: Lindsay Miglionica
Executive Marketing Manager: Kris Ellis-Levy
Marketing Coordinator: William J. Bliss
Executive Editor, MyLanguageLabs: Bob Hemmer
Senior Media Editor: Samantha Alducin
Development Editor: Judy Wyman Kelly
Development Editor for Assessment: Melissa Marolla Brown
Media Editor: Meriel Martinez
Senior Managing Editor for Product Development: Mary Rottino
Associate Managing Editor: Janice Stangel
Production Project Manager: Manuel Echevarria
Senior Manufacturing and Operations Manager, Arts and Sciences: Nick Sklitsis
Operations Specialist: Brian Mackey
Senior Art Director: Pat Smythe
Text and Cover Designer: Wanda España, Wee Design Group
Cover Image: Jochen Helle
Full-Service Project Management: Margaret Chan, Graphicraft Limited
Printer/Binder: Courier/Kendallville
Cover Printer: Lehigh-Phoenix Color/Hagerstown
Publisher: Phil Miller

Credits and acknowledgments borrowed from other sources and reproduced, with permission, in this textbook appear on page xxiv.

This book was set in 12/15 Sabon by Graphicraft Ltd., Hong Kong, and was printed and bound by Courier – Westford. The cover was printed by Phoenix Color Corp.

Library of Congress Cataloging-in-Publication Data

Wu, Sue-mei, 1968–
 Chinese link : intermediate Chinese, level 2, part 2 / Sue-mei Wu, Yueming Yu = [Zhong wén tian dì / Wu Suemei, Yu Yueming].
  p. cm.
 Parallel title also in Chinese characters.
 Includes index.
 ISBN 978-0-205-78279-6 (alk. paper)
 1. Chinese language—Textbooks for foreign speakers—English. I. Yu, Yueming, 1944– II. Title. III. Title: Intermediate Chinese. IV. Title: Zhong wén tian dì.
 PL1129.E5C4196 2012
 495.1'82421—dc22

2010044813

Printed in the United States of America
10 9 8 7 6 5 4 3 2 1

Prentice Hall
is an imprint of

www.pearsonhighered.com

ISBN 10: 0-205-78279-5
ISBN 13: 978-0-205-78279-6

目錄 (目录) CONTENTS

Scope and Sequence — 範圍和順序(范围和顺序) — vii

Preface — 前言(前言) — xiii

Acknowledgments — 致謝(致谢) — xxi

Abbreviations of Parts of Speech — 詞類簡稱(词类简称) — xxiii

Lesson 11 Caring for Others — 第十一課 關心他人 / 第十一课 关心他人 — 321

Lesson 12 Expressing Thanks and Appreciation — 第十二課 感謝和感激 / 第十二课 感谢和感激 — 357

Review Lesson 11 to Lesson 12 — 復習 第十一課至第十二課 / 复习 第十一课至第十二课 — 393

Lesson 13 Expressing Anger — 第十三課 生氣 / 第十三课 生气 — 395

Lesson 14 Prose and Poetic Expressions — 第十四課 散文和詩情表達 / 第十四课 散文和诗情表达 — 431

Review Lesson 13 to Lesson 14 — 復習 第十三課至第十四課 / 复习 第十三课至第十四课 — 466

Lesson 15 Music – Review — 第十五課 音樂-復習 / 第十五课 音乐-复习 — 469

Lesson 16 Etiquette and Manners — 第十六課 讚美與客套 / 第十六课 赞美与客套 — 501

Review Lesson 15 to Lesson 16 — 復習 第十五課至第十六課 / 复习 第十五课至第十六课 — 539

Lesson 17 Applying for a Job — 第十七課 申請工作 / 第十七课 申请工作 — 543

Lesson 18 The Interview
第十八課 面談
第十八课 面談   573

Review Lesson 17 to Lesson 18
復習 第十七課至第十八課
复习 第十七课至第十八课   604

Lesson 19 Choosing a Job
第十九課 選擇工作
第十九课 选择工作   607

Lesson 20 After Graduation – Review
第二十課 畢業以後-復習
第二十课 毕业以后-复习   637

Review Lesson 19 to Lesson 20
復習 第十九課至第二十課
复习 第十九课至第二十课   665

Traditional/Simplified Character Table
繁簡體字對照表
繁简体字对照表   A1

English Translations of Language in Use
課文英文翻譯(课文英文翻译)   A3

Language in Use with Pinyin
課文拼音(课文拼音)   A14

Pinyin Glossary
拼音索引(拼音索引)   A50

English Glossary
英文索引(英文索引)   A62

Characters in the Character Book
寫字簿的生字(写字簿的生字) A75

範圍和順序 (范围和顺序)
SCOPE AND SEQUENCE

Lessons & Topics 課程 & 主題 (课程 & 主题)	Objectives & Communications 教學目標 & 交際活動 (教学目标 & 交际活动)	Grammar 語法要點 (语法要点)	Idiom Story 成語故事 (成语故事)	Media Literacy 媒體文字通 (媒体文字通)	Culture Link 文化知識 (文化知识)
11 **Caring for Others** 關心他人 (关心他人) *p. 321*	■ Express concern for others ■ Respond when others show concern for you ■ Describe an unpleasant situation	I. Passive sentences 被動句(被动句) A. Unmarked in structure (notional passive sense) B. Marked in structure with 被, 叫, or 讓(让) II. 被 sentences versus 把 sentences	A bird frightened by the mere twang of a bow 驚弓之鳥 (惊弓之鸟)	Fee for designating specific doctor(s) to perform the surgery 手術點名費 (手术点名费)	**Culture Notes:** How the Chinese show concern for others 中國人怎麼表示對他人的關心 (中国人怎么表示对他人的关心) **Fun with Chinese:** Saying: 打是親, 罵是愛。(打是亲, 骂是爱。) **Let's Go:** Personal medicine bag 隨身藥包(随身药包)
12 **Expressing Thanks and Appreciation** 感謝和感激 (感谢和感激) *p. 357*	■ Express appreciation ■ Reply to/accept another's thanks ■ Describe a cause-and-effect situation ■ Describe a conditional situation ■ Write thank-you notes and invitations	I. Compound sentences 複合句 (复合句) A. Cause-and-effect conjunctions and their compound sentences 因果連詞和因果複合句 (因果连词和因果复合句) B. Conditional conjunctions and their compound sentences 條件連詞和條件複合句 (条件连词和条件复合句)	Pulling up the seedling to help it grow 拔苗助長 (拔苗助长)	Friends are an excellent remedy 朋友是良藥 (朋友是良药)	**Culture Notes:** Giving gifts and thanks 送禮和感謝(送礼和感谢) **Fun with Chinese:** Saying: 悔不當初 (悔不当初) **Let's Go:** Mailing a package 寄包裹 (寄包裹)

Lessons & Topics 課程 & 主題 (课程 & 主题)	Objectives & Communications 教學目標 & 交際活動 (教学目标 & 交际活动)	Grammar 語法要點 (语法要点)	Idiom Story 成語故事 (成语故事)	Media Literacy 媒體文字通 (媒体文字通)	Culture Link 文化知識 (文化知识)
13 **Expressing Anger** 生氣(生气) *p. 395*	■ Express anger and make complaints ■ Reply and listen to anger and complaints ■ Seek and provide advice	I. Pivotal constructions 兼語句 (兼语句) II. Causative sentences and pivotal constructions 使動用法和兼語句(使动用法和兼语句) III. Summary of interjections 感嘆詞 (感叹词)	Shooting two hawks with one arrow 一箭雙鵰 (一箭双雕)	The strange scene on Xi'an's highway 西安高速公路奇景 (西安高速公路奇景)	**Culture Notes:** Chinese fortune telling: another way to seek advice 算命(算命) **Fun with Chinese:** Saying: 吃虧是福 (吃亏是福) **Let's Go:** The lunar calendar 農民曆 (农民历)
14 **Prose and Poetic Expressions** 散文和詩情表達(散文和诗情表达) *p. 431*	■ Compose a prose essay ■ Sharpen verbal and written communication skills ■ Connect two verbal expressions ■ Express or accept an apology	I. Onomatopoeic words as adverbials or attributives 擬聲詞當修飾語(拟声词当修饰语) II. Conjunction 既……又 III. Summary of topic-comment sentences	To show mutual concern for people in the same boat 同舟共濟 (同舟共济)	Essential principles for a married couple: apologies and good communication 夫妻之道：道歉及溝通 (夫妻之道：道歉及沟通)	**Culture Notes:** Famous modern Chinese prose writers 中國有名的現代散文作家(中国有名的现代散文作家) **Fun with Chinese:** Saying: 急中生智 (急中生智) **Let's Go:** A rainy scene 雨中即景 (雨中即景)

Lessons & Topics 課程 & 主題 (课程 & 主题)	Objectives & Communications 教學目標 & 交際活動 (教学目标 & 交际活动)	Grammar 語法要點 (语法要点)	Idiom Story 成語故事 (成语故事)	Media Literacy 媒體文字通 (媒体文字通)	Culture Link 文化知識 (文化知识)
15 Music – Review 音樂–復習 (音乐–复习) *p. 469*	■ Request favors and respond to requests for favors ■ Understand Chinese omissions ■ Format email messages ■ Review—passive sentences and conjunctions	I. Review: Passive sentences II. Review: Conjunctions (1) III. Omissions in Chinese	To mend the stall after a sheep is lost 亡羊補牢 (亡羊补牢)	Saving pandas 拯救熊貓 (拯救熊猫)	**Culture Notes:** Traditional and contemporary music 傳統和現代音樂(传统和现代音乐) **Fun with Chinese:** Saying: 有驚無險 (有惊无险) **Let's Go:** Art performance 藝術演出 (艺术演出)
16 Etiquette and Manners 讚美與客套 (赞美与客套) *p. 501*	■ Give and reply to compliments ■ Say goodbye to guests and hosts in an appropriate manner ■ Use emphasis in conversations	I. Emphasis in Chinese sentences II. Summary: Serial verb constructions	To beat the drum once to boost morale 一鼓作氣 (一鼓作气)	Do kids really need to attend after-school learning centers? 補習班真的非上不可嗎? (补习班真的非上不可吗?)	**Culture Notes:** Chinese Etiquette 中國的客套話 (中国的客套话) **Fun with Chinese:** Saying: 禮多人不怪(礼多人不怪) **Let's Go:** Invitation to a university anniversary celebration 校慶請柬 (校庆请柬)

Lessons & Topics 課程 & 主題 (课程 & 主题)	Objectives & Communications 教學目標 & 交際活動 (教学目标 & 交际活动)	Grammar 語法要點 (语法要点)	Idiom Story 成語故事 (成语故事)	Media Literacy 媒體文字通 (媒体文字通)	Culture Link 文化知識 (文化知识)
17 **Applying for a Job** 申請工作 (申请工作) *p. 543*	■ Ask a rhetorical question ■ Describe procedures ■ Compose a Chinese résumé	I. Rhetorical questions II. Words and expressions indicating procedures	A person in the State of Qi worries that the sky may fall 杞人憂天 (杞人忧天)	Number of people seeking jobs rises in the third quarter 三季度求職人數上升 (三季度求职人数上升)	**Culture Notes:** The surge in Chinese students studying overseas 中國大學生的出國熱(中国大学生的出国热) **Fun with Chinese:** Saying: 萬事俱備，只欠東風 (万事俱备，只欠东风) **Let's Go:** Résumé/ Curriculum Vitae (C.V.) 個人簡歷 (个人简历)
18 **The Interview** 面談(面谈) *p. 573*	■ Market oneself for a job interview ■ Participate in a job interview ■ Review conjunctions ■ Express approximation	I. Review: Conjunctions (2) II. Expressions indicating approximation	To pretend to play a musical instrument in a group just to round out the number 濫竽充數 (滥竽充数)	Opening ceremony for college graduate employment services week 高校畢業生就業服務周開幕(高校毕业生就业服务周开幕)	**Culture Notes:** The service industry in China 中國的第三產業(中国的第三产业) **Fun with Chinese:** Saying: 毛遂自薦 (毛遂自荐) **Let's Go:** Job services advertisement 招聘廣告 (招聘广告)

Lessons & Topics 課程 & 主題 (课程 & 主题)	Objectives & Communications 教學目標 & 交際活動 (教学目标 & 交际活动)	Grammar 語法要點 (语法要点)	Idiom Story 成語故事 (成语故事)	Media Literacy 媒體文字通 (媒体文字通)	Culture Link 文化知識 (文化知识)
19 **Choosing a Job** 選擇工作 (选择工作) *p. 607*	■ Describe choices ■ Express agreement or disagreement ■ Use emphasis ■ Discuss job benefits	I. Adverbs expressing tone of voice/mood: 卻(却), 倒, 到底(究竟/終究)[(究竟/终究)] II. Conjunction 固然 III. Emphasis in Chinese sentences 非……不可	Saiweng lost his horse 塞翁失馬 (塞翁失马)	Narrating the story of what you encountered on the job market 講述你職場中的故事 (讲述你职场中的故事)	**Culture Notes:** Foreign businesses in China 中國的外資企業(中国的外资企业) **Fun with Chinese:** Saying: 百尺竿頭，更進一步。(百尺竿头，更进一步。) **Let's Go:** Bank advertisement 銀行廣告 (银行广告)
20 **After Graduation – Review** 畢業以後–復習(毕业以后–复习) *p. 637*	■ Ask for advice ■ Talk about the future ■ Review conjunctions ■ Review prepositions	I. Review: Conjunctions (3) 與其……不如 (与其……不如)，即使……也……，既然……就……，……，以免…… II. Review: Prepositions 對(对), 為(为), 給(给)	To show off one's carpentry skills in front of Lu Ban 班門弄斧 (班门弄斧)	Nursing major favored by male students 高校護理專業受到男生青睞(高校护理专业受到男生青睞)	**Culture Notes:** Employment of university graduates in China 中國大學畢業生的就業情況(中国大学毕业生的就业情况) **Fun with Chinese:** Saying: 吃得苦中苦，方為人上人。(吃得苦中苦，方为人上人。) **Let's Go:** Letter of Recommendation 推薦信(推荐信)

Appendices

Traditional/Simplified Character Table 繁簡體字對照表(繁简体字对照表) *p. A1*

English Translations of Language in Use 課文英文翻譯(课文英文翻译) *p. A3*

Language in Use with Pinyin 課文拼音(课文拼音) *p. A14*

Pinyin Glossary 拼音索引(拼音索引) *p. A50*

English Glossary 英文索引(英文索引) *p. A62*

Characters in the Character Book 寫字簿的生字(写字簿的生字) *p. A75*

前言（前言） PREFACE

CHINESE LINK: Zhongwen Tiandi 中文天地 (Intermediate Chinese) serves as the intermediate level in the *Chinese Link*: 中文天地 program. This series systematically emphasizes and integrates the "5Cs" principles of the National Standards for Foreign Language Education—Communication, Cultures, Comparisons, Connections, and Communities—throughout the program.

The intermediate curriculum encompasses 20 lessons. It is designed to be completed in an academic year of college-level study. This intermediate level program is designed to be well linked to the introductory level program by continuing to provide a practical, learner-centered, and enjoyable language and culture learning experience for intermediate level Chinese learners, as well as an efficient and comprehensive teaching resource for instructors.

While learners of Chinese at the intermediate level need to continue to build their mastery of commonly used vocabulary and grammatical structures, they also need to begin to train for advanced level language usage. Thus, there are two main goals for the intermediate level program:

1. The first goal is to continue to systematically build learners' abilities in the four skills of listening, speaking, reading, and writing so that they can reach the intermediate level of competence. The content and exercises in the intermediate level program build upon what has been studied in the introductory level program, gradually adding more sophisticated vocabulary and grammatical structures. Frequent consolidation and review exercises are included.

2. The second goal is to help the learners to get ready for advanced Chinese study by introducing formal and written expressions and increasing students' "media literacy." This is accomplished by providing exposure to common Chinese idioms and the stories behind them, and by including texts written in the style of newspaper, magazines, and Internet news articles.

What's New to this Edition

Thanks to the many instructors and students who provided valuable feedback on the first edition, the second edition incorporates several new features that we believe will make the materials more effective and easier to use. These new features are highlighted below:

1. In General

- Lessons have been revisited to provide greater balance among lessons, add more review and recycling of materials, enhance consistency, and emphasize student outcomes. More engaging and communicative exercises for learners have been added, and several of the Culture Notes have been updated.

2. Full-Color Design

- The use of a full-color design makes the text more appealing to today's learners by providing them with realistic images of China today and provides a clear delineation between various items within the chapter.

3. Lesson Opener

- Opening photos have been updated to show students more contemporary photos of China that also highlight the theme of the chapter.
- A new "Connections and Communities Preview" section has been added to help learners make connections to their daily life and build links among their communities. Questions focus on the lesson and Culture Link themes.

4. Sentence Patterns

- Key grammar points in the Sentence Pattern section are now highlighted to show the grammar in context and make it more explicit for the students.

5. Language Notes

- "Language Notes" are now in the margin next to the "Language in Use" dialogues, rather than in a separate section, to make them easier for students to reference while reading the dialogue.

6. Grammar

- Grammar explanations have been simplified to help learners more easily understand concepts.
- A new "Try it!" section has been added to provide guided communicative practice and reinforcement immediately following grammar presentation.

7. Supplementary Practice

- New questions have been added to aid students' reading comprehension of the supplementary texts.

8. Activities

- Activities have been updated and additional communicative activities have been added to the end of each chapter to support the aim of the text to help develop students' communicative competence.

9. Culture Notes

- Culture Notes, thematically linked to the content of the lesson, have been updated with new information and some new topics to ensure they will be of interest to today's students.
- A "Do You Know . . ." section of introductory questions has been added before the reading to engage student motivation, attention, and interest before reading the Culture Notes.
- Comparison questions following the reading help learners compare their own culture to Chinese culture and discuss the differences or similarities. Questions also encourage discussion on issues related to the readings and lesson's theme.

- Photos have been updated to present scenes related to the reading. Captions encourage students to reflect upon the information learned in the reading.

10. Fun with Chinese

- New activity questions have been added to highlight familiar words in the sayings and to help students to connect real-life situations with the sayings.

11. Let's Go!

- Information and activities have been updated to further the connection to the lesson's theme.

12. Student Activities Manual

- The *Student Activities Manual* incorporates listening, character, grammar, and comprehensive exercises into each lesson's homework.
- Situational dialogues have been created for each lesson to incorporate themes, expressions, and pragmatic settings of the lesson. Dialogues also contain some vocabulary and expressions that students have not yet studied.
- More challenging and authentic materials have been added to the listening exercises. The situational dialogues will challenge students from the very beginning and help them develop the skill of picking out useful information, even if they don't fully understand everything they hear. This helps develop an important survival skill for students who will encounter real life settings in Chinese societies through study abroad, travel, or interaction with Chinese communities in their own countries.
- A new "Progress Checklist" has been added to the end of each SAM chapter so that students can monitor their progress and the accomplishment of lesson goals and language competencies in each lesson.

13. Character Book

- The character exercises have been put into a separate volume to make it more convenient and efficient for students to work with characters.
- The *Character Book* provides the Chinese characters for the core vocabulary in every lesson to help student practice writing chinese characters.
- Both traditional and simplified characters are included, thus making the learning of both forms easy for the students.
- Blank boxes are also included for students to practice writing the character.
- As a handy reference, four **types of glossaries** are provided in the Character Book: (1) By number of strokes; (2) By Lesson number; (3) Alphabetical by Pinyin; (4) Common Radicals.

14. MyChineseLab™

- My **MyChineseLab™**, part of the award-winning Pearson's MyLanguageLabs™ suite, is a nationally hosted online learning system created for students and instructors of language courses. It brings together, in one convenient, easily navigable site, a wide array of language-learning tools and resources, including an electronic interactive version of the *Chinese Link* student text, *Student Activities Manual*, downloadable PDFs of the

Character Book, a file of the artwork in the text, and all materials from the audio programs. Readiness checks, chapter tests, and grammar tutorials personalize instruction to meet the unique needs of individual students. Instructors can use the system to make assignments, set grading parameters, listen to student-created audio recordings, and provide feedback on student work. Instructor access codes to MyChineseLab™ are available for purchase. Take a tour! Visit www.mylanguagelabs.com.

Features of CHINESE LINK: 中文天地 (Intermediate Chinese)

- The 5Cs (**National Standards**) are addressed consistently throughout the content, exercises, and homework in the intermediate level program.
- **Clearly and systematically linked** to the introductory level program. This helps Chinese learners reuse and review what they have learned, as well as continue to develop their skills in listening, speaking, reading, and writing for daily communication.
- **Topics** are selected to be **interesting and practical** from the students' point of view. Topics in the intermediate level program are expanded to **more abstract** and **more societal phenomena** to help learners better understand current Chinese society and be able to discuss, compare, and analyze cultural differences. Learners will also be exposed to various communicative situations that require them to develop and use skills such as basic summary, description, discussion, debate, and report.
- While equal emphasis is still given to both vocabulary and grammatical structures, students are guided to write **longer and more cohesive essays** in Chinese.
- Students learn to build from words and phrases, to sentences and cohesive passages, and then to application in **communicative tasks.**
- The **grammar points** and **core vocabulary** are presented naturally in the main texts. The main texts, in turn, provide model situations in which the grammar and vocabulary for each lesson are integrated into **realistic** communicative situations.
- Care has been taken to indicate regional differences in Chinese societies in expressions, pronunciation, and culture notes.

Highlights of the Differences between the Introductory and Intermediate Level Programs

Much of the lesson structure and pedagogical strategy of the introductory program has been incorporated in the intermediate level program. Key differences between these programs are summarized below:

- In the intermediate level the texts and examples are provided in both traditional and simplified characters in order to accommodate different users' needs and preferences.
- In order to help the learners become accustomed to reading Chinese characters without phonetic transliteration, in the intermediate level the Pinyin has been removed from under the characters in the core lesson texts. However, a Pinyin version of Language In Use section has been placed in an appendix for reference.

- An *Idiom Story* passage is provided as an interesting way to introduce Chinese history and traditions and expose learners to important formal and written expressions. Exercises are provided and are designed to link the learner's comprehension of the text to his/her personal experiences and opinions.
- *Media Literacy* is promoted in the intermediate level textbook through various channels such as idiom stories and articles written in the style of newspapers, magazines, and the internet.
- Review lessons follow every two lessons. These are specifically designed as grammar summary, review, and consolidation lessons. They require learners to apply what they have learned to interesting and practical communicative situations.

Organization of the Textbook

The intermediate level program is divided into two volumes: Level 2, Part 1 (Lesson 1 to Lesson 10) and Level 2, Part 2 (Lesson 11 to Lesson 20). Both volumes contain the **Core lessons** and **Appendices**.

Core Lessons

- **Lesson Opening:** Lesson objectives, related photo, and *Connections and Communities Preview* section.

The major sections of each lesson are described below:

- Core Vocabulary: Core vocabulary terms, which appear in the **Language Link** section, are introduced here. For each vocabulary item, traditional and simplified character forms are presented along with Pinyin pronunciation, grammatical function, and English meaning. This section also points out differences between Mainland China and Taiwan usage.
- Language Link: This section contains situations that incorporate the lesson's core vocabulary and grammar points. It is accompanied by an art program that adds context and makes the lesson more interesting. **Language Link** serves as a model of the correct usage of the vocabulary and grammar points introduced in the lesson. Notes are provided to further explain the text. For most of the lessons, **Language Link** includes dialogues; for some selections it includes essays, diaries, e-mail, and letters. The length of **Language Link** is carefully controlled, and gradually increases to provide pedagogical sufficiency and challenge.
- Grammar: Core Grammar points from **Language Link** are explained in this section. A broad variety of more advanced grammar points and expressions is introduced in order to strengthen students' ability to express themselves in Chinese. The **Grammar** section contains many examples and summary tables to organize the information for students. The intermediate level program also emphasizes frequent and systematic **review**, **summarization**, and **consolidation** of grammatical structures throughout the content and exercises.
- Supplementary Practice: Each lesson has a **Supplementary Practice** section with themes, vocabulary, and grammar similar to those found in **Language Link**. This allows students to practice immediately what they have learned from their study of the main text. Care has

been taken to use a different format from that found in **Language Link**. For example, if **Language Link** contains a dialogue, **Supplementary Practice** will include a prose format, and vice versa. The pedagogical purpose is to help students learn to use vocabulary and grammar structures in varying forms of communication.

- **Idiom Story** is carefully chosen and written to consolidate the core grammar points of that lesson. Its purpose is to introduce students to the rich Chinese cultural and literary tradition while reviewing what they have learned in yet another interesting way.

- **Media Literacy** texts, which are incorporated into Lessons 11–20, are short texts written in the style of newspapers, magazines, and Internet news articles. These texts introduce students to the formal grammatical structures common in these written genres. **Exercises** in this section include text skimming, comparing written and spoken expressions, translation, and finding examples of the lesson's grammar points in the article. This section will not only promote students' media literacy skills, but will also give them motivation and confidence toward becoming life-long independent readers of Chinese.

- **Activities:** This section is designed primarily for classroom use. Listening, character, grammar, and communicative exercises are included throughout the text. Care has been taken to provide balance between structural drills and real-life communicative tasks. The exercises integrate with the grammar points to provide a systematic extension of usage skills from vocabulary-item level to sentence level and on to discourse-level narration and description. Since these exercises are for class meeting time, they are designed to be dynamic and interactive. Most involve interaction between instructor and students, student and student, or group and group. Communicative activities are based on situations designed to elicit the grammar points and vocabulary students have learned in the lesson and in prior lessons. Visual aids are provided to help set the context for the communicative activities. Our goal in providing classroom exercises is to help save instructor time, which makes the text convenient and efficient for instructors to use.

- **Culture Link:** This section contains three components:
  - **Culture Notes:** The topics of the **Culture Notes** are carefully chosen to relate to those of the core lessons. It is hoped that the **Culture Notes** will help students to better understand Chinese societies, as well as how language reflects culture. Authentic photos are provided to create a vivid and interesting learning experience. The discussion questions are designed to encourage students to discuss and compare cultural differences by helping them to be aware of the features of their own culture while gaining understanding of other cultures.
  - **Fun with Chinese:** This section introduces a common slang expression, an idiom, or a motto that either utilizes new vocabulary presented in the lesson or is closely related to the theme of the lesson. Drawings are included to help students better understand the content in an eye-catching way. Discussion questions are provided to offer another fun way to relate the common Chinese expressions to the theme of the lesson.
  - **Let's Go!:** This section gives students an opportunity to interact with Chinese in an authentic context. It assists the students to connect themselves to authentic Chinese societies and communities. This section promotes students' motivation and helps them develop survival skills for life in authentic Chinese societies.

Appendices

The appendices serve as a learning resource for both students and teachers. They can also be used for review exercises in class or for self-study. The Appendices include the following:

- Traditional/Simplified Character Table
- English Translations of Language in Use
- Language in Use with Pinyin
- Glossaries (Pinyin and English)
- Characters in the Character Book

Program Components

Instructor Resources

Instructor's Resource Manual

The **Instructor's Resource Manual** provides sample syllabi, daily schedules, and the answer keys for in-class and homework exercises. This manual is available for download on the Instructor Resource Center (IRC) and MyChineseLab to qualified adopters. Upon adoption or to preview the online resources, please go to PearsonSchool.com/Access_Request and select "Online Teacher Supplements." You will be required to complete a one-time registration subject to verification. Upon verification of educator status, access information and instructions will be sent via e-mail.

Testing Program

A highly flexible testing program allows instructors to customize tests by selecting the modules they wish to use or by changing individual items. This complete testing program, available in electronic format via the IRC and MyChineseLab includes quizzes, chapter tests, and comprehensive examinations that tests speaking, reading, and writing skills as well as grammar, vocabulary, and cultural knowledge. For all elements in the testing program, detailed grading guidelines are provided.

Student Resources

Student Activities Manual

The **Student Activities Manual** contains homework assignments for each lesson in the main textbook. Homework activities are divided among listening, character recognition and writing, grammar exercises, and communicative tasks.

Character Book

The **Character Book** provides the Chinese characters for the core vocabulary in every lesson. It shows the following for each character:

1. Character with its stroke order indicated by numbers.
2. Traditional form of the character.
3. Simplified form of the character.
4. Pinyin pronunciation, grammatical usage, and sample sentences or phrases.

5. Stroke order illustrated by writing the character progressively.

6. Radical of the character with its Pinyin pronunciation and meaning.

7. Dotted graph lines to aid students' practice.

Blank boxes are also included for students to practice writing the character. As a handy reference, four types of glossaries are provided in the Character Book: (1) By number of strokes; (2) By Lesson number; (3) Alphabetical by Pinyin; (4) Common Radicals.

Audio Materials

The audio recording for all the lesson's texts, vocabulary, listening exercises, as well as listening exercises in the Student Activities Manual are provided in audio program either via the CW, CD's, or MyChineseLab.

Online Resources

Companion Web site, <www.pearsonhighered.com/chineselink>

This open-access robust site offers the resources to accompany the text, including parts of the audio program.

MyChineseLab™

Over 200,000 students use the award-winning MyLanguageLabs online learning and assessment system to succeed in their basic language courses. If your instructor has required use of MyChineseLab, you will have online access to an eText, an interactive Student Activities Manual, audio and video materials, and many more resources to help you succeed. For more information or to purchase access, visit www.mylanguagelabs.com.

致謝 (致谢)　ACKNOWLEDGMENTS

We are very happy to complete the *Chinese Link*: 中文天地 (Intermediate Chinese), second edition. We would like to take this opportunity to thank many individuals who offered us support, suggestions, and encouragement, all of which led to the improvement and development of this edition.

We are especially grateful to the folks at Pearson Education's World Languages team for bringing their talent and professional publishing experience to the *Chinese Link* project. Many thanks to: Rachel McCoy, Executive Acquisitions Editor, for her commitment and confidence to the Chinese Link program; Phil Miller, Publisher, for his support of Chinese Link; and Lindsay Miglionica, Editorial Assistant, for helping with every aspect of preparing the revision and ensuring the manuscripts were ready for production. Mary Rottino, Senior Managing Editor for Product Development, Janice Stangel, Associate Managing Editor, and Manuel Echevarria, Production Project Manager, have been wonderful conduits for channeling the vision of the second edition through development and into the final phase of production. Thanks also to Meriel Martinez, Media Editor, for carefully overseeing the production of the Audio program and Companion Web Site; Melissa Marolla Brown, Development Editor for Assessment, for providing guidance in preparing various manuscripts for MyChineseLab™; Samantha Alducin, Senior Media Editor, and Bob Hemmer, Executive Editor for MyLanguageLabs, for their skillful management of the excellent media products in MyChineseLab™; and Judy Wyman Kelly, Development Editor, who provided some suggestions that enabled this second edition to be more outstanding than the first. And a big thanks to our marketing team for their wonderful promotion of the second edition, Kris Ellis-Levy, Executive Marketing Manager, and William J. Bliss, Marketing Coordinator.

Our sincere appreciation goes to Margaret Chan, Project Manager, and her Graphicraft team members. Their hard work and dedication helped this project to reach final production. Thanks to Mark Haney for his assistance with English proofreading of the manuscript during the many different stages of preparation. With Mark's devotion and patience, the *Chinese Link* project moved along smoothly.

We wish to thank our families, without whose love and support this project would not have been possible. Many thanks to our husbands, Mark and Denny, for their patience and support. Thanks also to the *Chinese Link* Program lead author, Dr. Sue-mei Wu's children, Carrie, Marion, and baby Kevin, for their love and for giving up a lot of time with their mom so that this project could be completed.

We extend our sincere thanks and appreciation to the colleagues who reviewed the manuscript and provided valuable input. Their detailed comments and insightful suggestions helped us to further refine our manuscript.

Hsiu-hsien Chan – Yale University
Pei-Chia Chen – University of California, San Diego
Matthew B. Christensen – Brigham Young University

Doris Chun – City College of San Francisco

I-Ping Fu – Radford University & Virginia Tech

Wayne Wenchao He – The University of Rhode Island

Michael Gibbs Hill – University of South Carolina

Wenze Hu – US Naval Academy, MD

Alexander C. Y. Huang – Pennsylvania State University

Dela Xiao Jiao – New York University

Julia Hongwei Kessel – New Trier High School, IL

Wen-Chao Li – San Francisco State University

Hua-Fu Liu – San Jose City College

Weihsun Mao – Ohlone College

Kitty Shek – San Joaquin Delta College

Chao-mei Shen – Rice University, TX

Cindy Lee Shih – University of Arizona, Tucson

Mary-Ann Stadtler-Chester – Framingham State College, MA

Hongyin Tao – University of California, Los Angeles

Jean Wu – University of Oregon

Yun Xiao – Bryant University

John Yu – The City University of New York, Baruch College

Zheng-sheng Zhang – San Diego State University

Sue-mei Wu 吳素美, Ph.D.
Lead author of *Chinese Link*
Teaching Professor of Chinese Studies
Carnegie Mellon University

詞類簡稱 (词类简称)
ABBREVIATIONS OF PARTS OF SPEECH

Adj.	= adjective	形容詞(形容词) [xíngróngcí]	e.g., 好 [hǎo] (good) 美 [měi] (beautiful)
Adv.	= adverb	副詞(副词) [fùcí]	e.g., 很 [hěn] (very) 也 [yě] (also)
Aux.	= auxiliary verb (helping verb)	助動詞(助动词) [zhùdòngcí]	e.g., 會(会) [hui] (can)
Conj.	= conjunction	連詞(连词) [liáncí]	e.g., 可是 [kěshì] (but)
Int.	= interjection	嘆詞(叹词) [tàncí]	e.g., 啊 [a] (Ah?)
M.W.	= measure word (or classifier)	量詞(量词) [liàngcí]	e.g., 本 [běn] (used when counting books)
N.	= noun	名詞(名词) [míngcí]	e.g., 老師(老师) [laoshī] (teacher) 書(书) [shū] (book)
Num.	= numeral	數詞(数词) [shùcí]	e.g., 二 [èr] (two) 十 [shí] (ten)
Part.	= particle (word with grammatical function)	助詞(助词) [zhùcí]	e.g., 嗎(吗) [ma] (a word that turns a sentence into a question)
Prep.	= preposition	介詞(介词) [jiècí]	e.g., 在 [zài] (in; at) 從(从) [cóng] (from)
Pron.	= pronoun	代詞(代词) [dàicí]	e.g., 你 [nǐ] (you) 他 [tā] (he)
V.	= verb	動詞(动词) [dòngcí]	e.g., 學(学) [xué] (to study) 說(说) [shuō] (to speak) 跑 [pǎo] (to run)
V.O.	= verb + object	動賓(动宾) [dòng bīn]	e.g., 說中文(说中文) [shuō Zhōngwén] (to speak Chinese)
V.C.	= verb + complement	動補(动补) [dòng bǔ]	e.g., 搬過來(搬过来) [bān guò lái] (to move over) 打破 [dǎ pò] (to hit, broken)

圖片供應者 (图片供应者) PHOTO CREDITS

關心他人（关心他人）
Caring for Others

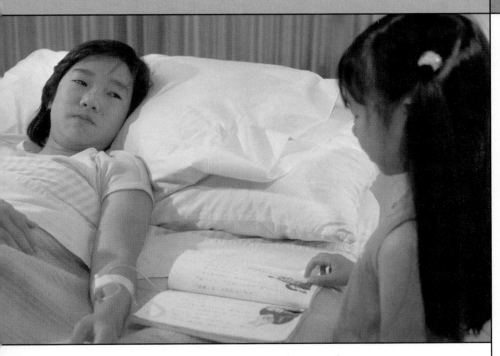

Caring for others is an important part of Chinese culture.

CONNECTIONS AND COMMUNITIES PREVIEW

Discuss the following questions with a partner or your class. What similarities and differences do you think there might be between Chinese culture and your own culture?

1. What are the common expressions in your culture to show concern for others?

2. How do you typically show concern for others?

教學目標（教学目标）OBJECTIVES

- Express concern for others
- Respond when others show concern for you
- Describe an unpleasant situation

生詞 (生词) VOCABULARY

核心詞 (核心词) Core Vocabulary

TRADITIONAL	SIMPLIFIED	PINYIN		
1. 被	被	bèi	Prep. N.	(introduces the agent in a passive sentence) quilt
2. 住院	住院	zhùyuàn	V.O.	to be hospitalized
3. 照顧	照顾	zhàogu	V.	to look after, give consideration to
4. 到底	到底	dàodǐ	Adv.	at last, finally, after all (used in an interrogative sentence to indicate an attempt to get to the bottom of the matter)
5. 回	回	huí	V. M.W.	to return, reply (measure word for indicating the frequency of action), (measure word [spoken form] for matters)
6. 唉	唉	ài	Int.	(a sigh of sadness or regret)
7. 事情	事情	shìqíng	N.	matter
8. 經過	经过	jīngguò	N.	process
9. 肚子	肚子	dùzi	N.	belly
10. 以為	以为	yǐwéi	V.	to think, consider
11. 管	管	guǎn	V.	to mind, control
12. 拖	拖	tuō	V.	to delay, pull, drag
13. 厲害	厉害	lìhai	Adj.	severe
14. 受不了	受不了	shòubuliǎo	Adj.	not be able to bear

	TRADITIONAL	SIMPLIFIED	PINYIN		
15.	剛好	刚好	gānghǎo	Adv.	it so happened that, just
16.	情況	情况	qíngkuàng	N.	situation
17.	救護車	救护车	jiùhùchē	N.	ambulance
18.	急診室	急诊室	jízhěnshì	N.	emergency room
19.	急性	急性	jíxìng	N.	acute
20.	盲腸炎 (闌尾炎)	盲肠炎 (阑尾炎)	mángchángyán (lánwěiyán)	N.	appendicitis
21.	開刀	开刀	kāidāo	V.O.	(spoken form) to perform or have an operation
22.	動手術	动手术	dòng shǒushù	V.O.	to have a surgical operation
23.	嚇死	吓死	xiàsǐ	V.C.	to be scared to death
24.	手術室	手术室	shǒushùshì	N.	operating room
25.	擔心	担心	dānxīn	V.	to worry, feel anxious
26.	進行	进行	jìnxíng	V.	to be in progress
27.	順利	顺利	shùnlì	Adv.	smoothly
28.	護士	护士	hùshì	N.	nurse
29.	推	推	tuī	N.	to push
30.	病房	病房	bìngfáng	N.	ward (of a hospital)
31.	休養	休养	xiūyǎng	V.	to recuperate
32.	通知	通知	tōngzhī	V.	to notify, inform
33.	家人	家人	jiārén	N.	family members
34.	怕	怕	pà	V.	to fear, be afraid of

TRADITIONAL	SIMPLIFIED	PINYIN		
35. 敢	敢	gǎn	V.	to dare
36. 結束	结束	jiéshù	V.	to end, finish
37. 不要緊	不要紧	búyàojǐn		it doesn't matter, it's not serious
38. 罵	骂	mà	V.	to scold
39. 頓	顿	dùn	M.W.	(measure word for meals or scolds)
40. 關心	关心	guānxīn	V. N.	to be concerned about concern
41. 可憐	可怜	kělián	Adj. V.	to be in a sorry situation to feel sorry for, to take pity on
42. 父母	父母	fùmǔ	N.	father and mother
43. 請假	请假	qǐngjià	V.O.	to ask for leave
44. 早日康復	早日康复	zǎorìkāngfù		get well soon, speedy recovery

專名 (专名) Proper Nouns

TRADITIONAL	SIMPLIFIED	PINYIN		
1. 小謝	小谢	Xiǎo Xiè	N.	(name) Little Xie (Xie is the surname). "Xiao Xie" is used to imply that Xiao Xie is younger than the speaker.
2. 常天	常天	Cháng Tiān	N.	(name) Chang is the surname
3. 明修	明修	Míngxiū	N.	(name) Mingxiu is the given name

語文知識 (语文知识) LANGUAGE LINK

Read and listen to the following sentence patterns. These patterns use vocabulary, expressions, and grammar that you will study in more detail in this lesson. After reading the sentence patterns, read and listen to the Language in Use section that follows.

句型 (句型) Sentence Patterns

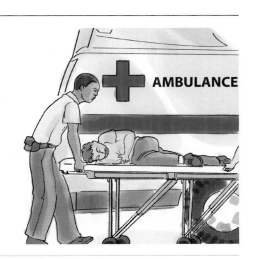

A: 到底是怎麼回事? 你怎麼住院了呢?
到底是怎么回事? 你怎么住院了呢?
Dàodǐ shì zěnme huíshì? Nǐ zěnme zhùyuàn le ne?

B: 我的肚子疼得厲害, 然後就被送進醫院了。
我的肚子疼得厉害, 然后就被送进医院了。
Wǒde dùzi téngde lìhai, ránhòu jiù bèi sòngjìn yīyuàn le.

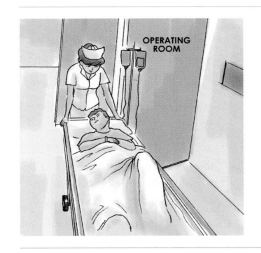

A: 是你把他送進急診室開刀的嗎?
是你把他送进急诊室开刀的吗?
Shì nǐ bǎ tā sòngjìn jízhěnshì kāidāo de ma?

B: 是的。手術完了以後, 他就讓護士
是的。手术完了以后, 他就让护士
Shìde. Shǒushù wánle yǐhòu, tā jiùràng hùshi

給推進病房休養了。
给推进病房休养了。
gěi tuījìn bìngfáng xiūyǎng le.

A: 你通知家人了嗎? 他們一定急死了。
你通知家人了吗? 他们一定急死了。
Nǐ tōngzhī jiārén le ma? Tāmen yídìng jísǐ le.

B: 通知了。可是, 我叫媽媽給罵了一頓,
通知了。可是, 我叫妈妈给骂了一顿,
Tōngzhī le. Kěshì, wǒ jiào māma gěi mà le yídùn,

說我怎麼這麼晚才告訴她。
说我怎么这么晚才告诉她。
shuō wǒ zěnme zhème wǎn cái gàosu tā.

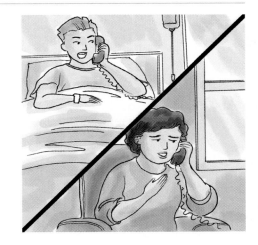

🔊 課文 Language in Use: My Unexpected Stay in Hospital
(繁體字 Traditional Character Version)

(小謝住院了，他的室友常天在旁邊照顧他，他的同學明修來了。)

明修： 怎麼樣，好多了嗎?

小謝： 好多了，沒事[1]了。你那麼忙還過來看我，真不好意思。

明修： 哪兒的話[2]，平安就好。到底是怎麼回事[3]? 你怎麼住院了呢?

小謝： 唉! 事情的經過是這樣的: 前幾天我就覺得肚子不舒服，以為是吃壞肚子了，吃了藥就會好了，也就沒管它[4]。但是有時候還是會疼，拖了一兩天。前天早上疼得屬害，受不了了。就這樣，我被送進醫院了。

常天： 是呀! 中明和我剛好沒課在家，看他疼得屬害，覺得情況不對，就馬上打電話叫救護車，把他送進急診室去了。

小謝： 醫生說是急性盲腸炎，要馬上開刀。一聽要動手術，就把我嚇死了，很快我就被送進手術室了。

常天： 我和中明在外面挺擔心的，不過還好，手術進行得很順利。手術完了以後，他就讓護士給推進病房休養了。

1. 沒事(没事)
"Nothing," "It's OK," "Fine." This phrase is used frequently in many situations, such as replying to concern by others, or an apology, thanks, or gesture of appreciation.

2. 哪兒的話(哪儿的话)
This is a humble way to reply to thanks or appreciation in Chinese. Literally it means, "Where are the words from?" It implies that the receiver does not feel deserving of the thanks.

3. 怎麼回事(怎么回事)
"What's wrong?" 回(回) is the measure word for 事(事) (matter), e.g. 一回事 (一回事). A relatively more formal measure word for 事(事) is "件(件)," e.g. 一件事 (一件事).

4. 沒管它(没管它)
"To not pay attention to it," "not care about it." 它(它) "it" is the third person singular pronoun for inanimate things in Chinese.

Continued on page 328

课文 Language in Use: My Unexpected Stay in Hospital
(简体字 Simplified Character Version)

(小谢住院了，他的室友常天在旁边照顾他，他的同学明修来了。)

明修： 怎么样，好多了吗？

小谢： 好多了，没事¹了。你那么忙还过来看我，真不好意思。

明修： 哪儿的话²，平安就好。到底是怎么回事³? 你怎么住院了呢？

小谢： 唉！事情的经过是这样的：前几天我就觉得肚子不舒服，以为是吃坏肚子了，吃了药就会好了，也就没管它⁴。但是有时候还是会疼，拖了一两天。前天早上疼得厉害，受不了了。就这样，我被送进医院了。

常天： 是呀！中明和我刚好没课在家，看他疼得厉害，觉得情况不对，就马上打电话叫救护车，把他送进急诊室去了。

小谢： 医生说是急性盲肠炎，要马上开刀。一听要动手术，就把我吓死了，很快我就被送进手术室了。

常天： 我和中明在外面挺担心的，不过还好，手术进行得很顺利。手术完了以后，他就让护士给推进病房休养了。

Continued on page 329

🔊 課文 Language in Use: My Unexpected Stay in Hospital
(繁體字 Traditional Character Version) —— 接第三百二十六頁

明修： 喔！原來是這樣的。對了，你通知家人了嗎？他們一定急死了。

小謝： 唉！本來我怕他們擔心，不敢告訴他們。昨天等手術結束以後，才給媽媽打電話，告訴她不要緊了，可是她還是擔心得很，還生氣呢。我還叫她在電話裡給罵了一頓，說我怎麼這麼晚才告訴她。

常天： 你媽媽是關心你啊！可憐天下父母心[5]！你看他們明天就要趕過來看你了。

5. 可憐天下父母心(可怜天下父母心)
"So sad! The hearts of the world's parents." It is a common Chinese saying indicating that all parents share the same worries and cares related to their children.

小謝： 說的也是。唉！我要好幾個星期都不能上課了，功課怎麼辦？

明修： 學校那邊，你不要擔心，我會幫你請假的。等你好了以後，我們再幫你復習。

常天： 是呀，現在就別管那麼多了。你好好地休養，才能早日康復。

小謝： 那就太謝謝你們了。

课文 Language in Use: My Unexpected Stay in Hospital
(简体字 Simplified Character Version) —— 接第三百二十七页

明修： 喔！原来是这样的。对了，你通知家人了吗？他们一定急死了。

小谢： 唉！本来我怕他们担心，不敢告诉他们。昨天等手术结束以后，才给妈妈打电话，告诉她不要紧了，可是她还是担心得很，还生气呢。我还叫她在电话里给骂了一顿，说我怎么这么晚才告诉她。

常天： 你妈妈是关心你啊！可怜天下父母心5！你看他们明天就要赶过来看你了。

小谢： 说的也是。唉！我要好几个星期都不能上课了，功课怎么办？

明修： 学校那边，你不要担心，我会帮你请假的。等你好了以后，我们再帮你复习。

常天： 是呀，现在就别管那么多了。你好好地休养，才能早日康复。

小谢： 那就太谢谢你们了。

語法 (语法) GRAMMAR

I. 被動句 (被动句) Passive Sentences

The passive sense in Chinese is similar to English. In Chinese, however, the passive sense sentence commonly occurs in the following two structures:

A. Unmarked in structure (notional passive sense.) It usually occurs as a topic-comment sentence.

Examples:

飯做好了。
饭做好了。
The meal is ready.

作業寫完了。
作业写完了。
The assignment is finished.

錢花光了。
钱花光了。
The money has all been spent.

信寄出去了。
信寄出去了。
The letter has been sent out.

B. Marked in structure with 被, 叫, or 讓(让) to indicate the passive sense.

This is commonly known as the "passive construction." The passive construction is illustrated below.

Object (receiver of action) +	被(被) 叫(叫) 讓(让)	+ Subject (doer) +	(給) [(给)] 給(给) 給(给)	+ V. + other elements

叫 and 讓(让) are more colloquial than 被. 給(给) is optional with 被 but usually is present with 叫 and 讓(让) to avoid ambiguity. (That's because 叫 could mean "to call, to order, to be named," or could be used as a passive sense marker; 讓(让) could mean "to let, to allow," or could be used as a passive sense marker.)

Examples:

我的鏡子被弟弟(給)打破了。
我的镜子被弟弟(给)打破了。

我的鏡子叫弟弟給打破了。
我的镜子叫弟弟给打破了。

我的鏡子讓弟弟給打破了。
我的镜子让弟弟给打破了。
My mirror was broken by my younger brother.

The doer (Subject) is required when using the marker 叫 and 讓(让), but is optional when using the marker 被.

Examples:

車子被(老王)撞壞了。
车子被(老王)撞坏了。
The car was smashed (by Lao Wang).

車子叫/讓老王給撞壞了。
车子叫/让老王给撞坏了。
The car was smashed by Lao Wang.

The following are some characteristics of the 被 sentences:

1. The "doer" is usually introduced or implied.

   他被老王打了。
   他被老王打了。
   He was hit by Lao Wang. (老王 is the doer)

   他被人打了。
   他被人打了。
   He was hit (by someone).

2. It commonly occurs in a narrative sentence to describe how something has happened to the object. For example, 鏡子被打破了(镜子被打破了) emphasizes that what has happened to the mirror is the result of someone's action (it has been broken by someone), while 鏡子打破了(镜子打破了) communicates the resulting fact that the mirror is broken.

3. The doer of the action can be animate or inanimate.

房子給壞人燒 ([shāo]: to burn) 光了。
房子给坏人烧光了。
The house was burned down by bad people. (壞人(坏人) <animate> is the doer.)

房子被火燒光了。
房子被火烧光了。
The house was burned down by fire. (火 <inanimate> is the doer.)

4. The 被 construction is often used to convey a sense of unhappiness, loss, surprise, or helplessness.

Examples:

- When the doer is unknown.

錢被偷了。
钱被偷了。
The money was stolen.

- To convey something unfortunate or unpleasant that has happened to the receiver.

小狗被車子撞死了。
小狗被车子撞死了。
The dog was killed by a car.

- To suggest surprise or astonishment.

這件事情怎麼會被他知道了?
这件事情怎么会被他知道了?
How could he know about this matter?

Note: Due to influences from the English language, Chinese sometimes has sentences which don't convey unpleasant situations but for which the 被 construction is used.

Example:
He was elected as president.

他被選為總統 ([zǒngtǒng]: president) 了。(with 被 construction)
他被选为总统了。

他當選 ([dāngxuǎn]: be elected) 為總統了。(without 被 construction)
他当选为总统了。

5. To negate the 被 construction, 沒有(没有) is placed before 被. Note that "不" cannot be used. There is no "了" used in the sentence.

Example:

錢沒有被偷 ([tōu]: to steal)。
钱没有被偷。

The money was not stolen.

6. The 被 construction cannot be used in a command except with the negative imperative particle (不要，別) ("don't") added.

Examples:

別被他騙 ([piàn]: to cheat) 了。
别被他骗了。

Don't be fooled by him.

不要被看見了。
不要被看见了。

Don't be seen!

7. Though the passive sense in Chinese is similar to English, some English passive sentences cannot be translated with the 被 passive construction.

Examples:

- "This book was written by Mr. Wang." A sentence of this type should be translated as:
  這本書是王先生寫的。
  这本书是王先生写的。
  (use the 是……的 pattern to emphasize that it is Mr. Wang who wrote the book)

- "Your check has been received." A sentence of this type should be translated as:
  你的支票收到了。
  你的支票收到了。
  (use topic-comment to convey the passive sense)

»Try it! With a partner, make two to three passive sentences to describe some unhappy situations. For example,

我的蛋糕叫妹妹給吃完了。
我的蛋糕叫妹妹给吃完了。

II. 被字句和把字句的比較 (被字句和把字句的比较)
被 Sentences versus 把 Sentences

把 (first introduced in *Chinese Link*, Beginning Chinese, Lesson 20) and 被 sentences are often mentioned together for comparison. The similarities and differences between 把 and 被 sentences can be summarized as follows:

1. Both 把 and 被 sentences indicate the notion of disposal. That is, they indicate that an action has some influence on the object.

2. The subject and object are in different positions in the two types of sentences.

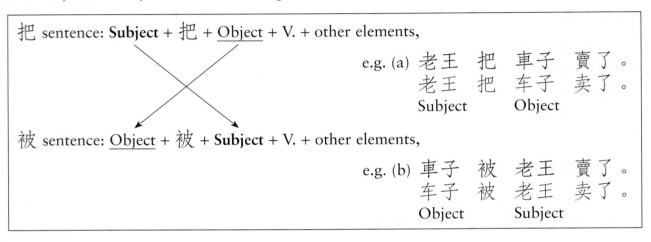

3. 把 and 被 sentences can be switched to provide a change in emphasis.

4. 被 sentences usually convey a sense of an unpleasant situation. 把 sentences do not convey this sense. In example (b) 車子被老王賣了(车子被老王卖了), the use of 被 implies that the car being sold by Lao Wang was not a happy thing.

5. 把 is commonly used with commands, but 被 is not.

Example:

把車賣了!
把车卖了!
Sell the car!

As mentioned above, 被 can only be used with the negative imperative 別 or 不要 in a command.

Example:

別(不要)被騙了。
別(不要)被骗了。

6. Perceptual verbs such as 聽見(听见), 看見(看见), and 知道 cannot be used with the 把 construction (for details, please refer to *Chinese Link*, Beginning Chinese, Lesson 20), but may be used in the 被 construction.

Example:

那件事情被他聽見/看見/知道了。

那件事情被他听见/看见/知道了。

(把 cannot be used here.)

»Try it!   With a partner, change the following 把 sentences into 被 sentences.

1. 爸爸把哥哥罵了一頓。
   爸爸把哥哥骂了一顿。

2. 他女朋友把他的錢全花光了。
   他女朋友把他的钱全花光了。

3. 壞人把他的車撞壞了。
   坏人把他的车撞坏了。

4. 小貓把弟弟的蛋糕吃了。
   小猫把弟弟的蛋糕吃了。

補充課文 (补充课文) SUPPLEMENTARY PRACTICE

Read the following passage. Then listen and repeat.

A Letter to Teacher Wang: Helping Xiao Xie Ask for Sick Leave
(繁體字 Traditional Character Version)

王老師，

　　您好。我們想告訴您小謝前天生病住院的消息。事情的經過是這樣子的：前幾天他就覺得肚子不舒服，以為是吃壞肚子了，也就沒管它。後來疼得厲害，受不了了，他就被送去醫院了。檢查出來，才知道是盲腸炎，要馬上開刀，不過還好，手術進行得很順利，我們也通知了他的家人。他媽媽已經趕過來照顧他了，您不用擔心，他現在已經平安沒事了。醫生說再過兩天，他就可以出院了。出院以後，他得待在家裡，好好休養，不能去上課。我們想告訴您這個消息，也想順便幫他請假。

　　謝謝。

您的學生
明修和常天

Notes:
檢查(检查) [jiǎnchá]: to check, examine, check-up, examination
出院(出院) [chūyuàn]: to be discharged from the hospital
順便(顺便) [shùnbiàn]: at one's convenience; without taking extra trouble

補充課文 (补充课文) SUPPLEMENTARY PRACTICE

Read the following passage. Then listen and repeat.

A Letter to Teacher Wang: Helping Xiao Xie Ask for Sick Leave (简体字 Simplified Character Version)

王老师，

您好。我们想告诉您小谢前天生病住院的消息。事情的经过是这样子的：前几天他就觉得肚子不舒服，以为是吃坏肚子了，也就没管它。后来疼得厉害，受不了了，他就被送去医院了。检查出来，才知道是盲肠炎，要马上开刀，不过还好，手术进行得很顺利，我们也通知了他的家人。他妈妈已经赶过来照顾他了，您不用担心，他现在已经平安没事了。医生说再过两天，他就可以出院了。出院以后，他得待在家里，好好休养，不能去上课。我们想告诉您这个消息，也想顺便帮他请假。

谢谢。

您的学生
明修和常天

Exercises: work with a partner or in small groups

1. 有哪些這一課的生詞和語法出現 ([chūxiàn]: to appear) 在這封信上？請把它們找出來。

   有哪些这一课的生词和语法出现在这封信上？请把它们找出来。

2. 請把這封信翻譯成 ([fānyì chéng]: to translate into) 英文。

   请把这封信翻译成英文。

成語故事 (成语故事) IDIOM STORY

驚弓之鳥 (惊弓之鸟) [jīng gōng zhī niǎo]

Meaning: A bird frightened by the mere twang of a bow.

Usage: This is used to describe a person who is seized with fear because of some frightening experience encountered in the past.

Example: 他上次肚子疼得厲害被送去醫院，還住院住了很長時間。現在，只要一聽到要去醫院，他就像 "驚弓之鳥" 一樣，嚇死了。

他上次肚子疼得厉害被送去医院，还住院住了很长时间。现在，只要一听到要去医院，他就像 "惊弓之鸟" 一样，吓死了。

Pay special attention to the passive sentences 被動句 (被, 叫, or 讓)[被动句 (被, 叫, or 让)] and the 把 sentences.

(繁體字 Traditional Character Version)

　　古時候有一個神箭手，他跟魏王出去玩兒。剛好有一隻鳥在空中飛過來飛過去，鳥的哭叫聲很可憐。
　　魏王問神箭手: 你能把那隻鳥射下來嗎?
　　神箭手說: 沒問題，我不用箭就可以把牠射下來。
　　神箭手把他的弓箭拿出來，撥動了一下弓弦，鳥就被他射下來了。
　　魏王看了覺得很奇怪，說: 你又沒有把你的箭射出去，怎麼那隻鳥就讓你給射下來了?
　　神箭手說: 事情是這樣子的，那是一隻被嚇壞的鳥，牠很累，也很可憐，牠怕弓箭。只要我把我的弓弦撥動一下，牠就以為牠叫弓箭給射中了，所以牠就自己掉下來了。

(简体字 Simplified Character Version)

古时候有一个神箭手，他跟魏王出去玩儿。刚好有一只鸟在空中飞过来飞过去，鸟的哭叫声很可怜。

魏王问神箭手：你能把那只鸟射下来吗？

神箭手说：没问题，我不用箭就可以把它射下来。

神箭手把他的弓箭拿出来，拨动了一下弓弦，鸟就被他射下来了。

魏王看了觉得很奇怪，说：你又没有把你的箭射出去，怎么那只鸟就让你给射下来了？

神箭手说：事情是这样子的，那是一只被吓坏的鸟，它很累，也很可怜，它怕弓箭。只要我把我的弓弦拨动一下，它就以为它叫弓箭给射中了，所以它就自己掉下来了。

Notes:

古時候(古时候) [gǔ shíhòu]: ancient times
神箭手(神箭手) [shénjiànshǒu]: great archer
魏王(魏王) [Wèi wáng]: the King of Wei
鳥(鸟) [niǎo]: bird
空中(空中) [kōngzhōng]: in the sky
哭叫聲(哭叫声) [kūjiào shēng]: cry
射下來(射下来) [shè xiàlái]: to shoot down
牠(它) [tā]: it (for animals)
弓箭(弓箭) [gōngjiàn]: bow and arrow
撥動(拨动) [bōdòng]: to pluck
弓弦(弓弦) [gōngxián]: bowstring
嚇壞(吓坏) [xiàhuài]: to be frightened
射中(射中) [shèzhòng]: to hit (intended target)

Exercises: work with a partner or in small groups

1. 找出有下面語法的句子：the passive sentences 被動句 (被，叫，or 讓) and the 把 sentences.
   找出有下面语法的句子：the passive sentences 被动句 (被，叫，or 让) and the 把 sentences.

2. 用你自己的話說說 "驚弓之鳥" 的故事。
   用你自己的话说说 "惊弓之鸟" 的故事。

3. 請用 "驚弓之鳥" 造一個句子或者說一個 "驚弓之鳥" 的例子。
   请用 "惊弓之鸟" 造一个句子或者说一个 "惊弓之鸟" 的例子。

4. "驚弓之鳥" 的故事，告訴了我們什麼？
   "惊弓之鸟" 的故事，告诉了我们什么？

練習 (练习) ACTIVITIES

I. Listening Exercises

 11-1 Listen to the passage and answer the following questions. Then check them with your partner.

Notes:
跑步(跑步) [pǎobù]: to run
突然(突然) [tūrán]: suddenly
繼續(继续) [jìxù]: to continue
淋溼(淋湿) [línshī]: to get wet
恢復(恢复) [huīfù]: to recover
傳染(传染) [chuánrǎn]: be contagious
拉肚子(拉肚子) [lādùzi]: diarrhea (spoken form)
腹瀉(腹泻) [fùxiè]: diarrhea (written form)

問題(问题):

1. 他要出去跑步的時候，發生了什麼事情?
   他要出去跑步的时候，发生了什么事情?

2. 他出去跑步的時候，又發生了什麼事情?
   他出去跑步的时候，又发生了什么事情?

3. 第二天起床的時候，他怎麼了?
   第二天起床的时候，他怎么了?

4. 他的室友幫他做了什麼? 他恢復得怎麼樣?
   他的室友帮他做了什么? 他恢复得怎么样?

5. 他的室友被他怎麼了? 有什麼症狀 ([zhèngzhuàng]: symptom)?
   他的室友被他怎么了? 有什么症状?

6. 他覺得他應該為他室友做什麼?
   他觉得他应该为他室友做什么?

11-2   Based on the short passage you have just listened to, complete the following sentences (pay attention to the 把 and 被 constructions). Then check them with your partner.

1. 他正在 ＿＿＿＿ 的時候，突然下雨了，雨 ＿＿＿＿ 他淋溼了。
   他正在 ＿＿＿＿ 的时候，突然下雨了，雨 ＿＿＿＿ 他淋湿了。

2. 他 ＿＿＿＿ 雨淋溼了以後，就 ＿＿＿＿ 了。
   他 ＿＿＿＿ 雨淋湿了以后，就 ＿＿＿＿ 了。

3. 他室友不小心也 ＿＿＿＿ 他 ＿＿＿＿ 傳染了。
   他室友不小心也 ＿＿＿＿ 他 ＿＿＿＿ 传染了。

4. 他覺得他室友很 ＿＿＿＿，他要在家好好地 ＿＿＿＿ 他室友。
   他觉得他室友很 ＿＿＿＿，他要在家好好地 ＿＿＿＿ 他室友。

II. Character Exercises

11-3   Work with a partner. Read the following words, phrases, and sentences.

顧 顾	厲 厉
照顧 照顾	厲害 厉害
在旁邊照顧他 在旁边照顾他	他疼得厲害 他疼得厉害
他室友在旁邊照顧他。 他室友在旁边照顾他。	他肚子疼得厲害。 他肚子疼得厉害。

Now with your partner, try to use the following characters to make words, phrases, and then sentences.

1. 底　　2. 被　　3. 管　　4. 拖　　5. 剛　　6. 況
   底　　　　被　　　　管　　　　拖　　　　剛　　　　況

7. 救　　8. 診　　9. 炎　　10. 擔　　11. 順　　12. 頓
   救　　　　诊　　　　炎　　　　担　　　　顺　　　　顿

11-4 Read aloud the following sentences. Write them out using traditional characters. Then check your answers with a partner.

1. 刚才肠子疼得厉害。 _____

2. 他被护士送到急诊室去了。 _____

3. 他很可怜，要动手术，情况很紧急。 _____

4. 你不用担心，好好休养。 _____

5. 他让医生给骂了一顿。 _____

11-5 Form groups and create phrases with the following words (pay attention to the various usages of each word).

Example:　塊：十五塊錢　　一塊鏡子，一塊麵包，一塊蛋糕
　　　　　　块：十五块钱　　一块镜子，一块面包，一块蛋糕

1. 院：_____ _____
   院：_____ _____

2. 經：_____ _____
   经：_____ _____

3. 拖：_____ _____
   拖：_____ _____

4. 養：_____ _____
   养：_____ _____

5. 通：_____ _____
   通：_____ _____

6. 緊：_____ _____
   紧：_____ _____

7. 結：_____ _____
   结：_____ _____

Homophones:

Example:　[shì]　士：護士
　　　　　　　士：护士

　　　　　　　是：你是誰?
　　　　　　　是：你是谁?

1. [　　] 脱：_____
　　　　 脱：_____

　　　　 拖：_____
　　　　 拖：_____

2. [　　] 肚：_____
　　　　 肚：_____

　　　　 度：_____
　　　　 度：_____

3. [　　] 管：_____
　　　　 管：_____

　　　　 館：_____
　　　　 馆：_____

4. [　　] 救：_____
　　　　 救：_____

　　　　 就：_____
　　　　 就：_____

5. [　　] 急：_____
　　　　 急：_____

　　　　 極：_____
　　　　 极：_____

　　　　 及：_____
　　　　 及：_____

6. [   ] 性: _____

　　　 性: _____

　　　 姓: _____

　　　 姓: _____

7. [   ] 束: _____

　　　 束: _____

　　　 數: _____

　　　 数: _____

　　　 樹: _____

　　　 树: _____

8. [   ] 敢: _____

　　　 敢: _____

　　　 感: _____

　　　 感: _____

III. Grammar Exercises

11-6   Form groups to rewrite the following sentences using 被/叫/讓(让).

1. 老師把學生罵了一頓。
   老师把学生骂了一顿。

2. 壞人把他銀行的存款全取走了。
   坏人把他银行的存款全取走了。

3. 老王騙 ([piàn]: to deceive) 了小英。
   老王騙了小英。

4. 老鼠 ([lǎoshǔ]: mouse) 把媽媽嚇了一跳 ([xiàyítiào]: be terribly frightened)。
   老鼠把妈妈吓了一跳。

5. 警察把他的車拖走 ([tuōzǒu]: to tow away) 了。
   警察把他的车拖走了。

6. 小狗把妹妹的蛋糕吃了。
   小狗把妹妹的蛋糕吃了。

7. 外面的噪音 ([zàoyīn]: noise) 把寶寶 ([bǎobao]: baby) 吵醒 ([chǎoxǐng]: awakened by noise) 了。

   外面的噪音把宝宝吵醒了。

8. 哥哥把妹妹罵哭 ([kū]: to cry) 了。

   哥哥把妹妹骂哭了。

11-7 Form groups to (i) read aloud the following passage (pay attention to the 把 sentences); (ii) answer the following questions; and (3) use your own words to retell the story using "被, 叫, or 讓(让)" sentences.

Passage:

謝進學： 我已經把你的車停在那棵大樹的旁邊了。
谢进学： 我已经把你的车停在那棵大树的旁边了。

常天： 說到那棵大樹，真不好意思！上次我搬進來的時候，
把那棵大樹撞壞了。
常天： 说到那棵大树，真不好意思！上次我搬进来的时候，
把那棵大树撞坏了。

夏中明： 是呀！我也把房東的鏡子打破了。房東很生氣，把我罵
了一頓，說我太不小心了。
夏中明： 是呀！我也把房东的镜子打破了。房东很生气，把我骂
了一顿，说我太不小心了。

謝進學： 沒事！罵不會疼！對了，謝謝你們的幫忙，這次搬家把
你們累壞了。今天晚上我請客！
谢进学： 没事！骂不会疼！对了，谢谢你们的帮忙，这次搬家把
你们累坏了。今天晚上我请客！

夏中明： 太好了！這附近有一家很不錯的中國飯館，可是我把地
址忘了。
夏中明： 太好了！这附近有一家很不错的中国饭馆，可是我把地
址忘了。

常天： 沒關係，我有，你們看，我找到了。
常天： 没关系，我有，你们看，我找到了。

謝進學： 太好了，咱們走吧！
谢进学： 太好了，咱们走吧！

With a partner, ask and answer the following questions.

1. 大樹讓誰給撞壞了？
   大树让谁给撞坏了？

2. 房東為什麼很生氣？中明被處罰 ([chǔfá]: to punish) 了嗎？是怎麼被處罰的？
   房东为什么很生气？中明被处罚了吗？是怎么被处罚的？

3. 他們為什麼累壞了？
   他们为什么累坏了？

4. 中國飯館的地址被誰給忘了，然後是誰找到的呢？
   中国饭馆的地址被谁给忘了，然后是谁找到的呢？

IV. Media Literacy

The short text below, written in the style of newspapers, magazines, or Internet news articles, will help you become familiar with the formal written expressions used in these genres.

手術點名費 (手术点名费)
Fee for Designating Specific Doctor(s) to Perform the Surgery

繁體字：

醫院手術點名費叫停
北京取消部分醫療服務收費

昨日，北京市發出《關於進一步規範及取消部分醫療服務項目收費》的通知，北京將從3月1日起，各家醫院取消點名手術費。此外，手術中使用的外用鹽水也被取消，將不再另行收費。

简体字:

医院手术点名费叫停
北京取消部分医疗服务收费

昨日，北京市发出《关于进一步规范及取消部分医疗服务项目收费》的通知，北京将从3月1日起，各家医院取消点名手术费。此外，手术中使用的外用盐水也被取消，将不再另行收费。

Notes:
點名(点名) [diǎnmíng]: to designate
手術點名費(手术点名费) [shǒushù diǎnmíng fèi]: fee paid (in advance) for designating specific doctor(s) to perform the surgery
取消(取消) [qǔxiāo]: to cancel

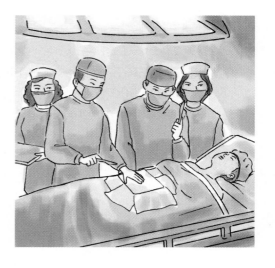

Exercises for the headlines: work with a partner or a group to ask and answer the following questions.

1. What can you tell about the news by skimming the headlines?

2. How would you translate the headlines into English?

3. Newspaper headlines are usually very concise, with many abbreviations, omissions, hints, metaphors, and written forms. Can you identify some of these in the headlines above?

Notes:
關於......的通知(关于......的通知) [guānyú . . . de tōngzhī]: notification on . . .
規範(规范) [guīfàn]: to standardize; standard
及(及) [jí]: and, to reach
此外(此外) [cǐwài]: moreover
外用鹽水(外用盐水) [wàiyòng yánshuǐ]: surgical IV
另行(另行) [lìngxíng]: separately

Exercises for the article: work with a partner or a group to ask and answer the following.

1. Can you guess why patients want to designate specific doctors?

2. When is the fee for designating doctors waived? What other fees are canceled?

3. Can you find any written-form expressions? Indicate the spoken counterparts for the following expressions:

昨日(昨日)   各(各)   將(将)   及(及)
從3月1日起(从3月1日起)   此外(此外)

4. Point out the sentences which contain Lesson 11 vocabulary (e.g. 手術(手术); 通知 . . .), then translate the sentences into English.

5. Locate the 被 sentences in this article. How many are there?

6. Do you think patients should be allowed to request that specific doctors perform their surgery? Why?

7. Try to use your own words to summarize the headlines and article.

V. Communicative Activities

11-8 學習中國朝代和歷史(学习中国朝代和历史): You are taking an ancient Chinese history course and have learned that Chinese recorded civilization dates back at least 5,000 years. Looking at the chart below, form groups to describe the relationships among dynasties using 把(把) and 被(被) sentences , for example,

A: 周朝是什麼時候建立的? 是怎麼建立的?
周朝是什么时候建立的? 是怎么建立的?

B: 周朝是在公元前1027年建立的。是周朝把商朝打敗的, 商朝是 叫周朝給滅亡的。
周朝是在公元前1027年建立的。是周朝把商朝打败的, 商朝是 叫周朝给灭亡的。

A: 我知道了, 也就是說, 商朝被周朝給打敗了, 然後周朝就建立 起來了。
我知道了, 也就是说, 商朝被周朝给打败了, 然后周朝就建立 起来了。

中國的主要朝代和時期(中国的主要朝代和时期)
Major Chinese Dynasties and Periods

夏(夏) [Xià] 2100–1600 B.C.

商(商) [Shāng] 1600–1028 B.C.

周(周) [Zhōu] 1027–256 B.C.

   西周(西周) [Xī Zhōu] 1027–771 B.C.

   東周(东周) [Dōng Zhōu] 770–256 B.C.

     春秋(春秋) [Chūnqiū] (Spring and Autumn) 722–468 B.C.

     戰國(战国) [Zhànguó] (Warring States) 403–221 B.C.

秦(秦) [Qín] 221–207 B.C.

漢(汉) [Hàn] 206 B.C.–8 A.D.

三國(三国) [Sānguó] (Three Kingdoms)

   (魏，蜀，吳 (魏，蜀，吴) [Wèi, Shǔ, Wú]) 220–280

六朝(六朝) [Liùcháo] (Six Dynasties) 222–589

晉(晋) [Jìn] 265–420

南北朝(南北朝) [Nánběicháo] (Southern and Northern Dynasties) 420–581

隋(隋) [Suí] 581–618

唐(唐) [Táng] 618–907

宋(宋) [Sòng] 960–1279

元(元) [Yuán] 1260–1368

明(明) [Míng] 1368–1644

清(清) [Qīng] 1644–1911

Notes:
建立(建立) [jiànlì]: to establish
朝/朝代(朝/朝代) [cháodài]: dynasty
打敗(打败) [dǎbài]: to defeat
滅亡(灭亡) [mièwáng]: to destroy
公元前(公元前) [gōngyuán qián]: B.C.
公元後(公元后) [gōngyuán hòu]: A.D.

Identify the correct dynasty(ies) for the following:

• when the Great Wall was built.
• when the movie *Hero* 英雄 was set.
• the Three Kingdoms.
• when the famous poet 李白 lived.

11-9   Your parents gave you and your younger brother a car to share. Unfortunately, the car has been stolen. With a partner, use 把 and 被 sentences to report the incident to your parents.

Situations

1. Your younger brother parked the car. (use 把)
2. The car was left unlocked in the parking lot. (use 把 or 被)
3. The car was stolen by two thieves. (use 把 or 被)
4. The car was found at the back of the park. (use 被)
5. The CD player was stolen. (use 把 or 被)
6. Money on the front seat was stolen. (use 把 or 被)
7. It has already been reported to the police and the insurance company. (use 把)

Notes:
偷走(偷走) [tōuzǒu]: to steal
拿走(拿走) [názǒu]: to take away
小偷(小偷) [xiǎotōu]: thief
停在(停在) [tíngzài]: to park at
鎖好(锁好) [suǒhǎo]: to lock
光碟機(光碟机) [guāngdiéjī]: CD player
前座(前座) [qiánzuò]: the front seat
警察(警察) [jǐngchá]: police
保險公司(保险公司) [bǎoxiǎn gōngsī]: insurance company

11-10   Your roommate didn't do well on his math mid-term test. You are asking him what happened. He is afraid that he will fail the course. You show your concern and try to encourage him.

Useful words and expressions:
順利(顺利)
期中考(期中考)
到底(到底)
及格(及格) [jígé]: to pass (a test)
被當(被当) [bèidàng]: to fail (a course)
被(被)/叫(叫)/讓(让)
把(把)
擔心(担心)
沒事(没事)
不要緊(不要紧)
沒管它(没管它)

文化知識 (文化知识) Culture Link

文化點滴 (文化点滴) CULTURE NOTES

中國人怎麼表示對他人的關心 (中国人怎么表示对他人的关心)
How the Chinese Show Concern for Others

When you sneeze among Chinese people they don't say "bless you," as Americans might expect. This doesn't mean that Chinese are not friendly and don't care about others. You might also find that the Chinese may ask you directly about personal information such as your age, salary, and marital status the first time you meet them. This isn't considered nosy or rude. They feel that to know you better is to treat you like a family member, and thus it is fine to ask you personal questions. Some might even try to be your matchmaker. These examples demonstrate some of the particular ways in which Chinese show their concern for others.

Chinese put others first, and sometimes treat guests even better than their family members. When dining at a restaurant, Chinese will almost always try to pay for the other person. Because everyone wants to show concern for each other, almost every meal at a restaurant will end up with a fight over the check. In Western culture, giving money instead of a present may indicate a lack of thoughtfulness. For the Chinese, however, giving money in a red envelope is a very common gift. When guests visit, they are always treated very well. They get the

> **Do you know...**
> - why Chinese feel comfortable asking personal questions?
> - what common expressions are used when saying goodbye, and what are the implications of these expressions?
>
> **Read and find out!**

best towels, the best linens, the best food, and so on. And when guests visit, they usually bring a gift for the host.

Chinese people show their concern for acquaintances through the use of formalities. Upon parting after an event, people will tell each other to "come over to our place and have tea." This is not usually an actual invitation, but a way to express good wishes and the desire to get together again some time. In Western culture, people show politeness to people they don't know that well by calling them "Miss" or "Mister," but in Chinese, they are referred to as "Auntie" or "Uncle." Even if they do not know a person that well, the Chinese will show their concern for acquaintances, and sometimes even strangers, by treating them as if they are close friends or family members.

Within the family, concern is shown mainly through actions. To show affection and respect for siblings, their relationship, such as "little sister" or "third brother," is generally used instead of the given name. Instead of saying "I love you" to their children, parents will often show their love through actions and sacrifices, such as paying for the child's college tuition. When sons and daughters grow up to have their own jobs, it is always expected that they will take care of their aging parents. Nursing homes are not a common option in Chinese culture. It is especially important to show concern for family members, something done primarily through actions.

Old friends get together to chat and care for each other at a busy outdoor teahouse in Sichuan Province. Why do Chinese fight over the check at a restaurant?

In Chinese culture, it is expected that aging parents will live with and be taken care of by their children.

問題討論 (问题讨论) *Discuss the following with a partner or in small groups.*

1. 你對中國人表示對他人關心的方式有什麼看法? 跟你的文化有什麼一樣或者不一樣的地方?

   你对中国人表示对他人关心的方式有什么看法? 跟你的文化有什么一样或者不一样的地方?

   What do you think of the ways that Chinese show their concern for others? What are the similarities or differences with your own culture?

2. 你比較喜歡哪一種表示關心、接受關心的方式呢?

   你比较喜欢哪一种表示关心、接受关心的方式呢?

   How do you prefer to express concern or accept the concern of others?

趣味中文 (趣味中文) FUN WITH CHINESE

打是親，罵是愛
打是亲，骂是爱

Hitting is the symbol of affection,
scolding is the symbol of love

dǎ	shì	qīn	mà	shì	ài
打	是	親	罵	是	愛
打	是	亲	骂	是	爱
to hit	is	affection	to scold	is	love

問題討論 (问题讨论) *Discuss the following with a partner or in small groups.*

Are there similar sayings in English or other languages indicating that your love or concern for someone might cause you to be more strict with them than with others?

行動吧! (行动吧!) LET'S GO!

隨身藥包 (随身药包) Personal Medicine Bag

小明要和朋友去自助旅行，媽媽不放心，怕他在旅途中生病或者發生意外，所以要幫他準備一個隨身藥包。以下是她在網上找到的隨身藥包表，我們一起來看看：

小明要和朋友去自助旅行，妈妈不放心，怕他在旅途中生病或者发生意外，所以要帮他准备一个随身药包。以下是她在网上找到的随身药包表，我们一起来看看：

隨身藥包表(随身药包表)
1. 綜合維生素。 　綜合維生素。
2. 要必備感冒藥，退燒藥，如果出現鼻塞、咳嗽、發燒等症狀，要立刻服藥或者去醫院治療。 　要必备感冒药，退烧药，如果出现鼻塞、咳嗽、发烧等症状，要立刻服药或者去医院治疗。
3. 常備藥：體溫計、創可貼、腹瀉藥。 　常备药：体温计、创可贴、腹泻药。
4. 自助旅行保健：多補充水份，睡眠要充足，帶著手機，保持聯絡。 　自助旅行保健：多补充水份，睡眠要充足，带着手机，保持联络。

Notes:

隨身藥包(随身药包) [suíshēn yàobao]: personal medicine bag

自助旅行(自助旅行) [zìzhù lǚxíng]: self-planned travel

意外(意外) [yìwài]: accident

綜合維生素(综合维生素) [zōnghé wéishēngsù]: multivitamin (In Taiwan, the term used is
　綜合維他命(综合维他命) [zōnghé wéitāmìng])

常備藥(常备药) [chángbèi yào]: common medicines

體溫計(体温计) [tǐwēnjì]: thermometer

創可貼(创可贴) [chuāngkětiē]: Band-Aid (in Taiwan, the term used is OK 絆 (OK 绊) [bàn])

保健(保健) [bǎojiàn]: health protection; health care

補充(补充) [bǔchōng]: to supplement; add to

睡眠(睡眠) [shuìmián]: (written expression) sleep

充足(充足) [chōngzú]: sufficient

保持(保持) [bǎochí]: to keep, maintain

聯絡(联络) [liánluò]: to contact; get in touch with

問題討論 (问题讨论) *Discuss the following with a partner or in small groups.*

1. 請用你自己的話說一說隨身藥包表的東西1–4。
   请用你自己的话说一说随身药包表的东西1–4。

2. Translate the following into English:

   要必備感冒藥，退燒藥，如果出現鼻塞、咳嗽、發燒等症狀，要立刻服藥或者去醫院治療。

   要必备感冒药，退烧药，如果出现鼻塞、咳嗽、发烧等症状，要立刻服药或者去医院治疗。

3. 你準備過隨身藥包嗎？你去中國旅行的時候，你會準備什麼樣的隨身藥包？

   你准备过随身药包吗？你去中国旅行的时候，你会准备什么样的随身药包？

12

感謝和感激 (感谢和感激)
Expressing Thanks and Appreciation

A young boy offers oranges (symbolizing luck) to his grandmother to thank her and wish her prosperity in the upcoming New Year.

CONNECTIONS AND COMMUNITIES PREVIEW

Discuss the following questions with a partner or your class. What similarities and differences do you think there might be between Chinese culture and your own culture?

1. What are the common expressions in your culture for showing appreciation?

2. What expressions or actions do you use to show gratitude?

教學目標 (教学目标) OBJECTIVES

- Express appreciation
- Reply to/accept another's thanks
- Describe a cause-and-effect situation
- Describe a conditional situation
- Write thank-you notes and invitations

生詞 (生词) VOCABULARY

核心詞 (核心词) Core Vocabulary

TRADITIONAL	SIMPLIFIED	PINYIN		
1. 由於	由于	yóuyú	Conj.	due to, because of
2. 幫助	帮助	bāngzhù	V. N.	to help help
3. 解決	解决	jiějué	V.	to solve
4. 答謝	答谢	dáxiè	V.	to thank
5. 煮	煮	zhǔ	V.	to cook
6. 恭喜	恭喜	gōngxǐ	V.	to congratulate
7. 出院	出院	chūyuàn	V.O.	to be discharged from the hospital
8. 恢復	恢复	huīfù	V.	to recover
9. 啦	啦	la	Int.	(used at the end of a sentence to indicate sighing, questioning, etc.)
10. 段	段	duàn	M.W.	(measure word for section, segment)
11. 亂跑	乱跑	luànpǎo	V.	to run around
12. 只好	只好	zhǐhǎo	Adv.	have to (no choice)
13. 待	待	dāi	V.	to stay
14. 躺	躺	tǎng	V.	to lie, recline
15. 整天	整天	zhěngtiān	N.	the whole day
16. 悶死	闷死	mēnsǐ	V.C.	to be extremely boring
17. 算了吧	算了吧	suànleba		let it be, just forget it
18. 如此	如此	rúcǐ		so, thus

	TRADITIONAL	SIMPLIFIED	PINYIN		
19.	何必	何必	hébì		there is no need
20.	當初	当初	dāngchū		in the first place, originally
21.	檢查	检查	jiǎnchá	V. N.	to examine checkup, examination
22.	地步	地步	dìbù	N.	condition
23.	哎呀	哎呀	āiya	Int.	ah!, gosh!, oh dear!
24.	後悔	后悔	hòuhuǐ	V.	to regret
25.	多虧	多亏	duōkuī		thanks to, luckily
26.	糟	糟	zāo	Adj.	in a terrible state, chaotic
27.	不幸	不幸	búxìng	N.	adversity, misfortune
28.	不然	不然	bùrán	Conj.	or else, otherwise, if not
29.	後果	后果	hòuguǒ	N.	consequence, aftermath
30.	不堪設想	不堪设想	bùkānshèxiǎng		cannot bear to think about it
31.	害	害	hài	V.	to harm, cause trouble for
32.	趟	趟	tàng	M.W.	(measure word for trips)
33.	麻煩	麻烦	máfan	Adj. V.	troublesome to put somebody to trouble
34.	順便	顺便	shùnbiàn	Adv.	conveniently, in passing
35.	出門在外	出门在外	chūménzàiwài		to be away from home
36.	保險	保险	bǎoxiǎn	N.	insurance
37.	證明	证明	zhèngmíng	V. N.	to prove, certify proof, certificate
38.	因此	因此	yīncǐ	Conj.	therefore
39.	缺席	缺席	quēxí	V.O. N.	to be absent absence

TRADITIONAL	SIMPLIFIED	PINYIN		
40. 輔導	辅导	fǔdǎo	V.	to give guidance in studying, coach
41. 補考	补考	bǔkǎo	N.	make-up test
42. 至於	至于	zhìyú	Prep.	as for, as to
43. 倒楣	倒霉	dǎoméi	Adj.	unlucky
44. 俗話	俗话	súhuà	N.	common saying, proverb
45. 靠	靠	kào	V.	to lean against, depend on
46. 友誼	友谊	yǒuyì	N.	friendship

語文知識 (语文知识) LANGUAGE LINK

Read and listen to the following sentence patterns. These patterns use vocabulary, expressions, and grammar that you will study in more detail in this lesson. After reading the sentence patterns, read and listen to the Language in Use section that follows.

句型 (句型) Sentence Patterns

A: 這次真是多虧了你們，不然事情可能會更糟呢。
这次真是多亏了你们，不然事情可能会更糟呢。
Zhècì zhēnshì duōkuīle nǐmen, bùrán shìqíng kěnéng huì gèngzāo ne.

B: 說的也是，還好有你們的幫助，
说的也是，还好有你们的帮助，
Shuōdeyěshì, háihǎo yǒu nǐmen de bāngzhù,

不然後果就不堪設想了。
不然后果就不堪设想了。
bùrán hòuguǒ jiù bùkān shèxiǎng le.

C: 沒什麼，你們太客氣了。
没什么，你们太客气了。
Méishénme, nǐmen tàikèqi le.

A: 小謝會不會被記缺席？
小谢会不会被记缺席？
Xiǎo Xiè huìbuhuì bèi jì quēxí?

B: 不會的，他有醫生證明，
不会的，他有医生证明，
Búhuìde, tā yǒu yīshēng zhèngmíng,

因此不會被記缺席。
因此不会被记缺席。
yīncǐ búhuì bèi jì quēxí.

A: 由於你們的幫助，倒楣事兒全沒了。
由于你们的帮助，倒霉事儿全没了。
Yóuyú nǐmen de bāngzhù, dǎoméi shèr quánméi le.

B: 是呀！事情能進行得這麼順利，是由於
是呀！事情能进行得这么顺利，是由于
Shìyā! Shìqíng néng jìnxíng de zhème shùnlì, shìyóuyú

你們的幫助。真是太麻煩你們了！
你们的帮助。真是太麻烦你们了！
nǐmen de bāngzhù. Zhēnshì tài máfan nǐmen le!

C: 小事兒，不麻煩，沒什麼。
小事儿，不麻烦，没什么。
Xiǎo shèr, bùmáfan, méishénme.

課文 Language in Use: A Special Thanks for Your Help!
(繁體字 Traditional Character Version)

(小謝病好了，為了要答謝大家的幫助，媽媽特地煮了一桌菜請明修、常天和中明來吃飯。)

明修： 小謝，恭喜你出院了。你看起來精神不錯，恢復得很好。

小謝： 還可以啦！希望我能跟以前一樣靈活。但是這段時間，我不能亂跑，只好待在家裡，差不多天天都躺在床上。整天被關在家裡，快把我悶死了！

媽媽： 算了吧！早知如此，何必當初[1]。你要是能多注意身體，早點兒去檢查，就不會到這樣的地步了。

小謝： 哎呀！我知道錯了，真後悔！下次真的不敢了！

爸爸： 說真的，這次真是多虧了你們[2]。要不是你們的幫助，事情可能會更糟呢。

媽媽： 說的也是，真是謝天謝地，不幸中的大幸[3]。還好有你們在，不然後果就不堪設想了。

小謝： 對不起，這次可把你們忙壞了，害你們跑了好幾趟醫院[4]。真是太麻煩你們了。

---

1. 早知如此，何必當初。
   (早知如此，何必当初。)

如此(如此) ([rúcǐ]: like this); 當初(当初) ([dāngchū]: originally, in the first place).

"If you (or I, or somebody) had known it would come to this, you (or I, or somebody) would have acted differently." This saying is commonly used to express regret.

---

2. 多虧了你們。(多亏了你们。)

多虧(多亏) ([duōkuī]: thanks to, luckily) "thanks to you all" or "we were lucky to have your help."

---

3. 謝天謝地，不幸中的大幸。
   (谢天谢地，不幸中的大幸。)

謝天謝地(谢天谢地) thank goodness, thank heavens.

不幸中的大幸(不幸中的大幸):
幸(幸) ([xìng]: good fortune) "In the midst of misfortune there is good fortune." This saying is commonly used to comfort somebody and lessen the impact of an unfortunate event.

---

4. 害你們跑了好幾趟醫院。
   (害你们跑了好几趟医院。)

害(害) ([hài]: to cause trouble for).

害你們跑了好幾趟醫院(害你们跑了好几趟医院) means "(we) have troubled you to make several trips to the hospital."

Continued on page 364

课文 Language in Use: A Special Thanks for Your Help!
(简体字 Simplified Character Version)

(小谢病好了，为了要答谢大家的帮助，妈妈特地煮了一桌菜请明修、
常天和中明来吃饭 。)

明修： 小谢，恭喜你出院了 。你看起来精
　　　神不错，恢复得很好 。

小谢： 还可以啦！希望我能跟以前一样灵
　　　活 。但是这段时间，我不能乱跑，
　　　只好待在家里，差不多天天都躺在
　　　床上 。整天被关在家里，快把我闷
　　　死了！

妈妈： 算了吧！早知如此，何必当初[1] 。
　　　你要是能多注意身体，早点儿去检
　　　查，就不会到这样的地步了 。

小谢： 哎呀！我知道错了，真后悔！下次真
　　　的不敢了！

爸爸： 说真的，这次真是多亏了你们[2] 。要不是你们的帮助，事情可能
　　　会更糟呢 。

妈妈： 说的也是，真是谢天谢地，不幸中的大幸[3] 。还好有你们在，
　　　不然后果就不堪设想了 。

小谢： 对不起，这次可把你们忙坏了，害你们跑了好几趟医院[4] 。真是
　　　太麻烦你们了 。

Continued on page 365

課文 Language in Use: A Special Thanks for Your Help!
(繁體字 Traditional Character Version) —— 接第三百六十二頁

常天： 沒什麼，不麻煩。我們沒幫什麼忙，你們太客氣了。

中明： 是呀！一點都不麻煩，醫院就在附近，我也是下課以後就順便過去看看。小事兒，沒什麼。

明修： 這是我們應該做的。出門在外，總是會有不方便的時候。

媽媽： 你們真好。對了，學校那邊，關於請假和保險的事情都解決了嗎?

明修： 都辦好了。小謝有醫生證明，因此不會被記缺席。等他回來上課以後，也可以參加輔導、補考。至於保險方面，因為小謝有健康保險，所以也沒問題。

小謝： 太好了！由於你們的幫助，這些倒楣事兒全沒了。

爸爸： 事情能進行得這麼順利，是由於你們的幫助。俗話說: "在家靠父母，出外靠朋友[5]"，真是一點兒也沒錯！

> 5. 在家靠父母，出外靠朋友。
> (在家靠父母，出外靠朋友。)
>
> "At home you have parents to count on; away from home you might need to count on friends." This saying emphasizes the value of friendship.

媽媽： 喔！不要只顧著說話，你們都餓了吧。來來來，請上座，菜可要涼了。

爸爸： 是呀！來來來，請坐，請坐。我們一起為我們的健康和友誼乾一杯吧。

爸爸、媽媽、小謝、中明、常天、明修: 好，乾杯!

课文 Language in Use: A Special Thanks for Your Help!
(简体字 Simplified Character Version) —— 接第三百六十三页

常天： 没什么，不麻烦。我们没帮什么忙，你们太客气了。

中明： 是呀！一点都不麻烦，医院就在附近，我也是下课以后就顺便过去看看。小事儿，没什么。

明修： 这是我们应该做的。出门在外，总是会有不方便的时候。

妈妈： 你们真好。对了，学校那边，关于请假和保险的事情都解决了吗？

明修： 都办好了。小谢有医生证明，因此不会被记缺席。等他回来上课以后，也可以参加辅导、补考。至于保险方面，因为小谢有健康保险，所以也没问题。

小谢： 太好了！由于你们的帮助，这些倒霉事儿全没了。

爸爸： 事情能进行得这么顺利，是由于你们的帮助。俗话说："在家靠父母，出外靠朋友[5]"，真是一点儿也没错！

妈妈： 喔！不要只顾着说话，你们都饿了吧。来来来，请上座，菜可要凉了。

爸爸： 是呀！来来来，请坐，请坐。我们一起为我们的健康和友谊干一杯吧。

爸爸、妈妈、小谢、中明、常天、明修： 好，干杯！

語法 (语法) GRAMMAR

I. 複合句 (复合句) Compound Sentences

A compound sentence is a sentence composed of two linked clauses which are related in theme. In Chinese, a compound sentence is usually linked with conjunctions (e.g. 因為......所以(因为 ......所以) because . . . therefore) or conjunctives (e.g. adverbs: 才, 就 and 卻(却) [què] but, yet, however). The linking conjunction or conjunctive indicates the relationship between the clauses. (Note: by clause we mean subject-predicate or topic-comment constructions which are part of a larger sentence. In this lesson, we refer to any sentence that is linked to another sentence as a clause.)

Conjunctions in Chinese usually occur as pairs. However, when the context is clear, one or both of the conjunctions may be omitted. A conjunctive which is an adverb may only occur in the second clause and is placed before a verbal phrase. For example,

A paired conjunction: 因為......所以......(因为 ......所以......)

Because you often help him, he is very appreciative.
因為你常幫助他，所以他很感激 [gǎnjī] (thankful)。
因为你常帮助他，所以他很感激 。

因為你常幫助他，他很感激 。
因为你常帮助他，他很感激 。

你常幫助他，所以他很感激 。
你常帮助他，所以他很感激 。

Conjunctives (adverb): 卻(却) [què] (but)

你常幫助他，他卻不感激 。
你常帮助他，他却不感激 。
You often help him, but he is not appreciative.

>>Try it! With a partner, use 因為......所以 (因为......所以) and 卻 (却) to make some compound sentences. For example,

我因為生病了，所以不能去上課。
我因为生病了，所以不能去上课。

他好好的，卻沒來上課。
他好好的，却没来上课。

A. 因果連詞和因果複合句 (因果连词和因果复合句)
Cause-and-Effect Conjunctions and Their Compound Sentences

When two clauses have a cause-and-effect relationship, the first clause usually indicates the cause (reason) and the second one usually indicates the effect (result). The following chart is a list of the most commonly used (paired) conjunctions in cause-and-effect compound sentences.

Cause-and-effect conjunctions	Features	Examples Because of your help, the matter has been resolved.
因為……，所以…… 因为……，所以…… *clause 1* *clause 2* because therefore	• When the context is clear, 因為 (因为) or 所以 (所以) can be omitted. • Sometimes the 因為(因为) clause (acting as an afterthought) follows the consequence clause. In this case 所以(所以) must be omitted.	<u>因為</u>你們的幫助， <u>因为</u>你们的帮助， <u>所以</u>事情都解決了。 <u>所以</u>事情都解决了。 <u>因為</u>你們的幫助，事情都解決了。 <u>因为</u>你们的帮助，事情都解决了。 事情都解決了，<u>因為</u>你們的幫助。 事情都解决了，<u>因为</u>你们的帮助。 (the 因為(因为) clause acts as an afterthought)
由於……，因此…… 由于……，因此…… *clause 1* *clause 2* because therefore	• 由於(由于)……因此(因此)…… is used more in writing than 因為(因为)……所以(所以). • 由於(由于) or 因此(因此) can be omitted.	<u>由於</u>你們的幫助， <u>由于</u>你们的帮助， <u>因此</u>事情都解決了。 <u>因此</u>事情都解决了。 <u>由於</u>你們的幫助，事情都解決了。 <u>由于</u>你们的帮助，事情都解决了。

Cause-and-effect conjunctions	Features	Examples Because of your help, the matter has been resolved.
由於……，…… 由于……，…… *clause 1　　clause 2* due to, because of	• 由於(由于) may also be used with 所以(所以).	由於你們的幫助，事情都解決了。 由于你们的帮助，事情都解决了。
由於……，所以…… 由于……，所以…… due to　　　therefore	• 由於(由于)……所以(所以) is used more in writing than 因為……所以…… (因为……所以……).	由於你們的幫助， 由于你们的帮助， 所以事情都解決了。 所以事情都解决了。
……，　　是由於 ……，　　是由于 *clause 1*　*clause 2* 　　　　is because 　　　　of . . .	• 是由於(是由于) occurs in the second clause to emphasize the cause or reason for something. • used more in writing	事情都解決了，是由於你們 事情都解决了，是由于你们 的幫助。 的帮助。
為了……，…… 为了……，……	• 為了(为了) occurs in the first clause to provide reason.	為了你的健康，你得馬上去檢查 为了你的健康，你得马上去检查 你的身體。 你的身体。
……，　　只好…… ……，　　只好…… *clause 1*　*clause 2* reason　　result, 　　　　have to, 　　　　be forced to	• 只好(只好) occurs in the second clause to indicate a result of the first clause.	事情越來越糟，我們解決不了， 事情越来越糟，我们解决不了， 只好請你們幫忙了。 只好请你们帮忙了。 The matter is getting worse, we cannot resolve it, (therefore) we have to ask for your help.

>>**Try it!** **With a partner, use the cause-and-effect conjunctions to make some compound sentences. For example,**

我由於生病了，所以沒去上課。
我由于生病了，所以没去上课。

B. 條件連詞和條件複合句 (条件连词和条件复合句) Conditional Conjunctions and Their Compound Sentences

Conditional compound sentences are linked by conjunctions that indicate a hypothesis and a conditional relationship between the clauses. The following chart lists the most commonly used (paired) conjunctions and conjunctives in conditional compound sentences.

Conditional conjunctions/ conjunctives	Features	Examples
要是......，就 要是......，就 *clause 1 clause 2* if . . . then . . . 如果(如果) [rúguǒ] 假使(假使) [jiǎshǐ] 假如(假如) [jiǎrú] 假若(假若) [jiǎruò]	• These five conjunctions share the same pattern and meaning. • They are listed in order from the most common spoken style, 要是(要是), to the one used mostly in writing, 假若(假若). • 就(就) occurs in the second clause and is placed after the subject and before a verbal phrase.	要是你們不幫忙， 要是你们不帮忙， 事情就會更糟了。 事情就会更糟了。 If you don't help, the matter will get worse.

Conditional conjunctions/ conjunctives	Features	Examples
......,　不然(不然) [bùrán] + clause 否則(否则) [fǒuzé] *clause 1 clause 2* otherwise, or	• 不然(不然) is used more in speaking than 否則(否则). • 不然/否則(不然/否则) occurs at the beginning of the second clause.	你們一定要幫忙，<u>不然</u> 你们一定要帮忙，<u>不然</u> (否則)事情會更糟。 (否则)事情会更糟。 You definitely need to help, otherwise the matter will get worse.
只有......，......才...... 只有......，......才...... *clause 1　　clause 2* (condition), (consequence) only if/when	• Conjunction 只有(只有) followed by 才(才) indicates an "if and only if" relationship between the clauses. • The second clause indicates a result that arises only under the condition set out in the first clause.	<u>只有</u>你們肯幫忙， <u>只有</u>你们肯帮忙， 事情<u>才</u>能解決。 事情<u>才</u>能解决。 Only if you agree to help can the matter be resolved. 肯(肯) [kěn] agree, be willing to
只要......，就...... 只要......，就...... as long as . . . , (then) . . .	• Conjunction 只要(只要) followed by 就(就) indicates an "as long as" relationship between the clauses. • 就(就) is placed after a subject and before a verbal phrase.	<u>只要</u>你們幫忙， <u>只要</u>你们帮忙， 事情<u>就</u>能解決了。 事情<u>就</u>能解决了。 As long as you help, the matter will be resolved.

Conditional conjunctions/ conjunctives	Features	Examples
沒有……，就沒有…… 没有……，就没有…… if without . . . , then it will be without . . .	• 沒有……，就沒有…… （没有……，就没有……） is a set pair of conjunctions indicating that the first clause is a necessary condition for the second clause. • is used more in speaking.	沒有你以前的幫忙， 没有你以前的帮忙， 就沒有現在的我們。 就没有现在的我们。 沒有國家就沒有人民。 没有国家就没有人民。

≫Try it! With a partner, use conditional conjunctions to make some compound sentences. For example,

要是我病好了，我一定去參加你的生日舞會。
要是我病好了，我一定去参加你的生日舞会。

補充課文 (补充课文) SUPPLEMENTARY PRACTICE

Read the following passage. Then listen and repeat.

"Thank You," and an Invitation to Dinner
(繁體字 Traditional Character Version)

明修和常天，

　　你們好，我是小謝。謝謝你們送我去醫院，還常常來看我。謝謝你們通知王老師，幫我請假，還幫我辦理保險的事情。由於你們的幫助，我可以安心地休養，現在恢復得很好，非常感謝你們的友誼和幫助。

　　我媽媽說這次真是太麻煩你們了，要不是你們的幫助，事情可能會更糟，所以她想請你們吃飯，好好地答謝你們。她要特地煮一桌菜請你們過來吃飯。告訴你們，我媽媽做的飯好吃極了，色香味俱全，你們一定會喜歡的。

　　這個星期六晚上七點，在我家。到時候，我可要好好地跟你們乾一杯。星期六晚上七點見！

小謝

Notes:
辦理(办理) [bànlǐ]: to take care of, handle
安心(安心) [ānxīn]: to have peace of mind, have no worries
煮(煮) [zhǔ]: to cook

補充課文 (补充课文) SUPPLEMENTARY PRACTICE

Read the following passage. Then listen and repeat.

"Thank You," and an Invitation to Dinner
(简体字 Simplified Character Version)

明修和常天，

　　你们好，我是小谢。谢谢你们送我去医院，还常常来看我。谢谢你们通知王老师，帮我请假，还帮我办理保险的事情。由于你们的帮助，我可以安心地休养，现在恢复得很好，非常感谢你们的友谊和帮助。

　　我妈妈说这次真是太麻烦你们了，要不是你们的帮助，事情可能会更糟，所以她想请你们吃饭，好好地答谢你们。她要特地煮一桌菜请你们过来吃饭。告诉你们，我妈妈做的饭好吃极了，色香味俱全，你们一定会喜欢的。

　　这个星期六晚上七点，在我家。到时候，我可要好好地跟你们干一杯。星期六晚上七点见！

　　　　　　　　　　　　　　　　　　　　　　　小谢

Exercises: work with a partner or in small groups

1. 有哪些這一課的語法和生詞出現在這張感謝邀請卡上? 請把它們找出來。
   有哪些这一课的语法和生词出现在这张感谢邀请卡上? 请把它们找出来。

2. 把這張感謝卡翻譯成英文。
   把这张感谢卡翻译成英文。

成語故事 (成语故事) IDIOM STORY

拔苗助長 (拔苗助长) [bá miáo zhù zhǎng]

Meaning: Pulling up the seedling to help it grow.

Usage: It implies spoiling things through excessive enthusiasm.

Example: 謝謝你告訴我媽媽，所以她沒有 "拔苗助長"，要我用兩年時間把大學讀完。

謝謝你告訴我媽媽，所以她没有 "拔苗助长"，要我用兩年時間把大学读完。

Pay special attention to the usage of cause-and-effect conjunctions and conditional conjunctions.

(繁體字 Traditional Character Version)

　　宋國有一個農夫，他覺得他的秧苗長得太慢了，把他急死了。他每天都在想著：要是我的秧苗能長得快一點兒，那就太好了。有一天，他想，秧苗自己長不快，我只好幫他們長快一點兒吧。他想到了一個好方法，他把每一個秧苗都拔高了一點，到了晚上他才回家吃飯。

　　他很高興地告訴他的家人說：今天把我累死了，因為田裡的秧苗長得太慢了，所以我就幫它們長高。現在，由於我的幫助，田裡的秧苗都長高了。

　　他的兒子覺得很好奇，就跑到田裡去看看，結果田裡的秧苗都開始枯萎了。

(简体字 Simplified Character Version)

　　宋国有一个农夫，他觉得他的秧苗长得太慢了，把他急死了。他每天都在想着：要是我的秧苗能长得快一点儿，那就太好了。有一天，他想，秧苗自己长不快，我只好帮他们长快一点儿吧。他想到了一个好方法，他把每一个秧苗都拔高了一点，到了晚上他才回家吃饭。

　　他很高兴地告诉他的家人说：今天把我累死了，因为田里的秧苗长得太慢了，所以我就帮它们长高。现在，由于我的帮助，田里的秧苗都长高了。

　　他的儿子觉得很好奇，就跑到田里去看看，结果田里的秧苗都开始枯萎了。

Notes:
宋國(宋国) [Sòngguó]: the State of Song
農夫(农夫) [nóngfū]: farmer
方法(方法) [fāngfǎ]: method
拔(拔) [bá]: to pull
好奇(好奇) [hàoqí]: curious
結果(结果) [jiéguǒ]: as a result of
枯萎(枯萎) [kūwěi]: to wither

Exercises: work with a partner or in small groups

1. 找出有下面語法的句子：the cause-and-effect conjunctions and the conditional conjunctions.

   找出有下面语法的句子：the cause-and-effect conjunctions and the conditional conjunctions.

2. 用你自己的話說說 "拔苗助長" 的故事。
   用你自己的话说说 "拔苗助长" 的故事。

3. 請用 "拔苗助長" 造一個句子或者說一個 "拔苗助長" 的例子。
   请用 "拔苗助长" 造一个句子或者说一个 "拔苗助长" 的例子。

4. "拔苗助長" 的故事，告訴了我們什麼?
   "拔苗助长" 的故事，告诉了我们什么?

練習 (练习) ACTIVITIES

I. Listening Exercises

 12-1 Listen to the dialogue between 友朋 and 小保 and then answer the following questions. Check them with your partner.

Notes:
路考(路考) [lùkǎo]: driving test
駕照(驾照) [jiàzhào]: driving license
考場(考场) [kǎochǎng]: test place
努力(努力) [nǔlì]: to make great efforts
載(载) [zài]: to give somebody a ride
慶祝(庆祝) [qìngzhù]: to celebrate

問題(问题):

1. 小保有什麼喜事?
   小保有什么喜事?

2. 友朋幫小保做了什麼事情?
   友朋帮小保做了什么事情?

3. 小保是怎麼說感謝友朋的話?
   小保是怎么说感谢友朋的话?

4. 友朋是怎麼回答小保的感謝?
   友朋是怎么回答小保的感谢?

5. 他們現在要去哪兒? 怎麼去?
   他们现在要去哪儿? 怎么去?

6. 下課以後他們要去做什麼? 怎麼去?
   下课以后他们要去做什么? 怎么去?

12-2 Based on the short passage you just listened to, fill in the blanks in the following sentences using the following conjunctions 是由於(是由于), 不然, 由於(由于), 因此, 因為(因为), or 為了(为了). Then check them with your partner.

1. 小保通過路考了, _____ 他拿到駕照了!
   小保通过路考了, _____ 他拿到驾照了!

2. 友朋常教小保練車，＿＿＿＿＿ 小保也不會通過路考。
   友朋常教小保练车，＿＿＿＿＿ 小保也不会通过路考。

3. 友朋說小保通過路考，＿＿＿＿＿ 小保的努力。
   友朋说小保通过路考，＿＿＿＿＿ 小保的努力。

4. 小保覺得很不好意思，＿＿＿＿＿ 他太麻煩友朋了。
   小保觉得很不好意思，＿＿＿＿＿ 他太麻烦友朋了。

5. 小保說：＿＿＿＿＿ 他有駕照了，＿＿＿＿＿ 他可以開車了。
   小保说：＿＿＿＿＿ 他有驾照了，＿＿＿＿＿ 他可以开车了。

II. Character Exercises

12-3 Work with a partner. Read the following words, phrases, and sentences.

答	煮
答	煮
答謝	煮了一桌菜
答谢	煮了一桌菜
要答謝你們的幫助	媽媽特地煮了一桌菜
要答谢你们的帮助	妈妈特地煮了一桌菜
為了要答謝你們的幫助，我請客。	媽媽特地煮了一桌菜，請他們吃飯。
为了要答谢你们的帮助，我请客。	妈妈特地煮了一桌菜，请他们吃饭。

Now with your partner, try to use the following characters to make words, phrases, and then sentences.

1. 恢　　2. 悶　　3. 害　　4. 堪　　5. 趙
   恢　　　 闷　　　 害　　　 堪　　　 赵

6. 險　　7. 輔　　8. 保　　9. 楣　　10. 靠
   险　　　 辅　　　 保　　　 霉　　　 靠

12-4 Read aloud the following sentences. Write them out using traditional characters. Then check your answers with a partner.

1. 由于你的帮助，我恢复得很好。

   _____

2. 这段时间，我不能乱跑，整天被关在家里，快把我闷死了！

   _____

3. 我错了，真后悔！不过，我也体会到一个道理。

   _____

4. 多亏了你们，不然后果就不堪设想了。

   _____

5. 关于请假和保险的事情，我都办好了。

   _____

6. 小谢有医生证明，因此不会被记缺席。等他回来上课以后，也可以参加辅导、补考。

   _____

   _____

12-5 Form groups and create phrases with the following words (pay attention to the various usages of each word).

Example: 塊：十五塊錢　　一塊鏡子，一塊麵包，一塊蛋糕
　　　　　块：十五块钱　　一块镜子，一块面包，一块蛋糕

1. 道：_____　　_____

   道：_____　　_____

2. 此：_____　　_____

   此：_____　　_____

3. 導：_____　　_____

   导：_____　　_____

4. 整： ＿＿＿＿＿＿ ＿＿＿＿＿＿＿＿＿＿＿＿＿

   整： ＿＿＿＿＿＿ ＿＿＿＿＿＿＿＿＿＿＿＿＿

5. 後： ＿＿＿＿＿＿ ＿＿＿＿＿＿＿＿＿＿＿＿＿

   后： ＿＿＿＿＿＿ ＿＿＿＿＿＿＿＿＿＿＿＿＿

6. 難： ＿＿＿＿＿＿ ＿＿＿＿＿＿＿＿＿＿＿＿＿

   难： ＿＿＿＿＿＿ ＿＿＿＿＿＿＿＿＿＿＿＿＿

Homophones:

Example: [shì] 士： 護士

   士： 护士

   是： 你是誰?

   是： 你是谁?

1. [   ] 助： ＿＿＿＿＿＿＿＿＿＿

   助： ＿＿＿＿＿＿＿＿＿＿

   祝： ＿＿＿＿＿＿＿＿＿＿

   祝： ＿＿＿＿＿＿＿＿＿＿

   住： ＿＿＿＿＿＿＿＿＿＿

   住： ＿＿＿＿＿＿＿＿＿＿

2. [   ] 公： ＿＿＿＿＿＿＿＿＿＿

   公： ＿＿＿＿＿＿＿＿＿＿

   恭： ＿＿＿＿＿＿＿＿＿＿

   恭： ＿＿＿＿＿＿＿＿＿＿

   工： ＿＿＿＿＿＿＿＿＿＿

   工： ＿＿＿＿＿＿＿＿＿＿

   功： ＿＿＿＿＿＿＿＿＿＿

   功： ＿＿＿＿＿＿＿＿＿＿

3. [   ] 出：＿＿＿＿＿＿＿＿＿＿

出：＿＿＿＿＿＿＿＿＿＿

初：＿＿＿＿＿＿＿＿＿＿

初：＿＿＿＿＿＿＿＿＿＿

4. [   ] 步：＿＿＿＿＿＿＿＿＿＿

步：＿＿＿＿＿＿＿＿＿＿

不：＿＿＿＿＿＿＿＿＿＿

不：＿＿＿＿＿＿＿＿＿＿

部：＿＿＿＿＿＿＿＿＿＿

部：＿＿＿＿＿＿＿＿＿＿

5. [   ] 設：＿＿＿＿＿＿＿＿＿＿

设：＿＿＿＿＿＿＿＿＿＿

舍：＿＿＿＿＿＿＿＿＿＿

舍：＿＿＿＿＿＿＿＿＿＿

攝：＿＿＿＿＿＿＿＿＿＿

摄：＿＿＿＿＿＿＿＿＿＿

6. [   ] 性：＿＿＿＿＿＿＿＿＿＿

性：＿＿＿＿＿＿＿＿＿＿

姓：＿＿＿＿＿＿＿＿＿＿

姓：＿＿＿＿＿＿＿＿＿＿

幸：＿＿＿＿＿＿＿＿＿＿

幸：＿＿＿＿＿＿＿＿＿＿

興：＿＿＿＿＿＿＿＿＿＿

兴：＿＿＿＿＿＿＿＿＿＿

III. Grammar Exercises

12-6 Compound Sentences

Situation: 明修 is searching for some tips on how to write Chinese characters beautifully. He posted a question online and received the following replies.

With your partner, use the following cause-and-effect conjunctions to translate the following replies orally.

因為……，所以……　　由於……　　因此……　　是由於　　為了　　只好
因为……，所以……　　由于……　　因此……　　是由于　　为了　　只好

明修's question on how to write Chinese characters beautifully.

怎麼樣才能寫出漂亮的漢字?
怎么样才能写出漂亮的汉字?

Replies.

1. I practice writing characters every day; therefore, my characters are beautifully written. (use 因為……所以……)

   _____

2. My characters do not look good either. I have to practice an hour every day. (use 只好)

   _____

3. Because I spend an hour every day practicing writing characters, now I can write them very well. (use 由於)

   _____

4. My Chinese characters look good because I write a love letter to my Chinese girlfriend every day. (use 是由於)

   _____

5. I write the characters slowly; therefore, I can write them well. (use 因此)

   _____

6. I review the characters in the character book every day; therefore, I can write them beautifully. (use 因此)

   _____

12-7 Situation: 明修 is using the key words (關鍵字(关键字) [guānjiànzì]) 健康，鍛煉(锻炼)，and 減肥(减肥) in an online search engine (網上搜尋引擎 (网上搜寻引擎) [wǎngshàng sōuxún yǐnqíng]). Here are some suggestions he collected. With your partner, use the following conditional conjunctions to translate them orally into compound sentences.

要是(如果，假如，假使，假若)......，就　　不然，　　否則
要是(如果，假如，假使，假若)......，就　　不然，　　否則

只有......，才　　只要......，就　　沒有......就沒有
只有......，才　　只要......，就　　沒有......就沒有

1. If you work out every day, you will be healthy. (use 要是......，就)

   _____

2. If you get up and go to bed early every day, then you will be healthy. (use 如果)

   _____

3. Without sleep you won't be healthy. (use 沒有......，就沒有)
   – 睡眠 [shuìmián]: sleep

   _____

4. Only if you don't smoke and don't drink will you be healthy. (use 只有......，才)

   _____

5. You need to quit smoking, otherwise you will be unhealthy. (use 否則)

   _____

6. As long as you work out every day, you will be able to lose weight.
   (use 只要......，就)

   _____

7. You need to eat less and get more exercise or you will get fatter and fatter.
   (use 不然)

   _____

IV. Media Literacy

The short text below, written in the style of newspapers, magazines, or Internet news articles, will help you become familiar with the formal written expressions used in these genres.

朋友是良藥 (朋友是良药) **Friends Are an Excellent Remedy**

繁體字：

朋友是良藥

"朋友是良藥，"專家告訴我們，治療疾病不僅靠藥物，還需要友誼和快樂。

專家把人們分成兩組做實驗，一組有寵物為伴，另一組則沒有。結果證明，前一組出現的健康問題比後一組少一半。朋友和寵物成為輔助治療的一個良藥。

简体字：

朋友是良药

"朋友是良药，"专家告诉我们，治疗疾病不仅靠药物，还需要友谊和快乐。

专家把人们分成两组做实验，一组有宠物为伴，另一组则没有。结果证明，前一组出现的健康问题比后一组少一半。朋友和宠物成为辅助治疗的一个良药。

Note:
良藥(良药) [liángyào]: excellent remedy

Exercises for the headlines: work with a partner or a group to ask and answer the following questions.

1. What can you tell about the news by skimming the headline?

2. How would you translate the headline into English?

3. What is the spoken counterpart for the written form "良"?

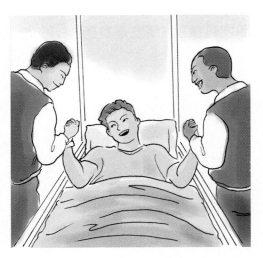

Notes:
專家(专家) [zhuānjiā]: experts
不僅......, 還......(不仅......, 还......): not only . . . but also
實驗(实验) [shíyàn]: experiment
組(组) [zǔ]: set, group
寵物(宠物) [chǒngwù]: pet
為伴(为伴) [wéibàn]: to keep company, as a companion
輔助治療(辅助治疗) [fǔzhù zhìliáo]: supplementary
   treatment

Exercises for the article: work with a partner or a group to ask and answer the following.

1. What was the experiment carried out by the experts? What was the result of the experiment?

2. What did the experts suggest?

3. Can you find any written expressions in the article? What are the spoken counterparts for the following expressions.

   不僅......, 還......(不仅......, 还......)
   成為(成为)

4. Point out the sentences which contain Lesson 12 vocabulary, then translate the sentences into English, for example, 友誼(友谊), 證明(证明).

5. How can pets help cure patients?

6. How do you feel about the importance of friendship?

7. Use your own words to summarize the headline and article.

V. Communicative Activities

Work with a partner or a group. Try to incorporate the following conjunctions to act out the situations below:

Cause-and-effect conjunctions

因為......，所以......　　由於......，因此　　是由於　　只好
因为......，所以......　　由于......，因此　　是由于　　只好

Conditional conjunctions

要是(如果，假如，假使，假若)......，就　　不然
要是(如果，假如，假使，假若)......，就　　不然

只有......，才　　只要......，就　　沒有......，就沒有
只有......，才　　只要......，就　　没有......，就没有

12-8 車子發不動了(车子发不动了)： You parked your car in the parking lot. You were in a hurry and forgot to turn off the lights. When you returned to your car after class your car wouldn't start and you realized that the battery had died. You call your friends, explain the situation, and ask for help.

Notes:
發動(发动) [fādòng]: to operate
電池(电池) [diànchí]: battery
發動器(发动器) [fādòngqì]: starter
電纜(电缆) [diànlǎn]: cable

麻煩　順便　後果　謝天謝地　後悔
沒什麼　俗話　靠　友誼

麻烦　顺便　后果　谢天谢地　后悔
没什么　俗话　靠　友谊

1. Call your friends and explain the situation.
2. Your friends drive their car over to give you a jump start.
3. You are very grateful and show your appreciation.
4. Your friends say that it's nothing, no trouble at all.

12-9 雪下得太大了，因此車子出不來。
雪下得太大了，因此车子出不来。

It is a cold winter. Last night there was a big snow storm. When you try to drive your car out of the driveway, you are blocked by deep snow. Your kind neighbor comes out to help shovel the snow and apply salt. You invite him inside for a cup of hot chocolate to show your appreciation.

Notes:
鄰居(邻居) [línjū]: neighbor
剷雪(铲雪) [chǎnxuě]: to shovel snow
除雪機(除雪机) [chúxuějī]: snow blower, snow plow
車道(车道) [chēdào]: driveway
走道(走道) [zǒudào]: footpath
深(深) [shēn]: deep
鹽(盐) [yán]: salt
撒鹽(撒盐) [sǎyán]: to scatter salt
結冰(结冰) [jiébīng]: freeze, ice up
冰冷的(冰冷的) [bīnglěngde]: icy
滑(滑) [huá]: slippery
熱巧克力(热巧克力) [rè qiǎokèlì]: hot chocolate

悶死　解決　順便　麻煩　害　俗話　靠　友誼
闷死　解决　顺便　麻烦　害　俗话　靠　友谊

1. You are working alone at first, then your kind neighbor comes out to help.
2. You are grateful and show your appreciation.
3. Your neighbor says that it's nothing.
4. You invite him inside to have hot chocolate, chat about the big snow storm, etc.

文化知識 (文化知识) Culture Link

文化點滴 (文化点滴) CULTURE NOTES

送禮和感謝 (送礼和感谢) Giving Gifts and Thanks

The ways in which Chinese people give and accept thanks are quite complex. Unlike the Western custom, compliments are not graciously accepted with a "thank you," but rather with a "not at all," or "it is nothing." Accepting direct praise or appreciation is considered poor etiquette.

In Western culture, a thank you or thank-you notes are acceptable ways to show appreciation. In China, however, a thank-you dinner or gift is preferred as a more tangible expression of gratitude. Gift giving may seem like a trivial matter, but there are actually many practices and traditions that go along with it in Chinese culture.

When it comes to gift giving, there are certain items that are generally considered to be bad choices. These items should be avoided, as they are typically associated with death, grief, and bad luck. For example, clocks should not be given as gifts because the phrase 送鐘 (送钟) [sòng zhōng] (give a clock) sounds like the phrase 送終 (送终) [sòng zhōng] (to see off the dead). Gifts related to the number four should also be avoided, since the word for four in Chinese 四 [sì] (four) sounds like the word for 死 [sǐ] (death).

Do you know...

- what items are generally considered to be bad gifts in Chinese culture? Why?
- whether the Chinese usually open gifts when they are received? Why?
- what are some common gifts among Chinese people?

Read and find out!

梨 [lí] (pears) and 傘 (伞) [sǎn] (umbrellas) are not given as gifts because they sound like the words for 離 (离) [lí] (to separate) and 散 [sàn] (to disperse). You should also avoid giving a handkerchief as a present, as it is believed to cause the recipient to cry. Sharp objects imply the severance of a relationship, so steer clear of knives and scissors. Avoid giving white or yellow flowers (especially chrysanthemums), which are used for funerals.

Once a suitable gift is found, care should be taken to present it in the proper manner. First, wrap the gift in a color symbolizing happiness or prosperity, such as red or gold. Avoid using black or white, colors generally used at funerals. When signing a card or note, avoid using red ink, since it symbolizes the end of a relationship. Gifts should be presented with two hands and given directly to the recipient. The Chinese usually do not open gifts at the time they are received, since to do so would seem greedy. Also, gifts should be given in private, not in front of other people. Otherwise, this can embarrass the recipient and imply that those not receiving a gift are less valued. Chinese etiquette requires that a person decline a gift or invitation two or three times before accepting. It is expected that the giver will persist, gently, until the gift is accepted. When giving a gift one should take into consideration how expensive it is. Giving a gift that would make it impossible for the receiver to reciprocate in kind would cause a loss of face and place them in a difficult position.

Some good ideas for gifts include jade, liquor, cigarettes, tea, artwork, or some local famous products. Modern choices also include health products, or beauty products for women.

A thank-you dinner is a more tangible form of showing appreciation. To pour tea for another is a courteous practice. What other ways do Chinese use to show their thanks and appreciation?

Herbal supplements are one of the common gifts among Chinese. What other gifts do the Chinese typically give?

問題討論 (问题讨论) *Discuss the following with a partner or in small groups.*

1. 在表達感謝和送禮方面，中西文化有什麼相似或者不同的地方？
   在表达感谢和送礼方面，中西文化有什么相似或者不同的地方？
   What similarities and differences are there between Chinese and Western culture regarding how to show and accept appreciation?

2. 在你們的文化當中，什麼是好的禮物？在送禮方面有什麼禁忌呢？
   在你们的文化当中，什么是好的礼物？在送礼方面有什么禁忌呢？
   Provide some examples from your culture of good gifts or gift taboos.

趣味中文 (趣味中文) FUN WITH CHINESE

悔不當初
悔不当初

To regret a previous mistake
Regret having done something

huǐ	bù	dāngchū
悔	不	當初
悔	不	当初
to regret	not	originally, at that time

問題討論 (问题讨论) *Discuss the following with a partner or in small groups.*

Are there any similar sayings in English or other languages that provide a similar expression of regret? How do you react to somebody's regret?

行動吧! (行动吧!) LET'S GO!

寄包裹 (寄包裹) Mailing a Package

常天的生日就要到了，他哥哥寄了一個包裹給他，裡面都是他的生日禮物。以下是包裹外面的郵件詳情單。

常天的生日就要到了，他哥哥寄了一个包裹给他，里面都是他的生日礼物。以下是包裹外面的邮件详情单。

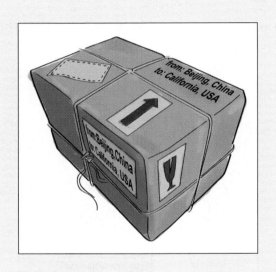

中华人民共和国邮政 国际特快专递邮件详情单
北京西区邮政

寄件人	
姓名: 常爱民	
地址: 北京市西大街10号	
电话: 010-588-11345	**邮政编码**: 100035
内容说明: 书，衣服和光碟	

收件人

姓名：	常天
地址：	5000 Forbes Ave., Pittsburgh, PA 15213, USA
电话：	412-268-9375

Notes:

包裹(包裹) [bāoguǒ]: package
郵政(邮政) [yóuzhèng]: post
郵件(邮件) [yóujiàn]: mail
詳情單(详情单) [xiángqíngdān]: detailed information form
寄件人(寄件人) [jìjiànrén]: sender
收件人(收件人) [shōujiànrén]: receiver
想像(想象) [xiǎngxiàng]: to imagine
填填看(填填看) [tiántian kàn]: try to fill in (the form)

問題討論 (问题讨论) *Discuss the following with a partner or in small groups.*

1. 寄件人是誰，包裹是從哪兒寄出的?
   寄件人是谁，包裹是从哪儿寄出的?

2. 包裹裡面是什麼東西?
   包裹里面是什么东西?

3. 以下的英文是什麼意思?
   以下的英文是什么意思?

   (a) 中華人民共和國郵政(中华人民共和国邮政)
   (b) 國際特快專遞郵件詳情單(国际特快专递邮件详情单)
   (c) 北京西區郵政(北京西区邮政)

4. 想像你在中國，也想寄一個包裹到美國，你來填填看：
   想象你在中国，也想寄一个包裹到美国，你来填填看：

寄件人
姓名：
地址：北京市西大街10号
电话：　　　　　　　　　　　邮政编码：
内容说明：

收件人
姓名：
地址：
电话：

復習 (复习) Review

LESSON 11 TO LESSON 12

I. Report

With your partner, use at least 15 sentences in Chinese to report an unpleasant experience you have had. Pay attention to your accuracy (e.g. pronunciation, grammar usage) and fluency.

Notes:

事情	經過	情況	生氣	擔心	罵	麻煩	順利	開心	可憐	結束
事情	经过	情况	生气	担心	骂	麻烦	顺利	开心	可怜	结束

> Object (receiver of action) + 被(被) + Subject (doer) + 給(给) + V. + other elements
> 叫(叫)   給(给)
> 讓(让)   給(给)

II. Dialogue

With your partner, use at least 15 sentences to talk in Chinese about a mistake you made previously and explain how you resolved the situation.

Useful cause-and-effect conjunctions:

因為……, 所以	由於……, 因此	是由於	為了	只好
因为……, 所以	由于……, 因此	是由于	为了	只好

Useful conditional conjunctions:

要是(如果，假如，假使，假若)……, 就   不然/否則
要是(如果，假如，假使，假若)……, 就   不然/否则

只有……, ……才	只要……, 就	沒有……, 就沒有
只有……, ……才	只要……, 就	没有……, 就没有

III. Picture Description

With your group, use the passive construction, cause-and-effect conjunctions, and conditional conjunctions to describe the pictures below:

(1)

(2)

IV. Traditional and Simplified Characters

With a partner, read each character aloud. Write its traditional form. Then make a phrase and a sentence using the character.

Example: 学 → 學 → 學生 → 我是學生。

L11: 顾 (　)   厉 (　)   刚 (　)   诊 (　)   术 (　)   吓 (　)   护 (　)

L12: 养 (　)   紧 (　)   骂 (　)   顿 (　)   怜 (　)

13

生氣（生气）
Expressing Anger

This 莫生氣(莫生气) [mò shēngqì] (don't be angry) calligraphy couplet can be used as a decoration as well as a motto.

CONNECTIONS AND COMMUNITIES PREVIEW

Discuss the following questions with a partner or your class. What similarities and differences do you think there might be between Chinese culture and your own culture?

1. What are the typical ways to express anger and make complaints in your culture?

2. How do you deal with your anger? Are there any resources available for anger management in your community?

教學目標 (教学目标) OBJECTIVES

- Express anger and make complaints

- Reply and listen to anger and complaints

- Seek and provide advice

生詞 (生词) VOCABULARY

🔊 核心詞 (核心词) Core Vocabulary

	TRADITIONAL	SIMPLIFIED	PINYIN		
1.	催	催	cuī	V.	to urge
2.	吵架	吵架	chǎojià	V.O.	to quarrel
3.	心情	心情	xīnqíng	N.	mood
4.	談談	谈谈	tántan	V.	to chat
5.	建議	建议	jiànyì	V. N.	to advise, recommend advice, recommendation
6.	怎麼搞的	怎么搞的	zěnmegǎode		what's wrong, what's the matter
7.	又	又	yòu	Adv.	again
8.	心事	心事	xīnshì	N.	something weighing on one's mind
9.	數碼相機 (數位相機)	数码相机 (数位相机)	shùmǎ xiàngjī (shùwèi xiàngjī)	N.	digital camera
10.	退貨	退货	tuìhuò	V.O.	to return merchandise
11.	陪	陪	péi	V.	to accompany
12.	掛	挂	guà	V.	to hang, hang up (telephone)
13.	交代	交代	jiāodài	V.	to tell, explain, make clear
14.	專心	专心	zhuānxīn	V.	to concentrate on
15.	高速公路	高速公路	gāosù gōnglù	N.	highway
16.	車禍	车祸	chēhuò	N.	car accident

	TRADITIONAL	SIMPLIFIED	PINYIN		
17.	碰到	碰到	pèngdào	V.C.	to run into
18.	塞車	塞车	sāichē	N.	traffic jam
19.	出口	出口	chūkǒu	N.	exit
20.	禁止	禁止	jìnzhǐ	V.	to prohibit, ban
21.	通過	通过	tōngguò	V.	to go through
22.	使	使	shǐ	V.	to make, cause
23.	完全	完全	wánquán	Adv.	totally, entirely
24.	動不了	动不了	dòngbuliǎo		cannot move
25.	剛剛	刚刚	gānggāng	Adv.	a moment ago, just now
26.	匆匆忙忙	匆匆忙忙	cōngcōng mángmáng	Adv.	in a hurry
27.	逼	逼	bī	V.	to force
28.	路肩	路肩	lùjiān	N.	shoulder (of a road)
29.	碰運氣	碰运气	pèngyùnqi		to try one's luck
30.	結果	结果	jiéguǒ	N.	result
31.	警察	警察	jǐngchá	N.	police
32.	抓住	抓住	zhuāzhù	V.C.	to catch
33.	罰單	罚单	fádān	N.	ticket, citation
34.	遲到	迟到	chídào	V.	to be late
35.	聲	声	shēng	N.	sound
36.	抱怨	抱怨	bàoyuàn	V.	to complain
37.	守時	守时	shǒushí	V.	to be on time

TRADITIONAL	SIMPLIFIED	PINYIN		
38. 脾氣	脾气	píqì	N.	temperament
39. 容易	容易	róngyì	Adj.	easy
40. 吃虧	吃亏	chīkuī	V.O.	to suffer losses, come to grief
41. 改	改	gǎi	V.	to change, revise
42. 道歉	道歉	dàoqiàn	V.O.	to apologize
43. 原諒	原谅	yuánliàng	V. / N.	to excuse, forgive / forgiveness

專名 (专名) Proper Nouns

TRADITIONAL	SIMPLIFIED	PINYIN		
1. 史文超	史文超	Shǐ Wénchāo	N.	(full name) Wenchao Shi
2. 何順強	何顺强	Hé Shùnqiáng	N.	(full name) Shunqiang He
3. 彩宜	彩宜	Cǎiyí	N.	(given name) Caiyi

語文知識 (语文知识) LANGUAGE LINK

Read and listen to the following sentence patterns. These patterns use vocabulary, expressions, and grammar that you will study in more detail in this lesson. After reading the sentence patterns, read and listen to the Language in Use section that follows.

句型 (句型) Sentence Patterns

A: 怎麼搞的，是不是又跟女朋友吵架啦？
怎么搞的，是不是又跟女朋友吵架啦？
Zěnmegǎo de, shìbushì yòu gēn nǚpéngyou chǎojià la?

B: 哎呀！你真厲害，馬上就知道我的心事了。
哎呀！你真厉害，马上就知道我的心事了。
Àiyā! Nǐ zhēn lìhài, mǎshàng jiù zhīdào wǒ de xīnshì le.

A: 她催我快一點兒，還交代我要專心開車。
她催我快一点儿，还交代我要专心开车。
Tā cuīwǒ kuài yìdiǎnr, hái jiāodài wǒ yào zhuānxīn kāichē.

B: 沒什麼問題呀！她好像很小心，不錯嘛！
没什么问题呀！她好像很小心，不错嘛！
Méishénme wèntí yā! Tā hǎoxiàng hěn xiǎoxīn, búcuò ma!

A: 出口關起來了，禁止車子通過，我逼自己
出口关起来了，禁止车子通过，我逼自己
Chūkǒu guānqǐlái le, jìnzhǐ chēzi tōngguò, wǒ bī zìjǐ

走路肩，使她生氣了。
走路肩，使她生气了。
zǒu lùjiān, shǐ tā shēngqì le.

B: 我建議你先向她道歉，她大概會原諒你。
我建议你先向她道歉，她大概会原谅你。
Wǒ jiànyì nǐ xiān xiàng tā dàoqiàn, tā dàgài huì yuánliàng nǐ.

課文 Language in Use: I Need Some Advice
(繁體字 Traditional Character Version)

(史文超和女朋友吵架了，心情很不好，他來找順強談談，請他給一些建議。)

史文超：順強，我能進來跟你談談嗎?

何順強(開門)：嘿，文超是你呀! 請進，怎麼搞的，是不是又跟女朋友吵架啦?

史文超：哎呀! 你真厲害[1]，馬上就知道我的心事了。是啊! 昨天我和彩宜吵架了!

何順強：喔! 你們倆昨天還好好的，怎麼今天就吵架了!

史文超：唉! 事情是這樣的：她買了一部數碼相機，出了一些問題。她想退貨，要我陪她去，我不小心睡過頭[2]了。她打電話來催我快一點兒，我掛了電話，馬上就開車去接她了。

何順強：那很好啊! 怎麼會到吵架的地步呢?

史文超：問題就出在後面啦! 她交代我要把手機帶著，不可以讓手機開著，這樣才能專心開車。

何順強：聽上去好像沒什麼問題呀! 她好像很小心，不錯嘛!

史文超：等我把故事說完你就知道了。我上高速公路以後，前面有一個小車禍，碰到塞車了。我想要從出口下去，可是旁邊的出口又關起來了，禁止車子通過，使我完全動不了了。原來想打手機通知她，但是剛剛匆匆忙忙地跑了出來，手機叫我給忘在家裡了。我怕她會等太久，就逼自己走路肩，想碰碰運氣。結果被警察抓住了，吃了一張罰單。

---

1. 你真厲害(你真厉害)

厲害(厉害) has two meanings. One meaning is "severe, serious," e.g. 我肚子疼得厲害(我肚子疼得厉害): "My belly is in severe pain." The other meaning is "very good, capable." 你真厲害(你真厉害) means "You are very capable" or "You are terrific!"

---

2. 睡過頭(睡过头)

睡過頭(睡过头): oversleep. 過頭(过头) means "to go beyond the limit, overdo." 過頭(过头) is usually formed into a construction with a verb or adjective: V. (Adj.) + 過頭(过头).

Examples:

我午飯吃過頭，太飽了!
我午饭吃过头，太饱了!
I overate at lunch; (I'm) too full!

小花越來越胖，已經胖過頭了。
小花越来越胖，已经胖过头了。
Xiaohua is getting fatter and fatter. She is already overweight.

Continued on page 402

课文 Language in Use: I Need Some Advice
(简体字 Simplified Character Version)

(史文超和女朋友吵架了，心情很不好，他来找顺强谈谈，请他给一些
建议。)

史文超： 顺强，我能进来跟你谈谈吗？

何顺强(开门)： 嘿，文超是你呀！请进，怎么搞的，是不是又跟女朋友
　　　　　　　吵架啦？

史文超： 哎呀！你真厉害[1]，马上就知道我
　　　　的心事了。是啊！昨天我和彩宜
　　　　吵架了！

何顺强： 喔！你们俩昨天还好好的，怎么
　　　　今天就吵架了！

史文超： 唉！事情是这样的：她买了一部
　　　　数码相机，出了一些问题。她想
　　　　退货，要我陪她去，我不小心睡
　　　　过头[2]了。她打电话来催我快一点
　　　　儿，我挂了电话，马上就开车去
　　　　接她了。

何顺强： 那很好啊！怎么会到吵架的地步
　　　　呢？

史文超： 问题就出在后面啦！她交代我要把手机带着，不可以让手机
　　　　开着，这样才能专心开车。

何顺强： 听上去好像没什么问题呀！她好像很小心，不错嘛！

史文超： 等我把故事说完你就知道了。我上高速公路以后，前面有一
　　　　个小车祸，碰到塞车了。我想要从出口下去，可是旁边的出口
　　　　又关起来了，禁止车子通过，使我完全动不了了。原来想打手
　　　　机通知她，但是刚刚匆匆忙忙地跑了出来，手机叫我给忘在
　　　　家里了。我怕她会等太久，就逼自己走路肩，想碰碰运气。
　　　　结果被警察抓住了，吃了一张罚单。

Continued on page 403

課文 Language in Use: I Need Some Advice
(繁體字 Traditional Character Version) —— 接第四百頁

何順強：喔！喔！真是的，吃虧[3]了吧！

史文超：是啊！真後悔，可是已經來不
及了。等我到的時候，已經遲
到了兩個鐘頭。不過，她還在
那兒等我。一見我就哼地一
聲，把我罵了一頓，說我總是
喜歡遲到。

何順強：她是說氣話嘛！

史文超：是啊！可是我剛剛叫警察給
開了罰單，心情很不好。一聽
她抱怨，我就生起氣來了。因
此我們就吵架了。

何順強：嗯！原來如此，不要緊的！聽
我說，你要記住，守時是最重要的；還有，你的脾氣比較急，
這樣是很容易吃虧的，應該改一改。至於彩宜呢，現在已經過
了一天了，她應該好多了。我建議你應該先向她道歉，陪她去
把退貨的事情辦好，然後再
請她去看個電影、吃頓飯什
麼的[4]。我想她大概就會原諒
你了。

史文超：好的，讓我再想想，謝謝你的
建議。

何順強：不用謝啦！祝你好運！

---

3. 吃虧(吃亏)

吃虧(吃亏) means "to suffer a loss or be taken advantage of." The verb 吃(吃) usually means "to eat." It also has the meaning "suffer, incur."

Examples:

他吃了一張罰單。
他吃了一张罚单。
He received a ticket.

他給小花吃苦頭。
他给小花吃苦头。
He made Xiaohua suffer.

他今天吃了敗仗。
他今天吃了败仗。
Today he suffered a defeat.

**4. 看個電影、吃頓飯什麼的
(看个电影、吃顿饭什么的)**

"Watch a movie, eat a meal, and so on." 什麼的(什么的) is more colloquial than 等等(等等).

课文 Language in Use: I Need Some Advice
(简体字 Simplified Character Version) —— 接第四百零一页

何顺强： 喔！喔！真是的，吃亏[3]了吧！

史文超： 是啊！真后悔，可是已经来不及了。等我到的时候，已经迟到了两个钟头。不过，她还在那儿等我。一见我就哼地一声，把我骂了一顿，说我总是喜欢迟到。

何顺强： 她是说气话嘛！

史文超： 是啊！可是我刚刚叫警察给开了罚单，心情很不好。一听她抱怨，我就生起气来了。因此我们就吵架了。

何顺强： 嗯！原来如此，不要紧的！听我说，你要记住，守时是最重要的；还有，你的脾气比较急，这样是很容易吃亏的，应该改一改。至于彩宜呢，现在已经过了一天了，她应该好多了。我建议你应该先向她道歉，陪她去把退货的事情办好，然后再请她去看个电影、吃顿饭什么的[4]。我想她大概就会原谅你了。

史文超： 好的，让我再想想，谢谢你的建议。

何顺强： 不用谢啦！祝你好运！

語法 (语法) GRAMMAR

I. 兼語句 (兼语句) Pivotal Constructions

In a pivotal construction a noun phrase serves as the object of a verb and simultaneously as the notional subject of a second verb. That is, the noun phrase functions as a pivot or center pin relating the two verbs. The pivotal constructions can be schematized as follows:

a) 我　　　請　　你們　　吃飯。
　　我　　　请　　你们　　吃饭。
　　Subj.　V.　　Obj.
　　　　　　　　Subj.　　V.

你們(你们) is the object of the first verb 請(请). 你們(你们) also serves as the notional subject of the second verb 吃飯(吃饭).

b) 我　　　恭喜　　小謝　　出院了。
　　我　　　恭喜　　小谢　　出院了。
　　Subj.　V.　　　Obj.
　　　　　　　　　Subj.　　V.

小謝(小谢) is the object of the first verb 恭喜, and 小謝(小谢) also serves as the notional subject of the second verb 出院.

c) 我　　　建議　　你　　向她道歉。
　　我　　　建议　　你　　向她道歉。
　　Subj.　V.　　　Obj.
　　　　　　　　　Subj.　　V.

你 is the object of the first verb 建議(建议). 你 also serves as the notional subject of the second verb 道歉.

Note: The pivotal construction is one type of serial verb construction 連動句(连动句) [liándòngjù]. In a serial verb construction a sentence contains two or more verb phrases or clauses placed side by side without any marker. The relationship of these verb phrases usually depends on the nature of the verbs and the context. For example, 我去圖書館看書 (我去图书馆看书). 去圖書館(去图书馆) is one verb phrase, and 看書(看书) is the other. It could mean "I went to the library, and studied" or "I went to the library in order to study." More details about serial verb constructions 連動句(连动句) will be presented in Lesson 16.

>>**Try it!** With a partner, use 請 (请), 恭喜 and 建議 (建议) to make some sentences for the pivotal constructions. For example,

A: 明天晚上我請你們看電影，去不去？
明天晚上我请你们看电影，去不去？

B: 好啊！我一定去。
好啊！我一定去。

II. 使動用法和兼語句 (使动用法和兼语句) Causative Sentences and Pivotal Constructions

In Chinese, verbs related to giving commands or making suggestions are used to form causative constructions. The causative construction can usually be schematized as a pivotal construction 兼語句(兼语句) [jiānyǔjù]. That is, the object of the first verb (e.g. 請(请), 要, and 叫 below) becomes the notional subject of a second verb phrase. Some verbs which are commonly used in causative constructions are listed below.

Verbs	Meaning	Examples (mainly from Lesson 13 text) Causative sentences/pivotal construction
1. 請(请) [qǐng]	to request, ask somebody to do something	你請她去看電影。 你请她去看电影。
2. 要(要) [yào]	to want	她要我陪她去退貨。 她要我陪她去退货。
3. 叫(叫) [jiào]	ask/get somebody to do something • 叫(叫) may be also followed by an adjective. • 叫(叫) is more spoken style than 使(使), 讓(让).	她叫我專心開車。 她叫我专心开车。 她叫我高興。 她叫我高兴。 She made me happy.
4. 讓(让) [ràng]	to let, make • 讓(让) may be also followed by an adjective.	他讓我把故事說完。 他让我把故事说完。 她讓我生氣。 她让我生气。 She made me angry.

Verbs	Meaning	Examples (mainly from Lesson 13 text) Causative sentences/pivotal construction
5. 使(使) [shǐ]	to make, cause • 使(使) may be also followed by an adjective.	前面塞車使我完全動不了了。 前面塞车使我完全动不了了。 她使我生氣。 她使我生气。 She made me angry.
6. 令(令) [lìng]	to make, cause • 令(令) is more written style. • 令(令) is also used with an adjective.	她的話令我很生氣。 她的话令我很生气。 令人滿意 令人满意 to make people satisfied
7. 命令(命令) [mìnglìng]	to order, command	她命令我快一點兒。 她命令我快一点儿。
8. 勸(劝) [quàn]	to advise, urge, try to persuade	她勸我要改脾氣。 她劝我要改脾气。
9. 允許(允许) [yǔnxǔ]	to permit, allow	她不允許我一面開車一面打手機。 她不允许我一面开车一面打手机。
10. 交代(交代) [jiāodài]	to tell, explain, make clear	她交代我不可以讓手機開著。 她交代我不可以让手机开着。
11. 吩咐(吩咐) [fēnfù]	to tell, instruct	她吩咐我把手機帶著。 她吩咐我把手机带着。
12. 催(催) [cuī]	to urge	她催我快一點兒。 她催我快一点儿。
13. 逼(逼) [bī]	to force	我逼自己走路肩。 我逼自己走路肩。
14. 禁止(禁止) [jìnzhǐ]	to prohibit, ban	出口那兒禁止車子通過。 出口那儿禁止车子通过。
15. 建議(建议) [jiànyì]	to suggest, recommend	我建議你應該先向她道歉。 我建议你应该先向她道歉。

>>**Try it!** With a partner, use 讓 (让), 使, 勸 (劝), 交代 , 催 and 禁止 to make some causative sentences and pivotal constructions. For example,

警察在出口那兒，禁止車子通過。
警察在出口那儿，禁止车子通过。

III. 感嘆詞 (感叹词) Summary of Interjections

Interjections are used to indicate the tone or mood of the speaker. Some commonly used interjections are listed below. Those in Group (1) usually stand alone or precede another sentence, and those in Group (2) are sentence-final-particles. (Please note that some of the functions and meanings of the interjections may change slightly due to the interpretation of the context.)

Group 1

Interjections 語氣詞(语气词)	Speaker's emotion	Examples
1. 嘿(嘿) [hēi]	delight	嘿，文超是你呀! 嘿，文超是你呀! Oh! It's you Wenchao! 嘿，她真漂亮! 嘿，她真漂亮! Wow, she is really pretty!
2. 哼(哼) [hēng]	angry or unhappy	哼! 你又遲到了! 哼! 你又迟到了! Humph! You are late again!
3. 唉(唉) [ài]	regret, sigh	唉! 他真倒楣! 唉! 他真倒霉! Oh! He had really bad luck.

Interjections 語氣詞(语气词)	Speaker's emotion	Examples
4. 哎呀(哎呀) [āiya]	• surprise • happy • unhappy	哎呀！我睡過頭了！ 哎呀！我睡过头了！ Ah! I overslept! 哎呀！你真棒！ 哎呀！你真棒！ Gosh! You are terrific! 哎呀！你們兩個怎麼又吵架了！ 哎呀！你们两个怎么又吵架了！ Oh dear! How could you two be quarreling again!
5. 呸(呸) [pēi]	• contempt, disregard	呸！胡說八道 [húshuōbādào]！ 呸！胡说八道！ Bah! Nonsense!
6. 喔(喔) [ō]	• realization	喔！原來是你呀！ 喔！原来是你呀！ Oh! So it's you!
7. 嗯(嗯) [ēn]	• acknowledgment in a conversation • agree	嗯！我知道了。 嗯！我知道了。 Hmm! I got it. 嗯！我同意你的看法。 嗯！我同意你的看法。 Hmm! I agree with you.

Interjections 語氣詞(语气词)	Speaker's emotion	Examples
8. 噢(噢) [ō]	• sudden realization	噢！已經很晚了，我得走了。 噢！已经很晚了，我得走了。 Oh! It's very late. I've got to go.
9. 啊(啊) [ā] [á] [ǎ] [à]	With different tones, 啊(啊) can imply different moods and emotions.	[ā] surprise 啊！這是我的。 啊！这是我的。 Oh! This is mine.
		[á] asking for confirmation 啊！你剛才說什麼？ 啊！你刚才说什么？ Pardon me, what did you just say?
		[ǎ] doubt and surprise 啊！你說她真的生氣了。 啊！你说她真的生气了。 Oh! You say she really got angry?
		[à] admire or agree 啊！多漂亮的長城啊！ 啊！多漂亮的长城啊！ Ah! How beautiful the Great Wall is!

Group 2

Sentence-final-particles (Interjections) 句尾語氣詞 (句尾语气词)	Speaker's tone and emotion	Examples
1. 呢(呢) [ne]	• makes the tone softer • response to expectation • strengthens the assertion or reality	怎麼搞的呢? 怎么搞的呢? Oh! What's up? 他遲到了三個鐘頭呢! 他迟到了三个钟头呢! (You see), he was three hours late. 她很生氣呢。 她很生气呢。 She is very mad.
2. 吧(吧) [ba]	• suggestion or assumption	我們走吧! 我们走吧! Let's go! 你是愛文吧! 你是爱文吧! You must be Aiwen.
3. 嘛(嘛) [ma]	• emphasizes obviousness • makes the tone softer	她是關心你嘛! 她是关心你嘛! She is concerned about you (you see)!
4. 啊(啊) [a]	• emphasizes obviousness	這就是我的故事啊! 这就是我的故事啊! This is my story (you see)!
5. 喔(喔) [ō]	• a friendly warning • often used to soften a command	別睡過頭喔! 别睡过头喔! Don't oversleep, OK? 要專心開車喔! 要专心开车喔! Concentrate on driving, OK?

Sentence-final-particles (Interjections) 句尾語氣詞 (句尾语气词)	Speaker's tone and emotion	Examples
6. 呀(呀) [ya]	• surprise, and makes the tone softer	是你呀! 是你呀! It's you!
7. 啦(啦) [la]	• makes the tone softer	不用謝啦! 不用谢啦! No need to thank me, OK?

>>Try it! With a partner, fill in the interjections for the following sentences and then read them aloud.

1. _____! 你今天真好看! _____ 原來是要跟女朋友去看電影 _____!
   _____! 你今天真好看! _____ 原来是要跟女朋友去看电影 _____!

2. 怎麼搞的 _____? _____! 你又睡過頭了!
   怎么搞的 _____? _____! 你又睡过头了!

3. _____! 太晚了，我得走了。
   _____! 太晚了，我得走了。

4. 開車要專心，小心 _____!
   开车要专心，小心 _____!

補充課文 (补充课文) SUPPLEMENTARY PRACTICE

Read the following passage. Then listen and repeat.

Diary: An Argument with My Girlfriend, Caiyi
(繁體字 Traditional Character Version)

二月七日　　　　星期二　　　　天氣：下雨

　　今天我和女朋友吵架了，心情很不好。我找順強談了，他給了我一些建議。

　　我原來答應我女朋友，今天要開車帶她去商店買東西。可是，我不小心睡過頭了。她打電話來催我快一點兒，我就馬上出門了。

　　我上高速公路以後，前面有一個小車禍，碰到塞車了。我想要從出口下去，可是旁邊的出口又關起來了，禁止車子通過，使我完全動不了了。我想打手機通知她，可是我急急忙忙地出來，也把手機忘在家裡了。真後悔。

　　後來我遲到了兩個鐘頭。我女朋友很生氣，把我罵了一頓，說我總是喜歡遲到。我一聽她抱怨，我也生起氣來了，因此我們就吵架了。

　　順強建議我應該先向我女朋友道歉，請她去看個電影，吃頓飯什麼的，這樣她大概就會原諒我了。明天我再想想該怎麼向她道歉吧。

補充課文 (补充课文) SUPPLEMENTARY PRACTICE

Read the following passage. Then listen and repeat.

Diary: An Argument with My Girlfriend, Caiyi
(简体字 Simplified Character Version)

二月七日　　　星期二　　　天气：下雨

　　今天我和女朋友吵架了，心情很不好。我找顺强谈了，他给了我一些建议。

　　我原来答应我女朋友，今天要开车带她去商店买东西。可是，我不小心睡过头了。她打电话来催我快一点儿，我就马上出门了。

　　我上高速公路以后，前面有一个小车祸，碰到塞车了。我想要从出口下去，可是旁边的出口又关起来了，禁止车子通过，使我完全动不了了。我想打手机通知她，可是我急急忙忙地出来，也把手机忘在家里了。真后悔。

　　后来我迟到了两个钟头。我女朋友很生气，把我骂了一顿，说我总是喜欢迟到。我一听她抱怨，我也生起气来了，因此我们就吵架了。

　　顺强建议我应该先向我女朋友道歉，请她去看个电影，吃顿饭什么的，这样她大概就会原谅我了。明天我再想想该怎么向她道歉吧。

Exercises: work with a partner or in small groups

1. 有哪些這一課的生詞和語法出現在這篇日記上？請把它們找出來。
   有哪些这一课的生词和语法出现在这篇日记上？请把它们找出来。

2. 請把這篇日記翻譯成英文。
   请把这篇日记翻译成英文。

成語故事 (成语故事) IDIOM STORY

一箭雙鵰 (一箭双雕) [yí jiàn shuāng diāo]

Meaning: Shooting two hawks with one arrow.

Usage: This is used to indicate that someone has received two positive results from one action. That is, to kill two birds with one stone.

Example: 這次由於他先向他女朋友道歉，他女朋友不但不生氣了，而且還請他吃飯，他真是 "一箭雙鵰"，不錯嘛！

這次由于他先向他女朋友道歉，他女朋友不但不生气了，而且还请他吃饭，他真是 "一箭双雕"，不错嘛！

Pay attention to:
1. Pivotal constructions 兼語句 (兼语句).
2. Causative sentences and pivotal constructions 使動用法和兼語句 (使动用法和兼语句).
3. Summary of interjections 感嘆詞 (感叹词).

(繁體字 **Traditional Character Version**)

　　從前有兩隻大鵰，牠們常常吵架。別的大鵰勸牠們要和好，否則牠們是會吃虧的。可是牠們不聽，還是常常吵架。

　　有一天，牠們正在為一塊肥肉，吵來吵去。國王看到了，就命令他的神箭手把這兩隻大鵰射下來。

　　當這兩隻大鵰咬住肥肉，打在一起的時候，神箭手一箭射出，同時射中這兩隻大鵰。別的大鵰知道了，都嘆氣說：哎呀！我們常建議牠們和好，勸牠們要把牠們的脾氣改一改，可是牠們完全不聽。唉！早知如此，何必當初啊！

(简体字 Simplified Character Version)

　　从前有两只大雕，它们常常吵架。别的大雕劝它们要和好，否则它们是会吃亏的。可是它们不听，还是常常吵架。

　　有一天，它们正在为一块肥肉，吵来吵去。国王看到了，就命令他的神箭手把这两只大雕射下来。

　　当这两只大雕咬住肥肉，打在一起的时候，神箭手一箭射出，同时射中这两只大雕。别的大雕知道了，都叹气说：哎呀！我们常建议它们和好，劝它们要把它们的脾气改一改，可是它们完全不听。唉！早知如此，何必当初啊！

Notes:

大鵰(大雕) [dàdiāo]: big vulture

勸(劝) [quàn]: to persuade

和好(和好) [héhǎo]: to reconcile

否則(否则) [fǒuzé]: otherwise

肥肉(肥肉) [féiròu]: fat meat

國王(国王) [guówáng]: king

命令(命令) [mìnglìng]: to order

神箭手(神箭手) [shénjiànshǒu]: great archer

射(射) [shè]: to shoot, discharge

咬住(咬住) [yǎozhù]: to bite into

嘆氣(叹气) [tànqì]: to sigh

Exercises: work with a partner or in small groups

1. 找出有下面語法的句子：(i) Pivotal constructions 兼語句; (ii) Causative sentences and pivotal constructions 使動用法和兼語句; (iii) Summary of interjections 感嘆詞。

   找出有下面语法的句子：(i) Pivotal constructions 兼语句; (ii) Causative sentences and pivotal constructions 使动用法和兼语句; (iii) Summary of interjections 感叹词。

2. 用你自己的話說說"一箭雙鵰"的故事。
   用你自己的话说说"一箭双雕"的故事。

3. 請用"一箭雙鵰"造一個句子或者說一個"一箭雙鵰"的例子。
   请用"一箭双雕"造一个句子或者说一个"一箭双雕"的例子。

4. "一箭雙鵰"的故事，告訴了我們什麼?
   "一箭双雕"的故事，告诉了我们什么?

練習 (练习) ACTIVITIES

I. Listening Exercises

 13-1 Listen to the passage, and answer the following questions. Then check them with your partner.

Notes:
和事佬(和事佬) [héshìlǎo]: peacemaker
溫柔(温柔) [wēnróu]: gentle and soft
很兇(很凶) [hěn xiōng]: very fierce, very mean
命令(命令) [mìnglìng]: to command
口氣(口气) [kǒuqì]: tone
和好(和好) [héhǎo]: to become reconciled
對方(对方) [duìfāng]: the other (opposite) side
分手(分手) [fēnshǒu]: to break up

問題(问题):

1. 發生了什麼事情?
   发生了什么事情?

2. 小花為什麼生氣了呢?
   小花为什么生气了呢?

3. 小花的男朋友抱怨小花有什麼毛病?
   小花的男朋友抱怨小花有什么毛病?

4. 如果這次他們不原諒對方,小花的室友會有什麼建議?
   如果这次他们不原谅对方,小花的室友会有什么建议?

5. 你同意小花室友的看法嗎? 如果你是小花的室友,你會怎麼做呢?
   你同意小花室友的看法吗? 如果你是小花的室友,你会怎么做呢?

13-2 Based on the short passage you just listened to, complete the following sentences. Then check them with your partner (pay attention to causative sentences and pivotal constructions).

1. 小花和他男朋友又 _____ 了, _____! 我真 _____!
   小花和他男朋友又 _____ 了, _____! 我真 _____!

2. 小花特別 _____ 她男朋友要準時到，結果他還是 _____ 了。
   小花特別 _____ 她男朋友要准时到，结果他还是 _____ 了。

3. 小花常 _____ 她的男朋友快一點兒，_____ 很不好，一點兒也不
   _____，很兇。
   小花常 _____ 她的男朋友快一点儿，_____ 很不好，一点儿也不
   _____，很凶。

4. 他們兩個人的個性不合，我想 _____ 他們分手吧！
   他们两个人的个性不合，我想 _____ 他们分手吧！

5. _____ 他們真的分手了，我也就沒事 _____！哎呀！真 _____！
   _____ 他们真的分手了，我也就没事 _____！哎呀！真 _____！

II. Character Exercises

13-3 Work with a partner. Read the following words, phrases, and sentences.

吵	建議
吵	建议
吵架	建議你向她道歉
吵架	建议你向她道歉
跟女朋友吵架啦？	我建議你先向她道歉。
跟女朋友吵架啦？	我建议你先向她道歉。
怎麼又跟女朋友吵架啦？	我建議你應該先向她道歉。
怎么又跟女朋友吵架啦？	我建议你应该先向她道歉。

Now with your partner, try to use the following characters to make words, phrases, and then sentences.

1. 退   2. 陪   3. 催   4. 吩   5. 速
   退   陪   催   吩   速

6. 禍   7. 禁   8. 罰   9. 守   10. 改
   祸   禁   罚   守   改

13-4 Read aloud the following sentences. Write them out using traditional characters. Then check your answers with a partner.

1. 他过来谈谈，请他给一些建议。

   _____

2. 她买了一部数码相机，出了一些问题。

   _____

3. 我睡过头了，她打电话来催我快一点儿，我挂了电话，马上就开车去了。

   _____

4. 她交代我不要让手机开着，这样才能专心开车。

   _____

5. 我逼自己走路肩，想碰碰运气，结果被警察抓住了，吃了一张罚单。

   _____

6. 我迟到了两个钟头，她一见我就哼地一声，把我骂了一顿。

   _____

13-5 Form groups and create phrases with the following words (pay attention to the various usages of each word).

Homophones:

Example: [shì] 士：護士
　　　　　　士：护士

　　　　　　是：你是誰?
　　　　　　是：你是谁?

1. [　　] 諒：_____
　　　　 谅：_____

　　　　 輛：_____
　　　　 辆：_____

2. [   ] 货： _____

　　　　货： _____

　　　　或： _____

　　　　或： _____

　　　　祸： _____

　　　　祸： _____

3. [   ] 肩： _____

　　　　肩： _____

　　　　間： _____

　　　　间： _____

　　　　堅： _____

　　　　坚： _____

4. [   ] 建： _____

　　　　建： _____

　　　　見： _____

　　　　见： _____

　　　　件： _____

　　　　件： _____

5. [   ] 遲： _____

　　　　迟： _____

　　　　持： _____

　　　　持： _____

6. [   ] 抱： _____

　　　　抱： _____

　　　　報： _____

　　　　报： _____

III. Grammar Exercises

13-6 You and your group are filling in a psychology survey about personality types. You are having fun checking with each other about the questions. (Pay attention to the pivotal constructions 兼語句(兼语句) [jiānyǔjù] and causative sentences 使動用法(使动用法) [shǐdòng yòngfǎ].)

請 要 叫 讓 使 令 命令 勸 允許 交代 吩咐 催 逼 禁止 建議
请 要 叫 让 使 令 命令 劝 允许 交代 吩咐 催 逼 禁止 建议

Try to use the verbs listed above to answer the questions.

1. 如果快來不及了，你會 ＿＿＿ 別人快一點兒嗎?
   如果快来不及了，你会 ＿＿＿ 别人快一点儿吗?

2. 在圖書館，如果有人大聲說話，你會 ＿＿＿ 他小聲一點兒嗎?
   在图书馆，如果有人大声说话，你会 ＿＿＿ 他小声一点儿吗?

3. 你的好朋友有不守時的毛病，你會 ＿＿＿ 他改嗎?
   你的好朋友有不守时的毛病，你会 ＿＿＿ 他改吗?

4. 你的室友常吸煙，你很不喜歡，你會 ＿＿＿ 他不要吸煙嗎?
   你的室友常吸烟，你很不喜欢，你会 ＿＿＿ 他不要吸烟吗?

5. 你最近不 ＿＿＿ 你自己做什麼事?
   你最近不 ＿＿＿ 你自己做什么事?

6. 如果你的薪資 ([xīnzī]: salary) 令你不滿意 ([mǎnyì]: satisfied)，你會 ＿＿＿ 你的老闆知道嗎?
   如果你的薪资令你不满意，你会 ＿＿＿ 你的老板知道吗?

7. 如果你的老闆常 ＿＿＿ 你做事，你會待在那家公司嗎?
   如果你的老板常 ＿＿＿ 你做事，你会待在那家公司吗?

8. 你的朋友太胖了，你會 ＿＿＿ 他減肥嗎?
   你的朋友太胖了，你会 ＿＿＿ 他减肥吗?

9. 最近 ([zuìjìn]: recently) 有人 ＿＿＿ 你生氣嗎? 是什麼事情 ＿＿＿ 你生氣的?
   最近有人 ＿＿＿ 你生气吗? 是什么事情 ＿＿＿ 你生气的?

10. 你會 ＿＿＿ 你自己做你不想做的事嗎?
    你会 ＿＿＿ 你自己做你不想做的事吗?

11. 你覺得大學應該 ＿＿＿ 學生喝酒嗎?
    你觉得大学应该 ＿＿＿ 学生喝酒吗?

12. 你最近常 ＿＿＿ 你的朋友開車不打手機嗎?
    你最近常 ＿＿＿ 你的朋友开车不打手机吗?

13-7 明學(明学) is watching a basketball game with his roommate 小保.
Unfortunately, 明學(明学)'s favorite team is beaten badly by 小保's team.
Below is their conversation. With your partner, fill in the blanks with interjections.
Then recite the dialogue with your partner.

嘿, 哼, 唉, 哎呀, 呸, 喔, 嗯, 噢, 啊, 呢, 吧, 嘛, 喔, 呀, 啦
嘿, 哼, 唉, 哎呀, 呸, 喔, 嗯, 噢, 啊, 呢, 吧, 嘛, 喔, 呀, 啦

Notes:
贏(赢) [yíng]: to win
得分(得分) [défēn]: score
投進(投进) [tóujìn]: to throw into
差(差) [chà]: bad, poor
輸定了(输定了) [shūdìngle]: be defeated for sure

小保: ＿＿＿, 太棒了! 我們的隊打得很好, 我們快要贏了呀!
小保: ＿＿＿, 太棒了! 我们的队打得很好, 我们快要赢了呀!

明學: ＿＿＿! 別高興得太早, 我們馬上就要得分了。
明学: ＿＿＿! 别高兴得太早, 我们马上就要得分了。

＿＿＿! 怎麼又沒投進去 ＿＿＿。＿＿＿! 這5號球員今天是怎麼
＿＿＿! 怎么又没投进去 ＿＿＿。＿＿＿! 这5号球员今天是怎么

搞的, 打得太差 ＿＿＿!
搞的, 打得太差 ＿＿＿!

小保: ＿＿＿! 是 ＿＿＿! 你的5號球員今天打得很差 ＿＿＿!
小保: ＿＿＿! 是 ＿＿＿! 你的5号球员今天打得很差 ＿＿＿!

＿＿＿! 你看, 我們又進了一球 ＿＿＿!
＿＿＿! 你看, 我们又进了一球 ＿＿＿!

明學: ＿＿＿! 我看我們是輸定了 ＿＿＿!
明学: ＿＿＿! 我看我们是输定了 ＿＿＿!

小保: 沒關係 ___! 打球總是會有輸贏的 ___!
小保: 没关系 ___! 打球总是会有输赢的 ___!

明學: ___，真可惜，就差那麼一球，___! 氣死人 ___!
明学: ___，真可惜，就差那么一球，___! 气死人 ___!

小保: ___! 球賽看完了，你一定也餓了 ___! 咱們去吃飯，怎麼樣?
小保: ___! 球赛看完了，你一定也饿了 ___! 咱们去吃饭，怎么样?

明學: ___! 好 ___! 別管球賽了，還是管我們的肚子 ___!
明学: ___! 好 ___! 别管球赛了，还是管我们的肚子 ___!

我快餓死 ___!
我快饿死 ___!

小保: 太好了，咱們走 ___!
小保: 太好了，咱们走 ___!

IV. Media Literacy

The short text below, written in the style of newspapers, magazines, or Internet news articles, will help you become familiar with the formal written expressions used in these genres.

🔊 **西安高速公路奇景 (西安高速公路奇景) The Strange Scene on Xi'an's Highway**

繁體字:

西安高速公路奇景：隨地大小便

為省錢圖方便　　形成 "天然公廁"

有外國觀光客詢問: "高速公路上可以大小便嗎? 在路邊小便是西安人的習俗嗎?" 這個問題使在場的西安人覺得臉上無光。從那以後只要有人被發現在咸陽機場的高速公路上隨便停車 "方便"，他們就會被罰寫悔過書，令其自我檢討。

简体字：

西安高速公路奇景：随地大小便

为省钱图方便   形成"天然公厕"

有外国观光客询问："高速公路上可以大小便吗？在路边小便是西安人的习俗吗？"这个问题使在场的西安人觉得脸上无光。从那以后只要有人被发现在咸阳机场的高速公路上随便停车"方便"，他们就会被罚写悔过书，令其自我检讨。

Notes:
西安(西安) [Xī'ān]: name of a city in China. It is a famous
　　tourism spot in north central China.
奇景(奇景) [qíjǐng]: strange scene
随地(随地) [suídì]: anywhere, everywhere
大小便(大小便) [dàxiǎobiàn]: 大便(大便) means "have a
　　bowel movement"; 小便(小便) means "urinate"
圖(图) [tú]: to pursue, seek
天然(天然) [tiānrán]: natural
公廁(公厕) [gōngcè]: public restroom

Exercises for the headlines: work with a partner or a group to ask and answer the following questions.

1. What can you tell about the news by skimming the headlines?

2. How would you translate the headlines into English?

3. Newspaper headlines are usually very concise, with many abbreviations, omissions, hints, metaphors, and written forms. Can you identify some of these in the headlines above?

Notes:
觀光客(观光客) [guānguāngkè]: tourist
詢問(询问) [xúnwèn]: to ask
習俗(习俗) [xísú]: custom
在場(在场) [zàichǎng]: be at the scene
臉上無光(脸上无光) [liǎnshàngwúguāng]: feel embarrassed or ashamed
咸陽機場(咸阳机场) [Xiányáng jīchǎng]: The Xianyang airport in 西安
悔過書(悔过书) [huǐguòshū]: a written statement of repentance
其(其) [qí]: written (ancient) form for pronouns he, she, it, they
自我檢討(自我检讨) [zìwǒjiǎntǎo]: self-criticism

Exercises for the article: work with a partner or a group to ask and answer the following.

1. What written forms can you find? What are their spoken counterparts?

   (e.g. 圖(图), 詢問(询问), 其)

2. How many causative sentences are used? (e.g. 使, 令)

3. Use your own words to retell the headline and article.

V. Communicative Activities

13-8 Talk about your experiences.

Try to incorporate the following in your report.

pivotal constructions 兼語句(兼语句) [jiānyǔjù] and causative sentences 使動用法(使动用法) [shǐdòng yòngfǎ]:

請 要 叫 讓 使 令 命令 勸 允許 交待 吩咐 催 逼 禁止 建議
请 要 叫 让 使 令 命令 劝 允许 交待 吩咐 催 逼 禁止 建议

interjections:

嘿，哼，唉，哎呀，呸，喔，嗯，噢，啊，呢，吧，嘛，喔，呀，啦
嘿，哼，唉，哎呀，呸，喔，嗯，噢，啊，呢，吧，嘛，喔，呀，啦

– Describe a situation which made you feel angry, sad, or embarrassed.
– How did you overcome it?

13-9 Seeking advice.

Try to incorporate the following in your report.

pivotal constructions 兼語句(兼语句) [jiānyǔjù] and causative sentences 使動用法(使动用法) [shǐdòng yòngfǎ]:

請 要 叫 讓 使 令 命令 勸 允許 交待 吩咐 催 逼 禁止 建議
请 要 叫 让 使 令 命令 劝 允许 交待 吩咐 催 逼 禁止 建议

interjections:

嘿，哼，唉，哎呀，呸，喔，嗯，噢，啊，呢，吧，嘛，喔，呀，啦
嘿，哼，唉，哎呀，呸，喔，嗯，噢，啊，呢，吧，嘛，喔，呀，啦

Notes:
抱怨 吃虧 建議 談談 怎麼搞的 心事 脾氣
抱怨 吃亏 建议 谈谈 怎么搞的 心事 脾气

Situation A: You are having trouble with your courses. Ask your friends for advice.

• talk about your troubles with the courses
• you have been trying to resolve them on your own but it hasn't worked well
• your friends are very nice and give you valuable advice

Situation B: You would like to move out from the dorm. Seek advice on how to tell your roommate and how to find a good apartment.

• give the reasons why you would like to move out of the dorm
• ask how to tell your roommate about your decision
• ask how to find a good apartment
• your good friends give you advice

Situation C: You had a quarrel with your boyfriend/girlfriend. You would like to break the ice. Seek advice from your best friend.

文化知識 (文化知识) Culture Link

文化點滴 (文化点滴) CULTURE NOTES

算命 (算命)
Chinese Fortune Telling: Another Way to Seek Advice

Fortune telling is a popular way for Chinese people to seek advice when facing dilemmas in life. Common topics for fortune telling include relationships, academic study, and business. The advice provided by fortune tellers often serves to give Chinese people peace of mind when confronted with an important decision.

Fortune tellers in Chinese society are usually located in or near temples. For a small fee or donation, a person can seek advice from a fortune teller who uses a person's date and time of birth to calculate the values of the five elements 五行 [Wǔxíng]: 金 [jīn] (metal), 木 [mù] (wood), 水 [shuǐ] (water), 火 [huǒ] (fire), and 土 [tǔ] (earth). The relationship between these five elements is critical in determining what advice the fortune teller should give in any particular circumstance. The relationship between the five elements can be classified into two categories: *affinity* and *enmity*. The *affinity*

Do you know...

- the common topics for fortune telling in Chinese culture?
- about the five elements 五行, and what is the relationship between these five elements?
- whether Chinese temples usually provide fortune telling services?

Read and find out!

relationship completes a cycle and can be defined as follows: water can help wood to grow; wood can be burnt by fire; the burnt wood creates ash (earth); ash forms rock (metal); and finally, these rocks hold water. On the other hand, an *enmity relationship* counters that effect: water puts out fire, but fire causes water to evaporate; a tree's (wood) roots break up the earth, but earth can bury wood; fire melts metal, but in the process metal decreases fire's heat; earth absorbs water, but water floods the land (earth); metals can be used to cut wood, but wood dulls the metal.

Self-interpretive methods of fortune telling are also available in temples. Fortunes can be gleaned from marked bamboo sticks shaken from a container or from crescent-shaped wooden pieces thrown on the ground. The fortunes can also be interpreted with the assistance of the resident fortune teller for a small fee or donation.

Temples are common places to worship or to seek fortunes in Chinese culture. What other methods do the Chinese use to get advice?

A local fortune teller in Ningxia (north central China). What are some other ways that Chinese fortune tellers provide advice?

問題討論 (问题讨论) *Discuss the following with a partner or in small groups.*

1. 你對中國人去算命有什麼看法？
   你对中国人去算命有什么看法？
   Why do you think Chinese people turn to fortune telling for advice?

2. 在你的文化或者其他文化當中有類似算命的做法嗎？
   在你的文化或者其他文化当中有类似算命的做法吗？
   Do you know of any similar practices or different types of fortune telling methods in your culture or in other cultures?

趣味中文 (趣味中文) FUN WITH CHINESE

吃虧是福
吃亏是福
To be at a disadvange is good fortune.

chī	kuī	shì	fú
吃	虧	是	福
吃	亏	是	福
to suffer	disadvantage	to be	good fortune

This Chinese saying is commonly used to provide advice or comfort to others who feel they have been treated unfairly. The aim is to help them feel better and be able to forgive and forget in order to avoid future conflicts.

問題討論 (问题讨论) *Discuss the following with a partner or in small groups.*

Are there any similar sayings in English or other languages that provide advice to comfort others and help avoid conflicts?

行動吧! (行动吧!) LET'S GO!

農民曆 (农民历) The Lunar Calendar

The Chinese Lunar Calendar (also known as the Farmer's Calendar) is often used for fortune telling. It is used to find appropriate days to do things such as travel, move to a new house, get married, or hold a funeral. It also contains information for finding your best love match, a lucky name for your baby, or even to predict a baby's gender before conception.

Below is one of the entries from a Lunar Calendar.

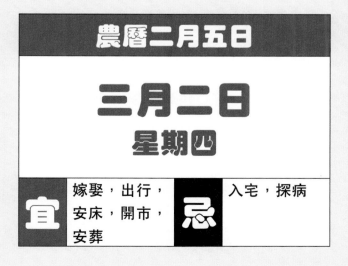

Notes:

農民曆(农民历) [nóngmín lì]: lunar calendar, farmer's calendar

農曆(农历) [nónglì]: lunar calendar. Another term for lunar calendar is 陰曆(阴历) [yīnlì].
   The solar calendar is called 陽曆(阳历) [yánglì] or 西曆(西历) [xīlì].

宜(宜) [yí]: suitable, appropriate, fitting

嫁娶(嫁娶) [jiàqǔ]: marriage

出行(出行) [chūxíng]: to travel

安床(安床) [ānchuáng]: to place a bed (in a room)

開市(开市) [kāishì]: (of a shop) re-open after cessation of business

安葬(安葬) [ānzàng]: to bury (the dead)

忌(忌) [jì]: to avoid

入宅(入宅) [rùzhái]: to move into a new dwelling

探病(探病) [tànbìng]: to visit sick people

問題討論 (问题讨论) *Discuss the following with a partner or in small groups.*

For the following questions, assume that today is the day shown on the lunar calendar.

1. According to the lunar calendar, would this be a good day to start a new business? Would it be a good date to move into a new dwelling?
2. 小明 is going to get married soon. Would today be a good date for him to invite his Chinese relatives to his wedding banquet?
3. Can you tell that the language used in the lunar calendar is very concise and uses written forms? Can you provide some examples with their equivalent spoken forms?
4. Translate the lunar calendar entry into English.
5. Would you like to consult the Chinese lunar calendar for some advice? Why or why not?

14

散文和詩情表達 (散文和诗情表达)
Prose and Poetic Expressions

Chinese students are introduced to famous writers at a young age.

教學目標 (教学目标) OBJECTIVES

- Compose a prose essay
- Sharpen verbal and written communication skills
- Connect two verbal expressions
- Express or accept an apology

CONNECTIONS AND COMMUNITIES PREVIEW

Discuss the following questions with a partner or your class. What similarities and differences do you think there might be between Chinese culture and your own culture?

1. Are writers and poets respected in your culture?

2. Do you know when prose writing first began in your culture?

3. Who is your favorite writer, or what is your favorite book?

生詞 (生词) VOCABULARY

核心詞 (核心词) Core Vocabulary

	TRADITIONAL	SIMPLIFIED	PINYIN		
1.	撲通撲通	扑通扑通	pūtōngpūtōng		*onomatopoeia*, e.g., flop, thump, splash, pit-a-pat
2.	跳	跳	tiào	V.	to jump, leap, bounce
3.	開口	开口	kāikǒu	V.O.	to open one's mouth, start to talk
4.	封	封	fēng	M.W.	(measure word for mailing letters)
5.	顯示	显示	xiǎnshì	V.	to show, display
6.	靈機一動	灵机一动	língjīyídòng	V.	to have a sudden inspiration
7.	聊天室	聊天室	liáotiānshì	N.	chat room
8.	諒解	谅解	liàngjiě	V.	to understand, make allowances for
9.	以下	以下	yǐxià	N.	below, the following
10.	對話	对话	duìhuà	N.	dialogue
11.	寫道	写道	xiědào	V.	to write
12.	是否	是否	shìfǒu	Conj.	whether or not, whether, if
13.	淅瀝淅瀝	淅沥淅沥	xīlìxīlì		*onomatopoeia*, e.g., the patter of rain, water
14.	溝通	沟通	gōutōng	V. N.	to communicate communication
15.	滴答滴答	滴答滴答	dīdādīdā		*onomatopoeia*, e.g., tick, tick-tock

TRADITIONAL	SIMPLIFIED	PINYIN		
16. 忍不住	忍不住	rěnbuzhù	V.	to be unable to bear, cannot help (doing something)
17. 傷心	伤心	shāngxīn	Adj.	sad, aggrieved, broken-hearted
18. 失望	失望	shīwàng	Adj.	disappointed
19. 說聲	说声	shuōshēng	V.O.	to say one word
20. 誤會	误会	wùhuì	V. N.	to misunderstand misunderstanding
21. 難過	难过	nánguò	Adj.	feel sorry, feel sad
22. 理	理	lǐ	V.	to pay attention to, show interest in
23. 哭	哭	kū	V.	to weep, cry
24. 委屈	委屈	wěiqū	V. Adj.	to put somebody to great inconvenience feel wronged
25. 淚眼汪汪	泪眼汪汪	lèiyǎnwāngwāng		(eyes) brimming with tears
26. 少來	少来	shǎolái		stop, quit it, cut it out
27. 在乎	在乎	zàihu	V.	to care about, mind
28. 感受	感受	gǎnshòu	V. N.	to be affected by, experience emotional feeling
29. 實在	实在	shízài	Adv.	indeed
30. 急急忙忙	急急忙忙	jíjímángmáng	Adj.	in a hurry, hurriedly
31. 理解	理解	lǐjiě	V.	to understand, comprehend
32. 出事	出事	chūshì	V.O.	to meet with a mishap, have an accident

TRADITIONAL	SIMPLIFIED	PINYIN		
33. 著急	着急	zháojí	V.	to worry, feel anxious
34. 安危	安危	ānwēi	N.	safety and danger, safety
35. 既……又	既……又	jì . . . yòu	Conj.	both . . . and, as well as
36. 感動	感动	gǎndòng	V.	to move, touch (emotions)
37. 不瞞你說	不瞞你说	bùmánnǐshuō		to tell you the truth 瞞 (to hide the truth from)
38. 自從	自从	zìcóng	Prep.	since
39. 清楚	清楚	qīngchǔ	Adj.	clear
40. 劈里啪啦	劈里啪啦	pīli pālā	Int.	*onomatopoeia*, e.g., crackle of firecracker, burst of gunfire
41. 平常	平常	píngcháng	Adv.	generally, usually
42. 準時	准时	zhǔnshí	Adj.	on time
43. 毛病	毛病	máobìng	N.	defect, shortcoming, trouble
44. 音樂會	音乐会	yīnyuèhuì	N.	concert
45. 保證	保证	bǎozhèng	V.	to pledge, guarantee, assure

語文知識 (语文知识) LANGUAGE LINK

Read and listen to the following sentence patterns. These patterns use vocabulary, expressions, and grammar that you will study in more detail in this lesson. After reading the sentence patterns, read and listen to the Language in Use section that follows.

句型 (句型) Sentence Patterns

雨淅瀝淅瀝地下著，我的心撲通撲通地跳著。
雨淅沥淅沥地下着，我的心扑通扑通地跳着。
Yǔ xīlìxīlì de xià zhe, wǒde xīn pūtōngpūtōng de tiào zhe.

時間滴答滴答地過去了。
时间滴答滴答地过去了。
Shíjiān dīdādīdā de guòqu le.

我劈里啪啦地把你罵了一頓。
我劈里啪啦地把你骂了一顿。
Wǒ pīli pālā de bǎ nǐ mà le yídùn.

 A: 我想向你道歉，說聲
我想向你道歉，说声
Wǒ xiǎng xiàng nǐ dàoqiàn, shuōshēng

"對不起！"，請你原諒我。
"对不起！"，请你原谅我。
"duìbuqǐ!", qǐng nǐ yuánliàng wǒ.

B: 沒關係，我也有錯，我不應該罵你。
没关系，我也有错，我不应该骂你。
Méi guānxi, wǒ yě yǒucuò, wǒ bù yīnggāi mà nǐ.

A: 我以為你出事了，非常著急，
我以为你出事了，非常着急，
Wǒ yǐwéi nǐ chūshì le, fēicháng zháojí,

人家是擔心你的安危呀！
人家是担心你的安危呀！
rénjiā shì dānxīn nǐ de ānwēi yā!

B: 聽你這麼說我是既感動又高興。
听你这么说我是既感动又高兴。
Tīng nǐ zhèmeshuō wǒ shì jì gǎndòng yòu gāoxìng.

課文 Language in Use: Please Accept My Apology
(繁體字 Traditional Character Version)

(聽了順強的建議以後，文超想打電話給彩宜，可是又不知道怎麼開口。他想寫一封電子郵件給她。剛好他的電腦顯示，彩宜也正在上網呢。他就靈機一動，希望能跟她在網上聊天室談談，得到她的諒解。以下是他們在網上的對話。)

史文超寫道：彩宜，是我，文超，你還好嗎? 是否還在生我的氣呢?

(彩宜第一次沒回)

史文超又寫道：親愛的彩宜，你好嗎? 我知道你正在上網。下雨了，外面的雨淅瀝淅瀝地下著，而我的心撲通撲通地跳著。我不知道該對你說些什麼好，我想跟你好好地溝通溝通。

(時間滴答滴答地過去了，彩宜還沒有回信……過了有一會兒[1]，彩宜才忍不住回信了……)

1. 有一會兒(有一会儿)
一會兒(一会儿) [yìhuěr] means "a little while." 有一會兒(有一会儿) means it has been a little while. Since 文超(文超) is anxious to get 彩宜(彩宜)'s reply, time seems to be passing slowly for him.

彩宜：　我還在傷心呢! 我們之間好像沒什麼好說的，你讓我很失望。

史文超：彩宜，是你啊! 真高興你終於開口了。唉! 其實，我也不想多說什麼，只想向你道歉，說聲 "對不起!" 昨天都是我的錯，是一場誤會呀!

彩宜：　我現在還是很難過，本來是不想理你的，但是看了你寫的話以後，我又忍不住哭起來了。

史文超：你一定是覺得很委屈才會傷心難過的。別哭，你淚眼汪汪的樣子，一定很可憐。

Continued on page 438

课文 Language in Use: Please Accept My Apology
(简体字 Simplified Character Version)

(听了顺强的建议以后，文超想打电话给彩宜，可是又不知道怎么开口。他想写一封电子邮件给她。刚好他的电脑显示，彩宜也正在上网呢。他就灵机一动，希望能跟她在网上聊天室谈谈，得到她的谅解。以下是他们在网上的对话。)

史文超写道：彩宜，是我，文超，你还好吗？是否还在生我的气呢？

(彩宜第一次没回)

史文超又写道：亲爱的彩宜，你好吗？我知道你正在上网。下雨了，外面的雨淅沥淅沥地下着，而我的心扑通扑通地跳着。我不知道该对你说些什么好，我想跟你好好地沟通沟通。

(时间滴答滴答地过去了，彩宜还没有回信……过了有一会儿[1]，彩宜才忍不住回信了……)

彩宜：　我还在伤心呢！我们之间好像没什么好说的，你让我很失望。

史文超：彩宜，是你啊！真高兴你终于开口了。唉！其实，我也不想多说什么，只想向你道歉，说声"对不起！"昨天都是我的错，是一场误会呀！

彩宜：　我现在还是很难过，本来是不想理你的，但是看了你写的话以后，我又忍不住哭起来了。

史文超：你一定是觉得很委屈才会伤心难过的。别哭，你泪眼汪汪的样子，一定很可怜。

Continued on page 439

🔊 **課文 Language in Use: Please Accept My Apology**
(繁體字 Traditional Character Version) —— 接第四百三十六頁

彩宜：　少來2，你一點兒都不在乎人家3的感受！

史文超：對不起，我實在是不知道說什麼好。我不應該遲到，害你等那麼久。我急急忙忙地出去，把手機給忘在家裡了。路上又碰到塞車，所以沒辦法通知你。然後走路肩又給警察開了罰單。那時候心情挺糟的，希望你能理解，接受我的道歉。

彩宜：　我等不到你的電話，以為你出事了，非常著急。人家是擔心你的安危呀！

史文超：聽你這麼說我是既感動又高興。感動的是，你為我等了那麼久，都沒離開。高興的是，覺得你還是很在乎我的喔！

彩宜：　不瞞你說，自從我們吵架以後，我也有一點兒後悔。我不應該沒問清楚就劈里啪啦地把你罵了一頓。

史文超：你罵我是應該的。我要是早點兒出門，平常準時一點兒，你也不會生這麼大的氣。

彩宜：　是啊！我覺得挺委屈的！你的老毛病4真的要改一改呀！

史文超：我一定會改的。對了，明天我沒事，我陪你去退貨，怎麼樣？

彩宜：　嗯！好呀！幾點？

史文超：下午三點，行嗎？

彩宜：　應該可以。

史文超：那你是接受我的道歉了！謝天謝地！退了貨以後，我們去吃飯，然後去聽音樂會，怎麼樣？

彩宜：　聽上去好像很不錯，行！說好了，可不能再遲到喔！

史文超：我保證，我一定會準時到的。明天見！

彩宜：　明天見！

---

2. 少來(少来)

少來(少来) stop it, quit it, cut it out. 彩宜(彩宜) is still mad, so she is using this tone to express her anger. This phrase is used mostly by women.

---

3. 人家(人家)

人家(人家) [rénjiā] has various meanings:

i. Household.

Example:

這裡住了三戶人家。
这里住了三户人家。
There are three households here.

ii. Others.

Example:

如果人家能，我們也能。
如果人家能，我们也能。
If other people can do it, so can we.

iii. The speaker herself. This meaning is used mostly by women, especially when acting 撒嬌(撒娇) [sājiāo] (pretending to be angry or displeased). In the text, 彩宜(彩宜) is using this tone when talking to her boyfriend 文超(文超).

课文 Language in Use: Please Accept My Apology
(简体字 Simplified Character Version) ── 接第四百三十七页

彩宜：　少来2，你一点儿都不在乎人家3的感受！

史文超：对不起，我实在是不知道说什么好。我不应该迟到，害你等那么久。我急急忙忙地出去，把手机给忘在家里了。路上又碰到塞车，所以没办法通知你。然后走路肩又给警察开了罚单。那时候心情挺糟的，希望你能理解，接受我的道歉。

彩宜：　我等不到你的电话，以为你出事了，非常着急。人家是担心你的安危呀！

史文超：听你这么说我是既感动又高兴。感动的是，你为我等了那么久，都没离开。高兴的是，觉得你还是很在乎我的喔！

彩宜：　不瞒你说，自从我们吵架以后，我也有一点儿后悔。我不应该没问清楚就劈里啪啦地把你骂了一顿。

史文超：你骂我是应该的。我要是早点儿出门，平常准时一点儿，你也不会生这么大的气。

彩宜：　是啊！我觉得挺委屈的！你的老毛病4真的要改一改呀！

史文超：我一定会改的。对了，明天我没事，我陪你去退货，怎么样？

4. 老毛病(老毛病)
毛病(毛病) [máobìng] is a colloquial word meaning shortcoming. Its more formal written form is 缺點(缺点) [quēdiǎn]. 老(老) means always doing something. For example, 他最近老想玩網上遊戲 (他最近老想玩网上游戏) (Recently all he thinks about is playing online games.) In the text here, the use of 老毛病(老毛病) indicates that 文超(文超) has a habit of not being on time.

彩宜：　嗯！好呀！几点？

史文超：下午三点，行吗？

彩宜：　应该可以。

史文超：那你是接受我的道歉了！谢天谢地！退了货以后，我们去吃饭，然后去听音乐会，怎么样？

彩宜：　听上去好像很不错，行！说好了，可不能再迟到喔！

史文超：我保证，我一定会准时到的。明天见！

彩宜：　明天见！

語法 (语法) GRAMMAR

I. 擬聲詞當修飾語 (拟声词当修饰语) Onomatopoeic Words as Adverbials or Attributives. (Another common term for "onomatopoeic words" is 像聲詞 (象声词))

Onomatopoeic expressions are words that imitate natural sounds. In general, onomatopoeic expressions are used in the following ways.

- adverbials which occur before a verb phrase (VP): Onomatopoeic words + 地 + VP

  Example: 時鐘滴答滴答地走著。
  时钟滴答滴答地走着。
  The clock is ticking.

- attributives which occur before a noun phrase (NP). Onomatopoeic words + NP (聲)(声) [shēng] sound, noise

  Example: 我聽見隆隆的雷聲。
  我听见隆隆的雷声。
  I heard the rumble of thunder.

Onomatopoeic expressions are commonly used in prose to make the writing more lively and more beautiful. Similar to other languages, Chinese has its own conventions to describe natural sounds. Common onomatopoeic expressions are listed below.

Onomatopoeic expression	Meaning	Examples
1. 嗶嗶 哔哔 [bībī]	sound of a whistle	哨子 "嗶嗶" 地響。 哨子 "哔哔" 地响。 The whistle is making a bi-bi sound. 原來是警察在禁止別人亂停車。 原来是警察在禁止别人乱停车。 It is the policeman prohibiting others from parking illegally.
2. 潺潺 潺潺 [chánchán]	murmur, babble (of water)	潺潺流水。 潺潺流水。 A murmuring stream.
3. 滴答滴答 滴答滴答 [dīdādīdā]	tick-tock (of a clock)	時鐘滴答滴答地走著。 时钟滴答滴答地走着。 The clock is ticking.

Onomatopoeic expression	Meaning	Examples
4. 滴滴答答 滴滴答答 [dīdīdādā]	drip drip (of water)	雨水滴滴答答地打在窗上。 雨水滴滴答答地打在窗上。 The rain is dripping on the window.
5. 叮噹 叮当 [dīngdāng]	ding-dong, jingle	門鈴叮噹地響著。 门铃叮当地响着。 The doorbell is making a ding-dong sound. 教堂鐘響起了一陣的叮噹聲， 教堂钟响起了一阵的叮当声， From the church came the sound of jingling bells 歡迎聖誕節。 欢迎圣诞节。 to welcome Christmas.
6. 呼呼 呼呼 [hūhū]	the sound of wind	風呼呼地颳著。 风呼呼地刮着。 The wind is howling.
7. 嘩啦嘩啦 哗啦哗啦 [huālā huālā]	the gurgling of a stream, bubbling sounds of water	大雨嘩啦嘩啦地下著。 大雨哗啦哗啦地下着。 A heavy rain is pouring down.
8. 嘰嘰喳喳 叽叽喳喳 [jījī zhāzhā]	the chirping of birds	嘰嘰喳喳的小鳥聲把孩子吵醒了。 叽叽喳喳的小鸟声把孩子吵醒了。 The chirping of the birds woke up the kids.
9. 哐啷 哐啷 [kuānglāng]	clanking noise	鍋子哐啷地掉在地上。 锅子哐啷地掉在地上。 The pot fell onto the floor with a clang.
10. 隆隆 隆隆 [lónglóng]	the rumble of thunder	我聽見隆隆的雷聲。 我听见隆隆的雷声。 I heard the rumble of thunder.
11. 喵喵 喵喵 [miāomiāo]	meow (of a cat)	小貓喵喵地叫著。 小猫喵喵地叫着。 The cat is meowing.

Onomatopoeic expression	Meaning	Examples
12. 喔喔喔 喔喔喔 [ō ō ō]	crowing sound (of a rooster)	公雞喔喔喔地叫著。 公鸡喔喔喔地叫着。 The rooster is crowing.
13. 砰砰 砰砰 [pēngpēng]	sound of knocking on a door, a door shutting, gunfire	砰的一聲，門關上了。 砰的一声，门关上了。 The door banged shut. 我聽見砰砰的槍聲。 我听见砰砰的枪声。 I heard the sound of gunfire.
14. 劈里啪啦 劈里啪啦 [pīli pālā]	crackle of firecrackers	外面一陣劈里啪啦的鞭炮聲。 外面一阵劈里啪啦的鞭炮声。 There is a crackle of firecrackers outside.
15. 撲通撲通 扑通扑通 [pūtōngpūtōng]	to plop (into water); a heartbeat (e.g., nervous, fear)	青蛙撲通撲通地跳下水。 青蛙扑通扑通地跳下水。 The frog plopped into the water. 我的心在撲通撲通地跳著。 我的心在扑通扑通地跳着。 My heart is going pitter-patter.
16. 嗡嗡 嗡嗡 [wēngwēng]	humming (of a bee)	蜜蜂嗡嗡地飛著。 蜜蜂嗡嗡地飞着。 The bees are humming by.
17. 淅瀝淅瀝 淅沥淅沥 [xīlìxīlì]	patter (of rain, water)	小雨淅瀝淅瀝地下著。 小雨淅沥淅沥地下着。 The rain is pattering down.

»Try it!   **With a partner, use "onomatopoeic expressions" to describe some situations. For example,**

外面下雨了，大雨嘩啦嘩啦地下著。
外面下雨了，大雨哗啦哗啦地下着。

II. Conjunction 既......又 "both . . . and, as well as"

既......又 is a conjunction which joins two verbal expressions (verbs or adjectives). The elements which 既......又 connects are usually very similar in structure.

Examples: 聽了你的話，讓我既高興又感動。
听了你的话，让我既高兴又感动。

他既會說中文，又會唱中文歌。
他既会说中文，又会唱中文歌。

The following table presents several conjunctions which connect parallel verbal elements, and highlights the subtle differences between them.

Conjunctions	Features	Examples
既......又 既......又	"both.. .and, as well as"	他既會說中文，又會唱中國歌。 他既会说中文，又会唱中国歌。
既......也 既......也	"both.. .and, as well as"	他既會說中文，也會唱中國歌。 他既会说中文，也会唱中国歌。
既......且	"both.. .and, as well as" • more written style than 既......又(也) • only used to connect monosyllabic adjectives	這個大樓既高且大。 这个大楼既高且大。 This building is both tall and big. 這條河既寬且深。 这条河既宽且深。 This river is both wide and deep.
也......也	"not only . . .but also"	她在晚會上也唱歌也跳舞。 她在晚会上也唱歌也跳舞。 She was not only singing, but also dancing at the party.
又......又	"not only.. .but also" • stronger than 也......也	她在晚會上又唱歌又跳舞。 她在晚会上又唱歌又跳舞。 She was not only singing, but also dancing at the party.

Note: If the subjects are different but with the same predicate, 既......又(且，也) cannot be used. In that case the 不但......也 pattern is used.

他生氣了，我也生氣了。→ 不但他生氣了，我也生氣了。
他生气了，我也生气了。→ 不但他生气了，我也生气了。

»Try it! With a partner, use the "both . . . and" conjunctions to describe what you or your friends are good at, or what you or your friends like. For example,

我室友既會唱歌，又會跳舞。
我室友既会唱歌，又会跳舞。

III. Summary of Topic-Comment Sentences

Chinese is known as a topic-prominent language. That is, the "topic" notion plays an important role in explaining some Chinese grammatical structures. As illustrated below, Chinese sentences may be divided into two categories: subject-predicate and topic-comment.

Subject-predicate sentences	– generally used for narrative purpose – mainly express an action	我們　常做中國飯。 我们　常做中国饭。 *subject　predicate* We often cook Chinese food.
Topic-comment sentence	– describe or provide further comment related to the topic – mainly express a state	做中國飯　是我們的愛好。 做中国饭　是我们的爱好。 *topic　　　comment* Cooking Chinese food is our hobby. (As for cooking Chinese food, that is our hobby.)

In a topic-comment sentence the topic is the shared information in the context while the comment that follows it provides further information related to the topic. The topic can be a noun, pronoun, verbal phrase, or clause. The topic may be translated beginning with "As for . . . ." The comments may be a verbal phrase or a clause. See the examples in the table.

Topic	Comment	Features
那棵樹 那棵树	葉子大。 叶子大。	葉子大(叶子大): serves as the comment. It also has a part (葉子)[叶子] to whole (樹)[树] relationship. Speaking of the tree, its leaves are big.
我 我	頭疼。 头疼。	This is also a part to whole relationship. I have a headache. (As for me, my head hurts.)

Topic	Comment	Features
昨天 昨天	是一場誤會。 是一场误会。	As for yesterday, it was a misunderstanding.
第三課的語法 第三课的语法	我有兩個問題。 我有两个问题。	As for the grammar points of Lesson 3, I have two questions.
他的女朋友 他的女朋友	眼睛大，頭髮長，很漂亮。 眼睛大，头发长，很漂亮。	A topic may be followed by several comments. (We are talking about his girlfriend.) As for his girlfriend, her eyes are big, (her) hair is long, and (she is) beautiful.

Note that as we mentioned in Lesson 11, the unmarked notional passive sentence usually occurs as a topic-comment sentence. See the examples in the table.

Topic	Comment	English
飯 饭	做好了。 做好了。	The meal is ready. (As for the meal, it is ready.)
作業 作业	寫完了。 写完了。	The assignment is finished. (As for the assignment, it is finished.)
錢 钱	花光了。 花光了。	The money is all spent. (As for the money, it is all spent.)
信 信	寄出去了。 寄出去了。	The letter has been sent. (As for the letter, it has been sent.)
你的支票 你的支票	收到了。 收到了。	Your check has been received. (As for your check, it has been received.)

»Try it! With a partner, use the "topic-comment" notion to make 2–3 sentences. For example,

這學期的中文課，功課很多，可是考試不難。
这学期的中文课，功课很多，可是考试不难。

補充課文 (补充课文) SUPPLEMENTARY PRACTICE

Read the following passage. Then listen and repeat.

The Rain in March (繁體字 Traditional Character Version)

三月裡的小雨，淅瀝瀝瀝瀝瀝，淅瀝瀝瀝下個不停。

山谷裡的小溪，嘩啦啦啦啦啦，嘩啦啦啦流個不停。

小雨為誰飄，小溪為誰流，帶著滿懷的淒清。

三月裡的小雨，淅瀝瀝瀝瀝瀝，淅瀝瀝瀝下個不停。

山谷裡的小溪，嘩啦啦啦啦啦，嘩啦啦啦流個不停。

小雨陪伴我，小溪聽我訴，可知我滿懷的寂寞。

請問小溪，誰代我追尋，追尋那一顆愛我的心，

追尋那一顆愛我的心……

Notes:

山谷(山谷) [shāngǔ]: mountain valley
小溪(小溪) [xiǎoxī]: creek
流(流) [liú]: to flow
飄(飘) [piāo]: to drizzle, fall slowly, drift
滿懷(满怀) [mǎnhuái]: have one's heart filled with
淒清(凄清) [qīqīng]: lonely and sad
陪伴(陪伴) [péibàn]: to accompany
寂寞(寂寞) [jìmò]: lonely
代(代) [dài]: to do something on someone's behalf
追尋(追寻) [zhuīxún]: to pursue
顆(颗) [kē]: (measure word for hearts)

補充課文 (补充课文) SUPPLEMENTARY PRACTICE

Read the following passage. Then listen and repeat.

The Rain in March (简体字 Simplified Character Version)

三月里的小雨，淅沥沥沥沥沥，淅沥沥沥下个不停。

山谷里的小溪，哗啦啦啦啦啦，哗啦啦啦流个不停。

小雨为谁飘，小溪为谁流，带着满怀的凄清。

三月里的小雨，淅沥沥沥沥沥，淅沥沥沥下个不停。

山谷里的小溪，哗啦啦啦啦啦，哗啦啦啦流个不停。

小雨陪伴我，小溪听我诉，可知我满怀的寂寞。

请问小溪，谁代我追寻，追寻那一颗爱我的心，

追寻那一颗爱我的心……

Exercises: work with a partner or in small groups

1. 把出現的擬聲詞 (onomatopoeic expressions) 找出來。
   把出现的拟声词找出来。

2. 這首歌在說什麼，請用你自己的話再說一遍。
   这首歌在说什么，请用你自己的话再说一遍。

3. 把這首歌的歌詞翻譯成英文。
   把这首歌的歌词翻译成英文。

成語故事 (成语故事) IDIOM STORY

同舟共濟 (同舟共济) [tóng zhōu gòng jì]

Meaning: To show mutual concern for people in the same boat.

Usage: It is used to indicate people helping each other to reach the same goal.

Example: 你們應該互相諒解，"同舟共濟"，一起完成這個報告。

你们应该互相谅解，"同舟共济"，一起完成这个报告。

Pay attention to:
1. Onomatopoeia as adverbials or attributives 擬聲詞當修飾語(拟声词当修饰语)
2. Conjunctions 既……又
3. Summary of topic-comment sentences.

(繁體字 Traditional Character Version)

　　古代吳國和越國的人常常不喜歡對方。有一天，兩國的人既同時要去河的對岸又坐同一條船。船剛開走的時候，他們很不喜歡對方，好像要吵架的樣子。船開到河的中間的時候，突然遇到大風雨，隆隆地打雷聲，風呼呼地颳著。很快地，大雨就嘩啦嘩啦地下起來了，他們的船很快就要翻了。兩國的人心裡既緊張地撲通撲通地跳著，又不知道應該怎麼辦才好。最後，為了保住自己的生命，他們就互相幫助、合作，最後終於安全地到了河的對岸。

(简体字 **Simplified Character Version**)

　　古代吴国和越国的人常常不喜欢对方。有一天，两国的人既同时要去河的对岸又坐同一条船。船刚开走的时候，他们很不喜欢对方，好像要吵架的样子。船开到河的中间的时候，突然遇到大风雨，隆隆地打雷声，风呼呼地刮着。很快地，大雨就哗啦哗啦地下起来了，他们的船很快就要翻了。两国的人心里既紧张地扑通扑通地跳着，又不知道应该怎么办才好。最后，为了保住自己的生命，他们就互相帮助、合作，最后终于安全地到了河的对岸。

Notes:
古代(古代) [gǔdài]: ancient times
吳國(吴国) [Wúguó]: the State of Wu
越國(越国) [Yuèguó]: the State of Yue
對方(对方) [duìfāng]: the other party
河(河) [hé]: river
對岸(对岸) [duì'àn]: opposite shore
突然(突然) [tūrán]: suddenly
遇到(遇到) [yùdào]: to run into
雷(雷) [léi]: thunder
颳(刮) [guā]: (of wind) to blow
翻(翻) [fān]: to turn over
緊張(紧张) [jǐnzhāng]: nervous
生命(生命) [shēngmìng]: life

Exercises: work with a partner or in small groups

1. 找出有下面語法的句子：(i) Onomatopoeic words as adverbials or attributives;
   (ii) Conjunctions 既……又; (iii) Topic-comment sentences.

   找出有下面語法的句子：(i) Onomatopoeic words as adverbials or attributives;
   (ii) Conjunctions 既……又; (iii) Topic-comment sentences.

2. 用你自己的話說說 "同舟共濟" 的故事。
   用你自己的话说说 "同舟共济" 的故事。

3. 請用 "同舟共濟" 造一個句子或者說一個 "同舟共濟" 的例子。
   请用 "同舟共济" 造一个句子或者说一个 "同舟共济" 的例子。

4. "同舟共濟" 的故事，告訴了我們什麼？
   "同舟共济" 的故事，告诉了我们什么？

練習 (练习) ACTIVITIES

I. Listening Exercises

 14-1 Listen to the passage and then answer the following questions. Check them with your partner.

Notes:
亂七八糟(乱七八糟) [luànqībāzāo]: in a mess
停車位(停车位) [tíngchēwèi]: parking space
拖吊(拖吊) [tuōdiào]: to tow away
警察局(警察局) [jǐngchájú]: police station
消息(消息) [xiāoxi]: news
砰砰(砰砰) [pēngpēng]: sound of knocking on a door
解釋(解释) [jiěshì]: to explain

問題(问题):

1. 昨天他為什麼要開他室友的車子去學校，路上碰到了什麼事情?
   昨天他为什么要开他室友的车子去学校，路上碰到了什么事情?

2. 他考完試出去一看，又發生了什麼事情?
   他考完试出去一看，又发生了什么事情?

3. 他很著急，以為車子怎麼了? 他做了什麼事情?
   他很着急，以为车子怎么了? 他做了什么事情?

4. 回家以後，他告訴他室友什麼事情? 他室友的反應 [fǎnyìng]
   (reaction) 是什麼?

   回家以后，他告诉他室友什么事情? 他室友的反应是什么?

5. 後來車子到底怎麼了?
   后来车子到底怎么了?

6. 他為什麼既高興又難過?
   他为什么既高兴又难过?

14-2 Based on the short passage you have just listened to, complete the following sentences. Then check them with your partner.

1. 我不小心睡過頭了，＿＿ 地開了室友的車子去學校。
   我不小心睡过头了，＿＿ 地开了室友的车子去学校。

2. 車子不見了。我很 ＿＿，打電話到 ＿＿ 局那兒問，也沒有 ＿＿。
   车子不见了。我很 ＿＿，打电话到 ＿＿ 局那儿问，也没有 ＿＿。

3. 我不知道該怎麼 ＿＿ 我室友 ＿＿，一路上，我的心是 ＿＿ 地跳著，不知道怎麼 ＿＿。
   我不知道该怎么 ＿＿ 我室友 ＿＿，一路上，我的心是 ＿＿ 地跳着，不知道怎么 ＿＿。

4. 我 ＿＿ 地敲著他的門，告訴他，他的車子 ＿＿ 的事情。
   他很 ＿＿，＿＿ ＿＿ 地把我罵了一頓。

   我 ＿＿ 地敲着他的门，告诉他，他的车子 ＿＿ 的事情。
   他很 ＿＿，＿＿ ＿＿ 地把我骂了一顿。

5. 他說：我 ＿＿ 你的道歉！我聽了以後是 ＿＿＿＿＿＿。
   他说：我 ＿＿ 你的道歉！我听了以后是 ＿＿＿＿＿＿。

II. Character Exercises

14-3 Work with a partner. Read the following words, phrases, and sentences.

顯	聊
显	聊
顯示	聊天室
显示	聊天室
電腦顯示	在網上聊天室談談。
电脑显示	在网上聊天室谈谈。
電腦顯示，他也正在上網呢。	希望能跟她在網上聊天室談談。
电脑显示，他也正在上网呢。	希望能跟她在网上聊天室谈谈。

Now with your partner, try to use the following characters to make words, phrases, and then sentences.

1. 諒   2. 否   3. 浙   4. 撲   5. 滴
   谅   否   淅   扑   滴

6. 忍   7. 傷   8. 委   9. 汪   10. 既
   忍   伤   委   汪   既

14-4 Read aloud the following sentences. Write them out using traditional characters. Then check your answers with a partner.

1. 他灵机一动，希望能跟她在网上聊天室谈谈。

_____

2. 雨是淅沥淅沥地下着，而我的心是扑通扑通地跳着，我想跟你沟通沟通。

_____

3. 她还在伤心呢！我想说一声"对不起！"这是我的错，是一场误会。

_____

4. 你泪眼汪汪的样子，一定很可怜。

_____

5. 我要是早点儿出门，平常准时一点儿，你也不会生这么大的气。

_____

6. 我保证，我一定会准时到的。

_____

14-5 Form groups and create phrases with the following words (pay attention to the various usages of each word).

Example: 塊：十五塊錢　　一塊鏡子，一塊麵包，一塊蛋糕
　　　　　　块：十五块钱　　一块镜子，一块面包，一块蛋糕

1. 毛：＿＿＿＿＿＿＿＿＿＿　＿＿＿＿＿＿＿＿＿＿＿＿＿＿＿＿＿＿

　毛：＿＿＿＿＿＿＿＿＿＿　＿＿＿＿＿＿＿＿＿＿＿＿＿＿＿＿＿＿

2. 通：＿＿＿＿＿＿＿＿＿＿　＿＿＿＿＿＿＿＿＿＿＿＿＿＿＿＿＿＿

　通：＿＿＿＿＿＿＿＿＿＿　＿＿＿＿＿＿＿＿＿＿＿＿＿＿＿＿＿＿

3. 準：＿＿＿＿＿＿＿＿＿＿　＿＿＿＿＿＿＿＿＿＿＿＿＿＿＿＿＿＿

　准：＿＿＿＿＿＿＿＿＿＿　＿＿＿＿＿＿＿＿＿＿＿＿＿＿＿＿＿＿

4. 危：＿＿＿＿＿＿＿＿＿＿　＿＿＿＿＿＿＿＿＿＿＿＿＿＿＿＿＿＿

　危：＿＿＿＿＿＿＿＿＿＿　＿＿＿＿＿＿＿＿＿＿＿＿＿＿＿＿＿＿

Homophones:

Example: [shì] 士：護士
　　　　　　　　　 士：护士

　　　　　　　　　 是：你是誰?
　　　　　　　　　 是：你是谁?

1. [　　] 瀝：＿＿＿＿＿＿＿＿＿＿＿＿

　　　　沥：＿＿＿＿＿＿＿＿＿＿＿＿

　　　　利：＿＿＿＿＿＿＿＿＿＿＿＿

　　　　利：＿＿＿＿＿＿＿＿＿＿＿＿

　　　　麗：＿＿＿＿＿＿＿＿＿＿＿＿

　　　　丽：＿＿＿＿＿＿＿＿＿＿＿＿

　　　　歷：＿＿＿＿＿＿＿＿＿＿＿＿

　　　　历：＿＿＿＿＿＿＿＿＿＿＿＿

2. [   ] 失: _____

　　　　失: _____

　　　　師: _____

　　　　师: _____

　　　　詩: _____

　　　　诗: _____

3. [   ] 聲: _____

　　　　声: _____

　　　　生: _____

　　　　生: _____

4. [   ] 維: _____

　　　　维: _____

　　　　為: _____

　　　　为: _____

5. [   ] 淚: _____

　　　　泪: _____

　　　　累: _____

　　　　累: _____

6. [   ] 低: _____

　　　　低: _____

　　　　滴: _____

　　　　滴: _____

III. Grammar Exercises

14-6 Form groups and fill in the blanks with the following onomatopoeic expressions:

1. 嗶嗶(哔哔) [bībī]
2. 潺潺(潺潺) [chánchán]
3. 滴答滴答(滴答滴答) [dīdādīdā]
4. 滴滴答答(滴滴答答) [dīdīdādā]
5. 叮噹(叮当) [dīngdāng]
6. 呼呼(呼呼) [hūhū]
7. 嘩啦嘩啦(哗啦哗啦) [huālā huālā]
8. 嘰嘰喳喳(叽叽喳喳) [jījī zhāzhā]
9. 哐啷(哐啷) [kuānglāng]
10. 隆隆(隆隆) [lónglóng]
11. 喵喵(喵喵) [miāomiāo]
12. 喔喔喔(喔喔喔) [ō ō ō]
13. 砰砰(砰砰) [pēngpēng]
14. 劈里啪啦(劈里啪啦) [pīli pālā]
15. 撲通撲通(扑通扑通) [pūtōngpūtōng]
16. 嗡嗡(嗡嗡) [wēngwēng]
17. 淅瀝淅瀝(淅沥淅沥) [xīlìxīlì]
18. 汪汪(汪汪) [wāngwāng]

Notes:
散文(散文) [sǎnwén]: prose
外婆(外婆) [wàipó]: grandmother (mother's side)
鄉下(乡下) [xiāngxià]: village
接觸(接触) [jiēchù]: to contact
大自然(大自然) [dàzìrán]: the natural world
公雞(公鸡) [gōngjī]: rooster
鄰居(邻居) [línjū]: neighbor
釣魚(钓鱼) [diàoyú]: go fishing
青蛙(青蛙) [qīngwā]: frog
打雷(打雷) [dǎléi]: thunder
木柴(木柴) [mùchái]: firewood
取暖(取暖) [qǔnuǎn]: warm oneself (e.g., by a fire)
天晴(天晴) [tiānqíng]: it's clearing up (of weather)
小鳥(小鸟) [xiǎoniǎo]: little birds

(繁體字 Traditional Character Version)

一篇散文：去外婆家

　　我的外婆住在鄉下，我最喜歡去她那兒，因為可以接觸大自然，很棒喔！一大早，就會聽到公雞 ＿＿＿＿ 的聲音，鄰居的小狗也會 ＿＿＿＿ 地叫著，外婆養了一隻貓，小貓總是跑到我的床上 ＿＿＿＿ 地叫我起床。

　　吃了早飯以後，爸爸會帶我去河邊釣魚。河邊很安靜，可以聽到小河 ＿＿＿＿ 的水聲，有時候會有幾隻青蛙 ＿＿＿＿ 地跳下水。

　　下午的時候，有時候會打雷，我最怕打雷了，＿＿＿＿ 的雷聲，使我心裡 ＿＿＿＿ 地跳著，真讓我害怕。外婆會燒著木柴取暖，木柴讓火燒得 ＿＿＿＿＿ 地響著，很好聽。

　　我喜歡坐在窗戶旁邊聽著 ＿＿＿＿＿ 的雨聲，希望趕快天晴，然後我就可以出去玩了！

　　過一會兒，雨停了，小鳥出來了，＿＿＿＿＿ 地叫著，我也高高興興地出去玩了。

(简体字 Simplified Character Version)

一篇散文：去外婆家

　　我的外婆住在乡下，我最喜欢去她那儿，因为可以接触大自然，很棒喔！一大早，就会听到公鸡 ＿＿＿＿ 的声音，邻居的小狗也会 ＿＿＿＿ 地叫着，外婆养了一只猫，小猫总是跑到我的床上 ＿＿＿＿ 地叫我起床。

　　吃了早饭以后，爸爸会带我去河边钓鱼。河边很安静，可以听到小河 ＿＿＿＿ 的水声，有时候会有几只青蛙 ＿＿＿＿ 地跳下水。

　　下午的时候，有时候会打雷，我最怕打雷了，＿＿＿＿ 的雷声，使我心里 ＿＿＿＿ 地跳着，真让我害怕。外婆会烧着木柴取暖，木柴让火烧得 ＿＿＿＿＿ 地响着，很好听。

　　我喜欢坐在窗户旁边听着 ＿＿＿＿＿ 的雨声，希望赶快天晴，然后我就可以出去玩了！

　　过一会儿，雨停了，小鸟出来了，＿＿＿＿＿ 地叫着，我也高高兴兴地出去玩了。

14-7　Topic-comment sentences

Work with your partner. Analyze the following sentences from the text. Indicate which part is the topic and which part is the comment.

1. 外面的雨是淅瀝淅瀝地下著，而我的心是撲通撲通地跳著。
   外面的雨是淅沥淅沥地下着，而我的心是扑通扑通地跳着。

2. 昨天都是我的錯，是一場誤會。
   昨天都是我的错，是一场误会。

3. 你淚眼汪汪的樣子，一定很可憐。
   你泪眼汪汪的样子，一定很可怜。

4. 聽你這麼說我是既感動又高興。
   听你这么说我是既感动又高兴。

5. 你的老毛病真的要改一改呀！
   你的老毛病真的要改一改呀！

IV. Media Literacy

The short text below, written in the style of newspapers, magazines, or Internet news articles, will help you become familiar with the formal written expressions used in these genres.

 夫妻之道: 道歉及溝通 (夫妻之道: 道歉及沟通)
Essential Principles for a Married Couple: Apologies and Good Communication

繁體字：

夫妻之道：道歉及溝通

王先生以前常和妻子發生爭執及冷戰，在朋友的勸說之下，夫妻互相道歉，並達成協議：多溝通，多在乎對方的感受，犯錯一方必須先向對方道歉，絕不在孩子面前吵架……等等。如今因夫妻同心協力，五年來未有爭吵事情發生。

简体字:

夫妻之道：道歉及沟通

王先生以前常和妻子发生争执及冷战，在朋友的劝说之下，夫妻互相道歉，并达成协议：多沟通，多在乎对方的感受，犯错一方必须先向对方道歉，绝不在孩子面前吵架……等等。如今因夫妻同心协力，五年来未有争吵事情发生。

Notes:
夫妻(夫妻) [fūqī]: married couple
道(道) [dào]: principle

Exercises for the headlines: work with a partner or a group to ask and answer the following questions.

1. How does the literal translation of the headline differ from what would sound natural in your native language?

2. What are the spoken counterparts for some of the words in the headline?

Notes:
爭執(争执) [zhēngzhí]: disagreement
冷戰(冷战) [lěngzhàn]: cold war
達成(达成) [dáchéng]: to reach
協議(协议) [xiéyì]: to agree on, agreement
如今(如今) [rújīn]: nowadays, now
同心協力(同心协力) [tóngxīn xiélì]: to work together with one heart

Exercises for the article: work with a partner or a group to ask and answer the following.

1. Can you find any expressions used solely in writing? What are their spoken counterparts (e.g., 如今, 未有)?

2. Point out the sentences which contain Lesson 14 vocabulary, then translate the sentences into your native language (e.g., 道歉; 溝通(沟通); 吵架).

3. Use your own words in Chinese to retell the meaning of the headline and article.

V. Communicative Activities

14-8   Tell a story or describe an experience you have had. Use some of the following onomatopoetic words, topic-comment sentences, and 既……又 in your report.

1. 嗶嗶(哔哔) [bībī]
2. 潺潺(潺潺) [chánchán]
3. 滴答滴答(滴答滴答) [dīdādīdā]
4. 滴滴答答(滴滴答答) [dīdīdādā]
5. 叮噹(叮当) [dīngdāng]
6. 呼呼(呼呼) [hūhū]
7. 嘩啦嘩啦(哗啦哗啦) [huālā huālā]
8. 嘰嘰喳喳(叽叽喳喳) [jījī zhāzhā]
9. 哐啷(哐啷) [kuānglāng]
10. 隆隆(隆隆) [lónglóng]
11. 喵喵(喵喵) [miāomiāo]
12. 喔喔喔(喔喔喔) [ō ō ō]
13. 砰砰(砰砰) [pēngpēng]
14. 劈里啪啦(劈里啪啦) [pīli pālā]
15. 撲通撲通(扑通扑通) [pūtōngpūtōng]
16. 嗡嗡(嗡嗡) [wēngwēng]
17. 淅瀝淅瀝(淅沥淅沥) [xīlìxīlì]

14-9 You made a mistake and would like to seek forgiveness. With a partner,

1. Explain the mistake you made and then apologize.
2. Listen, provide comments, and then accept the apology.

Notes:

開口(开口)	諒解(谅解)	傷心(伤心)	失望(失望)
說一聲(说一声)	對不起(对不起)	誤會(误会)	難過(难过)
道歉(道歉)	理解(理解)	既……又(既……又)	感動(感动)
毛病(毛病)	保證(保证)		

14-10 集體創作(集体创作) ([jítǐ chuàngzuò]: collective creation)

Would you like to be a writer? Now you can try with your group.

1. Form groups to compose a prose essay. Use some of the onomatopoeic expressions from this lesson to make your work more lively.
2. Read your work aloud to the class.

文化知識 (文化知识) Culture Link

文化點滴 (文化点滴) CULTURE NOTES

中國有名的現代散文作家 (中国有名的现代散文作家)
Famous Modern Chinese Prose Writers

散文 [sǎnwén] (prose), that is stories written in the vernacular language, only became popular in China around a century ago during the 五四運動 (五四运动) [Wǔsì Yùndòng] (May Fourth Movement), the important literary revolution that began in 1919. Chinese prose often includes flowery and poetic language, such as the onomatopoeic expressions introduced in this lesson. A main leader of this movement was 魯迅(鲁迅) [Lǔ Xùn] (1881–1936), one of China's most famous modern writers. Initially studying to become a doctor, China's widespread corruption inspired Lu Xun to abandon medicine for writing—a medium he hoped would help to heal what he saw to be China's dying soul. His prolific and satirical writings addressed social problems in China, such as the negative impact of modernization, the oppression of superstitious traditions, and overall

> **Do you know...**
> - what the May Fourth Movement represented?
> - the names of any famous modern Chinese prose writers?
>
> *Read and find out!*

issues of social and economic justice. His characterization was precise, and he favored the use of caricatures to represent China's ills.

Another important modern writer is 徐志摩 [Xú Zhìmó] (1897–1931), a renowned lyrical poet. While studying in the United States and England, he was influenced by Tagore, an Indian poet, and Shelley and Keats. 徐志摩 used his flowery and ornate writings as a way to express his political views in the monthly magazine he edited, 新月 [Xīn Yuè]. Other famous prose writers include 朱自清 [Zhū Zìqīng] (1898–1948) and 冰心 [Bīng Xīn] (1900–1999).

In modern China, many famous writers have addressed current issues and ideas in their writings, making literature a significant tool for change as well as a record of issues and views in contemporary Chinese culture and society.

Lu Xun in his office, 1928. What social problems did he address in his writings?

Chinese children enjoy reading the works of famous writers. What do you think this teaches them?

問題討論 (问题讨论) *Discuss the following with a partner or in small groups.*

1. 你最喜歡的作家是誰？你最近看了什麼樣的小說？你最難忘的，
   覺得最有趣的情節是什麼？

   你最喜欢的作家是谁？你最近看了什么样的小说？你最难忘的，
   觉得最有趣的情节是什么？

   Who is your favorite writer? What is the most recent book you have read? What are the most unforgettable/interesting aspects of that book?

2. 你曾經想當作家嗎？如果你是一個作家，你想寫什麼樣的故事？
   為什麼？

   你曾经想当作家吗？如果你是一个作家，你想写什么样的故事？
   为什么？

   Have you ever dreamed of being a writer? If you were a writer, what types of stories would you like to write? Why?

趣味中文 (趣味中文) FUN WITH CHINESE

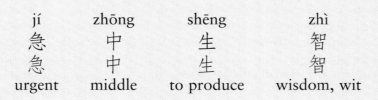

急中生智
急中生智

To suddenly hit upon a way out of a predicament

jí	zhōng	shēng	zhì
急	中	生	智
急	中	生	智
urgent	middle	to produce	wisdom, wit

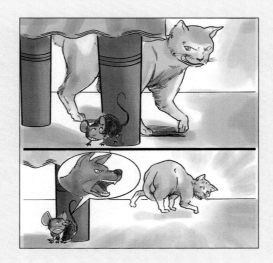

問題討論 (问题讨论) *Discuss the following with a partner or in small groups.*

Do you have a story or experience which illustrates this saying? Please share it.

行動吧! (行动吧!) LET'S GO!

雨中即景 (雨中即景) A Rainy Scene

小花最近買了一個 iPod。她常下載一些她喜歡的歌。小花在網上聽到了這首 "雨中即景" 的 MP3，歌詞裡面有很多擬聲詞，很有意思。以下是這首歌的歌詞。

小花最近买了一个 iPod。她常下载一些她喜欢的歌。小花在网上听到了这首 "雨中即景" 的 MP3，歌词里面有很多拟声词，很有意思。以下是这首歌的歌词。

(繁體字 Traditional Character Version)

雨中即景

嘩啦啦啦啦，下雨了，看到大家都在跑。
叭叭叭叭叭，計程車，他們的生意是特別好。
(你有錢坐不到)
嘩啦啦啦啦，淋濕了，好多人臉上嘛失去了笑。
無奈何望著天，嘆嘆氣把頭搖。
感覺天色不對，最好把雨傘帶好。
不要等雨來了，見你又躲又跑。
轟隆隆隆隆，打雷了，膽小的人都不敢跑。(怕怕)
無奈何望著天，嘆嘆氣把頭搖。

(简体字 Simplified Character Version)

雨中即景

哗啦啦啦啦，下雨了，看到大家都在跑。
叭叭叭叭叭，计程车，他们的生意是特别好。
(你有钱坐不到)
哗啦啦啦啦，淋湿了，好多人脸上嘛失去了笑。
无奈何望着天，叹叹气把头摇。
感觉天色不对，最好把雨伞带好。
不要等雨来了，见你又躲又跑。
轰隆隆隆隆，打雷了，胆小的人都不敢跑。(怕怕)
无奈何望着天，叹叹气把头摇。

Notes:

下載(下载) [xiàzǎi]: to download
擬聲詞(拟声词) [nǐshēngcí]: onomatopoeia
歌詞(歌词) [gēcí]: lyrics
生意(生意) [shēngyì]: business
淋濕(淋湿) [línshī]: to get wet
無奈何(无奈何) [wúnàihé]: cannot help but
望(望) [wàng]: to look
搖(摇) [yáo]: to shake
天色(天色) [tiānsè]: sky
雨傘(雨伞) [yǔsǎn]: umbrella
躲(躲) [duǒ]: to avoid, dodge

問題討論 (问题讨论) *Discuss the following with a partner or in small groups.*

1. 把出現的擬聲詞 (onomatopoeic expressions) 找出來。
   把出现的拟声词找出来。

2. 這首歌在說什麼，請用你自己的話說一說。
   这首歌在说什么，请用你自己的话说一说。

3. 把這首歌的歌詞翻譯成英文。
   把这首歌的歌词翻译成英文。

4. Do you know any songs that contain onomatopoeic expressions (in English or in your native language)? What are they about? What kinds of onomatopoeic expressions do the songs use?

復習 (复习) Review

LESSON 13 TO LESSON 14

I. Conversation

We learned two common Chinese sayings in "Fun with Chinese" in Lessons 13 and 14.

吃虧是福(吃亏是福) [chī kuī shì fú] (To be at a disadvantage is good fortune) and 急中生智(急中生智) [jí zhōng shēng zhì] (To suddenly hit upon a way out of a predicament)

Work with your partner.

1. Use your own words in Chinese to explain what these two sayings mean and imply.
2. Use these two sayings in Chinese sentences.
3. Tell a story or experience in Chinese to illustrate these two sayings (use at least 15 sentences).

Try to incorporate the following grammar points and expressions.

Grammar points: pivotal constructions 兼語句(兼语句) [jiānyǔ jù] and causative sentences 使動用法(使动用法) [shǐdòng yòngfǎ]

請 要 叫 讓 使 令 命令 勸 允許 交待 吩咐 催 逼 禁止 建議
请 要 叫 让 使 令 命令 劝 允许 交待 吩咐 催 逼 禁止 建议

Interjections (嘿，哼，唉，哎呀，呸，喔，嗯，噢，啊); sentence-final particles (呢，吧，嘛，喔，呀，啦).

Interjections (嘿，哼，唉，哎呀，呸，喔，嗯，噢，啊); sentence-final particles (呢，吧，嘛，喔，呀，啦).

(1)

(2)

II. Description

描述(描述) [miáoshù]: to describe; description
風景(风景) [fēngjǐng]: scenic view

Work with your partner. Describe a person, event, or a scenic view (use at least 15 sentences). Try to use some of the following expressions to make your description more lively and more elegant.

> *Notes:* Use onomatopoeic words, topic-comment sentences, and 既......又 in your story.
>
> 1. 嗶嗶(哔哔) [bībī]
> 2. 潺潺(潺潺) [chánchán]
> 3. 滴答滴答(滴答滴答) [dīdādīdā]
> 4. 滴滴答答(滴滴答答) [dīdīdādā]
> 5. 叮噹(叮当) [dīngdāng]
> 6. 呼呼(呼呼) [hūhū]
> 7. 嘩啦嘩啦(哗啦哗啦) [huālā huālā]
> 8. 嘰嘰喳喳(叽叽喳喳) [jījī zhāzhā]
> 9. 哐啷(哐啷) [kuānglāng]
> 10. 隆隆(隆隆) [lónglóng]
> 11. 喵喵(喵喵) [miāomiāo]
> 12. 喔喔喔(喔喔喔) [ō ō ō]
> 13. 砰砰(砰砰) [pēngpēng]
> 14. 劈里啪啦(劈里啪啦) [pīli pālā]
> 15. 撲通撲通(扑通扑通) [pūtōngpūtōng]
> 16. 嗡嗡(嗡嗡) [wēngwēng]
> 17. 淅瀝淅瀝(淅沥淅沥) [xīlìxīlì]

III. Storytelling

With your group, try to use the expressions provided above to create your own story based on the following pictures (at least three sentences for each picture).

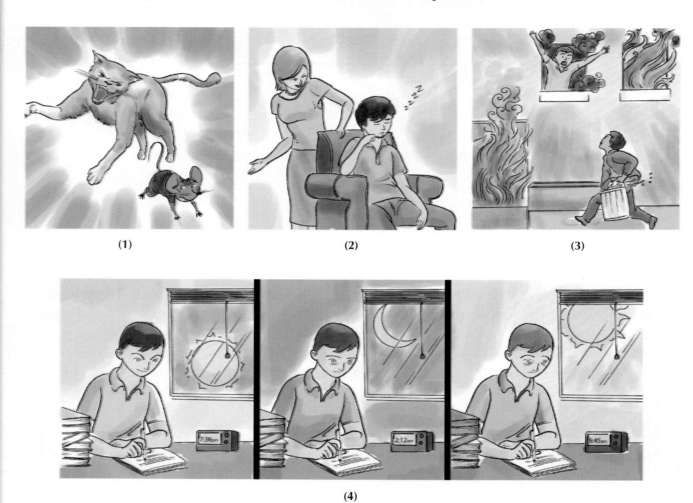

(1)   (2)   (3)

(4)

IV. Traditional and Simplified Characters

With a partner, read each character aloud. Write its traditional form. Then make a phrase and a sentence using the character.

Example: 学 → 學 → 學生 → 我是學生。

L13: 议 ( )   专 ( )   祸 ( )   罚 ( )   迟 ( )

L14: 扑 ( )   显 ( )   沥 ( )   沟 ( )   伤 ( )   声 ( )   泪 ( )

15

音樂－復習（音乐－复习）
Music – Review

A Chinese musician plays the pipa, a traditional Chinese lute.

CONNECTIONS AND COMMUNITIES PREVIEW

Discuss the following questions with a partner or your class. What similarities and differences do you think there might be between Chinese culture and your own culture?

1. How do you request favors or respond to requests for favors in your culture?

2. What kinds of music are most popular in your culture or community? Does this vary depending on age?

3. What is your favorite type of music or favorite musician?

教學目標（教学目标）OBJECTIVES

- Request favors and respond to requests for favors
- Understand Chinese omissions
- Format email messages
- Review—passive sentences and conjunctions

生詞 (生词) VOCABULARY

核心詞 (核心词) Core Vocabulary

	TRADITIONAL	SIMPLIFIED	PINYIN		
1.	求	求	qiú	V.	to beg, seek
2.	發件	发件	fājiàn	V.O.	to send mail
3.	收件	收件	shōujiàn	V.O.	to receive mail
4.	主題	主題	zhǔtí	N.	subject
5.	磁帶	磁带	cídài	N.	(magnetic) tape
6.	發送	发送	fāsòng	V.	to dispatch (letters, etc.)
7.	聯絡	联络	liánluò	V.	to contact
8.	卻	却	què	Adv.	but, yet, however
9.	遇	遇	yù	V.	to meet with
10.	和好	和好	héhǎo	V.	to make up (after a fight)
11.	盤	盘	pán	N. M.W.	tray, plate, dish (measure word for tray-shaped items, e.g., cassette tapes)
12.	錄音機	录音机	lùyīnjī	N.	tape recorder
13.	絞	绞	jiǎo	V.	to twist, entangle
14.	用力	用力	yònglì	V.O.	to exert one's strength
15.	反而	反而	fǎn'ér	Adv.	instead, on the contrary
16.	同樣	同样	tóngyàng	Adj.	of the same

TRADITIONAL	SIMPLIFIED	PINYIN		
17. 還	还	huán	V.	to return
18. 遍	遍	biàn	Adj.	all over
19. 愛好者	爱好者	àihàozhě	N.	amateur, enthusiast, fan
20. 光碟	光碟	guāngdié	N.	compact disc
21. 然而	然而	rán'ér	Conj.	yet, but, however
22. 歌	歌	gē	N.	song
23. 流行	流行	liúxíng	Adj.	prevalent, popular
24. 搜索	搜索	sōusuǒ	V.	to search for
25. 購	购	gòu	V.	to purchase
26. 帖子	帖子	tiězi	N.	a brief note
27. 總之	总之	zǒngzhī	Conj.	in a word, in short, in brief

專名 (专名) Proper Nouns

TRADITIONAL	SIMPLIFIED	PINYIN		
1. 高新遠	高新远	Gāo Xīnyuǎn	N.	(name) Xinyuan Gao
2. 貓王	猫王	Māowáng	N.	(nickname) Elvis Presley

語文知識 (语文知识) LANGUAGE LINK

Read and listen to the following sentence patterns. These patterns use vocabulary, expressions, and grammar that you will study in more detail in this lesson. After reading the sentence patterns, read and listen to the Language in Use section that follows.

句型 (句型) Sentence Patterns

因為太用力了，磁帶不但沒有被取出來，
因为太用力了，磁带不但没有被取出来，
Yīnwèi tài yònglì le, cídài búdàn méiyǒu bèi qǔ chūlai,

反而還讓我給拉壞了。
反而还让我给拉坏了。
fǎn'ér hái ràng wǒ gěi lā huài le.

你一定要幫我的忙呀！
你一定要帮我的忙呀！
Nǐ yídìng yào bāng wǒ de máng yā!

不然彩宜是不會原諒我的！
不然彩宜是不会原谅我的！
Bùrán Cǎiyí shì búhuì yuánliàng wǒ de!

我找不到貓王的磁帶，然而卻
我找不到猫王的磁带，然而却
Wǒ zhǎobudào Māowáng de cídài, rán'ér què

買到了同樣的音樂光碟。
买到了同样的音乐光碟。
mǎi dào le tóngyàng de yīnyuè guāngdié.

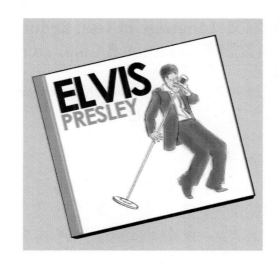

我跟你說了那麼多，總之，
我跟你说了那么多，总之，
Wǒ gēn nǐ shuō le nàme duō, zǒngzhī,

事情都解決了。
事情都解决了。
shìqing dōu jiějué le.

課文 Language in Use: Requesting a Favor
(繁體字 Traditional Character Version)

發件人：史文超 <wenchao@zhongwen.edu>
主題：請幫我買磁帶

收件人：高新遠 <xinyuan@hanyu.edu>
發送時間：4/21 3:45 P.M.

新遠：

　　很久沒有跟你聯絡了，好不容易[1]
給你寫信卻是有事要找你幫忙，真不好
意思。我最近遇到一件麻煩事，如果可
以的話，能不能請你幫個忙？

　　上個星期，我和女朋友彩宜為了一
個小誤會而吵架了。我們剛剛才和好，可是現在又出問題了。

　　事情的經過是這樣的：彩宜把一盤"貓王"的磁帶借給我聽，這是
她最喜歡的一盤磁帶了。當她把磁帶給我的時候，還交代我一定要小
心，我也向她保證沒問題。可是我在聽磁帶的時候，我的老錄音機把磁
帶絞了。當我急急忙忙地想把磁帶從錄音機裡拿出來的時候，又因為太
用力，磁帶不但沒有被取出來，反而讓我給拉壞了。我不敢把這件事告
訴彩宜，一想到她淚眼汪汪的樣子，我就不知道該怎麼辦才好。

　　我想再買一盤同樣的磁帶還給她，等買到新磁帶以後再把這件事
告訴她，向她道歉。但是這兩天我找遍了我這兒的商店，就是找不到同
樣的磁帶，所以我現在只好求你幫忙了。

　　你能不能幫我在你那兒的商店找找看？希望我能買到貓王的磁帶，
不然彩宜是不會原諒我的呀！

　　太麻煩你了，謝謝！

文超

> **1. 好不容易(好不容易)**
>
> 好不容易(好不容易) is an idiomatic
> expression meaning "quite difficult."
> "好(好)" means "quite, very."

Continued on page 476

课文 Language in Use: Requesting a Favor
(简体字 Simplified Character Version)

发件人：史文超 <wenchao@zhongwen.edu>　　收件人：高新远 <xinyuan@hanyu.edu>
主题：请帮我买磁带　　　　　　　　　　　　发送时间：4/21 3:45 P.M.

新远：

　　很久没有跟你联络了，好不容易[1]给你
写信却是有事要找你帮忙，真不好意思。我
最近遇到一件麻烦事，如果可以的话，能不
能请你帮个忙？

　　上个星期，我和女朋友彩宜为了一个
小误会而吵架了。我们刚刚才和好，可是现
在又出问题了。

　　事情的经过是这样的：彩宜把一盘"猫
王"的磁带借给我听，这是她最喜欢的一盘
磁带了。当她把磁带给我的时候，还交代我
一定要小心，我也向她保证没问题。可是我
在听磁带的时候，我的老录音机把磁带绞了。当我急急忙忙地想把磁带
从录音机里拿出来的时候，又因为太用力，磁带不但没有被取出来，反
而让我给拉坏了。我不敢把这件事告诉彩宜，一想到她泪眼汪汪的样
子，我就不知道该怎么办才好。

　　我想再买一盘同样的磁带还给她，等买到新磁带以后再把这件事
告诉她，向她道歉。但是这两天我找遍了我这儿的商店，就是找不到同
样的磁带，所以我现在只好求你帮忙了。

　　你能不能帮我在你那儿的商店找找看？希望我能买到猫王的磁带，
不然彩宜是不会原谅我的呀！

　　太麻烦你了，谢谢！

　　　　　　　　　　　　　　　　　　　　　　　　　　　　文超

Continued on page 477

課文 Language in Use: Requesting a Favor
(繁體字 Traditional Character Version) —— 接第四百七十四頁

發件人: 高新遠 <xinyuan@hanyu.edu>　　　收件人: 史文超 <wenchao@zhongwen.edu>
主題: 買到了光碟　　　　　　　　　　　　發送時間: 4/25 11:23 P.M.

文超:

　　不用擔心，我已經買到你要的東西了。我雖然找不到貓王的磁帶，然而卻買到了同樣的音樂光碟。

　　我一收到你的電子郵件就去附近的商店找。雖然貓王很有名，但是貓王的歌已經不像以前那麼流行了，所以我一直找不到。我上網搜索，還是找不到。最後我只好在網上發了求購貓王磁帶的帖子[2]。今天下午我終於收到了一封電子郵件，說有貓王的光碟。我想光碟更好，就幫你把它買下來了。

　　總之，事情解決了。你應該很快就能收到光碟了。

新遠

---

2. 發帖子(发帖子)

發帖子(发帖子) means "to post a message (on an Internet bulletin board or forum)." In mainland China, 發(发) is used as a short form of 發送(发送) (to send) and 帖子(帖子) is used to mean "a message"; conversely "replying to a post" is expressed as 回帖子(回帖子). In Taiwan, a message is called 消息，文章(消息，文章) and therefore the corresponding phrases are expressed as 發佈消息/文章 (发布消息/文章) (post a message) and 回覆消息/文章(回复消息/文章) (to reply to a post).

课文 Language in Use: Requesting a Favor
(简体字 Simplified Character Version) —— 接第四百七十五页

发件人：高新远 <xinyuan@hanyu.edu>   收件人：史文超 <wenchao@zhongwen.edu>
主题：买到了光碟   发送时间：4/25 11:23 P.M.

文超：

　　不用担心，我已经买到你要的东西了。我虽然找不到猫王的磁带，然而却买到了同样的音乐光碟。

　　我一收到你的电子邮件就去附近的商店找。虽然猫王很有名，但是猫王的歌已经不像以前那么流行了，所以我一直找不到。我上网搜索，还是找不到。最后我只好在网上发了求购猫王磁带的帖子[2]。今天下午我终于收到了一封电子邮件，说有猫王的光碟。我想光碟更好，就帮你把它买下来了。

　　总之，事情解决了。你应该很快就能收到光碟了。

新远

語法 (语法) GRAMMAR

Review of the main grammar points from Lesson 11 to Lesson 14.

I. Review: Passive Sentences 被動句 (被动句) (See Lesson 11 for more details)

There are two types of passive sense sentences that commonly occur: (1) unmarked in structure, called "notional passive sense"; and (2) marked in structure with 被, 叫, or 讓(让). The second type, the marked passive sense construction, can be summarized as follows:

Object (receiver of action) + 被(被) + Subject (doer) + (給) [(给)] + V. + other elements 　　　　　　　　　　　　　叫(叫)　　　　　　　　　 給(给) 　　　　　　　　　　　　　讓(让)　　　　　　　　　 給(给)

Examples:　我的蛋糕<u>被</u>弟弟吃完了。
　　　　　　我的蛋糕<u>被</u>弟弟吃完了。

　　　　　　姐姐的新衣服<u>叫</u>妹妹<u>給</u>拿走了。
　　　　　　姐姐的新衣服<u>叫</u>妹妹<u>给</u>拿走了。

　　　　　　他的車子<u>讓</u>他女朋友<u>給</u>撞壞了。
　　　　　　他的车子<u>让</u>他女朋友<u>给</u>撞坏了。

>>Try it!　With a partner, use 被, 叫, or 讓 (让) to describe some unhappy situations. For example,

A: 你室友好像很生氣!
　　你室友好像很生气!

B: 是啊! 我室友的電腦被他女朋友拿走了。
　　是啊! 我室友的电脑被他女朋友拿走了。

II. Review: Conjunctions (1) 連詞 (连词) (See Lessons 12 and 14 for more details)

Conjunctions	Features	Examples
因為......所以 因为......所以 because . . . therefore (由於)......因此； (由于)......因此； 是由於(是由于) 由於(由于) due to, because of 為了(为了) due to, because of 只好(只好) (result) have to 從而(从而) therefore	Connects cause-and-effect elements ● 從而(从而) indicates the result or further action of the first clause (See Lesson 12)	事情越來越糟，我解決不了了， 事情越来越糟，我解决不了了， 只好求你幫忙了。 只好求你帮忙了。 小王通過 [tōngguò] (through)同學們的幫助從而拿到了好成績 [chéngjì] (grade)。 小王通过同学们的帮助从而拿到了好成绩。
要是(如果，假如，假使，假若)......就 要是(如果，假如，假使，假若)......就 if . . . then 不然，否則 不然，否则 otherwise, or 只有......才 只有......才 only if 只要......就 只要......就 as long as . . . (then) 沒有......就沒有 没有......就没有 if without . . . then it will be without . . .	Connects conditional elements (See Lesson 12)	要是你們不幫忙， 要是你们不帮忙， 事情就會更糟了。 事情就会更糟了。 你們一定要幫忙， 你们一定要帮忙， 不然/否則事情會更糟。 不然/否则事情会更糟。

Conjunctions	Features	Examples
既......又(也，且) 既......又(也，且) both . . . and; as well as 也......也；又......又 也......也；又......又 both . . . and; not only . . . but also 不但......而且 不但......而且 not only . . . but also	Connects "parallel" elements (See Lesson 14)	他既會說中文，又會唱歌。 他既会说中文，又会唱歌。 她在晚會上又唱歌又跳舞。 她在晚会上又唱歌又跳舞。 她不但漂亮，而且很可愛。 她不但漂亮，而且很可爱。
並且，而且，此外 并且，而且，此外 and, besides, moreover	並且(并且)，而且 (而且)，and 此外 (此外) occur in the second clause to provide further information related to the first clause • 此外(此外) is used more in writing	他對人很好，此外他還常常 他对人很好，此外他还常常 幫助別人。 帮助别人。
和/跟/與/以及 和/跟/与/以及	And/with: connects two noun phrases. • 與(与) is used more in writing • 以及(以及) is more formal than 和(和), and is usually used to connect a list of items	老師和同學們都在上課。 老师和同学们都在上课。 我跟我室友都學中文。 我跟我室友都学中文。 語法與漢字都很難。 语法与汉字都很难。 游泳、打球、跑步以及滑雪都 游泳、打球、跑步以及滑雪都 是他喜歡的運動。 是他喜欢的运动。

Conjunctions	Features	Examples
而(而) but, and, therefore. There are various semantic relations between the phrases or clauses which 而(而) connects	"But": connects two words or clauses with opposite meanings	南方已經很暖和，而北方還在 南方已经很暖和，而北方还在 下大雪。 下大雪。
	"And": the second word or clause provides additional meaning to the first word or clause	這輛車跑得快而穩 [wěn] (stable)。 这辆车跑得快而稳。
	"Therefore": the following word or clause is a result of the first	他為了上學方便而搬家了。 他为了上学方便而搬家了。
雖然……但是/ 可是/不過/然而 虽然……但是/ 可是/不过/然而 although . . . (but)	Connects "concession/yield" elements • 然而(然而) is used more in writing	雖然她很美，對我也不錯， 虽然她很美，对我也不错， 可是我還是不喜歡她。 可是我还是不喜欢她。
卻(却) but, yet, however	卻(却) is an (conjunctive) adverb which occurs after a subject and before a verb phrase	她很美，對你也不錯， 她很美，对你也不错， 你卻不喜歡她。 你却不喜欢她。
或者(或者) 還是(还是) or 要麼……要麼 要么……要么 either . . . or 不是……就是 不是……就是 either . . . or	Connects "alternative choices" elements • 或者(或者) is used in statements, while 還是(还是) is used in questions • 要麼……要麼 (要么……要么) is used more in speech than 不是……就是 (不是……就是)	我想去中國或者日本旅行。 我想去中国或者日本旅行。 你要紅茶還是要綠茶? 你要红茶还是要绿茶? 我要麼今年要麼明年去中國。 我要么今年要么明年去中国。 我不是今年就是明年去中國。 我不是今年就是明年去中国。

Conjunctions	Features	Examples
不但……反而 不但……反而 not only . . . but even (on the contrary)	Emphasizes that what follows 不但(不但) is unexpected or contrary to logic, and what follows 反而(反而) is even more so	你幫助他那麼多。他<u>不但</u>沒 你帮助他那么多。他<u>不但</u>没 感謝你，<u>反而</u>還要害你。 感谢你，<u>反而</u>还要害你。 You helped him so much. (But) not only did he not express his appreciation, but (on the contrary) he is (still) out to get you.
總之，總而言之 总之，总而言之 in a word, in short, in brief	• used to introduce a summary • 總之(总之) is the abbreviation of 總而言之(总而言之)	我跟你說了那麼多，<u>總之</u>， 我跟你说了那么多，<u>总之</u>， 事情都解決了。 事情都解决了。

> **>>Try it!** With a partner make several sentences with conjunctions. For example,

他是個好學生，<u>此外</u>他還常常幫助別人。
他是个好学生，<u>此外</u>他还常常帮助别人。

III. Omissions in Chinese

Omissions are common in Chinese sentences. When the context is clear and the information is shared between the speaker and the listener(s), some grammatical elements may be omitted in the sentence (e.g., subject, object, or conjunction), especially in speech. Below are some examples of this phenomenon.

1. When talking about the weather:

下雨了。
下雨了。
It's raining.

下雪了。
下雪了。
It's snowing.

2. In answer to questions:

A: 你吃飯了嗎?
你吃饭了吗?

B: 吃了。
吃了。

A: 你想不想吃中國飯?
你想不想吃中国饭?

B: 想。
想。

(The subject 我 is omitted)

3. When the meaning is clear from shared context:

小玲把房間收拾好，(她)出門旅行了。
小玲把房间收拾好，(她)出门旅行了。

(The subject 她 is omitted)

爸爸給妹妹買了一條裙子。妹妹穿上(裙子)以後漂亮極了。
爸爸给妹妹买了一条裙子。妹妹穿上(裙子)以后漂亮极了。

(The object 裙子 is omitted)

前段時間(由於)我的考試很多，休息不夠，(所以)我感冒了。
前段时间(由于)我的考试很多，休息不够，(所以)我感冒了。

(The conjunctions 由於 and 所以 are omitted)

>>**Try it!** | With a partner compose several sentences with omissions (e.g., omissions of the subject, object, or conjunction). For example,

他把他最喜歡的磁帶借給了我，(他)還特別交代(我)，(不但)要好好
地聽，(而且)要很小心。

他把他最喜欢的磁带借给了我，(他)还特别交代(我)，(不但)要好好
地听，(而且)要很小心。

補充課文 (补充课文) SUPPLEMENTARY PRACTICE

Read the following passage. Then listen and repeat.

Thanks So Much for Your Help! (繁體字 Traditional Character Version)

(新遠幫文超買到了貓王的光碟以後的第三天，他們在網上的MSN上遇到了，文超向他感謝。)

文超：新遠，真是太謝謝你了！多虧你幫忙，不然我一定會讓彩宜給罵死。

新遠：不客氣，很高興這次能幫上你的忙。彩宜是個通情達理的人，因此我相信她一定能理解磁帶被絞的事。

文超：是啊！昨天晚上我把彩宜約出來了，把事情的經過告訴她，還把你幫我買的光碟交給她了。雖然她開始有點生氣，但是最後還是原諒我了。這次多虧你幫忙，不然事情就會更糟了。

新遠：沒什麼，不用謝啦。

文超：好了，我得走了，再見。

Notes:
相信(相信) [xiāngxìn]: to believe
理解(理解) [lǐjiě]: to understand
約(约) [yuē]: to make an appointment
交(交) [jiāo]: to submit, deliver

補充課文 (补充课文) SUPPLEMENTARY PRACTICE

Read the following passage. Then listen and repeat.

Thanks So Much for Your Help! (简体字 Simplified Character Version)

(新远帮文超买到了猫王的光碟以后的第三天，他们在网上的MSN上遇到了，文超向他感谢。)

文超： 新远，真是太谢谢你了！多亏你帮忙，不然我一定会让彩宜给骂死。

新远： 不客气，很高兴这次能帮上你的忙。彩宜是个通情达理的人，因此我相信她一定能理解磁带被绞的事。

文超： 是啊！昨天晚上我把彩宜约出来了，把事情的经过告诉她，还把你帮我买的光碟交给她了。虽然她开始有点生气，但是最后还是原谅我了。这次多亏你帮忙，不然事情就会更糟了。

新远： 没什么，不用谢啦。

文超： 好了，我得走了，再见。

Exercises: work with a partner or in small groups

1. 文超為什麼要謝謝新遠？
   文超为什么要谢谢新远？

2. 彩宜生氣了嗎？
   彩宜生气了吗？

3. 彩宜原諒文超了嗎？為什麼？
   彩宜原谅文超了吗？为什么？

成語故事 (成语故事) IDIOM STORY

亡羊補牢 (亡羊补牢) [wángyáng bǔláo]

Meaning: To mend the stall after a sheep is lost.

Usage: It implies taking a precaution after suffering a loss: it is never too late.

Example: 請你幫幫忙，幫我想想辦法，"亡羊補牢"，現在應該還來得及補救的。

請你帮帮忙，帮我想想办法，"亡羊补牢"，现在应该还来得及补救的。

Pay attention to the usages of passive voice, conjunctions, pivotal constructions, and interjections.

(繁體字 Traditional Character Version)

　　有一個農夫他有很多羊。有一天，他的一個鄰居看到他的羊圈破了一個很大的洞，就建議他補羊圈，說："你最好把羊圈補一下，不然羊是會被狼吃掉的。"可是那個人卻不聽鄰居的話，沒有去補羊圈。結果過了兩天，農夫的羊少了一隻。

　　這時，那個鄰居又來告訴他應該補羊圈。他不但不聽鄰居的話，反而還說："哎呀，羊才少了一隻，補什麼羊圈嘛?"

　　第二天，又有一隻羊被狼吃了。農夫這才覺得如果他還不快點兒把羊圈補好，羊就會被狼一隻一隻地吃完。所以，他馬上把羊圈修好。從那以後，羊就不再少了。

　　這個故事告訴我們，發現錯誤以後，如果及時補救就可以避免發生更大的錯誤。

(简体字 **Simplified Character Version**)

　　有一个农夫他有很多羊。有一天，他的一个邻居看到他的羊圈破了一个很大的洞，就建议他补羊圈，说："你最好把羊圈补一下，不然羊是会被狼吃掉的。"可是那个人却不听邻居的话，没有去补羊圈。结果过了两天，农夫的羊少了一只。

　　这时，那个邻居又来告诉他应该补羊圈。他不但不听邻居的话，反而还说："哎呀，羊才少了一只，补什么羊圈嘛？"

　　第二天，又有一只羊被狼吃了。农夫这才觉得如果他还不快点儿把羊圈补好，羊就会被狼一只一只地吃完。所以，他马上把羊圈修好。从那以后，羊就不再少了。

　　这个故事告诉我们，发现错误以后，如果及时补救就可以避免发生更大的错误。

Notes:

農夫(农夫) [nóngfū]: peasant, farmer
鄰居(邻居) [línjū]: neighbor
羊圈(羊圈) [yángjuàn]: sheep's stall
洞(洞) [dòng]: hole
補(补) [bǔ]: to mend, repair
狼(狼) [láng]: wolf
吃掉(吃掉) [chīdiào]: eat up

發現(发现) [fāxiàn]: to discover
錯誤(错误) [cuòwù]: mistake
及時(及时) [jíshí]: in time
補救(补救) [bǔjiù]: to correct a fault or deficiency
避免(避免) [bìmiǎn]: to avoid
發生(发生) [fāshēng]: to happen

Exercises: work with a partner or in small groups

1. 找出有下面語法的句子：passive voice, conjunctions, pivotal constructions, and interjections and omissions.

   找出有下面语法的句子：passive voice, conjunctions, pivotal constructions, and interjections and omissions.

2. 用你自己的話說說"亡羊補牢"的故事。
   用你自己的话说说"亡羊补牢"的故事。

3. 請用"亡羊補牢"造一個句子或者說一個"亡羊補牢"的例子。
   请用"亡羊补牢"造一个句子或者说一个"亡羊补牢"的例子。

4. "亡羊補牢"的故事，告訴了我們什麼？
   "亡羊补牢"的故事，告诉了我们什么？

練習 (练习) ACTIVITIES

I. Listening Exercises

15-1 In the blanks provided, write the Pinyin, with tones, for the words you hear. Then check them with your partner.

1. 小李 ＿＿＿ 同學抄 [chāo] (to copy) 中文作業，＿＿＿ 老師發現了，兩個人的功課都得了零分，還 ＿＿＿ 老師 ＿＿＿ 批評 [pīpíng] (to criticize) 了一頓。

   小李 ＿＿＿ 同学抄中文作业，＿＿＿ 老师发现了，两个人的功课都得了零分，还 ＿＿＿ 老师 ＿＿＿ 批评了一顿。

2. ＿＿＿ ＿＿＿ 路上塞車，＿＿＿ ＿＿＿ 順強沒趕上班機。

   ＿＿＿ ＿＿＿ 路上塞车，＿＿＿ ＿＿＿ 顺强没赶上班机。

3. 他 ＿＿＿ 女朋友的生日忘了，＿＿＿ 女朋友罵了 ＿＿＿ ＿＿＿ 。

   他 ＿＿＿ 女朋友的生日忘了，＿＿＿ 女朋友骂了 ＿＿＿ ＿＿＿ 。

4. 他的錢 ＿＿＿ ＿＿＿ 了，沒錢買午餐 [wǔcān] (lunch)，＿＿＿ ＿＿＿ 餓了一頓。

   他的钱 ＿＿＿ ＿＿＿ 了，没钱买午餐，＿＿＿ ＿＿＿ 饿了一顿。

5. 你現在都知道了。＿＿＿ ＿＿＿ ，小文給女朋友送花是為了 ＿＿＿ 她高興。

   你现在都知道了。＿＿＿ ＿＿＿ ，小文给女朋友送花是为了 ＿＿＿ 她高兴。

6. 這部電影 ＿＿＿ ＿＿＿ 場面壯觀，＿＿＿ ＿＿＿ 讓人很感動。

   这部电影 ＿＿＿ ＿＿＿ 场面壮观，＿＿＿ ＿＿＿ 让人很感动。

15-2 Listen to the story and then answer the questions. Check your answers with a partner.

Notes:

價錢(价钱) [jiàqián]: price
打折(打折) [dǎzhé]: on sale
出差(出差) [chūchāi]: to be on a business trip
商場(商场) [shāngchǎng]: the mall
叫醒(叫醒) [jiàoxǐng]: to wake up, awaken
罰金(罚金) [fájīn]: fine
拖(拖) [tuō]: to tow
趕緊(赶紧) [gǎnjǐn]: hasten
發現(发现) [fāxiàn]: to discover

問題(问题):

1. 麗麗一直想買什麼? 她買了嗎? 為什麼?
   丽丽一直想买什么? 她买了吗? 为什么?

2. 學明要幫麗麗做什麼? 為什麼?
   学明要帮丽丽做什么? 为什么?

3. 今天學明是什麼時候起床的? 他是怎麼醒的?
   今天学明是什么时候起床的? 他是怎么醒的?

4. 學明把車停在哪兒了?
   学明把车停在哪儿了?

5. 警察做什麼了? 學明怎麼辦?
   警察做什么了? 学明怎么办?

6. 學明買到麗麗要的東西了嗎? 為什麼?
   学明买到丽丽要的东西了吗? 为什么?

II. Character Exercises

15-3 Work with a partner. Read the following words, phrases, and sentences.

磁   卻
磁   却

磁帶   他卻不原諒我
磁带   他却不原谅我

把磁帶絞了   可是他卻不原諒我
把磁带绞了   可是他却不原谅我

老錄音機把磁帶絞了   我跟他道歉了，可是他卻不原諒我。
老录音机把磁带绞了   我跟他道歉了，可是他却不原谅我。

我的老錄音機把磁帶絞了。   我已經跟他道歉了，可是他卻不原
我的老录音机把磁带绞了。   諒我。
                                          我已经跟他道歉了，可是他却不原
                                          谅我。

Now with your partner, try to use the following characters to make words, phrases, and then sentences.

1. 求	2. 聯	3. 絞	4. 力	5. 反
求	联	绞	力	反

6. 碟	7. 錄	8. 遇	9. 遍	10. 購
碟	录	遇	遍	购

15-4 Form groups and create phrases with the following words (pay attention to the various usages of each word).

Example: 因：因為，因此
　　　　　　 因：因为，因此

1. 開：＿＿＿＿＿＿＿＿＿＿＿＿＿＿＿＿＿＿＿＿＿＿＿＿＿
　 开：＿＿＿＿＿＿＿＿＿＿＿＿＿＿＿＿＿＿＿＿＿＿＿＿＿

2. 保：_____

保：_____

3. 發：_____

发：_____

4. 然：_____

然：_____

5. 心：_____

心：_____

6. 復：_____

复：_____

7. 機：_____

机：_____

8. 過：_____

过：_____

III. Grammar Exercises

15-5 With your partner read the story, then complete the exercises that follow.

Notes:
過期(过期) [guòqī]: to be overdue
罰款(罚款) [fákuǎn]: to impose a fine or penalty
施工(施工) [shīgōng]: construction
挖(挖) [wā]: to dig
坑(坑) [kēng]: hole
標記(标记) [biāojì]: sign, symbol
掉(掉) [diào]: to fall
受傷(受伤) [shòushāng]: to be injured
剛好(刚好) [gānghǎo]: happened to; it so happened that
心疼(心疼) [xīnténg]: to be distressed
筆(笔) [bǐ]: (measure word for amount of money)
賠款(赔款) [péikuǎn]: indemnity

(繁體字 Traditional Character Version)

　　小明從圖書館借了一本書，明天就要過期了，＿＿ ＿＿ (if) 還晚了就要被罰款十元。已經是晚上十點了，＿＿ ＿＿ (but) 小明還要騎自行車急急忙忙地去還書。

　　學校圖書館前邊的道路正在施工，被挖了一個坑。＿＿ ＿＿ (because) 天太黑，＿＿ ＿＿ (also) 坑的前邊也沒有標記，＿＿ ＿＿ (thus) 小明沒有看到坑，不小心掉進坑裡，受傷了。

　　同學小王剛好從圖書館出來，看到小明身上有很多血，嚇死了。馬上把他送進醫院，還好沒有什麼大事。小明的女朋友聽說了非常心疼，眼淚嘩啦嘩啦地流了下來。

　　學校知道以後不但道歉了，＿＿ ＿＿ (besides) 還在坑的前邊放了一個大標記。＿＿ ＿＿ (although) 小明的書還晚了，＿＿ ＿＿ (but) 他 ＿＿ ＿＿ (not only) 不用被罰款，＿＿ ＿＿ (but also) 還得到了一筆賠款，＿＿ ＿＿ (therefore) 買了一輛新自行車。

(简体字 Simplified Character Version)

　　小明从图书馆借了一本书，明天就要过期了，＿＿ ＿＿ (if) 还晚了就要被罚款十元。已经是晚上十点了，＿＿ ＿＿ (but) 小明还要骑自行车急急忙忙地去还书。

学校图书馆前边的道路正在施工，被挖了一个坑。＿＿ ＿＿ (because) 天太黑，＿＿ ＿＿ (also) 坑的前边也没有标记，＿＿ ＿＿ (thus) 小明没有看到坑，不小心掉进坑里，受伤了。

同学小王刚好从图书馆出来，看到小明身上有很多血，吓死了。马上把他送进医院，还好没有什么大事。小明的女朋友听说了非常心疼，眼泪哗啦哗啦地流了下来。

学校知道以后不但道歉了，＿＿ ＿＿ (besides) 还在坑的前边放了一个大标记。＿＿ ＿＿ (although) 小明的书还晚了，＿＿ ＿＿ (but) 他 ＿＿ ＿＿ (not only) 不用被罚款，＿＿ ＿＿ (but also) 还得到了一笔赔款，＿＿ ＿＿ (therefore) 买了一辆新自行车。

1. With the help of the English clues, fill in the blanks with the appropriate Chinese conjunction words.
2. Form groups to take turns retelling the story in your own words.
3. Circle the markers of passive sentences.
4. Point out the places where the subject or object have been omitted in the story.

IV. Media Literacy

The short text below, written in the style of newspapers, magazines, or Internet news articles, will help you become familiar with the formal written expressions used in these genres.

 拯救熊貓 (拯救熊猫) Saving Pandas

繁體字：

拯救熊貓

在80年代，有30隻小熊貓被發現時，因無母親在身邊，所以被人們從野外帶回圈養。但是科學家發現，母熊貓外出覓食時，經常會把小熊貓單獨留下，所以當小熊貓被單獨發現時，不應將其帶回圈養。

简体字:

拯救熊猫

在80年代，有30只小熊猫被发现时，因无母亲在身边，所以被人们从野外带回圈养。但是科学家发现，母熊猫外出觅食时，经常会把小熊猫单独留下，所以当小熊猫被单独发现时，不应将其带回圈养。

Notes:

拯救(拯救) [zhěngjiù]: to save, rescue
熊貓(熊猫) [xióngmāo]: panda
年代(年代) [niándài]: a decade
發現(发现) [fāxiàn]: to find, discover
母親(母亲) [mǔqīn]: mother
身邊(身边) [shēnbiān]: at (or by) one's side
野外(野外) [yěwài]: open country, field
圈養(圈养) [juànyǎng]: to nurture (animals) in an enclosure
科學家(科学家) [kēxuéjiā]: scientist
外出(外出) [wàichū]: to go out
覓食(觅食) [mìshí]: to find food
經常(经常) [jīngcháng]: constantly, often
單獨(单独) [dāndú]: alone, by oneself
留下(留下) [liúxià]: to remain, leave

Exercises for the article: work with a partner or a group to ask and answer the following.

1. What characters can you find that are used mainly in writing? What are their spoken counterparts?
   Example: 母親(母亲), 圈養(圈养), 覓食(觅食), 經常(经常), 其

2. Circle the 把 and 被 sentences in the text. Identify the objects of the 把 sentences and the subjects of the 被 sentences.

3. Underline the conjunctions used in the text.

4. Use Chinese to retell the article in your own words.

V. Communicative Activities

15-6 算閏年(算闰年) [suàn rùnnián] (Calculating Leap Years).

Your nephew asks you how to calculate leap years. Using 被, explain to him the rules for calculating leap year listed in the chart below. Then work together to figure out which years are leap years. Form pairs to perform this exercise.

> *Rules for Calculating Leap Years*
> 1. Every year divisible by four is a leap year;
> 2. with the exception that years divisible by 100 are not leap years;
> 3. and years divisible by 400 are leap years.

Notes:
算(算) [suàn]: to calculate
閏年(闰年) [rùnnián]: leap year
根據(根据) [gēnjù]: on the basis of, according to
規則(规则) [guīzé]: rule, regulation, regular
整除(整除) [zhěngchú]: (math.) to be divided with no
   remainder

雖然……但是……，因為……所以……，
可是，而，然而，從而，此外，總之
虽然……但是……，因为……所以……，
可是，而，然而，从而，此外，总之

它們是閏年嗎? 為什麼?
它们是闰年吗? 为什么?

1996年　1897年　1249年　2001年　2008年　894年　2016年

(e.g. 根據規則(1)，因為2000年能被4整除，所以它可能是閏年。然而根據規則(2),2000能被100整除，所以可能它又不是閏年。最後根據規則(3),2000能被400整除，所以它還是閏年。總之，我們最後算出來2000年是閏年。)

(e.g. 根据规则(1)，因为2000年能被4整除，所以它可能是闰年。然而根据规则(2),2000能被100整除，所以可能它又不是闰年。最后根据规则(3),2000能被400整除，所以它还是闰年。总之，我们最后算出来2000年是闰年。)

15-7 Form groups to act out the following scene. Identify which clues are important for solving the case.

After returning from a business trip you discover that your house has been broken into. Call the police immediately. When the police arrive, describe what has happened and answer the questions.

1. A mirror has been broken.
2. A letter has been opened.
3. A document in the computer has been read.
4. Half a cup of water has been drunk.
5. The television has been moved from the living room to the bedroom.

Notes:

被打壞了，被打開了，雖然……但是……，因為……所以……，可是，而，然而，
從而，此外，總之

被打坏了，被打开了，虽然……但是……，因为……所以……，可是，而，然而，
从而，此外，总之

文化知識 (文化知识) Culture Link

文化點滴 (文化点滴) CULTURE NOTES

傳統和現代音樂 (传统和现代音乐) Traditional and Contemporary Music

Traditional Chinese music is as old as Chinese recorded civilization, spanning a time period of more than 5,000 years. An important part of Chinese culture and even philosophy, it was believed that music influenced the harmony of the universe and could serve as the best means to purify thoughts and nurture character. Although traditional music remains popular today in China, the contemporary music scene has also been influenced by other types of music, including Western classical, jazz, pop, rock, hip hop, and heavy metal.

Traditional music falls into several categories—imperial, literati, and folk. Imperial music was performed during ritual ceremonies and other important events involving the emperor, as well as for banquets and recreational outings. Literati music, together with calligraphy, painting, and poetry, defined the unique culture of the scholar elite in traditional China. A mastery of the 琴 [qín] (a traditional musical instrument), 棋 [qí] (chess), 書(书) [shū] (calligraphy), and 畫(画) [huà] (painting) was a requirement for any highly educated person, and among these four skills the 琴, representing music, was listed first. Folk music, including folk songs, "talk-singing,"

Do you know...

- the different categories of Chinese traditional music?
- any traditional Chinese musical instruments?
- the types of music that are popular in China nowadays?

Read and find out!

and opera, reflected the life and sentiments of ordinary people. Countless folk songs and more than 360 kinds of Chinese opera were passed down orally from one generation to the next. All of traditional music depended on Chinese traditional instruments, several hundred in number, made of materials ranging from metal to gourds to bone to even leaves.

Although traditional music is still popular in China today, increasingly it is Western classical music that enjoys the greatest following, and in cities a fair number of heavy metal and modern avant-garde bands have joined the music scene. Western classical music first gained a footing in China nearly one hundred years ago, followed by Western jazz several decades later. In the post-Mao era of the late 20th century, Western pop, rock and roll, and most recently hip hop, rap, and fusions of Western modern and Chinese traditional music have emerged. Western pop icon Elvis Presley, while unknown in China during his heyday, has enjoyed a surge in popularity since the official introduction of his music to the mainland in 1991, with "Love Me Tender" his most popular song. Unlike the Cultural Revolution era, when anything Western was banned, the current trend toward Western classical music is officially sanctioned and even encouraged by the Chinese government.

Much of this music and many contemporary Chinese musicians and composers were spotlighted during the 2008 Olympics in Beijing.

A Chinese musician in traditional dress plays the erhu (a two-stringed violin). What are some other common Chinese bowed strings instruments?

An all-women Chinese rock band performance.

問題討論 (问题讨论) *Discuss the following with a partner or in small groups.*

1. 你試過琴棋書畫嗎? 如果試過, 其中你最喜歡哪一個?
   你试过琴棋书画吗? 如果试过, 其中你最喜欢哪一个?

   Have you ever tried playing the 琴 [qín] (a traditional musical instrument), 棋 [qí] (chess), or Chinese 書(书) [shū] (calligraphy), or 畫(画) [huà] (painting)? If you have, which one do you like the best?

2. 你彈奏過中國的傳統樂器嗎? 如果彈奏過, 請和同學們分享你的經歷。
   你弹奏过中国的传统乐器吗? 如果弹奏过, 请和同学们分享你的经历。

   Have you ever played any traditional Chinese instruments? If you have, share your experiences with your classmates.

3. 你喜歡中國的流行歌嗎? 如果喜歡, 你最喜歡哪首歌和哪個歌星?
   你喜欢中国的流行歌吗? 如果喜欢, 你最喜欢哪首歌和哪个歌星?

   Do you like Chinese pop music? If so, what is your favorite song and who is your favorite singer?

趣味中文 (趣味中文) FUN WITH CHINESE

有驚無險
有惊无险

Adventurous but not dangerous

yǒu	jīng	wú	xiǎn
有	驚	無	險
有	惊	无	险
have	scare	no	risk

問題討論 (问题讨论) *Discuss the following with a partner or in small groups.*

1. Have you had any experiences that were adventurous, but not dangerous? If so, share them with your classmates.
2. Can you identify some sports activities that are adventurous, but not dangerous?

行動吧! (行动吧!) LET'S GO!

藝術演出 (艺术演出) Art Performance

中明 went to China. Walking on the street, he saw a lot of advertisements about a series of art performances. He was eager to find out how to get tickets to these performances. Can you read the Chinese in the advertisement with him and help him find out how to get tickets?

Notes:

藝術(艺术) [yìshù]: art
演出(演出) [yǎnchū]: performance
中外(中外) [Zhōngwài]: China and foreign countries
場(场) [chǎng]: (measure word for performance)
經典(经典) [jīngdiǎn]: classics
隆重(隆重) [lóngzhòng]: grand
登場(登场) [dēngchǎng]: come on stage
量(量) [liàng]: quantity
有限(有限) [yǒuxiàn]: limited
即止(即止) [jí zhǐ]: immediately stop
詳情(详情) [xiángqíng]: detailed information
查詢(查询) [cháxún]: to inquire about

問題討論 (问题讨论) Discuss the following with a partner or in small groups.

1. 這些演出是哪家公司辦的？這是一家什麼公司？
   这些演出是哪家公司办的？这是一家什么公司？
   What company organized these performances? What kind of company is it?

2. Translate the following sentences:

   (1) 50多場經典藝術，隆重登場。
       50多场经典艺术，隆重登场。

   (2) 票量有限，先到先得，賣完即止。
       票量有限，先到先得，卖完即止。

3. What are the spoken forms of these words?
   即，止，至

4. Use your own words in Chinese to explain the advertisement.

16

讚美與客套（赞美与客套）
Etiquette and Manners

A statue of Confucius, one of China's leading philosophers and teacher of ethics.

CONNECTIONS AND COMMUNITIES PREVIEW

Discuss the following questions with a partner or your class. What similarities and differences do you think there might be between Chinese culture and your own culture?

1. How do people in your country respond to compliments?

2. How do these responses differ in your culture compared to Chinese culture?

教學目標（教学目标） OBJECTIVES

- Give and reply to compliments
- Say goodbye to guests and hosts in an appropriate manner
- Use emphasis in conversations

生詞 (生词) VOCABULARY

🔊 核心詞 (核心词) Core Vocabulary

	TRADITIONAL	SIMPLIFIED	PINYIN		
1.	非......不可	非......不可	fēi . . . bùkě		have to, must
2.	年級	年级	niánjí	N.	grade
3.	往年	往年	wǎngnián	N.	(in) former years
4.	趁	趁	chèn	Prep.	avail oneself of
5.	叮噹	叮当	dīngdāng		*onomatopoeia*, e.g., jingle (of a bell)
6.	門鈴	门铃	ménlíng	N.	doorbell
7.	響	响	xiǎng	V.	to make a sound, ring
8.	提起	提起	tíqǐ	V.	to mention
9.	用功	用功	yònggōng	Adj.	hard-working, studious
10.	上進	上进	shàngjìn	Adj.	to aspire to improve
11.	成就感	成就感	chéngjiùgǎn	N.	sense of achievement
12.	包括	包括	bāokuò	V.	to include, comprise
13.	待人處世	待人处世	dàirénchǔshì		the way one acts with others and conducts oneself in public
14.	道理	道理	dàolǐ	N.	principle, argument
15.	寶貴	宝贵	bǎoguì	Adj.	precious
16.	懂事	懂事	dǒngshì	Adj.	intelligent, sensible
17.	當	当	dàng	V.	to regard as, treat as
18.	退休	退休	tuìxiū	V.	to retire
19.	期待	期待	qīdài	V.	to expect, await

	TRADITIONAL	SIMPLIFIED	PINYIN		
20.	毛筆	毛笔	máobǐ	N.	calligraphy brush
21.	佩服	佩服	pèifú	V.	to admire
22.	學問	学问	xuéwèn	N.	knowledge, scholarship
23.	懂	懂	dǒng	V.	to understand, grasp
24.	教書	教书	jiāoshū	V.O.	to teach
25.	看齊	看齐	kànqí	V.	to keep up with, emulate
26.	繼續	继续	jìxù	V.	to continue
27.	讀	读	dú	V.	to read, attend school
28.	經濟學	经济学	jīngjìxué	N.	economics
29.	碩士	硕士	shuòshì	N.	master
30.	教授	教授	jiàoshòu	N.	professor
31.	將來	将来	jiānglái	N.	future
32.	前途無量	前途无量	qiántúwúliàng		great expectations
33.	過獎	过奖	guòjiǎng	V.	to give undeserved compliment
34.	講	讲	jiǎng	V.	to talk
35.	經驗	经验	jīngyàn	N.	experience
36.	所學的	所学的	suǒxuéde	N.	what has been learned
37.	應用	应用	yìngyòng	V. N.	to apply application
38.	網絡	网络	wǎngluò	N.	Internet, network
39.	磨練	磨练	móliàn	V.	to temper oneself
40.	決心	决心	juéxīn	V. N.	to be determined to determination, resolution

	TRADITIONAL	SIMPLIFIED	PINYIN		
41.	番	番	fān	M.W.	(measure word for cause)
42.	事業	事业	shìyè	N.	cause, undertaking, enterprise
43.	以……為榮	以……为荣	yǐ . . . wéiróng		to be proud of
44.	加油	加油	jiāyóu	V.O.	to make an extra effort, "Go! Go!"
45.	打擾	打扰	dǎrǎo	V.	to disturb

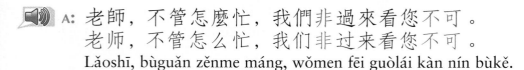

語文知識 (语文知识) LANGUAGE LINK

Read and listen to the following sentence patterns. These patterns use vocabulary, expressions, and grammar that you will study in more detail in this lesson. After reading the sentence patterns, read and listen to the Language in Use section that follows.

句型 (句型) Sentence Patterns

A: 老師，不管怎麼忙，我們非過來看您不可。
老师，不管怎么忙，我们非过来看您不可。
Lǎoshī, bùguǎn zěnme máng, wǒmen fēi guòlái kàn nín bùkě.

B: 你們這些孩子們都很懂事，
你们这些孩子们都很懂事，
Nǐmen zhèxiē háizimen dōu hěn dǒngshì,

不能不讓我感動。
不能不让我感动。
bùnéngbú ràng wǒ gǎndòng.

A: 老師是很喜歡寫書法嗎？
老师是很喜欢写书法吗？
Lǎoshī shì hěn xǐhuān xiě shūfǎ ma?

B: 是，當他拿著毛筆寫書法的時候，
是，当他拿着毛笔写书法的时候，
Shì, dāng tā ná zhe máobǐ xiě shūfǎ de shíhou,

會專心得連飯都忘了吃。
会专心得连饭都忘了吃。
huì zhuānxīn de lián fàn dōu wàng le chī.

A: 你畢業以後打算要做什麼？
你毕业以后打算要做什么？
Nǐ bìyè yǐhòu dǎsuàn yào zuò shénme?

B: 我要上研究生院繼續學習。
我要上研究生院继续学习。
Wǒ yào shàng yánjiūshēngyuàn jìxù xuéxí.

A: 很高興你們來看我。請慢走！
很高兴你们来看我。请慢走！
Hěn gāoxìng nǐmen lái kàn wǒ. Qǐng màn zǒu!

B: 您多保重！請留步。再見！
您多保重！请留步。再见！
Nín duō bǎozhòng! Qǐng liúbù. Zàijiàn!

課文 Language in Use: Visiting Teacher Xie
(繁體字 Traditional Character Version)

(放春假了，大學四年級的張建明、夏玲跟往年一樣，到謝老師家拜訪。張建明也趁這個機會，把女朋友吳小麗帶過來認識認識謝老師。)

("叮噹"，門鈴響了。謝老師去開門。)

張建明、夏玲： 老師，您好！好久不見，我們過來看您了！

謝老師： 喔！你們都來了，太好了，來，來，快請進。

張建明： 小麗，這位就是我常跟你提起的謝老師。老師，這是我的女朋友小麗。

吳小麗： 謝老師，您好，很高興認識您。建明老說著您呢，說您是他最好的老師。您的學生沒有不喜歡您的。

謝老師： 沒有啦！他們都是好學生，既用功又上進。我教他們教得很有成就感呢。

張建明： 老師您教了我們很多東西，其中還包括待人處世的道理，這些東西可真寶貴呀！

夏玲： 是呀！我們老想著您，不管怎麼忙，我們非過來看您不可。

謝老師： 你們這些孩子們都很懂事，是很有心[1]的，每年都不忘過來看我，不能不讓我感動。來，大家請坐，別客氣。就把這兒當[2]成自己的家吧。

---

1. 很有心(很有心)

Literally 有心(有心) means to "have heart." It is an adjective used to show a person's concern for others. Such adjectives using "有(有) + noun" can be modified by adverbs indicating degree, such as "很(很), 挺(挺), 最(最)."

Examples:

很有用(很有用)
very useful

非常有幫助(非常有帮助)
extraordinarily helpful

完全有道理(完全有道理)
absolutely reasonable

十分有抱負(十分有抱负)
extremely ambitious

挺有錢(挺有钱)
quite rich

最有趣(最有趣)
the most interesting

Continued on page 508

课文 Language in Use: Visiting Teacher Xie
(简体字 Simplified Character Version)

(放春假了，大学四年级的张建明、夏玲跟往年一样，到谢老师家拜访。张建明也趁这个机会，把女朋友吴小丽带过来认识认识谢老师。)

("叮当"，门铃响了。谢老师去开门。)

张建明、夏玲： 老师，您好！好久不见，我们过来看您了！

谢老师： 喔！你们都来了，太好了，来，来，快请进。

张建明： 小丽，这位就是我常跟你提起的谢老师。老师，这是我的女朋友小丽。

吴小丽： 谢老师，您好，很高兴认识您。建明老说着您呢，说您是他最好的老师。您的学生没有不喜欢您的。

谢老师： 没有啦！他们都是好学生，既用功又上进。我教他们教得很有成就感呢。

张建明： 老师您教了我们很多东西，其中还包括待人处世的道理，这些东西可真宝贵呀！

夏玲： 是呀！我们老想着您，不管怎么忙，我们非过来看您不可。

谢老师： 你们这些孩子们都很懂事，是很有心[1]的，每年都不忘过来看我，不能不让我感动。来，大家请坐，别客气。就把这儿当[2]成自己的家吧。

---

2. 当(当) [dàng, dāng]

当(当) is pronounced as [dàng] when used as a short form of the verb "当做(当做)/当成(当成)" (regard as, treat as) and is followed by an object. It is generally used in "把(把)" or "被(被)" construction sentences.

Example:

謝老師把學生當自己的孩子了。
谢老师把学生当自己的孩子了。
Xie Laoshi regards his students as his children.

Other uses of "当(当)" pronounced as [dāng] that we have studied are as follows:

当然(当然)　of course

当……的時候(当……的时候)
at that time, when

当天(当天)　on that day

当個教授(当个教授)　to work as

Continued on page 509

課文 Language in Use: Visiting Teacher Xie
(繁體字 Traditional Character Version) —— 接第五百零六頁

張建明： 老師，聽說您明年就要退休了。退休以後，打算做什麼呢？

謝老師： 我是很期待退休以後的日子的。我想多寫寫書法，多學習學習。

夏玲： 我記得您很喜歡寫書法，每當您拿著毛筆寫書法的時候，就非常專心。有時候專心得連飯都忘了吃，真讓人佩服。

吳小麗： 老師您已經很有學問了，為什麼還要學習呢？

謝老師： 是活到老，學到老[3]！你們要記住，當我們學得越多的時候，就會越覺得自己懂的實在太少了。我雖然二十多歲就開始教書，到現在已經當了三十幾年的老師了，但是我也很喜歡當學生，可以多學習、多長知識。

> **3. 活到老，學到老(活到老，学到老)**
>
> 活到老，學到老(活到老，学到老) is an idiomatic Chinese phrase that literally means "live to old age and learn to old age." The phrase emphasizes that the pursuit of knowledge is a lifelong effort.

張建明： 我們可要好好地向您看齊呀！對了，夏玲也打算上研究生院繼續學習呢！

謝老師： 是嗎？夏玲，你要上什麼研究生院？

夏玲： 我要去讀經濟學碩士，碩士以後我還要再繼續學習，希望以後能當個經濟學教授。

謝老師： 不錯，將來一定是前途無量[4]。

夏玲： 您過獎了。對了，建明說畢業後，要自己開公司呢！建明，你來講講你的計畫吧。

> **4. 前途無量(前途无量)**
>
> 前途無量(前途无量) means to "have boundless prospects." It is commonly used to extend good wishes or to comment on the great expectations of young people. A similar Chinese expression, 前途遠大 (前途远大) "have far and broad possibilities," is also used for good wishes.

張建明： 好的。老師您是知道的，我每年暑假都去電腦公司實習，在那兒學了不少知識和經驗。因此畢業以後，我想把我所學的，好好地應用一下。我想開個電腦網絡公司，給自己一個機會，磨練磨練。

Continued on page 510

课文 Language in Use: Visiting Teacher Xie
(简体字 Simplified Character Version) —— 接第五百零七页

张建明： 老师，听说您明年就要退休了。退休以后，打算做什么呢？

谢老师： 我是很期待退休以后的日子的。我想多写写书法，多学习学习。

夏玲： 我记得您很喜欢写书法，每当您拿着毛笔写书法的时候，就非常专心。有时候专心得连饭都忘了吃，真让人佩服。

吴小丽： 老师您已经很有学问了，为什么还要学习呢？

谢老师： 是活到老，学到老[3]！你们要记住，当我们学得越多的时候，就会越觉得自己懂的实在太少了。我虽然二十多岁就开始教书，到现在已经当了三十几年的老师了，但是我也很喜欢当学生，可以多学习、多长知识。

张建明： 我们可要好好地向您看齐呀！对了，夏玲也打算上研究生院继续学习呢！

谢老师： 是吗？夏玲，你要上什么研究生院？

夏玲： 我要去读经济学硕士，硕士以后我还要再继续学习，希望以后能当个经济学教授。

谢老师： 不错，将来一定是前途无量[4]。

夏玲： 您过奖了。对了，建明说毕业后，要自己开公司呢！建明，你来讲讲你的计划吧。

张建明： 好的。老师您是知道的，我每年暑假都去电脑公司实习，在那儿学了不少知识和经验。因此毕业以后，我想把我所学的，好好地应用一下。我想开个电脑网络公司，给自己一个机会，磨练磨练。

Continued on page 511

課文 Language in Use: Visiting Teacher Xie
(繁體字 Traditional Character Version) —— 接第五百零八頁

吳小麗： 他還下定決心，非要在三十歲以前做出一番事業不可。

謝老師： 很好，你們都是年輕有為[5]，祝你們成功！我會以你們為榮的，好好加油。對了，小麗呢，你也是今年畢業嗎?

5. 年輕有為(年轻有为)
年輕有為(年轻有为) means "young and promising." It is used to comment on a young person's promising future.

吳小麗： 不，他們都要畢業了，只有我今年還不能畢業。我是學醫的，我們學醫的非得學六年不可!

(謝老師和學生們繼續聊天。兩個小時以後，學生們要走了。)

張建明(看了看時間)： 喔！時間不早了，我們打擾您太久了，該走了。

謝老師： 還早呢！沒關係，再待一會兒吧。

夏玲： 不了，老師，我們是真的該走了。下次有空再來看您。

謝老師： 那，好吧！很高興你們來看我。請慢走[6]!

6. 請慢走(请慢走)
請慢走(请慢走) literally means "please walk slowly." It is usually said by the host when the guests are about to leave. Similar English expressions are "please take care" and "drive carefully."

吳小麗： 您多保重，請留步[7]。再見!

课文 Language in Use: Visiting Teacher Xie
(简体字 Simplified Character Version) —— 接第五百零九页

吴小丽：　他还下定决心，非要在三十岁以前做出一番事业不可。

谢老师：　很好，你们都是年轻有为5，祝你们成功！我会以你们为荣
　　　　　的，好好加油。对了，小丽呢，你也是今年毕业吗？

吴小丽：　不，他们都要毕业了，只有我今年还不能毕业。我是学医的，
　　　　　我们学医的非得学六年不可！

(谢老师和学生们继续聊天。两个小时以后，学生们要走了。)

张建明(看了看时间)：喔！时间不早了，我们打扰您太久了，该走了。

谢老师：　还早呢！没关系，再待一会儿吧。

夏玲：　　不了，老师，我们是真的该走
　　　　　了。下次有空再来看您。

谢老师：　那，好吧！很高兴你们来看
　　　　　我。请慢走6！

吴小丽：　您多保重，请留步7。再见！

7. 请留步(請留步)
請留步(请留步) literally "please keep your footsteps," is said by guests when the host is seeing them off. The implied meaning is "I will see myself out. Thank you."

語法 (语法) GRAMMAR

I. Emphasis in Chinese Sentences

Emphasis can be conveyed in various ways. It is commonly expressed by stressing a particular word or phrase in the sentence. It can also be realized through using adverbs and different sentence constructions.

Emphasis words/ constructions	Features	Examples
"非⋯⋯不可 (非⋯⋯不可)" Construction (for more detail, see Lesson 19)	used to indicate "must, have to"	這個星期六媽媽非去看弟弟不可。 这个星期六妈妈非去看弟弟不可。 Mom has to visit (our) little brother this Saturday. 今天妹妹非吃藥不可。 今天妹妹非吃药不可。 (Our) little sister has to take her medicine today.
"連⋯⋯也/都⋯⋯ (连⋯⋯也/都⋯⋯)" Construction (for more detail, see Lesson 8)	used to indicate "even"	
	連 + N. + 也/都 连 + N. + 也/都	這個問題太難了，連老師都不知道怎麼回答。 这个问题太难了，连老师都不知道怎么回答。 This question is too difficult. Even the teacher doesn't know how to answer it. 他急急忙忙地走了，連晚飯也沒來得及吃。 他急急忙忙地走了，连晚饭也没来得及吃。 He left hastily and didn't even have time to eat dinner. 他太忙了，連吃飯的時間也沒有。 他太忙了，连吃饭的时间也没有。 He is too busy, and doesn't even have time to eat.

Emphasis words/ constructions	Features	Examples
	連 + V. + 也/都 连 + V. + 也/都	這麼大的工程，我連想都不敢想，他卻一個人完成了。 这么大的工程，我连想都不敢想，他却一个人完成了。 I don't even dare to think about such a big project, but he finished it by himself.
	連 + clause + 也/都 连 + clause + 也/都	我連他住在哪兒都忘了。 我连他住在哪儿都忘了。 I've even forgotten where he lives.
	連(连) + NP with measure words 也/都 (也/都)	房間裡連一個人都沒有。 房间里连一个人都没有。 There is not a single person in the room. 她連一條裙子也沒有。 她连一条裙子也没有。 She doesn't have even one skirt.
Adverb "就(就)"	The adverb 就(就) is used to emphasize that an event occurred earlier than expected. Time modifiers and other adverbs must be used before 就(就).	我六歲的時候就認識她了。 我六岁的时候就认识她了。 I've known her since I was six years old.
	就(就) + 是(是)/ 在(在) is used to provide emphasis to a simple statement	這就是我的宿舍。 这就是我的宿舍。 This place is my dorm. 花店就在醫院旁邊。 花店就在医院旁边。 The flower store is right beside the hospital.

Emphasis words/ constructions	Features	Examples
	就(就) + V. is used to indicate a strong and unchangeable will. 就(就) is usually stressed in speaking.	媽媽叫我吃藥，我<u>就</u>不想吃藥。 妈妈叫我吃药，我<u>就</u>不想吃药。 Mom asked me to take medicine, but I just don't want to take medicine. 媽媽叫小王去坐車，可是他<u>就</u>要走路去上課。 妈妈叫小王去坐车，可是他<u>就</u>要走路去上课。 Mom asked Xiao Wang to take the bus, but he just wants to walk to class.
Adverb "可(可)"	The adverb 可(可) is frequently used in spoken language to provide emphasis	
	In statements	那個三歲的孩子吃得<u>可</u>不少。 那个三岁的孩子吃得<u>可</u>不少。 That three-year-old kid eats quite a lot. 買電腦<u>可</u>不能只看價錢 [jiàqián] (price)，貴的電腦<u>可</u>不一定好用。 买电脑<u>可</u>不能只看价钱，贵的电脑<u>可</u>不一定好用。 Don't just focus on price when purchasing a computer. Expensive computers are not necessarily the best ones.
	In rhetorical sentences	這麼大的地方，<u>可</u>去哪兒找他呀? 这么大的地方，<u>可</u>去哪儿找他呀? How can we find him in such a vast area?

Emphasis words/ constructions	Features	Examples
	In imperative sentences	你<u>可</u>要好好學中文呀！ 你<u>可</u>要好好学中文呀！ You have to learn Chinese well. 你<u>可</u>不能一邊開車一邊打手機呀！ 你<u>可</u>不能一边开车一边打手机呀！ You must not drive while talking on the cell phone.
Double negative structure	"不能不(不能不)、不會不(不会不)" are used to express a high possibility or strong obligation	小美的父母明天要來，她<u>不能不</u>整理房間。 小美的父母明天要来，她<u>不能不</u>整理房间。 Xiaomei's parents are coming tomorrow. She has to clean up the house. 小謝的朋友<u>不會不</u>幫他搬家的。 小谢的朋友<u>不会不</u>帮他搬家的。 It's not possible that Xiao Xie's friends won't help him move.
	"沒有……不 (没有……不)" is used to indicate "all"	<u>沒有人</u><u>不</u>喜歡他。 <u>没有人</u><u>不</u>喜欢他。 There isn't anyone who doesn't like him. 他<u>沒有一天</u><u>不</u>喝茶。 他<u>没有一天</u><u>不</u>喝茶。 He drinks tea every single day.

Emphasis words/ constructions	Features	Examples
Intensifier "是(是)" and the construction "是……的 (是……的)" (for details see *Chinese Link*, Level 1, Lesson 6)	In sentences referring to events that happened in the past, the "是……的 (是……的)" construction is applied to emphasize when, where, or how the actions occurred	我是在北京學中文的。 我是在北京学中文的。 It was in Beijing that I studied Chinese. 他是去年來的。 他是去年来的。 It was last year that he arrived.
	The intensifier 是(是) is used in sentences referring to the continuous present or future to indicate affirmation. 是(是) is not a predicate in the sentences and is usually stressed. 是(是) + word + (omitted particle 的) is used in a specific context to emphasize the fact of the subject	今天是冷。 今天是冷。 It is indeed cold today. 姚明是很高。 姚明是很高。 Yao Ming is very tall indeed.
	是(是) + clause	你的房間是比我的大。 你的房间是比我的大。 Your room is indeed larger than mine.
"……也/都 (……也/都)" or "……也沒/不 (……也没/不)" construction	Used to indicate "entirely" or "not at all"	同學們全都回家了。 同学们全都回家了。 All the classmates went home. 我一次也沒去過中國。 我一次也没去过中国。 I have not been to China once.

Emphasis words/ constructions	Features	Examples
Rhetorical questions (detailed usages will be introduced in Lesson 17)	Rhetorical questions are used to state an obvious fact or to intensify the tone. Typical constructions include: • "不是......嗎 (不是......吗)" • "沒......嗎 (没......吗)" • "難道...... (难道......)"	你<u>不是</u>去過上海<u>嗎</u>? 給我介紹一下那兒的小吃店吧。 你<u>不是</u>去过上海<u>吗</u>? 给我介绍一下那儿的小吃店吧。 Haven't you been to Shanghai? Then tell me about some snackbars there. 你<u>沒</u>聽出來<u>嗎</u>? 他<u>是</u>英國人。 你<u>没</u>听出来<u>吗</u>? 他<u>是</u>英国人。 Can't you tell from his accent that he is British? 你昨天<u>難道</u>沒看見我? 你昨天<u>难道</u>没看见我? Didn't you see me yesterday?

>>**Try it!**   With a partner, practice using the patterns for emphasis above. Make sure that you make at least one sentence with each of the patterns. For example,

1. 他是一個好老師，我們班的學生沒有一個不喜歡他的。
   他是一个好老师，我们班的学生没有一个不喜欢他的。

2. 你難道不想去看看老師嗎?
   你难道不想去看看老师吗?

II. Summary: Serial Verb Constructions

In Lesson 13 we learned about the pivotal construction, a type of serial verb construction 連動句(连动句) [liándòngjù]. A serial verb construction is a sentence consisting of two or more verb phrases or clauses juxtaposed without any marker or conjunctional devices. Common semantic relationships between the verb phrases (or clauses) in serial verb constructions are summarized in the table below.

Semantic relationship	Features	Examples
I. Sequence	• one action is completed and then followed by a second action	我下課回家。 我下课回家。 I finished my classes and then went home.
	• two or more separate events	我刷了牙、洗了臉，上床睡覺。 我刷了牙、洗了脸，上床睡觉。 I brushed my teeth, washed my face, and then went to bed.
II. Purpose	• the latter action provides the purpose of the first action	我們到老師家拜訪他。 我们到老师家拜访他。 We went to the teacher's house (in order) to visit him. (Visiting him is the purpose of going to the teacher's house.) 我們去中國學中文。 我们去中国学中文。 We went to China (in order) to study Chinese. (Studying Chinese was the purpose of going to China.)
III. Alternating	• the subject alternates between two actions	她每天唱歌跳舞。(她每天跳舞唱歌。) 她每天唱歌跳舞。(她每天跳舞唱歌。) She sings and dances every day.
IV. Circumstance	• the first action provides the circumstance in which the second action occurs	他開車出事了。 他开车出事了。 He had an accident while driving. (Driving the car provides the circumstance in which the accident occurred.)

Semantic relationship	Features	Examples
V. **Instrument or vehicle**	• the first action provides the means with which the second action is carried out	他用筷子吃飯。 他用筷子吃饭。 He eats with chopsticks. ("Use chopsticks" is the instrument of the action "eating.")
VI. **Accompanying circumstances**	• the first action is marked with 著(着), indicating that it occurs at the same time as the second action	他拿著毛筆寫書法。 他拿着毛笔写书法。 He is holding a brush while doing calligraphy. 她笑著對我說 "再見。" 她笑着对我说 "再见。" She smiled while saying "goodbye" to me.

Note: A serial verb construction sentence might be interpreted as more than one type of semantic relationship listed above. The context and the type of verb may provide clues to the semantic relationship between the two actions. For example, 他上樓睡覺(他上楼睡觉) may belong to type (I) Sequence (two separate events: he went upstairs and slept) or type (II) Purpose (he went upstairs in order to go to sleep).

>>Try it!   With a partner, practice making short dialogues using the serial verb construction sentences. For example,

A: 你下午做什麼去了?
你下午做什么去了?

B: 我下午坐車去買禮物送給我姐姐。
我下午坐车去买礼物送给我姐姐。

補充課文 (补充课文) SUPPLEMENTARY PRACTICE

Read the following passage. Then listen and repeat.

Our School Centennial Celebration (繁體字 Traditional Character Version)

百年校慶

三月十五日是我們大學的百年校慶，我們已經畢業十年了，這次校慶不能不說是一個讓大家重聚的好機會。那天，校園裡到處都是校友，每個人看上去都很開心。

老同學見面以後的第一件事就是一起去看看老師和師母。十年過去了，老師的頭髮都白了，可還是那麼健康，充滿活力。他還記得每個學生的名字，不能不讓人感動。在老師和老同學身邊，大家一起談天說地，好像又回到了美好的大學時光。

我們校園的變化也非常大，很多地方我們都認不出來了。以前的運動場，現在已經是一座漂亮的體育場了。有的地方可一點兒都沒變。還記得我們當年最愛去的 "真好吃" 飯館嗎? 我們又回那兒吃飯了! 飯館還是原來的飯館，老闆也是原來的老闆，連招牌菜也沒有變。我們坐在一起談著笑著。同學們都說，我們可一定要把同學們的友誼繼續下去不可。

這就是我們美麗的大學，可愛的老師和同學們。祝我們的大學更加發展，祝我們的老師永遠健康，祝我們的友誼萬古長青!

Notes:

校友(校友) [xiàoyǒu]: alumnus or alumna
充滿(充满) [chōngmǎn]: to be full of
活力(活力) [huólì]: vigor, energy
感動(感动) [gǎndòng]: move, touch
時光(时光) [shíguāng]: time
友誼(友谊) [yǒuyì]: friendship
萬古長青(万古长青) [wàngǔchángqīng]: to be everlasting

補充課文 (补充课文) SUPPLEMENTARY PRACTICE

Read the following passage. Then listen and repeat.

Our School Centennial Celebration (简体字 Simplified Character Version)

百年校庆

三月十五日是我们大学的百年校庆，我们已经毕业十年了，这次校庆不能不说是一个让大家重聚的好机会。那天，校园里到处都是校友，每个人看上去都很开心。

老同学见面以后的第一件事就是一起去看看老师和师母。十年过去了，老师的头发都白了，可还是那么健康，充满活力。他还记得每个学生的名字，不能不让人感动。在老师和老同学身边，大家一起谈天说地，好像又回到了美好的大学时光。

我们校园的变化也非常大，很多地方我们都认不出来了。以前的运动场，现在已经是一座漂亮的体育场了。有的地方可一点儿都没变。还记得我们当年最爱去的"真好吃"饭馆吗？我们又回那儿吃饭了！饭馆还是原来的饭馆，老板也是原来的老板，连招牌菜也没有变。我们坐在一起谈着笑着。同学们都说，我们可一定要把同学们的友谊继续下去不可。

这就是我们美丽的大学，可爱的老师和同学们。祝我们的大学更加发展，祝我们的老师永远健康，祝我们的友谊万古长青！

Exercises: work with a partner or in small groups

1. 有哪些這一課的語法出現在這篇短文裡？請把它們找出來。
   有哪些这一课的语法出现在这篇短文里？请把它们找出来。

2. 老師的身體怎麼樣？他還記得同學們嗎？
   老师的身体怎么样？他还记得同学们吗？

3. 學校和同學們有哪些地方變了？哪些地方沒有變？
   学校和同学们有哪些地方变了？哪些地方没有变？

成語故事 (成语故事) IDIOM STORY

一鼓作氣 (一鼓作气) [yìgǔ zuò qì]

Meaning: To beat the drum once to boost morale.

Usage: It means to get something done in one vigorous or sustained effort.

Example: 他現在很用功，想要 "一鼓作氣"，非要在明年畢業不可。

他现在很用功，想要 "一鼓作气"，非要在明年毕业不可。

Pay special attention to the usages of emphasis words/constructions and serial verb constructions.

(繁體字 Traditional Character Version)

　　古時候，齊國要攻打魯國。面對強大的齊國，連魯國的國王也害怕。正在這時，曹劌去見了國王，說："沒有什麼好害怕的，我們非戰勝他們不可。"

　　曹劌和國王的軍隊遇到了齊軍。齊軍擊鼓要來攻打魯軍，魯王聽見後馬上也要擊鼓迎戰。但曹劌卻說："現在不是出擊的時候，一定要等一會兒才行。"過了不久，齊軍第二次擊鼓。魯王說再不擊鼓迎戰就不行了，但曹劌又一次阻止了他。

　　當齊軍發起第三次進攻的時候，曹劌才對魯王說："現在趕快擊鼓，命令士兵一定要快速攻擊齊軍。"結果，魯國打了勝仗。

　　打了勝仗以後，魯王問曹劌為什麼開始的時候不讓他擊鼓，曹劌說："打仗主要是靠士兵的士氣。第一次擊鼓的時候，士兵的士氣一定是最高的。第二次擊鼓的時候，士氣就弱一點兒了。第三次擊鼓的時候，就更弱了。因此，當齊軍第一次、第二次擊鼓的時候我不得不反對你擊鼓，要你等等。直到第三次時，才同意你擊鼓。"

(简体字 **Simplified Character Version**)

　　古时候，齐国要攻打鲁国。面对强大的齐国，连鲁国的国王也害怕。正在这时，曹刿去见了国王，说："没有什么好害怕的，我们非战胜他们不可。"

　　曹刿和国王的军队遇到了齐军。齐军击鼓要来攻打鲁军，鲁王听见后马上也要击鼓迎战。但曹刿却说："现在不是出击的时候，一定要等一会儿才行。"过了不久，齐军第二次击鼓。鲁王说再不击鼓迎战就不行了，但曹刿又一次阻止了他。

　　当齐军发起第三次进攻的时候，曹刿才对鲁王说："现在赶快击鼓，命令士兵一定要快速攻击齐军。"结果，鲁国打了胜仗。

　　打了胜仗以后，鲁王问曹刿为什么开始的时候不让他击鼓，曹刿说："打仗主要是靠士兵的士气。第一次击鼓的时候，士兵的士气一定是最高的。第二次击鼓的时候，士气就弱一点儿了。第三次击鼓的时候，就更弱了。因此，当齐军第一次、第二次击鼓的时候我不得不反对你击鼓，要你等等。直到第三次时，才同意你击鼓。"

Notes:

古時候(古时候) [gǔshíhòu]: in the old days
齊國(齐国) [Qíguó]: the State of Qi
出擊(出击) [chūjī]: to dispatch troops
攻打(攻打) [gōngdǎ]: to attack
魯國(鲁国) [Lǔguó]: the State of Lu
戰勝(战胜) [zhànshèng]: to conquer
擊鼓(击鼓) [jīgǔ]: to beat the drum
迎戰(迎战) [yíngzhàn]: to meet the enemy head on
阻止(阻止) [zǔzhǐ]: to inhibit, prevent, stop
趕快(赶快) [gǎnkuài]: to hurry up
攻擊(攻击) [gōngjī]: to attack
士氣(士气) [shìqì]: morale
弱(弱) [ruò]: weak
反對(反对) [fǎnduì]: to oppose
同意(同意) [tóngyì]: to agree

Exercises: work with a partner or in small groups

1. 找出有下面語法的句子：emphasis words/constructions and serial verb constructions.

   找出有下面語法的句子：emphasis words/constructions and serial verb constructions.

2. 用你自己的話說說 "一鼓作氣" 的故事。
   用你自己的话说说 "一鼓作气" 的故事。

3. 請用 "一鼓作氣" 造一個句子或者說一個 "一鼓作氣" 的例子。
   请用 "一鼓作气" 造一个句子或者说一个 "一鼓作气" 的例子。

4. "一鼓作氣" 的故事，告訴了我們什麼?
   "一鼓作气" 的故事，告诉了我们什么?

練習 (练习) ACTIVITIES

I. Listening Exercises

 16-1 In the blanks provided, write the Pinyin, with tones, for the words you hear. Then check them with your partner.

Emphasis in Chinese Sentences

1. 他一次 ____ ____ 去過上海，____ 要去那兒看看 ____ ____ 。
   他一次 ____ ____ 去过上海，____ 要去那儿看看 ____ ____ 。

2. 他 ____ 想買一輛美國車，而不是日本車。
   他 ____ 想买一辆美国车，而不是日本车。

3. ____ 誰叫你到這兒來的?
   ____ 谁叫你到这儿来的?

4. 我忙得 ____ 一口水 ____ ____ 喝。
   我忙得 ____ 一口水 ____ ____ 喝。

Serial Verb Constructions

5. 他每天 ＿＿＿ 自行車 ＿＿＿ 學校。
   他每天 ＿＿＿ 自行车 ＿＿＿ 学校。

6. 老師 ＿＿＿ 小朋友們 ＿＿＿ 公園照相。
   老师 ＿＿＿ 小朋友们 ＿＿＿ 公园照相。

7. 她 ＿＿＿ 著 ＿＿＿ 電話。
   她 ＿＿＿ 着 ＿＿＿ 电话。

8. 我要 ＿＿＿ 銀行 ＿＿＿ 錢。
   我要 ＿＿＿ 银行 ＿＿＿ 钱。

 **16-2** Listen to the story and answer the questions. Then check them with your partner.

Notes:
仲永(仲永) [Zhòngyǒng]: a person's name
故事(故事) [gùshi]: story
從前(从前) [cóngqián]: in the past
忽然(忽然) [hūrán]: suddenly
首(首) [shǒu]: (measure word for songs or poems)
詩(诗) [shī]: poetry; poem
相信(相信) [xiāngxìn]: to believe in
無論(无论) [wúlùn]: no matter what
驚奇(惊奇) [jīngqí]: to be amazed
於是(于是) [yúshì]: consequently
爭(争) [zhēng]: to contend
普通人(普通人) [pǔtōngrén]: everyman, average person
聰明(聪明) [cōngmíng]: clever

問題(问题):

1. 仲永是從幾歲開始寫詩的?
   仲永是从几岁开始写诗的?

2. 仲永出名以後, 他的爸爸還讓他讀書嗎?
   仲永出名以后, 他的爸爸还让他读书吗?

3. 仲永十二歲的時候詩寫得怎麼樣? 二十歲呢?
   仲永十二岁的时候诗写得怎么样? 二十岁呢?

4. 這個故事告訴了我們什麼?
   这个故事告诉了我们什么?

II. Character Exercises

16-3 Work with a partner. Read the following words, phrases, and sentences.

齊 齐	番 番
看齊 看齐	一番 一番
向老師看齊 向老师看齐	一番事業 一番事业
好好地向老師看齊 好好地向老师看齐	做出一番事業 做出一番事业
我們可要好好地向老師看齊。 我们可要好好地向老师看齐。	他非要做出一番事業不可。 他非要做出一番事业不可。

Now with your partner, try to use the following characters to make words, phrases, and then sentences.

1. 鈴　　2. 響　　3. 提　　4. 講　　5. 懂
　　铃　　　　响　　　　提　　　　讲　　　　懂

6. 佩　　7. 獎　　8. 磨　　9. 量　　10. 決
　　佩　　　　奖　　　　磨　　　　量　　　　　决

16-4 Form groups and create phrases with the following words (pay attention to the various usages of each word).

Example:　留：留學，留步，留言
　　　　　　留：留学，留步，留言

1. 門：_____

　　门：_____

2. 經：_____

　　经：_____

3. 用：_____

   用：_____

4. 理：_____

   理：_____

5. 學：_____

   学：_____

6. 心：_____

   心：_____

7. 進：_____

   进：_____

8. 貴：_____

   贵：_____

9. 感：_____

   感：_____

10. 休：_____

    休：_____

III. Grammar Exercises

16-5 Serial Verb Constructions 連動句(连动句)

Form groups and complete the following.

1. Translate the following serial verb construction sentences into Chinese orally.
2. Identify the semantic relationship of the serial verb constructions (use the grammar notes section as your reference) in the sentences.

   (I) Sequence   (II) Purpose   (III) Alternating
   (IV) Circumstance   (V) Instrument or vehicle   (VI) Accompanying circumstances

   (a) I bought a ticket to watch a movie.

   _____

(b) We came over to visit you.

_____

(c) They used Chinese to chat.

_____

(d) He was not careful and got sick.

_____

(e) He hugged the child and said "I love you."   – 抱 [bào]: to hug

_____

(f) She sings and dances every day.

_____

(g) She rides a bicycle to school every day.

_____

(h) He drove his car and had an accident.

_____

16-6 Read the story, then with your partner complete the exercises that follow:

Notes:

數學(数学) [shùxué]: mathematics

成績(成绩) [chéngjì]: grade

仍然(仍然) [réngrán]: still

努力(努力) [nǔlì]: to make great efforts

早餐(早餐) [zǎocān]: breakfast

功夫不負有心人(功夫不负有心人) [gōngfu búfù yǒuxīnrén]: everything comes to one who makes an effort

微笑(微笑) [wēixiào]: to smile

分數(分数) [fēnshù]: grade, score

把臉一沉(把脸一沉) [bǎliǎnyìchén]: (literally: to sink the face) to suddenly look serious

難過(难过) [nánguò]: to feel bad

(繁體字 Traditional Character Version)

　　明明的數學成績不太好，可是他仍然在很努力地學習。他下定決心要在下次的數學考試 ＿＿ (must)考80分以上 ＿＿ ＿＿。於是他每天一早起來就做數學題，經常忙得 ＿＿ (even)吃早餐的時間 ＿＿ 沒有。功夫不負有心人，這次明明的數學考試終於得了82分。他拿著成績單高興地跳了起來，這 ＿＿ (truly is)是他這個學期以來最好的成績。放學的時候，明明一路跑著回家，他一進門就把成績單給媽媽，心裡想這次媽媽 ＿＿ (must)誇獎他 ＿＿ ＿＿。媽媽拿到明明的成績單，先是微笑著，然後就問班上的平均分，還有他的好朋友小亮的分數是多少。聽完以後她把臉一沉，說："＿＿ (but)別太高興了。你考得 ＿＿ (indeed)比以前好，但是你們班有十幾個人比你的成績高，＿＿ (even)小亮 ＿＿ 考得比你好呢。"媽媽的話讓明明難過得哭了。他心裡想：別人是別人，我是我，媽媽為什麼總是拿我跟別人比呢？

(简体字 Simplified Character Version)

　　明明的数学成绩不太好，可是他仍然在很努力地学习。他下定决心要在下次的数学考试 ＿＿ (must)考80分以上 ＿＿ ＿＿。于是他每天一早起来就做数学题，经常忙得 ＿＿ (even)吃早餐的时间 ＿＿ 没有。功夫不负有心人，这次明明的数学考试终于得了82分。他拿着成绩单高兴地跳了起来，这 ＿＿ (truly is)是他这个学期以来最好的成绩。放学的时候，明明一路跑着回家，他一进门就把成绩单给妈妈，心里想这次妈妈 ＿＿ (must)夸奖他 ＿＿ ＿＿。妈妈拿到明明的成绩单，先是微笑着，然后就问班上的平均分，还有他的好朋友小亮的分数是多少。听完以后她把脸一沉，说："＿＿ (but)别太高兴了。你考得 ＿＿ (indeed)比以前好，但是你们班有十几个人比你的成绩高，＿＿ (even)小亮 ＿＿ 考得比你好呢。"妈妈的话让明明难过得哭了。他心里想：别人是别人，我是我，妈妈为什么总是拿我跟别人比呢？

1. With the help of the English clues, fill in the blanks with appropriate words that emphasize the tone of the sentences.
2. Underline the serial verb constructions in the text.
3. Do you think that the mother was truly not satisfied with Mingming's grade? What were the mother's true thoughts?
4. Do you agree with how the mother handled Mingming's test scores? What do you think she should have done?

IV. Media Literacy

The short text below, written in the style of newspapers, magazines, or Internet news articles, will help you become familiar with the formal written expressions used in these genres.

 補習班真的非上不可嗎? (补习班真的非上不可吗?)
Do Kids Really Need to Attend After-School Learning Centers?

繁體字:

補習班真的非上不可嗎?

老師們開補習班,不但減輕了老師的教學壓力,還可以賺取高額補習費。有的補習班,很多人花錢都進不去,非得託關係找門路才行。不少家長抱怨,這種做法完全是本末倒置。

简体字:

补习班真的非上不可吗?

老师们开补习班,不但减轻了老师的教学压力,还可以赚取高额补习费。有的补习班,很多人花钱都进不去,非得托关系找门路才行。不少家长抱怨,这种做法完全是本末倒置。

Notes:

補習班(补习班) [bǔxíbān]: after-school learning center
減輕(减轻) [jiǎnqīng]: to lighten, alleviate
壓力(压力) [yālì]: pressure
賺取(赚取) [zhuànqǔ]: to make a profit, earn
花錢(花钱) [huāqián]: to spend money
託(托) [tuō]: entrust, plead
關係(关系) [guānxi]: relationship
門路(门路) [ménlù]: social connections
家長(家长) [jiāzhǎng]: the parent or guardian of a child
抱怨(抱怨) [bàoyuàn]: to complain
本末倒置(本末倒置) [běnmòdàozhì]: to put the cart before
  the horse

Exercises for the article: work with a partner or a group to ask and answer the following.

1. What are the meanings of 託關係(托关系) and 找門路(找门路)?

2. Identify and underline the serial verb constructions in the text.

3. Circle the words or constructions emphasized in the sentences.

4. Retell the story in your own words.

V. Communicative Activities

16-7 Dining out.

Work with your partner and act out the following.

To thank a friend who helped you remove a computer virus, you invite him/her to dine out at a famous Chinese restaurant. The restaurant is so famous that you had to reserve seats a week in advance. During the meal, emphasize how popular and how busy the restaurant is. Compliment your friend's computer skills.

Notes:
病毒(病毒) [bìngdú]: virus
清理(清理) [qīnglǐ]: to clear up

可……(可……)，連……都……(连……都……)，是……(是……)，
非……不可(非……不可)，沒有……不……(没有……不……)

16-8 You are visiting the house of your roommate's grandparents during spring break. Your roommate's grandparents are very healthy. They often go jogging. Work in groups to talk about how important it is to maintain good health.

Notes:
可……(可……), 連……都……(连……都……),
是……(是……), 非……不可(非……不可),
沒有……不……(没有……不……)

16-9 Work with your partner and act out the following.

You have brought a friend to meet your old high-school classmates. Please introduce everyone and ask your old classmates how they are doing.

文化知識 (文化知识) Culture Link

文化點滴 (文化点滴) CULTURE NOTES

中國的客套話 (中国的客套话) Chinese Etiquette

The Chinese language is full of polite phrases. Chinese people use them frequently to compliment each other or to speak humbly during social interactions. Chinese recorded history can be traced back as early as 3,000 years ago, and people unfamiliar with Chinese culture often find themselves overwhelmed or even confused by the ubiquitous polite phrases. The importance of learning about and understanding Chinese etiquette cannot be overemphasized, especially when doing business or hoping for a closer relationship with a Chinese person, or seeking a deeper understanding of Chinese society. Some common examples of Chinese polite phrases are listed in the table below.

Do you know...

- how far back Chinese culture can be traced?
- what is important if you seek a closer relationship with a Chinese friend?
- what are the consequences of overusing polite phrases?

Read and find out!

Chinese	English	Situation
久仰大名(久仰大名) [jiǔyǎng dàmíng]	I have long admired your significant name.	Meeting someone for the first time
有失遠迎(有失远迎) [yǒushī yuǎnyíng]	I am sorry for not welcoming you from afar.	Welcoming a guest
恭候光臨(恭候光临) [gōnghòu guānglín]	I am patiently waiting for your glorious arrival.	Welcoming a guest
賜教(赐教) [cìjiào]	Please bestow on me some instruction.	Asking for advice
高見(高见) [gāojiàn]	A far-reaching opinion.	Praising someone's opinion
打擾(打扰) [dǎrǎo]	To disturb you.	Troubling somebody to do something
拜託(拜托) [bàituō]	To humbly entreat you.	Requesting someone to do something
拜訪(拜访) [bàifǎng]	To humbly visit.	Referring to visiting someone

Chinese	English	Situation
慢走(慢走) [mànzǒu]	Walk slowly	Seeing off a guest
奉陪(奉陪) [fèngpéi]	To accompany	Referring to accompanying friends
恭候(恭候) [gōnghòu]	To await respectfully	Referring to waiting for a guest
光顧(光顾) [guānggù]	Illustrious patronage	Welcoming customers
久違(久违) [jiǔwéi]	Haven't seen you in a long time.	Greeting a friend you haven't seen in a long time
包涵(包涵) [bāohán]	A fault or embarrassment	Pleading for forgiveness
借光(借光) [jièguāng]	Excuse me	Asking someone to move out of the way, to yield passage
恭喜(恭喜) [gōngxǐ]	Congratulations	Congratulating someone
下次再來(下次再来) [xiàcì zàilái]	Come again next time	A polite way to say goodbye
失陪(失陪) [shīpéi]	To miss your company	To leave during the middle of a gathering
留步(留步) [liúbù]	Save steps	Telling the host he/she needn't come all the way to the door to see you off.
奉還(奉还) [fènghuán]	Respectfully give back	When returning something

The wording of 客套話(客套话) might sound extreme and flowery to the non-native ear. For example, people say "久仰大名" (I have long admired your significant name) to each other, although they have never met before. Some 客套話(客套话) are used to deflect attention from the abilities of the speaker and show humility. For example, some esteemed scholars often describe themselves as "才疏學淺(才疏学浅)" [cáishū xuéqiǎn] (my ability is limited and my knowledge is shallow) in the book prefaces they write. But if the preface of the book is written by the author's friend or colleague, what you find there would be totally different. There would be words such as "學界泰斗(学界泰斗)" [xuéjiè tàidǒu] (guru of the academic field). It means that this author is a very brilliant scholar, and his knowledge is not shallow at all.

Nonetheless, 客套話(客套话) should not be overused. Using some 客套話(客套话) between friends is appropriate, but too frequent use of 客套話(客套话) will embarrass the listeners, make them feel that the speaker is only paying lip service, and thus may cause them to consider the speaker insincere. Therefore, if one wants to strengthen a friendship, it is best to know how to use 客套話(客套话) appropriately.

There are many special ways to address senior citizens, who are revered in Chinese culture. Are there any special polite phrases used for senior citizens in your own culture?

Confucius's teachings on ethics and morality are deeply rooted in Chinese people's minds. Have you heard of any of his teachings? Can you share some similar teachings from your own country or culture?

問題討論 (问题讨论) *Discuss the following with a partner or in small groups.*

1. 除了文章中所講的客套話以外，你還知道什麼別的客套話？請舉出一些例子。

   除了文章中所讲的客套话以外，你还知道什么别的客套话？请举出一些例子。

   Besides the 客套話(客套话) mentioned above, what other Chinese 客套話(客套话) do you know? Provide some examples.

2. 在你說的語言裡有什麼客套話嗎？請與同學們分享一下。

   在你说的语言里有什么客套话吗？请与同学们分享一下。

   What are some polite phrases in your language? Share them with your classmates.

趣味中文 (趣味中文) FUN WITH CHINESE

禮多人不怪
礼多人不怪
Courtesy costs nothing.

lǐ	duō	rén	bú	guài
禮	多	人	不	怪
礼	多	人	不	怪
courtesy	much	people	not	blame

問題討論 (问题讨论) *Discuss the following with a partner or in small groups.*

1. What do you think about 禮多人不怪(礼多人不怪)?
2. Are there any similar sayings in English or in your native language?

行動吧! (行动吧!) LET'S GO!

校慶請柬 (校庆请柬) Invitation to a University Anniversary Celebration

建明(建明)'s father received an invitation from 東華大學(东华大学), his alma mater, to attend the anniversary celebration. Since it is the first time 建明 has read an invitation in formal Chinese, it is hard for him to understand everything. Read the card and explain it to him.

(繁體字 Traditional Character Version)

> ∽ **請柬** ∽
>
> 欣逢本校百年校慶，謹訂8月15日(星期日)上午9時於本校紀念堂舉行『校慶慶祝大會』。
>
>   恭請　光臨
>
>   東華大學　　校長
>
>   張振國　　敬邀

(简体字 Simplified Character Version)

∽请柬∾

欣逢本校百年校庆，谨订8月15日(星期日)上午9时于本校纪念堂举行『校庆庆祝大会』。

　　恭请　光临

　　　　　　　　　　　　　东华大学　　校长

　　　　　　　　　　　　　张振国　　敬邀

Notes:
請柬(请柬) [qǐngjiǎn]: (formal) invitation card
欣逢(欣逢) [xīn féng]: happy to meet, come upon
本校(本校) [běnxiào]: one's own school
校慶(校庆) [xiàoqìng]: anniversary of a school
謹(谨) [jǐn]: sincerely
訂(订) [dìng]: to be scheduled
於(于) [yú]: be at, be in
紀念堂(纪念堂) [jìniàntáng]: memorial hall
舉行(举行) [jǔxíng]: to hold (a meeting, ceremony, etc.)
慶祝(庆祝) [qìngzhù]: to celebrate
大會(大会) [dàhuì]: a grand meeting
恭請(恭请) [gōngqǐng]: to respectfully invite
光臨(光临) [guānglín]: (polite) presence (of a guest, etc.)
校長(校长) [xiàozhǎng]: school principal, school president
敬邀(敬邀) [jìngyāo]: to respectfully invite

問題討論 (问题讨论) *Discuss the following with a partner or in small groups.*

1. 這是東華大學的第幾年校慶？
   这是东华大学的第几年校庆？

2. 校慶是在哪一天？在哪兒舉行？
   校庆是在哪一天？在哪儿举行？

3. 你來找找看，請柬中有哪些禮貌用語或者正式用語。
   你来找找看，请柬中有哪些礼貌用语或者正式用语。

4. 請用英文向建明說一說請柬的內容。
   请用英文向建明说一说请柬的内容。

復習 (复习) Review

LESSON 15 TO LESSON 16

I. Retelling a story

In small groups, listen to the following conversation and then retell the story in your own words. Pay attention to the usage of "把" and "被", conjunctions, and omission of subjects and objects.

Notes:

化學(化学) [huàxué]: chemistry
金幣(金币) [jīnbì]: gold coin
指(指) [zhǐ]: to point to
液體(液体) [yètǐ]: liquid, solution
剛才(刚才) [gāngcái]: just now
扔(扔) [rēng]: to throw
溶化(溶化) [rónghuà]: to dissolve
內容(内容) [nèiróng]: content

(繁體字 **Traditional Character Version**)

(化學課上)

 老師(拿出一個金幣，指著瓶子裡的液體)："剛才我已經給你們講過這種液體了。現在，如果我把這個金幣扔進去。你們想一想：金幣會被溶化掉嗎？"

(孩子們你看看我，我看看你，誰也答不出來。)

(小明站起來)說："一定不會！"

老師："你回答得很好。今天只有你聽懂了我講的內容。"
小明："不，老師，我沒有聽懂。我什麼都不懂。"
老師："那你怎麼知道金幣不會被溶化呢？"
小明："老師，如果這種液體真的能把金幣溶化，您怎麼會把金幣扔進去呢？"

(简体字 Simplified Character Version)

(化学课上)

老师(拿出一个金币，指着瓶子里的液体)："刚才我已经给你们讲过这种液体了。现在，如果我把这个金币扔进去。你们想一想：金币会被溶化掉吗？"

(孩子们你看看我，我看看你，谁也答不出来。)

(小明站起来)说："一定不会！"

老师："你回答得很好。今天只有你听懂了我讲的内容。"
小明："不，老师，我没有听懂。我什么都不懂。"
老师："那你怎么知道金币不会被溶化呢？"
小明："老师，如果这种液体真的能把金币溶化，您怎么会把金币扔进去呢？"

II. Dialogue

Work with a partner. Talk about your experience of buying something online or from a store. How did you manage to return or exchange it when you found the item had defects? (Use at least 15 sentences.)

Notes:

Cause-and-effect:

因為……所以……，因此，由於，是由於，為了，只好，從而
因为……所以……，因此，由于，是由于，为了，只好，从而

Conditional:

要是(如果，假如，假使，假若)……才，
不然，只有……才，只要……就
要是(如果，假如，假使，假若)……才，
不然，只有……才，只要……就

Parallel-element conjunctions:

既……又(也，而)，不但……而且……，
此外，和/跟/與/以及
既……又(也，而)，不但……而且……，
此外，和/跟/与/以及

Concession:

然而，卻
然而，却

Alternative:

或者，還是，要麼……要麼，不是……就是
或者，还是，要么……要么，不是……就是

Summary:

總之，總而言之
总之，总而言之

III. Picture Description

Work in small groups to talk about the benefits the Internet brings to the modern world.

Notes:

非……不可，連……也/都……，就，可，不能/會/得不，沒有……不……，是……的
非……不可，连……也/都……，就，可，不能/会/得不，没有……不……，是……的

(1)

(2)

(3)

(4)

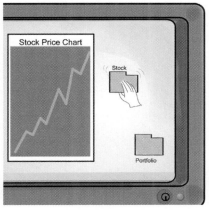

(5)

IV. Traditional and Simplified Characters

Work with your partner to read each character aloud and write out its traditional form. Then make a phrase and a sentence using the character.

Example: 学 → 學 → 學生 → 我是學生。

L15: 联 (　) 　涂 (　) 　闹 (　) 　断 (　) 　尽 (　) 　录 (　)
　　绞 (　) 　购 (　)

L16: 响 (　) 　宝 (　) 　齐 (　) 　继 (　) 　济 (　) 　验 (　)
　　扰 (　) 　荣 (　)

17

申請工作 (申请工作)
Applying for a Job

Online job applications are now common in China.

CONNECTIONS AND COMMUNITIES PREVIEW

Discuss the following questions with a partner or your class. What similarities and differences do you think there might be between Chinese culture and your own culture?

1. How do you prepare to apply for a job? Can you describe it in Chinese?

2. List some differences between job applications in China and in your country or community.

教學目標 (教学目标) OBJECTIVES

- Ask a rhetorical question
- Describe procedures
- Compose a Chinese résumé

生詞 (生词) VOCABULARY

🔊 核心詞 (核心词) Core Vocabulary

	TRADITIONAL	SIMPLIFIED	PINYIN		
1.	難道	难道	nándào	Adv.	Isn't it true . . .
2.	就業	就业	jiùyè	N.	employment
3.	中心	中心	zhōngxīn	N.	center
	就業中心	就业中心	jiùyè zhōngxīn	N.	career center
4.	講座	讲座	jiǎngzuò	N.	lecture
5.	如何	如何	rúhé	Pron.	how
6.	簡歷	简历	jiǎnlì	N.	résumé, curriculum vitae (C.V.)
7.	忘記	忘记	wàngjì	V.	to forget
8.	複雜	复杂	fùzá	Adj.	complicated, complex
9.	首先	首先	shǒuxiān	Adv.	first of all
10.	性質	性质	xìngzhì	N.	characteristic, quality, nature
11.	要求	要求	yāoqiú	V.	to require
				N.	requirement
12.	調整	调整	tiáozhěng	V.	to adjust
				N.	adjustment
13.	寫法	写法	xiěfǎ	N.	style of writing, format
14.	突出	突出	tūchū	V.	to make conspicuous
				Adj.	outstanding
15.	重點	重点	zhòngdiǎn	N.	focus, major point
16.	拒絕	拒绝	jùjué	V.	to refuse, reject

TRADITIONAL	SIMPLIFIED	PINYIN		
17. 仔仔細細	仔仔细细	zǐzǐxìxì	Adj.	very carefully
18. 修改	修改	xiūgǎi	V. N.	to revise revision
19. 招聘	招聘	zhāopìn	V.	to hire
20. 信息	信息	xìnxī	N.	information, message
21. 直接	直接	zhíjiē	Adv.	directly
22. 下載	下载	xiàzǎi	V.	to download
23. 表格	表格	biǎogé	N.	form
24. 推薦信	推荐信	tuījiànxìn	N.	recommendation letter
25. 恐怕	恐怕	kǒngpà	Adv.	I am afraid that . . .
26. 趕快	赶快	gǎnkuài	Adv.	speedily
27. 有限	有限	yǒuxiàn	Adj.	limited
28. 考慮	考虑	kǎolǜ	V.	to consider
29. 安排	安排	ānpái	V. N.	to arrange arrangement
30. 相信	相信	xiāngxìn	V.	to believe, to be sure
31. 樂意	乐意	lèyì	V.	to be willing to
32. 聰明	聪明	cōngmíng	Adj.	smart
33. 能幹	能干	nénggàn	Adj.	capable
34. 條件	条件	tiáojiàn	N.	qualifications
35. 但願	但愿	dànyuàn	V.	to wish

 專名 (专名) **Proper Nouns**

TRADITIONAL	SIMPLIFIED	PINYIN		
1. 史如影	史如影	Shǐ Rúyǐng	N.	(name) Ruying Shi
2. 張華利	张华利	Zhāng Huálì	N.	(name) Huali Zhang

語文知識 (语文知识) LANGUAGE LINK

Read and listen to the following sentence patterns. These patterns use vocabulary, expressions, and grammar that you will study in more detail in this lesson. After reading the sentence patterns, read and listen to the Language in Use section that follows.

句型 (句型) Sentence Patterns

 A: 你不是去年申請實習了嗎?
你不是去年申请实习了吗?
Nǐ búshì qùnián shēnqǐng shíxí le ma?

B: 哪兒啊! 你難道忘記了我沒有去成嗎?
哪儿啊! 你难道忘记了我没有去成吗?
Nǎr a! Nǐ nándào wàngjìle wǒ méiyou qù chéng ma?

A: 說說看，簡歷怎麼寫？
说说看，简历怎么写？
Shuōshuo kàn, jiǎnlì zěnmexiě?

B: 首先，你要清楚自己要申請
首先，你要清楚自己要申请
Shǒuxiān, nǐ yào qīngchǔ zìjǐ yào shēnqǐng

什麼性質的工作，然後再
什么性质的工作，然后再
shénme xìngzhì de gōngzuò, ránhòu zài

調整自己的簡歷。
调整自己的简历。
tiáozhěng zìjǐde jiǎnlì.

A: 那就是說，申請的工作不同，
那就是说，申请的工作不同，
Nà jiùshì shuō, shēnqǐng de gōngzuò bùtóng,

簡歷的寫法也要不同，是嗎？
简历的写法也要不同，是吗？
jiǎnlìde xiěfǎ yě yào bùtóng, shì ma?

B: 正是如此。
正是如此。
Zhèngshì rúcǐ.

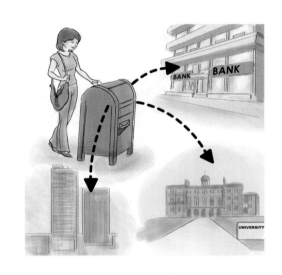

A: 你那麼聰明、能幹，條件那麼好。
你那么聪明、能干，条件那么好。
Nǐ nàme cōngmíng, nénggàn, tiáojiàn nàme hǎo.

不用擔心，你一定能找到工作。
不用担心，你一定能找到工作。
Búyòng dānxīn, nǐ yídìng néng zhǎodào gōngzuò.

B: 但願如此。
但愿如此。
Dànyuàn rúcǐ.

課文 Language in Use: Let Me Help You Apply for an Internship (繁體字 Traditional Character Version)

史如影： 昨天學校的就業中心有一個講座，介紹了如何寫簡歷，如何申請工作或者研究生院，很有幫助。

張華利： 來，說說看[1]，簡歷該怎麼寫？今年暑假我想申請去公司實習。

史如影： 你不是去年申請了嗎？

張華利： 哪兒啊[2]？你難道忘記了去年我沒有去成[3]嗎？就是因為我沒有把簡歷寫好。

史如影： 其實寫簡歷不複雜。首先，你要清楚自己想申請什麼性質的工作。然後，根據不同的工作要求調整自己的簡歷。

張華利： 那就是說[4]申請的工作不同，簡歷的寫法也要不同，是嗎？

史如影： 正是如此[5]。寫簡歷一定要突出重點。你去年不是這樣寫的嗎？

張華利： 沒有！怪不得去年我被拒絕了！我一定要仔仔細細地把簡歷修改一下。對了，你不是今年夏天也打算去實習的嗎？

史如影： 是的，可是我還不知道哪些公司在招聘。

張華利： 網上有很多信息，你不知道嗎？我今晚就給你發一些過去。唉，難道昨天他們沒有給你們介紹網站嗎？

---

1. 說說看(说说看)

說說看(说说看): "Come on, tell me." This is a very colloquial expression used to elicit comments.

---

2. 哪兒啊(哪儿啊)

哪兒啊(哪儿啊): an idiomatic expression used to express disagreement with what was previously said. It is often used together with "才不是呢(才不是呢)" to imply "what you just said is not true."

---

3. 去成(去成)

去成(去成): to succeed in going. V. + 成(成) is a verb + resultative complement phrase used to mean "to succeed in doing (something)." 成(成) means "to succeed in doing something."

Continued on page 550

课文 Language in Use: Let Me Help You Apply for an Internship
(简体字 Simplified Character Version)

史如影： 昨天学校的就业中心有一个
讲座，介绍了如何写简历，
如何申请工作或者研究生
院，很有帮助。

张华利： 来，说说看¹，简历该怎么
写？今年暑假我想申请去公
司实习。

史如影： 你不是去年申请了吗？

张华利： 哪儿啊²？你难道忘记了去年
我没有去成³吗？就是因为我
没有把简历写好。

史如影： 其实写简历不复杂。首先，
你要清楚自己想申请什么性
质的工作。然后，根据不同的
工作要求调整自己的简历。

张华利： 那就是说⁴申请的工作不同，
简历的写法也要不同，是吗？

史如影： 正是如此⁵。写简历一定要突
出重点。你去年不是这样写
的吗？

张华利： 没有！怪不得去年我被拒绝
了！我一定要仔仔细细地把
简历修改一下。对了，你不是
今年夏天也打算去实习的吗？

史如影： 是的，可是我还不知道哪些公司在招聘。

张华利： 网上有很多信息，你不知道吗？我今晚就给你发一些过去。
唉，难道昨天他们没有给你们介绍网站吗？

---

4. 那就是說(那就是说)

那就是說(那就是说): "Which is to say."
One can also say "這就是說(这就是说)"
or "也就是說(也就是说)".

---

5. 正是如此(正是如此)

正是如此(正是如此): "如此(如此)" is
an expression meaning "這樣(这样)" and
正是如此(正是如此) means "exactly so"
or "exactly like this."

Continued on page 551

課文 Language in Use: Let Me Help You Apply for an Internship
(繁體字 Traditional Character Version) —— 接第五百四十八頁

史如影: 介紹了。他們說我們可以直接從網上下載申請表格，填好以後把表格寄出去，也可以就在網上填表申請。

張華利: 對，我就是在網上申請的。

史如影: 下一步我還需要幾封推薦信。

張華利: 你還沒有找教授談過嗎? 恐怕要趕快了，教授們的時間是有限的。

史如影: 我已經考慮好了，準備安排一下兒，過幾天就去找一些教授談一談。希望他們能同意為我寫推薦信。

張華利: 我相信他們一定會很樂意幫你寫推薦信的。你那麼聰明、能幹，條件那麼好。不用擔心。

史如影: 但願如此[6]。

6. 但願如此(但愿如此)
但願如此(但愿如此): "I wish it were true/ that were the case."

课文 Language in Use: Let Me Help You Apply for an Internship
(简体字 Simplified Character Version) —— 接第五百四十九页

史如影： 介绍了。他们说我们可以直接从网上下载申请表格，填好以后把表格寄出去，也可以就在网上填表申请。

张华利： 对，我就是在网上申请的。

史如影： 下一步我还需要几封推荐信。

张华利： 你还没有找教授谈过吗？恐怕要赶快了，教授们的时间是有限的。

史如影： 我已经考虑好了，准备安排一下儿，过几天就去找一些教授谈一谈。希望他们能同意为我写推荐信。

张华利： 我相信他们一定会很乐意帮你写推荐信的。你那么聪明、能干，条件那么好。不用担心。

史如影： 但愿如此6。

語法 (语法) GRAMMAR

I. Rhetorical Questions

A rhetorical question refers to a question asked to confirm something or to elicit more information. It generally takes the form of "不……嗎? (不……吗?)", "……不是……嗎? (……不是……吗?)" or "……(難道)沒有……嗎? (……(难道)没有……吗?)" It is usually translated as "isn't it true that . . . ?" or "don't (didn't) you . . . ?"

Examples:

你不是去年申請實習了嗎?
你不是去年申请实习了吗?

Isn't it true that you applied for an internship last year? (Didn't you apply for an internship last year?)

他不是已經找到工作了嗎?
他不是已经找到工作了吗?

Isn't it true that he has found a job? (Hasn't he already found a job?)

你不知道我昨天很忙嗎?
你不知道我昨天很忙吗?

Don't you know that I was very busy yesterday?

他沒聽說我已經畢業了嗎?
他没听说我已经毕业了吗?

Didn't he hear people say that I had already graduated?

你(難道)沒有招聘網站的地址嗎?
你(难道)没有招聘网站的地址吗?

Don't you have a website address for job opportunities?

他(難道)昨天沒有去聽講座嗎?
他(难道)昨天没有去听讲座吗?

Didn't he go to the lecture yesterday?

Notes:

- These kinds of rhetorical questions are only used when you want to confirm what you think is true or you think you may need more information to prove you are right.
- Rhetorical questions are usually used for emphasis.
- The negative words "不" or "沒有" are only used before the major verb of the question while "不是" is usually placed before what is emphasized.

Examples:

他昨天不是<u>去</u>了嗎？
他昨天不是<u>去</u>了吗？
Didn't he GO yesterday? (emphasizing "去")

他不是<u>昨天</u>去了嗎？
他不是<u>昨天</u>去了吗？
Didn't he go YESTERDAY? (emphasizing "昨天")

不是<u>你</u>告訴我這件事的嗎？
不是<u>你</u>告诉我这件事的吗？
Wasn't it YOU who told me this? (emphasizing "你")

你上午看到的不是<u>他</u>嗎？
你上午看到的不是<u>他</u>吗？
Wasn't it HE who you saw in the morning? (emphasizing "他")

- In spoken Chinese, the word or expression being emphasized by "不是" should be stressed.

»Try it! With a partner, practice using rhetorical questions in short dialogues. For example,

A: 你知道小王在哪兒嗎？
   你知道小王在哪儿吗？

B: 他沒有跟你在一起嗎？
   他没有跟你在一起吗？

A: 沒有啊！
   没有啊！

B: 難道他回家了嗎？
   难道他回家了吗？

II. Words and Expressions Indicating Procedures

As in English, there are special words and expressions in Chinese that are used to indicate procedures. The following are the expressions used most often.

1. (首)先……，(然)後……，最後…… (首)先……，(然)后……，最后……	first (of all) . . . , and then . . . , finally . . .
2. 首先……，然後……，接下去……， 再接下去……，最後…… 首先……，然后……，接下去……， 再接下去……，最后……	first of all . . . , then . . . , after that . . . , and after that . . . , and finally . . .
3. 第一……，第二……，然後……， 接下去……，最後…… 第一……，第二……，然后……， 接下去……，最后……	first . . . , second . . . , and then . . . , after that . . . , and finally . . .
4. 第一步……，第二步/下一步…… 再下一步……，最後…… 第一步……，第二步/下一步…… 再下一步……，最后……	the first step (is) . . . , the second step/the next step . . . , the next step . . . , and finally . . .

Examples:

<u>首先</u>，你要清楚自己有什麼條件，<u>然後</u>再調整簡歷。
<u>首先</u>，你要清楚自己有什么条件，<u>然后</u>再调整简历。

<u>首先</u>，你要找一個公司，<u>然後</u>，從網上了解公司的情況，<u>接下去</u>，填表申請。
<u>首先</u>，你要找一个公司，<u>然后</u>，从网上了解公司的情况，<u>接下去</u>，填表申请。

<u>第一</u>，查網站，<u>第二</u>，寫簡歷，<u>第三</u>，找教授寫推薦信，<u>然後</u>把表格寄出去。
<u>第一</u>，查网站，<u>第二</u>，写简历，<u>第三</u>，找教授写推荐信，<u>然后</u>把表格寄出去。

<u>第一步</u>要了解實習的機會，<u>第二步/下一步</u>把申請表填好，<u>最後</u>把表格寄出去。
<u>第一步</u>要了解实习的机会，<u>第二步/下一步</u>把申请表填好，<u>最后</u>把表格寄出去。

Sometimes, when the order is not arranged based on time but on the degree of importance, the expressions 首先......，其次...... should be used meaning "firstly . . . , secondly . . . ."

Example:

首先，你要清楚招聘公司需要什麼樣的人，其次，得把簡歷寫好。
首先，你要清楚招聘公司需要什麼樣的人，其次，得把簡歷寫好。

However, the difference between these expressions is not very distinct, and often they can be used interchangeably.

> **≫Try it!** With a partner, practice using short dialogues to talk about procedures. Make sure that you use words and expressions indicating procedures, e.g. 首先, 其次, etc. Take the following dialogue as an example,

A: 申請工作要做什麼？
申请工作要做什么？

B: 首先，你要上網去找需要招聘人員的公司，然後，把簡歷寫好，再找教授給你寫推薦信。
首先，你要上网去找需要招聘人员的公司，然后，把简历写好，再找教授给你写推荐信。

補充課文 (补充课文) SUPPLEMENTARY PRACTICE

Read the following passage. Then listen and repeat.

A Job Seminar (繁體字 Traditional Character Version)

昨天下午學校就業中心的張女士為四年級的學生做了一個申請工作的講座。下面是她講座的主要內容:

　　同學們好! 還有三個月你們就要畢業了。畢業以後,你們都要找工作了。今天,我給你們介紹一下如何寫簡歷,如何申請工作的步驟。

　　第一步,你們要把簡歷寫好。簡歷是你們對自己的介紹,如果寫得好,招聘的公司就會對你感興趣,所以一定要把簡歷寫好。那麼,如何寫好簡歷呢? 首先,你要清楚地知道你想申請什麼樣的工作、自己的能力如何、有什麼好的條件。然後,要根據不同的工作性質調整你的簡歷。

　　第二步,你們要仔細了解有哪些公司在招聘員工。這些信息在網上都查得到,我們的就業中心也可以給你們介紹一些招聘網站。這些網站上有很多信息,也有申請表格讓你們下載。

　　除了寫簡歷、填表以外,你還需要有推薦信。要是你的教授能給你寫推薦信,那是最好不過的。不過,請記住,你一定要早一點告訴你的教授,這樣他們才能有足夠的時間幫你寫推薦信。

　　好,祝大家好運,找到你們喜歡的工作。

Notes:
女士(女士) [nǚshì]: lady, madam
內容(内容) [nèiróng]: content
能力(能力) [nénglì]: ability
了解(了解) [liǎojiě]: to know, understand
除了……以外(除了……以外) [chúle . . . yǐwài]: besides, except (for)
足夠(足够) [zúgòu]: enough

補充課文 (补充课文) SUPPLEMENTARY PRACTICE

Read the following passage. Then listen and repeat.

A Job Seminar (简体字 Simplified Character Version)

昨天下午学校就业中心的张女士为四年级的学生做了一个申请工作的讲座。下面是她讲座的主要内容：

同学们好！还有三个月你们就要毕业了。毕业以后，你们都要找工作了。今天，我给你们介绍一下如何写简历，如何申请工作的步骤。

第一步，你们要把简历写好。简历是你们对自己的介绍，如果写得好，招聘的公司就会对你感兴趣，所以一定要把简历写好。那么，如何写好简历呢？首先，你要清楚地知道你想申请什么样的工作、自己的能力如何、有什么好的条件。然后，要根据不同的工作性质调整你的简历。

第二步，你们要仔细了解有哪些公司在招聘员工。这些信息在网上都查得到，我们的就业中心也可以给你们介绍一些招聘网站。这些网站上有很多信息，也有申请表格让你们下载。

除了写简历、填表以外，你还需要有推荐信。要是你的教授能给你写推荐信，那是最好不过的。不过，请记住，你一定要早一点告诉你的教授，这样他们才能有足够的时间帮你写推荐信。

好，祝大家好运，找到你们喜欢的工作。

Exercises: work with a partner or in small groups

1. 他們在什麼地方？做什麼？參加的人是誰？
   他们在什么地方？做什么？参加的人是谁？

2. 找出有下面語法的句子：rhetorical questions, words, and expressions indicating procedures.

   找出有下面语法的句子：rhetorical questions, words, and expressions indicating procedures.

3. 用你自己的話再把這個講座說一遍。
   用你自己的话再把这个讲座说一遍。

成語故事 (成语故事) IDIOM STORY

杞人憂天 (杞人忧天) [qǐrén yōutiān]

Meaning: A person in the State of Qi worries that the sky might fall.

Usage: It is used to describe someone who has groundless worries or anxiety.

Example: A: 明年我就要畢業了，真擔心找不到工作。

明年我就要毕业了，真担心找不到工作。

B: 你別"杞人憂天"了，你的條件那麼好，又聰明又能幹，一定能找得到工作的。

你別"杞人忧天"了，你的条件那么好，又聪明又能干，一定能找得到工作的。

Pay attention to the usages of rhetorical questions, words, and expressions indicating procedures.

(繁體字 Traditional Character Version)

很久很久以前，在中國有一個地方叫杞國。杞國有一個人，他每天都愁眉苦臉的。他的朋友問他："你現在每天有吃有喝的，你難道還不高興嗎？"他說他擔心天會塌下來，地會陷下去，所以他想要搬到別的地方去。可是搬到哪兒去好呢？他也找不到一個好地方，可以讓他放心地住在那兒。

朋友聽了以後，就告訴他："你難道不知道天上都是空氣嗎？你每天都在空氣裡呼吸，難道空氣也會塌下來嗎？"他聽了以後就問："那就是說，天是塌不下來的。那麼天上的太陽、月亮和星星會不會掉下來呢？"朋友說："首先，它們離我們太遠了，是掉不下來的。其次，如果星星會掉下來，還沒到我們這兒，它就會完全消失了，你擔心什麼呢？"

但是他還是不放心，又問："那麼地陷下去怎麼辦呢？"他的朋友說："你難道沒有看見地上都是泥土和石頭嗎？你不是每天都在上面走嗎？地怎麼會陷下去呢？"

他聽了朋友的話以後，仔細地想了想，覺得很對，也就不再擔心了。

這個故事告訴我們平時不要沒有根據地擔心憂愁。

(简体字 **Simplified Character Version**)

很久很久以前，在中国有一个地方叫杞国。杞国有一个人，他每天都愁眉苦脸的。他的朋友问他："你现在每天有吃有喝的，你难道还不高兴吗？"他说他担心天会塌下来，地会陷下去，所以他想要搬到别的地方去。可是搬到哪儿去好呢？他也找不到一个好地方，可以让他放心地住在那儿。

朋友听了以后，就告诉他："你难道不知道天上都是空气吗？你每天都在空气里呼吸，难道空气也会塌下来吗？"他听了以后就问："那就是说，天是塌不下来的。那么天上的太阳、月亮和星星会不会掉下来呢？"朋友说："首先，它们离我们太远了，是掉不下来的。其次，如果星星会掉下来，还没到我们这儿，它就会完全消失了，你担心什么呢？"

但是他还是不放心，又问："那么地陷下去怎么办呢？"他的朋友说："你难道没有看见地上都是泥土和石头吗？你不是每天都在上面走吗？地怎么会陷下去呢？"

他听了朋友的话以后，仔细地想了想，觉得很对，也就不再担心了。

这个故事告诉我们平时不要没有根据地担心忧愁。

Notes:

杞國(杞国) [Qǐguó]: the State of Qi in ancient China

愁眉苦臉(愁眉苦脸) [chóuméi kǔliǎn]: to pull a long face due to worries

塌(塌) [tā]: to fall down

陷(陷) [xiàn]: to sink

空氣(空气) [kōngqì]: air

呼吸(呼吸) [hūxī]: to breathe

太陽(太阳) [tàiyáng]: the sun

月亮(月亮) [yuèliang]: the moon

星星(星星) [xīngxing]: the stars

掉(掉) [diào]: to fall

消失(消失) [xiāoshī]: to disappear

泥土(泥土) [nítǔ]: earth, clay

石頭(石头) [shítou]: stone

根據(根据) [gēnjù]: foundation, ground, basis

憂愁(忧愁) [yōuchóu]: to be worried

Exercises: work with a partner or in small groups

1. 找出有下面語法的句子：rhetorical questions "難道不是(沒有)......嗎?"
   找出有下面语法的句子：rhetorical questions "难道不是(没有)......吗?"

2. 杞國的這個人為什麼每天愁眉苦臉的?
   杞国的这个人为什么每天愁眉苦脸的?

3. 請用 "杞人憂天" 造一個句子或者說一個 "杞人憂天" 的例子。
   请用 "杞人忧天" 造一个句子或者说一个 "杞人忧天" 的例子。

4. 這個故事告訴了我們什麼?
   这个故事告诉了我们什么?

練習 (练习) ACTIVITIES

I. Listening Exercises

 17-1 Listen to the passage and then work with your partner to complete the exercises below:

Notes:
步驟(步骤) [bùzhòu]: step, procedure
另外(另外) [lìngwài]: in addition
總算(总算) [zǒngsuàn]: finally, eventually
回音(回音) [huíyīn]: reply, response
心想事成(心想事成) [xīnxiǎngshìchéng]: every wish comes true

1. Read each of the following statements. Mark a "✓" if it is correct, and an "✗" if it is incorrect. When completed, check with your partner.

   a. ☐ 再過幾個月我就要從研究生院畢業了。
       再过几个月我就要从研究生院毕业了。

   b. ☐ 申請研究生院的步驟很複雜，也很花時間。
       申请研究生院的步骤很复杂，也很花时间。

   c. ☐ 因為我的簡歷沒有突出重點，所以我把簡歷修改了好幾次。
       因为我的简历没有突出重点，所以我把简历修改了好几次。

d. ☐ 我的教授一直到昨天才告訴我他們很忙，沒有時間幫我寫
推薦信。

我的教授一直到昨天才告诉我他们很忙，没有时间帮我写
推荐信。

e. ☐ 我的男朋友很擔心我申請不到研究生院。
我的男朋友很担心我申请不到研究生院。

2. Form groups. Retell the paragraph in your own words.

II. Character Exercises

17-2 Work with a partner. Read the following words, phrases, and sentences.

雜	求
杂	求
複雜	要求
复杂	要求
不複雜	工作要求
不复杂	工作要求
不太複雜	不同的工作要求
不太复杂	不同的工作要求
寫簡歷不太複雜	公司有不同的工作要求
写简历不太复杂	公司有不同的工作要求
其實寫簡歷不太複雜	不同的公司有不同的工作要求
其实写简历不太复杂	不同的公司有不同的工作要求

Now with your partner, try to use the following characters to make words, phrases, and then sentences.

1. 成	2. 歷	3. 清	4. 突	5. 招	6. 首
成	历	清	突	招	首

7. 授	8. 慮	9. 薦	10. 聘	11. 聰	12. 願
授	虑	荐	聘	聪	愿

17-3 Read aloud the following paragraph. Write the traditional character form of the underlined characters. Then check your answers with a partner.

昨天下午就<u>业</u>中心的<u>讲</u>座很不<u>错</u>，我们了解了很多信息。我正在申请实习，所以很想知道怎么<u>写简历</u>，找信息，怎么在<u>网</u>上填表，直接<u>发</u>出去。我还要找教授写推<u>荐</u>信。我考<u>虑</u>了一下，想找王教授给我写，可是有时候我有些<u>担</u>心，怕他不同意。不过我觉得我的<u>条件</u>还不错，他可能不会拒<u>绝</u>我的。

1. _____   2. _____   3. _____   4. _____   5. _____

6. _____   7. _____   8. _____   9. _____   10. _____

11. _____   12. _____   13. _____   14. _____   15. _____

17-4 Each of the following pairs consists of homophones. Work in pairs to write out the Pinyin, with tones, and make as many phrases as you can with the following words.

Homophones:

Example: 慮(虑) [lǜ]   考慮(考虑)
            綠(绿) [lǜ]   綠茶(绿茶)

1. 條(条) [   ] _____
   調(调) [   ] _____

2. 歷(历) [   ] _____
   利(利) [   ] _____

3. 跟(跟) [   ] _____
   根(根) [   ] _____

4. 據(据) [   ] _____
   劇(剧) [   ] _____

17-5 Work with a partner. Fill in the blanks with an appropriate verb that goes with "成" to indicate "succeed in doing something."

1. 上個星期的講座你 _____ 成了嗎?
   上个星期的讲座你 _____ 成了吗?

2. 昨天的球賽你 _____ 成了嗎?
   昨天的球赛你 _____ 成了吗?

3. 你的簡歷 _____ 成了嗎?
   你的简历 _____ 成了吗?

4. 去年夏天的暑期中文班你 _____ 成了嗎?
   去年夏天的暑期中文班你 _____ 成了吗?

III. Grammar Exercises

17-6 Two months ago 華康(华康) and his girlfriend 小美 decided to participate in a summer Chinese program in Beijing. But suddenly, 小美 told 華康(华康) that she wanted to change the plans. 華康(华康) is confused and asks her questions to clarify the situation. Work in pairs to act out this question-answer exercise based on the clues given below. Use rhetorical questions.

Example:

What 小美 wants to do	Your questions to her
1. 決定申請去公司實習 決定申请去公司实习	1. 你不是決定去北京的暑期班學中文嗎? 你不是决定去北京的暑期班学中文吗?

Why 小美 wants to do the things mentioned above	Her questions to you
1. You told her several times that her major requires that she participate in an internship.	1. 你不是告訴我幾次,你的專業需要你去實習嗎? 你不是告诉我几次,你的专业需要你去实习吗?

Do the same with these new clues.

What 小美 wants to do	Your questions to her
1. 請你告訴她怎麼申請實習 请你告诉她怎么申请实习	
2. 她還沒有寫簡歷 她还没有写简历	
3. 她沒有招聘信息 她没有招聘信息	
4. 找哪個教授寫推薦信 找哪个教授写推荐信	

Why 小美 wants to do the things mentioned above	Her questions to you
1. She told you two weeks ago that she was too busy to go to the lecture at the Career Center.	
2. She showed you her résumé last week and you did not think it was good enough.	
3. You knew she did not have time to browse the web.	
4. She thinks the professors are all very busy.	

17-7 Work with your partner. The following is a checklist provided by the career center at your university about the specific procedures to go through when applying for a job or a graduate program. Take this as a reference and explain to your friends the procedures for the application. Please use words and expressions for the procedures.

申請工作或學校需要做的事情
(申请工作或学校需要做的事情)

1. 在網上查公司/學校的信息(在网上查公司/学校的信息)
2. 決定去哪個公司/學校(决定去哪个公司/学校)
3. 寫簡歷(写简历)
4. 找教授寫推薦信(找教授写推荐信)
5. 從網上下載表格(从网上下载表格)
6. 填表(填表)
7. 把表格發出去(把表格发出去)

IV. Media Literacy

The short text below, written in the style of newspapers, magazines, or Internet news articles, will help you become familiar with the formal written expressions used in these genres.

三季度求職人數上升 (三季度求职人数上升)
Number of People Seeking Jobs Rises in the Third Quarter

繁體字:

三季度求職人數上升

人事部發佈三季度求職市場信息。信息顯示，與二季度相比，招聘職位下降3%，求職登記人數上升2.8%。三季度招聘職位與求職登記人數比為1：2.19。

简体字:

三季度求职人数上升

人事部发布三季度求职市场信息。信息显示，与二季度相比，招聘职位下降3%，求职登记人数上升2.8%。三季度招聘职位与求职登记人数比为1 : 2.19。

Notes:

季度(季度) [jìdù]: season, quarter (of years)
求職(求职) [qiúzhí]: to seek jobs
上升(上升) [shàngshēng]: to rise
人事部(人事部) [rénshìbù]: human resources department
發佈(发布) [fābù]: to release, announce
市場(市场) [shìchǎng]: market
顯示(显示) [xiǎnshì]: to show
與……相比(与……相比) [yǔ . . . xiāngbǐ]: to compare with
招聘(招聘) [zhāopìn]: to invite applications for a job
職位(职位) [zhíwèi]: position
下降(下降) [xiàjiàng]: to decline
登記(登记) [dēngjì]: to register

Exercises for the article: work with a partner or a group to ask and answer the following.

1. Find the abbreviations and omissions usages (e.g. when subject, object, or conjunctions are omitted in the sentences) in the article.

2. Can you find any written expressions? What are their spoken counterparts (e.g. 與……相比(与……相比); 與(与); 為(为))

3. Use your own words to retell the headline and article.

V. Communicative Activities

17-8 Work in groups. Two of you are in your junior year and are preparing to apply for a summer internship. You have invited a senior to come and tell you about his/her experience applying for jobs. The senior has worked as an intern at two companies and has now found a job. Let him/her introduce the procedures first, and then start the question-and-answer session. Please use the following patterns, words, and expressions.

1. Rhetorical questions.

2. V. + 成 pattern.

3. 如何，至少，步驟，考慮，首先，要求，條件，同意，能力，對⋯⋯感興趣，被⋯⋯拒絕

   如何，至少，步骤，考虑，首先，要求，条件，同意，能力，对⋯⋯感兴趣，被⋯⋯拒绝

17-9 Pair work: you are now talking with your professor about your intention to apply for a master's degree program in your field. You ask him/her questions regarding the application and the professor explains to you how to proceed. Use the following as clues.

1. You are graduating in a few months.
2. You want to continue your studies in a master's program.
3. You ask your professor about the procedures to apply for the program.
4. You ask your professor about his willingness to write a recommendation letter for you.
5. You promise you will let him know the results of your application.

文化知識 (文化知识) Culture Link

文化點滴 (文化点滴) CULTURE NOTES

中國大學生的出國熱 (中国大学生的出国热)
The Surge in Chinese Students Studying Overseas

Over a century ago, inspired by the industrial advancement of Western countries, many Chinese students went overseas to study. Today another 出國熱(出国热) [chūguórè] (surge of studying abroad) is developing among university students in China. The reasons for studying abroad are threefold: (1) students hope it will give them a competitive edge for securing a better job in China; (2) ambitious students are attracted by the advanced technology, research atmosphere, and educational conditions in the United States and other developed countries; and (3) some less academically competitive high-school students see international study as a way to continue their studies without the pressure of the Chinese national college entrance exam.

After decades of isolation from the outside world following the founding of the People's Republic in 1949, China started to open its doors again at the end of the 1970s. The sharp contrast between China and more developed countries motivated the younger generation in China to go abroad to pursue higher education and work, thereby creating opportunities for a better future in China or elsewhere. The more open and lenient policy

Do you know...

- when China entered its second surge of students studying abroad?
- which countries Chinese students prefer to go?
- which traditional Chinese values have driven this trend?

Read and find out!

of the Chinese government made it possible for this to happen, and as a result the number of students going overseas increased greatly during the 1980s and 1990s. According to statistics compiled by 聯合國教科文組織 (联合国教科文组织) [Liánhéguó Jiàokēwén Zǔzhī] (the UN Educational, Scientific and Cultural Organization), China is the world's largest source of international students. In 2002, it was estimated that more than 460,000 Chinese students were studying in at least 103 countries and regions throughout the world.

The United States has been the favorite destination for Chinese students since the early 1980s. With the improvement in China's relations with other countries, however, recent years have witnessed a trend of students going to Japan, Australia, Canada, various European countries, and other developed nations. In 2002 alone, the number of Chinese students in Great Britain increased by 70 percent, and by 50 percent in Australia and Canada. Countries such as Germany and France, which have comparatively low educational and living expenses, are attractive to Chinese students from 中等家庭 [zhōngděng jiātíng] (middle-class families). Other recently popular countries include Russia, South Africa, Italy, New Zealand, Singapore, Malaysia, and South Korea.

Given the Chinese respect for education and the willingness of many parents to make sacrifices in order to support their children's study overseas programs, the trend is expected to continue.

The average age of Chinese students going abroad to study has got younger. In your country, at what age do students typically study abroad?

In China, there are many agencies helping overseas students. Are there such agencies in your country? What kind of services do they offer?

問題討論 (问题讨论) *Discuss the following with a partner or in small groups.*

1. 為什麼中國的大學生想出國留學? 你呢? 你也想出國留學嗎?
   为什么中国的大学生想出国留学? 你呢? 你也想出国留学吗?
   Why do Chinese college students want to study abroad? What about you? Do you also hope to study abroad?

2. 你知道中國的大學生出國留學要過幾道關嗎?
   你知道中国的大学生出国留学要过几道关吗?
   Do you know how many obstacles a Chinese college student needs to overcome in order to study abroad?

   道(道) [dào] (measure word for obstacles)
   關(关) [guān] obstacles
   過關(过关) [guòguān] to pass/overcome obstacles

3. 在你的國家, 出國留學能幫助你找到更好的工作嗎?
   在你的国家, 出国留学能帮助你找到更好的工作吗?
   Will study abroad enhance your job opportunities in your home country?

趣味中文 (趣味中文) FUN WITH CHINESE

萬事俱備，只欠東風。
万事俱备，只欠东风。
Everything is ready except for what is crucial.

wàn	shì	jù	bèi	zhǐ	qiàn	dōng	fēng
萬	事	俱	備	只	欠	東	風
万	事	俱	备	只	欠	东	风
ten thousand	things	all	ready	only	missing	east	wind

問題討論 (问题讨论) *Discuss the following with a partner or in small groups.*

1. Have you ever been in a situation like this? Give some examples.
2. Do you know a saying with the same or a similar meaning in your culture or another culture?

行動吧! (行动吧!) LET'S GO!

個人簡歷 (个人简历) Résumé/Curriculum Vitae (C.V.)

還有兩個月張小美就要畢業了。她已經把她的簡歷寫好了,可是她不知道她的簡歷寫得好不好。請你幫她看一看。你看了她的簡歷以後,能用英語回答下面的問題嗎?

还有两个月张小美就要毕业了。她已经把她的简历写好了,可是她不知道她的简历写得好不好。请你帮她看一看。你看了她的简历以后,能用英语回答下面的问题吗?

毕业生个人简历		
姓名: 张小美	**性别:** 女	**出生年月:** 1988 年 3 月 3 日
教育背景: 2007 年 9 月– 2011 年 7 月 广州理工大学		**专业:** 企业管理
通信地址: 广东省广州市中山一路10号		**邮编:** 513426
联系电话: 020-78645321	**移动寻呼:** 00810-0293857	**求職意向:** 商业文秘
技能总结		
英语水平	能熟练地进行听、说、读、写,通过国家英语四级考试,擅长撰写和回复英文商业信函。	
计算机水平	熟悉网路和电子商务,能熟练地操作计算机。	
实习经历总结	2009 年 7 月–9 月:广州网站电子商务实习。主要工作是在互联网上查阅国内以及国外的资讯,搜集、整理中英文资料,翻译英文资料等等。	

Notes:

個人(个人) [gèrén]: personal

性別(性别) [xìngbié]: gender

背景(背景) [bèijǐng]: background

理工(理工) [lǐgōng]: science and technology

企業管理(企业管理) [qǐyè guǎnlǐ]: business management

通信地址(通信地址) [tōngxìn dìzhǐ]: contact address

聯係(联系) [liánxì]: to keep in contact with

移動尋呼(移动寻呼) [yídòng xúnhū]: mobile & pager

意向(意向) [yìxiàng]: intention

文秘(文秘) [wénmì]: secretary

技能總結(技能总结) [jìnéng zǒngjié]: skills summary

水平(水平) [shuǐpíng]: level

熟練(熟练) [shúliàn]: skillfully

通過(通过) [tōngguò]: to pass

擅長(擅长) [shàncháng]: to be good at

撰寫(撰写) [zhuànxiě]: to compose, write

回復(回复) [huífù]: to reply

信函(信函) [xìnhán]: letters

操作(操作) [cāozuò]: to operate

互聯網(互联网) [hùliánwǎng]: the Internet, WWW

搜集(搜集) [sōují]: to collect

整理(整理) [zhěnglǐ]: to sort

問題討論 (问题讨论) Discuss the following with a partner or in small groups.

1. 張小美是從什麼大學畢業的? 她的專業是什麼?
   张小美是从什么大学毕业的? 她的专业是什么?

2. 她的英語水平怎麼樣? 她能用英語做什麼?
   她的英语水平怎么样? 她能用英语做什么?

3. 她會用電腦嗎? 她的電腦水平怎麼樣?
   她会用电脑吗? 她的电脑水平怎么样?

4. 她做過什麼實習工作?
   她做过什么实习工作?

第十八課 (第十八课)
LESSON

18

面談 (面谈)
The Interview

Group interviews are common in China.

教學目標 (教学目标) OBJECTIVES

- Market oneself for a job interview
- Participate in a job interview
- Review conjunctions
- Express approximation

CONNECTIONS AND COMMUNITIES PREVIEW

Discuss the following questions with a partner or your class. What similarities and differences do you think there might be between Chinese culture and your own culture?

1. What do you know about the job market in your country?

2. Have you had any experience looking for a job? If so, share some of your thoughts on preparing for a job interview.

生詞 (生词) VOCABULARY

🔊 核心詞 (核心词) Core Vocabulary

	TRADITIONAL	SIMPLIFIED	PINYIN		
1.	員工	员工	yuángōng	N.	employee
2.	左右	左右	zuǒyòu		more or less
3.	主任	主任	zhǔrèn	N.	director
4.	學位	学位	xuéwèi	N.	academic degree
5.	商務	商务	shāngwù	N.	business
6.	科學	科学	kēxué	N.	science
7.	月份	月份	yuèfèn	N.	(a certain) month
8.	從商	从商	cóngshāng	V.	to engage in business
9.	影響	影响	yǐngxiǎng	V. N.	to influence influence
10.	了解	了解	liǎojiě	V.	to know, understand
11.	咨詢	咨询	zīxún	V. N.	to consult consultation
12.	開發	开发	kāifā	V.	to develop
13.	軟件	软件	ruǎnjiàn	N.	software
14.	技術	技术	jìshù	N.	technology
15.	提供	提供	tígōng	V.	to provide
16.	大量	大量	dàliàng	N.	large quantity
17.	儘管	尽管	jǐnguǎn	Conj.	although
18.	上市	上市	shàngshì	V.	to go public, to list on the market

	TRADITIONAL	SIMPLIFIED	PINYIN		
19.	業務	业务	yèwù	N.	business
20.	開展	开展	kāizhǎn	V.	to carry on
21.	除了……以外	除了……以外	chúle . . . yǐwài	Conj.	besides, except (for)
22.	主修	主修	zhǔxiū	N.	major
23.	專業	专业	zhuānyè	N.	major subject
24.	副修	副修	fùxiū	N.	minor
25.	平均	平均	píngjūn	Adj.	average
26.	成績	成绩	chéngjì/chéngjī	N.	grade, score, result, success
27.	曾經	曾经	céngjīng	Adv.	once
28.	嘉獎	嘉奖	jiājiǎng	V. / N.	to award / award
29.	擔任	担任	dānrèn	V.	to take the position of
30.	學生會	学生会	xuéshēnghuì	N.	student committee
31.	主席	主席	zhǔxí	N.	chairman
32.	組織	组织	zǔzhī	V. / N.	to organize / organization
33.	凡是	凡是	fánshì	Adv.	all, every
34.	之一	之一	zhīyī		one of
35.	項目	项目	xiàngmù	N.	project (a project is called 計畫(计划) in Taiwan)
36.	論文	论文	lùnwén	N.	research paper, thesis
37.	出差	出差	chūchāi	V.O.	to go on a business trip
38.	哪怕	哪怕	nǎpà	Conj.	even if

專名 (专名) **Proper Nouns**

	TRADITIONAL	SIMPLIFIED	PINYIN		
1.	文如華	文如华	Wén Rúhuá	N.	(name) Ruhua Wen

語文知識 (语文知识) LANGUAGE LINK

Read and listen to the following sentence patterns. These patterns use vocabulary, expressions, and grammar that you will study in more detail in this lesson. After reading the sentence patterns, read and listen to the Language in Use section that follows.

句型 (句型) Sentence Patterns

A: 我今年五月份畢業，還有差不多一個月左右。
我今年五月份毕业，还有差不多一个月左右。
Wǒ jīnnián wǔyuèfèn bìyè, hái yǒu chàbuduō yíge yuè zuǒyòu.

B: 我們現在的員工有三百個左右。
我们现在的员工有三百个左右。
Wǒmen xiànzài de yuángōng yǒu sānbǎige zuǒyòu.

A: 我知道你們是一家上市公司。
我知道你们是一家上市公司。
Wǒ zhīdào nǐmen shì yìjiā shàngshì gōngsī.

B: 沒錯，儘管我們去年才開始
没错，尽管我们去年才开始
Méicuò, jǐnguǎn wǒmen qùnián cái kāishǐ

上市，可是業務發展得很快。
上市，可是业务发展得很快。
shàngshì, kěshì yèwù fāzhǎn de hěnkuài.

我組織過很多活動，凡是學校的重要活動，我都是組織人之一。
我组织过很多活动，凡是学校的重要活动，我都是组织人之一。
Wǒ zǔzhī guo hěnduō huódòng, fánshì xuéxiào de zhòngyào huódòng, wǒ dōushì zǔzhīrén zhī yī.

A: 這份工作要常常出差。
这份工作要常常出差。
Zhèfèn gōngzuò yào chángcháng chūchāi.

B: 那我是求之不得呀。哪怕要天天
那我是求之不得呀。哪怕要天天
Nà wǒ shì qiúzhībùdé ya. Nǎ pà yào tiāntiān

在外面走，我也會很高興。
在外面走，我也会很高兴。
zài wàimiàn zǒu, wǒ yě huì hěn gāoxìng.

🔊 課文 **Language in Use: "Why Are You Interested in This Job?"**
(繁體字 Traditional Character Version)

陳主任： 文小姐，你好。很高興你對我們公司感興趣。

文如華： 您好，陳主任。謝謝您給我這個機會。

陳主任： 我看了你的簡歷，你有雙學位[1]，電子商務和計算機科學，今年畢業，是嗎?

文如華： 是的。我今年五月份畢業，還有差不多一個月左右。

陳主任： 你為什麼對商學感興趣[2]呢?

文如華： 因為我爸爸是從商[3]的，受爸爸的影響，所以我從小就對商業感興趣。

陳主任： 能不能說一說你為什麼想來我們公司工作?

文如華： 我查了一下你們公司的網站，了解到你們是一家電腦諮詢公司。你們不但自己開發軟件技術，而且還提供大量的咨詢服務。

陳主任： 是的。我們公司儘管只有六年的歷史，可是發展得很快。現在公司的員工有三百個左右。

文如華： 聽說你們是上[4]市公司，是嗎?

---

1. 雙學位(双学位)

雙學位(双学位): a double major. We already know that 雙(双) can be used as a measure word for pairs, such as shoes, socks, hands, eyes, etc. It can also be used as a numeral to mean "double" or "both," e.g., "雙學位(双学位)" and "雙方(双方)."

---

2. 對…… 感興趣(对…… 感兴趣)

對……感興趣(对……感兴趣): "to be interested in . . . ." The object of "對(对)" can be either people or things. We may also use "對……有興趣(对……有兴趣)," e.g., i) 我對他妹妹有興趣。(我对他妹妹有兴趣。) ii) 我對中文感興趣。(我对中文感兴趣。)

---

3. 從商(从商)

"從(从)" here is used as a verb to mean 從事(从事) (to be engaged in), e.g., "從商(从商)" (to be engaged in business), "從軍(从军)" [cóngjūn] (to be engaged in military service), and "從政(从政)" [cóngzhèng] (to be engaged in politics).

---

4. 上(上)

上(上): to attend. It is used as a verb here. This is an idiomatic usage of 上(上), e.g., 上市(上市), 上學(上学), 上課(上课), 上班(上班), 上醫院(上医院), 上教堂(上教堂) [jiàotáng] church.

Continued on page 580

课文 Language in Use: "Why Are You Interested in This Job?"
(简体字 Simplified Character Version)

陈主任： 文小姐，你好。很高兴你对我们公司感兴趣。

文如华： 您好，陈主任。谢谢您给我这个机会。

陈主任： 我看了你的简历，你有双学位[1]，
电子商务和计算机科学，今年毕
业，是吗？

文如华： 是的。我今年五月份毕业，还有
差不多一个月左右。

陈主任： 你为什么对商学感兴趣[2]呢？

文如华： 因为我爸爸是从商[3]的，受爸爸的
影响，所以我从小就对商业感兴
趣。

陈主任： 能不能说一说你为什么想来我们
公司工作？

文如华： 我查了一下你们公司的网站，了
解到你们是一家电脑咨询公司。你们不但自己开发软件技
术，而且还提供大量的咨询服务。

陈主任： 是的。我们公司尽管只有六年的历史，可是发展得很快。现在
公司的员工有三百个左右。

文如华： 听说你们是上[4]市公司，是吗？

Continued on page 581

🔊 課文 Language in Use: "Why Are You Interested in This Job?"
(繁體字 Traditional Character Version) —— 接第五百七十八頁

接第五百七十八頁

陳主任： 一點兒也沒錯[5]。我們雖然去
年年初才開始上市，不過業
務開展得很好。對了，能不能
談談你自己的情況？

> **5. 一點兒也沒錯(一点儿也没错)**
>
> 一點兒也沒錯(一点儿也没错): exactly.
> It literally means "not wrong at all," but is
> usually used to express complete agreement.

文如華： 好的。我是中華大學的學生，
除了商學和計算機兩個主修專業以外，我還有一個中文副
修。我的平均成績很高，曾經多次得到過學校的嘉獎，還擔任
過商學院的學生會主席，組織過很多活動。凡是學校的重要
活動，我都是組織人之一。

陳主任： 你參加過研究項目嗎？

文如華： 參加過。從去年開始，我一直在跟教授做研究，現在正在寫畢
業論文。

陳主任： 除了學習以外，你還喜歡做什麼呢？

文如華： 我喜歡很多東西。不過，我最喜歡旅行。

陳主任： 那好，我們這份工作就是要
常常出差。

文如華： 那我是求之不得[6]呀！哪怕天
天在外面走，我也會很高興。

> **6. 求之不得(求之不得)**
>
> 求之不得(求之不得): all that one could
> wish for. 之(之) is a word from classical
> Chinese. It can be used as a pronoun or a
> possessive marker. It is still used in some
> set phrases in modern Chinese to mean
> "的(的)" as in "......之一(......之一)"
> (one of . . .) or as an objective pronoun
> "他/她/它(他/她/它)" as in "求之不得
> (求之不得)." Other examples are 之間
> (之间) which means "......的中間
> (.....的中间)" and 學而時習之(学而时
> 习之) which means "study and review what
> has been studied from time to time."

陳主任： 你還有什麼問題嗎？

文如華： 請問，你們什麼時候能做決
定呢？

陳主任： 下個星期一吧。我們會給你
打電話的。

文如華： 好，我等你們的電話。再次感
謝您給我這個機會。

课文 Language in Use: "Why Are You Interested in This Job?"
(简体字 Simplified Character Version) —— 接第五百七十九页

陈主任：一点儿也没错⁵。我们虽然去年年初才开始上市，不过业务开展得很好。对了，能不能谈谈你自己的情况？

文如华：好的。我是中华大学的学生，除了商学和计算机两个主修专业以外，我还有一个中文副修。我的平均成绩很高，曾经多次得到过学校的嘉奖，还担任过商学院的学生会主席，组织过很多活动。凡是学校的重要活动，我都是组织人之一。

陈主任：你参加过研究项目吗？

文如华：参加过。从去年开始，我一直在跟教授做研究，现在正在写毕业论文。

陈主任：除了学习以外，你还喜欢做什么呢？

文如华：我喜欢很多东西。不过，我最喜欢旅行。

陈主任：那好，我们这份工作就是要常常出差。

文如华：那我是求之不得⁶呀！哪怕天天在外面走，我也会很高兴。

陈主任：你还有什么问题吗？

文如华：请问，你们什么时候能做决定呢？

陈主任：下个星期一吧。我们会给你打电话的。

文如华：好，我等你们的电话。再次感谢您给我这个机会。

語法 (语法) GRAMMAR

I. Review: Conjunctions (2)

As we mentioned in Lesson 12, compound sentences are sentences that consist of two or more clauses. We also reviewed some of the commonly used conjunctions in Lesson 15. Below is a second review of some other conjunctions.

Conjunctions	Features	Examples
一邊……一邊 一边……一边 一面……一面 一面……一面 . . . while at the same time . . .	• connects two simultaneous actions	我喜歡一邊開車，一邊聽音樂。 我喜欢一边开车，一边听音乐。
不是……而是 不是……而是 not . . . but . . .	• indicates an alternative relation	不是我不在乎你的感受，而是我太忙了，所以現在不能理你。 不是我不在乎你的感受，而是我太忙了，所以现在不能理你。
一……就…… 一……就…… as soon as . . . then . . . (首)先……，然後…… (首)先……，然后…… first . . . , then . . .	• connects two actions which occur in sequence	她一畢業就找到了工作。 她一毕业就找到了工作。 首先你要查網站，然後你要把簡歷寫好。 首先你要查网站，然后你要把简历写好。
不管……，……都…… 不管……，……都…… 不管……， ……還是…… 不管……， ……还是…… no matter	• connects two clauses, the first indicating a condition and the second a result	不管我多忙，我都要去看他。 不管我多忙，我都要去看他。 不管我多忙，我還是要去看他。 不管我多忙，我还是要去看他。

Conjunctions	Features	Examples
無論……，也(都) 无论……，也(都) 不論……，也(都) 不论……，也(都) no matter 凡是……，…… 凡是……，…… whatever	• indicates an all-inclusive situation	無論你同意還是不同意，我都要去參加。 无论你同意还是不同意，我都要去参加。 凡是他想做的事，他一定能做好。 凡是他想做的事，他一定能做好。
除了 A 以外， ……還/也 B 除了 A 以外， ……还/也 B "besides . . . also . . ." (the same subject)	• indicates "inclusion" (both A and B are covered) • 以外(以外) can be omitted • if the number of items after 除了(除了) is long, 以外(以外) is usually present	除了商學以外，我還修中文。 除了商学以外，我还修中文。 Besides business, I also study Chinese. [study both 商學(商学) and 中文(中文)]
除了(除了) Subject 1 以外(以外), Subject 2 都(都) V. "except . . . for" (different subjects)	• to indicate "exclusion" • exclusion of Subject 1 before making a general truth • the general truth is marked by 都(都), and the exception is marked by 除了(除了)	除了他以外，我們都學中文。 除了他以外，我们都学中文。 Except for him, we all study Chinese. (他 is the "exclusion")

>>**Try it!** With a partner, select the correct conjunctions from above to ask and answer the questions.

A: _____ 這個公司 _____，你還申請了什麼公司？
_____ 这个公司 _____，你还申请了什么公司？

B: _____ 網站上的公司，我都申請了。
_____ 网站上的公司，我都申请了。

A: 現在找工作難嗎？
现在找工作难吗？

B: _____ 你是學電腦的，_____ 學工程的，現在找工作都很不容易。
_____ 你是学电脑的，_____ 学工程的，现在找工作都很不容易。

II. Expressions Indicating Approximation

A. 左右 and 上下 are expressions to indicate "approximation" for a number. They are used when the speaker is not sure of the exact number or does not think it is necessary to give the exact number of something.

Examples:

我們公司的員工有三百個上下。
我们公司的员工有三百个上下。

這盤光碟要二十元上下。
这盘光碟要二十元上下。

這個學校的教授有八百個左右。
这个学校的教授有八百个左右。

今天早上九點左右他要來參加我們的討論。
今天早上九点左右他要来参加我们的讨论。

Notes:

- 左右 and 上下 can only be placed after the number they modify. They are never placed before the number (see examples #1, #2, and #3 above).
- 左右 and 上下 can be used interchangeably when the number they modify indicates quantity or amount. But only 左右 is used for approximation of time (see example #4 above).

B. 大概, 大約(大约), and 差不多 are adverbs used for the same purpose.

Examples:

我們公司的員工<u>大概</u>有三百個上下。
我们公司的员工<u>大概</u>有三百个上下。

今天早上<u>大約</u>有十個人要來參加我們的討論。
今天早上<u>大约</u>有十个人要来参加我们的讨论。

這盤光碟<u>差不多</u>要二十元左右。
这盘光碟<u>差不多</u>要二十元左右。

However, while 左右 and 上下 are only used for numbers, 大概, 大約(大约), and 差不多 can also be used for situations.

Examples:

我<u>大概</u>明天可以接到他的電話了。
我<u>大概</u>明天可以接到他的电话了。

他<u>大約</u>已經決定了。
他<u>大约</u>已经决定了。

他們<u>差不多</u>都同意我的建議。
他们<u>差不多</u>都同意我的建议。

Notes:

- 大概, 大約(大约), and 差不多 are used before the major verb of the sentence.
- They can be used together with 左右 or 上下, but 左右 or 上下 can be omitted as well.

Examples:

A: 你們公司有多少員工?
你们公司有多少员工?

B: 大概(有)三百個(上下/左右)。
大概(有)三百个(上下/左右)。

A: 你們什麼時候可以決定?
你们什么时候可以决定?

B: 大約(在)星期一左右。
大约(在)星期一左右。

A: 這兒的房租是多少?
这儿的房租是多少?

B: 每個月差不多(是)五百元(左右)。
每个月差不多(是)五百元(左右)。

C. It is also common to place 多 or 幾 after a number to indicate approximation.

Example:

她今年二十多(幾)歲了。
她今年二十多(几)岁了。
She is 20-something this year.

D. It is also common to use two adjacent numbers together to indicate approximation.

Examples:

她今年二十三、四歲了。
她今年二十三、四岁了。
She is 23 or 24 this year.

這台電腦要八、九百塊錢。
这台电脑要八、九百块钱。
This computer costs 800 or 900 dollars.

>>**Try it!** With a partner, practice questions and answers with expressions indicating approximation. For example,

A: 你們的學院有多少專業?
你们的学院有多少专业?

B: 大概有七、八個專業吧。
大概有七、八个专业吧。

A: 學生呢?
学生呢?

B: 有一千五百個左右。
有一千五百个左右。

補充課文 (补充课文) SUPPLEMENTARY PRACTICE

Read the following passage. Then listen and repeat.

A Job Application Cover Letter (繁體字 Traditional Character Version)

尊敬的新華科技咨詢公司人事部:

　　在招聘網站上，我看到了貴公司正在招聘一個電腦軟件開發人員。我對這個工作非常感興趣，希望貴公司能考慮我的申請。

　　我現在是中華大學四年級的學生，主修計算機和商學兩個專業。四年來，我不但在計算機和商學方面學到了很多有用的知識，而且在好幾家公司參加了實習，得到了不少工作經驗。除此以外，我還擔任了商學院的學生會主席，組織了很多活動。凡是學校的重要活動，我都是組織人之一。

　　從貴公司的網站中，我了解到貴公司大概有五、六年的歷史，業務發展得非常快，現在已經是一家上市公司了。貴公司不但自己開發軟件技術，而且還為其他公司提供咨詢服務。我非常希望能用所學的知識為貴公司服務。如果貴公司能接受我的申請，我一定會努力地做好我的工作，為公司的發展做出貢獻。

　　此致

申請人: 文如華

Notes:
尊敬的(尊敬的) [zūnjìngde]: respected
科技(科技) [kējì]: hi-tech
人事部(人事部) [rénshìbù]: department of human resources
人員(人员) [rényuán]: personnel; staff
方面(方面) [fāngmiàn]: aspect
業務(业务) [yèwù]: business activities
其他(其他) [qítā]: other; else
為……服務(为……服务) [wèi . . . fúwù]: to serve
貢獻(贡献) [gòngxiàn]: to contribute to; contribution
此致(此致) [cǐzhì]: respectfully

補充課文 (补充课文) SUPPLEMENTARY PRACTICE

Read the following passage. Then listen and repeat.

A Job Application Cover Letter (简体字 Simplified Character Version)

尊敬的新华科技咨询公司人事部：

　　在招聘网站上，我看到了贵公司正在招聘一个电脑软件开发人员。我对这个工作非常感兴趣，希望贵公司能考虑我的申请。

　　我现在是中华大学四年级的学生，主修计算机和商学两个专业。四年来，我不但在计算机和商学方面学到了很多有用的知识，而且在好几家公司参加了实习，得到了不少工作经验。除此以外，我还担任了商学院的学生会主席，组织了很多活动。凡是学校的重要活动，我都是组织人之一。

　　从贵公司的网站中，我了解到贵公司大概有五、六年的历史，业务发展得非常快，现在已经是一家上市公司了。贵公司不但自己开发软件技术，而且还为其他公司提供咨询服务。我非常希望能用所学的知识为贵公司服务。如果贵公司能接受我的申请，我一定会努力地做好我的工作，为公司的发展做出贡献。

　　此致

申请人：文如华

Exercises: work with a partner or in small groups

1. 有哪些這一課的生詞和語法出現在這封信上？請把它們找出來。
   有哪些这一课的生词和语法出现在这封信上？请把它们找出来。

2. 她在大學四年裡，學到了什麼知識，參加過什麼活動？
   她在大学四年里，学到了什么知识，参加过什么活动？

3. 她要申請的是一家什麼樣的公司？
   她要申请的是一家什么样的公司？

4. 用你的話，再把每一段說一遍。
   用你的话，再把每一段说一遍。

成語故事 (成语故事) IDIOM STORY

濫竽充數 (滥竽充数) [lànyú chōngshù]

Meaning: To pretend to play a musical instrument in a group just to round out the number.

Usage: This is used to describe someone who is holding a post without the necessary qualifications just to round out the number. It is also often used as a humble way to reply to compliments about your promotion.

Examples: 1. 那個人什麼都不會，在公司裡面只是 "濫竽充數" 罷了。
那个人什么都不会，在公司里面只是 "滥竽充数" 罢了。

     2. A: 恭喜你拿到這個主任的工作！
恭喜你拿到这个主任的工作！

       B: 沒什麼，我只是很幸運，"濫竽充數" 罷了。
没什么，我只是很幸运，"滥竽充数" 罢了。

Pay attention to the usages of conjunctions 凡是, 不管……都……, 一邊……一邊……(一边……一边……), and ways of expressing approximation.

(繁體字 Traditional Character Version)

    兩千四百年以前，中國有一個齊 [Qí] 國。它的國王是齊宣王 [Qí Xuānwáng]。齊宣王非常喜歡音樂，特別喜歡聽很多人一起吹竽。他有一個很大的樂隊，每天有三百個左右的人一起吹竽給他聽。凡是吹竽的人，不管是誰，都能拿到很多錢。

    有一個南郭 [Nánguō] 先生。他不會吹竽，可是為了賺錢，他也混在樂隊裡面，假裝跟大家一起吹竽，看起來好像吹得很好似的。齊宣王並不知道他是假裝的，所以也給了他很多錢。就這樣，南郭先生在樂隊裡混了三、四年。

    後來，齊宣王死了，他的兒子當了國王，叫齊湣王 [Qí Mǐnwáng]。齊湣王也喜歡聽吹竽。但是他不喜歡聽大樂隊一起演奏，他喜歡聽樂師一個一個地吹。這樣，南郭先生就不能再混下去了，只好自己偷偷地走了。

    這個故事告訴我們一個人如果沒有真正的能力，只想混，最後還是騙不了人的。

(简体字 **Simplified Character Version**)

　　两千四百年以前，中国有一个齐国。它的国王是齐宣王。齐宣王非常喜欢音乐，特别喜欢听很多人一起吹竽。他有一个很大的乐队，每天有三百个左右的人一起吹竽给他听。凡是吹竽的人，不管是谁，都能拿到很多钱。

　　有一个南郭先生。他不会吹竽，可是为了赚钱，他也混在乐队里面，假装跟大家一起吹竽，看起来好像吹得很好似的。齐宣王并不知道他是假装的，所以也给了他很多钱。就这样，南郭先生在乐队里混了三、四年。

　　后来，齐宣王死了，他的儿子当了国王，叫齐湣王。齐湣王也喜欢听吹竽。但是他不喜欢听大乐队一起演奏，他喜欢听乐师一个一个地吹。这样，南郭先生就不能再混下去了，只好自己偷偷地走了。

　　这个故事告诉我们一个人如果没有真正的能力，只想混，最后还是骗不了人的。

Notes:

國王(国王) [guówáng]: ruler, king of a state in ancient China
吹(吹) [chuī]: to blow, play
竽(竽) [yú]: a musical instrument in ancient China
樂隊(乐队) [yuèduì]: band, orchestra
賺錢(赚钱) [zhuànqián]: to make money
混(混) [hùn]: to sneak in, pass off as
假裝(假装) [jiǎzhuāng]: to pretend
好像……似的(好像……似的) [hǎoxiàng . . . shìde]: as if . . .
死(死) [sǐ]: to die
偷偷地(偷偷地) [tōutōude]: stealthily
真正(真正) [zhēnzhèng]: genuine; real
能力(能力) [nénglì]: ability
騙(骗) [piàn]: to deceive

Exercises: work with a partner or in small groups

1. 找出有這一課語法的句子。
   找出有这一课语法的句子。

2. 為什麼在齊宣王的時候，南郭先生可以混在吹竽的樂隊裡?
   为什么在齐宣王的时候，南郭先生可以混在吹竽的乐队里?

3. 後來南郭先生為什麼要偷偷地走了?
   后来南郭先生为什么要偷偷地走了?

4. 這個故事告訴我們什麼? 你能用這個成語造一個句子嗎?
   这个故事告诉我们什么? 你能用这个成语造一个句子吗?

練習 (练习) ACTIVITIES

I. Listening Exercises

 18-1 史如影 is making a phone call to her mother. Listen to what she says and then complete the exercises below. When completed, check with your partner.

Notes:
成立(成立) [chénglì]: to establish
國際(国际) [guójì]: international
友好(友好) [yǒuhǎo]: friendly
總算(总算) [zǒngsuàn]: finally, eventually
心想事成(心想事成) [xīnxiǎngshìchéng]: every wish comes true

1. Decide whether the following statements are correct or not. Mark the correct statements with a "✓" and the incorrect statements with "✗".

a. ☐ 半個小時以前，我給中華咨詢公司打了一個電話申請工作。

半个小时以前，我给中华咨询公司打了一个电话申请工作。

b. ☐ 雖然中華咨詢公司的業務發展很快，可是還不是一家上市公司。

虽然中华咨询公司的业务发展很快，可是还不是一家上市公司。

c. ☐ 中華咨詢公司主要是提供咨詢服務，他們自己沒有軟件技術。

中华咨询公司主要是提供咨询服务，他们自己没有软件技术。

d. ☐ 人事部的陳主任和員工們都說希望我去那兒工作。

人事部的陈主任和员工们都说希望我去那儿工作。

e. ☐ 這份工作要常常出差，可是我很怕天天坐飛機。

这份工作要常常出差，可是我很怕天天坐飞机。

2. Work with your partner to answer the following questions orally.

   a. 為什麼史如影今天那麼高興?
      为什么史如影今天那么高兴?

      _____

   b. 她為什麼喜歡這份工作?
      她为什么喜欢这份工作?

      _____

II. Character Exercises

18-2   Work with a partner. Read the following words, phrases, and sentences.

技 技	獎 奖
技術 技术	嘉獎 嘉奖
軟件技術 软件技术	得到嘉獎 得到嘉奖
公司開發軟件技術 公司开发软件技术	他得到學校的嘉獎 他得到学校的嘉奖
公司大量開發軟件技術 公司大量开发软件技术	他多次得到學校的嘉獎 他多次得到学校的嘉奖
公司自己大量開發軟件技術 公司自己大量开发软件技术	他曾經多次得到學校的嘉獎 他曾经多次得到学校的嘉奖

Now with your partner, try to use the following characters to make words, phrases, and then sentences.

1. 除   2. 均   3. 咨   4. 務   5. 修   6. 儘
   除   均   咨   务   修   尽

7. 曾   8. 任   9. 擔   10. 凡   11. 項   12. 展
   曾   任   担   凡   项   展

18-3 Read the following paragraph. Circle each simplified character that matches its traditional form below and write the number beside it. Then check with your partner.

我们公司有六年的历史了。最近几年，业务发展得非常快，从去年开始上市。我们不但为客户提供咨询服务，也一直在开发新的软件技术。我们需要有领导能力的人。你在学校的成绩很好，又组织过很多活动，曾经多次受到嘉奖，看起来你的条件不错。

1. 歷   2. 導   3. 績   4. 條   5. 開   6. 業   7. 術   8. 務
9. 軟   10. 發   11. 動   12. 錯   13. 獎   14. 經   15. 詢

18-4 Each of the following words has two different pronunciations. Work with your partner to write out the Pinyin of each character, with tones, and the meaning of each word or phrase.

Example: 很<u>好</u> [hǎo] very good
很<u>好</u> [hǎo] very good

愛<u>好</u> [hào] hobby
爱<u>好</u> [hào] hobby

1. <u>教</u>授 [   ] _____
教授 [   ] _____
<u>教</u>書 [   ] _____
<u>教</u>书 [   ] _____

2. 旅<u>行</u> [   ] _____
旅<u>行</u> [   ] _____
<u>行</u>業 [   ] _____
<u>行</u>业 [   ] _____

3. <u>差</u>不多 [   ] _____
<u>差</u>不多 [   ] _____
出<u>差</u> [   ] _____
出<u>差</u> [   ] _____

4. 求之不<u>得</u> [   ] _____
求之不<u>得</u> [   ] _____
<u>得</u>去接人 [   ] _____
<u>得</u>去接人 [   ] _____

18-5 The following words are used in two different ways in our lesson. Work in groups, first to find from the text two phrases that indicate the different meanings of these words, and then to explain them in English. If you know more examples, include them as well.

Example: 開(开)：開始(开始) to begin
開(开)：開發(开发) to develop

1. 從(从)：_____ _____
   從(从)：_____ _____
   從(从)：_____ _____
   從(从)：_____ _____

2. 上(上)：_____ _____
   上(上)：_____ _____
   上(上)：_____ _____
   上(上)：_____ _____

III. Grammar Exercises

18-6 Form groups to combine the following sentences using appropriate conjunctions.

1. 警察給我開了罰單；他告訴我開車要小心。(indicating two simultaneous actions)
   警察给我开了罚单；他告诉我开车要小心。

   _____

2. 他不是來道歉的；他是來還我光碟的。(making an alternative)
   他不是来道歉的；他是来还我光碟的。

   _____

3. 你們需要我去哪兒；我願意去。(indicating conditional relation)
   你们需要我去哪儿；我愿意去。

   _____

4. 他拿到了博士學位；他開了一家電腦公司。(indicating sequence)
   他拿到了博士学位；他开了一家电脑公司。

   _____

5. 他學中文；他也學計算機。(indicating inclusion)
他学中文；他也学计算机。

_____

6. 我們都學計算機；只有他不學計算機。(indicating exclusion)
我们都学计算机；只有他不学计算机。

_____

18-7 陳華(陈华) is a person with a carefree personality who often uses the word "approximately." Today his girlfriend is discussing with him a job she wants to apply. Guess how he answers the following questions of hers. With a partner, act it out.

1. 你知道這家公司有多少年歷史了?
你知道这家公司有多少年历史了?

2. 你聽說這家公司有多少員工?
你听说这家公司有多少员工?

3. 你知道他們這次要招聘多少新的員工?
你知道他们这次要招聘多少新的员工?

4. 你覺得他們接受我的可能性 ([kěnéngxìng]: possibility) 有多大? (Use %)
你觉得他们接受我的可能性有多大? (Use %)

18-8 Form groups and complete the following sentences based on the context given below. Remember, 凡是 here is used to indicate all-inclusiveness.

1. 我最喜歡李連杰這個演員，凡是 _____
我最喜欢李连杰这个演员，凡是 _____

2. 我覺得我的男朋友非常聰明、能幹，凡是 _____
我觉得我的男朋友非常聪明、能干，凡是 _____

3. 他對中國非常有興趣，凡是 _____
他对中国非常有兴趣，凡是 _____

IV. Media Literacy

The short text below, written in the style of newspapers, magazines, or Internet news articles, will help you become familiar with the formal written expressions used in these genres.

高校畢業生就業服務周開幕 (高校毕业生就业服务周开幕)
Opening Ceremony for College Graduate Employment Services Week

繁體字：

高校畢業生就業服務周開幕

今日高校畢業生就業服務周開幕，擬招聘人數為22萬人。本次共有20多家舉辦網絡招聘會，現場招聘會將舉辦90多場，全國各地參加招聘的用人單位將超過18000家。

简体字：

高校毕业生就业服务周开幕

今日高校毕业生就业服务周开幕，拟招聘人数为22万人。本次共有20多家举办网络招聘会，现场招聘会将举办90多场，全国各地参加招聘的用人单位将超过18000家。

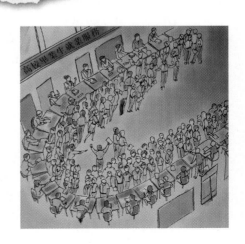

Notes:
開幕(开幕) [kāimù]: opening ceremony
擬(拟) [nǐ]: to intend to
舉辦(举办) [jǔbān]: to hold (a meeting)
現場(现场) [xiànchǎng]: on the spot
各地(各地) [gèdì]: various places
場(场) [chǎng]: session (for meetings, exhibitions, etc.)
用人單位(用人单位) [yòngréndānwèi]: employer

Exercises for the article: work with a partner or a group to ask and answer the following.

1. What is a "服務周"? What kind of "服務周" is being held here?

2. How many applicants are estimated to attend? How many companies will participate?

3. Can you find any written expressions? What are their spoken counterparts (e.g. 擬(拟); 以下(以下) . . . etc.)?

4. Use your own words to retell the headline and article.

V. Communicative Activities

18-9   Work in pairs. You are at a job fair and you see a company that interests you. You are talking with the recruiter to try to find out as much as you can about the company, and are trying to convince him/her that you have the appropriate qualifications for the job. One of you will be the recruiter and the other a job applicant. Please use (but do not be limited to) the following expressions:

機會　　對……感興趣　　了解　　開發　　提供　　受……影響/嘉獎
机会　　对……感兴趣　　了解　　开发　　提供　　受……影响/嘉奖

擔任　　參加　　組織
担任　　参加　　组织

不但……而且……　　儘管……可是……
不但……而且……　　尽管……可是……

哪怕……也……　　凡是……都……
哪怕……也……　　凡是……都……

除了……以外
除了……以外

18-10   You have received a job offer. Now you are at your professor's office to thank him/her for his/her help with your application. What are you going to say to him/her? Work with your partner and act out this conversation.

文化知識 (文化知识) Culture Link

文化點滴 (文化点滴) CULTURE NOTES

中國的第三產業 (中国的第三产业) The Service Industry in China

In the past few decades, China has moved from a centrally planned to a market economy. This has changed the 經濟形態 (经济形态) [jīngjì xíngtài] (economic patterns) of the country, and the 服務業 (服务业) [fúwùyè] (service industry), also called the third industry, has greatly expanded, creating new kinds of job opportunities.

The fast development of the services industry is partly the result of the market economy forcing state-owned businesses into bankruptcy, resulting in large numbers of unemployed workers. In order to ease these unemployment pressures, the government has developed new job positions, mainly in service businesses, for the 下崗人員 (下岗人员) [xiàgǎng rényuán] (laid-off workers).

With the rapid development of the economy, daily life for ordinary people has also become more fast-paced. Many working people are no longer able to spend as much time as they used to taking care of household chores or elderly parents. This has created, in turn, a need for new services such as certified housekeepers, care providers for the sick and the elderly, and daily companions

Do you know...

- why the service industry in China has greatly expanded during recent decades?
- how the Chinese government has tried to ease the pressures caused by unemployment?
- the scope of China's service industry? Can you list some services typical in China but not in other countries?

Read and find out!

whose job is to read newspapers to or chat with elderly people who feel lonely because their children are too busy to keep them company.

As China has opened further to the outside world, the service industry has become even more expansive, with new services, such as nannies who speak foreign languages, appearing as a result of the increasing number of foreign diplomats, business people, and foreign students living and working in China. Other services typically found in Chinese cities include 網吧 (网吧) [wǎngbā] (Internet bars), filled with young adults around the clock; 氧吧 [yǎngbā] (oxygen bars), where people refresh their lungs with oxygen or other breathing systems; and 陶吧 [táobā] (ceramics or pottery bars), popular with young people for expressing their artistic creativity. 足部按摩中心 [zúbù ànmó zhōngxīn] (foot massaging centers), for receiving Chinese herbal medical treatment for feet, have also become extremely popular. Of course, the service industry also includes conventional services such as advertising, finance and banking, insurance, real estate, law, and restaurants and shopping.

The service industry in China is very broad. Here, some women make silk flowers.

These women work at a foot-massage spa. Do these kinds of spas exist in your country? Can you give some examples of the kinds of services available?

問題討論 (问题讨论) *Discuss the following with a partner or in small groups.*

1. 請說說美國有什麼樣的服務業?
   请说说美国有什么样的服务业?
   Name some service industries that exist in the US.

2. 在你的國家和文化, 如果有人失業 ([shīyè]: unemployed) 了, 他會想怎麼做?
   在你的国家和文化, 如果有人失业了, 他会想怎么做?
   What kinds of services for the unemployed exist in your country or community?

趣味中文 (趣味中文) FUN WITH CHINESE

毛遂自薦
毛遂自荐

To offer one's services (as Mao Sui did)

Máo	Suì	zì	jiàn
毛	遂	自	薦
毛	遂	自	荐
Mao	Sui	self	to recommend

問題討論 (问题讨论) *Discuss the following with a partner or in small groups.*

1. In traditional Chinese culture, modesty is a virtue. Therefore, Chinese generally do not recommend themselves for jobs. What are your comments on this?

2. What is the situation in your culture? Find an expression in your language that indicates a similar or opposite meaning.

行動吧! (行动吧!) LET'S GO!

招聘廣告 (招聘广告) Job Services Advertisement

This is an advertisement for a company that provides employment services. Read it and answer the questions below.

工作天地
招聘广告/职业介绍

这里的岗位都只有3000元/月及以下薪酬：

行政文员，店长，营业员，收银员，保安员，电话销售，客户服务，销售代表(业务员)，派遣员工，宾馆酒店餐饮服务员，普工等等，都是这儿的主角。

最低薪酬800元只是起点！
向高收入挑战才具有您生活意义！来吧！

或者是来招聘，或者是来求职，
工作天地会圆您的人生之梦！

Notes:
岗位(岗位) [gǎngwèi]: post, position
薪酬(薪酬) [xīnchóu]: salary, pay
行政(行政) [xíngzhèng]: administrative
文員(文员) [wényuán]: civilian personnel
收銀員(收银员) [shōuyínyuán]: cashier
保安員(保安员) [bǎo'ānyuán]: security guard
代表(代表) [dàibiǎo]: representative
業務員(业务员) [yèwùyuán]: business representatives
派遣(派遣) [pàiqiǎn]: to dispatch
普工(普工) [pǔgōng]: general, non-skilled workers
主角(主角) [zhǔjué]: leading role
起點(起点) [qǐdiǎn]: starting point

問題討論 (问题讨论) *Discuss the following with a partner or in small groups.*

1. What is the full name of the company?
2. What kinds of jobs are available?
3. How much can you expect to earn each month?
4. What is the minimum monthly salary of the jobs provided here?
5. What does 圓您的人生之夢(圆您的人生之梦) mean here?

復習 (复习) Review

LESSON 17 TO LESSON 18

I. Dialogue

Suppose both you and your good friend are graduating in a few months and you are now preparing to apply for jobs. Yesterday, you attended a lecture given at the career center of your university. Now you are sharing with your friend what you have learned about job applications. Work with your partner to act out the conversation. Please use the following in your talk.

1. Useful expressions: 講座，簡歷，複雜，突出，重點，招聘，信息，下載，
   讲座，简历，复杂，突出，重点，招聘，信息，下载，

   表格，推薦，條件，就業中心
   表格，推荐，条件，就业中心

2. Grammar:

   a. Rhetorical sentence pattern 難道不是(沒有)......了嗎?
      难道不是(没有)......了吗?

   b. Procedural conjunctions 首先......然後......最後/接下去......
      首先......然后......最后/接下去......

      or 第一步......，第二步......，然後......，最後......
      第一步......，第二步......，然后......，最后......

II. Conversation

You just came back from an interview at a consulting company. Now you are telling your mother about the interview. Work with your partner to act out the conversation. The following are the clues you need to follow.

1. Explain the nature of the job you are applying for.
2. Give a short introduction about the company.
3. Say why you think you are qualified for the job.

Notes:
對......感興趣，受......影響/嘉獎，求之不得，除了......以外
对......感兴趣，受......影响/嘉奖，求之不得，除了......以外

Conjunctions:

不管……都……，無論……也……，不是……而是……，
不管……都……，无论……也……，不是……而是……，

一邊……一邊……，凡是……
一边……一边……，凡是……

III. Picture Description

Work in small groups to describe the following pictures using procedural expressions and at least three (sets of) conjunctions you have learned. Remember that you need to rearrange the order of these pictures.

(1)

(2)

(3)

(4)

(5)

IV. Traditional and Simplified Characters

Work in small groups. Read each character aloud and write its traditional form. Then make a phrase and a sentence using the character.

Example: 难 → 難 → 難道 → 難道你沒有申請工作嗎?

L17: 实 (　)　　历 (　)　　讲 (　)　　荐 (　)　　简 (　)　　业 (　)
　　　复 (　)　　虑 (　)　　乐 (　)

L18: 兴 (　)　　响 (　)　　发 (　)　　术 (　)　　尽 (　)　　专 (　)
　　　担 (　)　　织 (　)　　论 (　)

19

選擇工作 (选择工作)
Choosing a Job

Working in a foreign company is a dream job for young people in China.

教學目標 (教学目标) OBJECTIVES

- Describe choices
- Express agreement or disagreement
- Use emphasis
- Discuss job benefits

CONNECTIONS AND COMMUNITIES PREVIEW

Discuss the following questions with a partner or your class. What similarities and differences do you think there might be between Chinese culture and your own culture?

1. Are there foreign companies in your country? Do your fellow citizens like to work there?

2. Which is more important to you—salary, work environment, or potential for professional development?

生詞 (生词) VOCABULARY

🔊 核心詞 (核心词) Core Vocabulary

	TRADITIONAL	SIMPLIFIED	PINYIN		
1.	寧願	宁愿	nìngyuàn	Conj.	would rather . . . than
2.	金融	金融	jīnróng	N.	finance
3.	考慮	考虑	kǎolǜ	V. / N.	to consider / consideration
4.	市場	市场	shìchǎng	N.	market
5.	景氣	景气	jǐngqì	Adj.	prosperous
6.	競爭	竞争	jìngzhēng	V. / N.	to compete / competition
7.	祝賀	祝贺	zhùhè	V. / N.	to congratulate / congratulations
8.	謙虛	谦虚	qiānxū	Adj.	modest
9.	幸運	幸运	xìngyùn	Adj.	lucky
10.	工資	工资	gōngzī	N.	salary
11.	金	金	jīn	N.	gold
12.	飯碗	饭碗	fànwǎn	N.	rice bowl
13.	穩定	稳定	wěndìng	Adj.	stable
14.	待遇	待遇	dàiyù	N.	salary and benefits
15.	年薪	年薪	niánxīn	N.	annual salary
16.	起薪	起薪	qǐxīn	N.	starting salary
17.	萬	万	wàn	Num.	ten thousand

TRADITIONAL	SIMPLIFIED	PINYIN		
18. 股份	股份	gǔfèn	N.	stock
19. 婆婆媽媽	婆婆妈妈	pópomāmā		wordy, over-elaborate
20. 究竟	究竟	jiūjìng	Adv.	after all
21. 醫療	医疗	yīliáo	N.	medical treatment
22. 補貼	补贴	bǔtiē	V. N.	to compensate allowance
23. 修(課)	修(课)	xiū (kè)	V.	to study, take (a class)
24. 學費	学费	xuéfèi	N.	tuition
25. 福利	福利	fúlì	N.	welfare, benefit
26. 猶豫	犹豫	yóuyù	V.	to hesitate
27. 固然	固然	gùrán	Conj.	admittedly, though of course
28. 環境	环境	huánjìng	N.	environment, surroundings
29. 確實	确实	quèshí	Adv.	indeed, really
30. 融洽	融洽	róngqià	Adj.	harmonious
31. 上司	上司	shàngsī	N.	boss, supervisor
32. 賺	赚	zhuàn	V.	to earn or make (money)

專名 (专名) Proper Nouns

TRADITIONAL	SIMPLIFIED	PINYIN		
1. 周華信	周华信	Zhōu Huáxìn	N.	(name) Huaxin Zhou
2. 金新民	金新民	Jīn Xīnmín	N.	(name) Xinmin Jin

語文知識 (语文知识) LANGUAGE LINK

Read and listen to the following sentence patterns. These patterns use vocabulary, expressions, and grammar that you will study in more detail in this lesson. After reading the sentence patterns, read and listen to the Language in Use section that follows.

句型 (句型) Sentence Patterns

現在就業市場不太景氣，可是卻
现在就业市场不太景气，可是却
Xiànzài jiùyè shìchǎng bú tài jǐngqì, kěshì què

有三個公司要你，你真了不起！
有三个公司要你，你真了不起！
yǒu sānge gōngsī yào nǐ, nǐ zhēn liǎobuqǐ!

 要找好的工作非要有好的
要找好的工作非要有好的
Yào zhǎo hǎode gōngzuò fēiyào yǒu hǎode

條件不可。誰的條件不好都不行！
条件不可。谁的条件不好都不行！
tiáojiàn bùkě. Shéi de tiáojiàn bù hǎo dōu bùxíng!

A: 那家大咨詢公司給的工資比較高。
那家大咨询公司给的工资比较高。
Nàjiā dà zīxún gōngsī gěi de gōngzī bǐjiào gāo.

B: 我倒寧願去金融銀行。
我倒宁愿去金融银行。
Wǒ dào nìngyuàn qù jīnróng yínháng.

A: 要我說，只要拿的錢多
要我说，只要拿的钱多
Yào wǒ shuō, zhǐ yào ná de qián duō

就行了。
就行了。
jiù xíng le.

B: 這我倒不太同意。錢固然重要，
这我倒不太同意。钱固然重要，
Zhè wǒ dào bú tài tóngyì. Qián gùrán zhòngyào,

可還有比它更重要的。
可还有比它更重要的。
kě háiyǒu bǐ tā gèng zhòngyào de.

🔊 **課文** Language in Use: "Have You Had Any Job Offers?"
(**繁體字** Traditional Character Version)

周華信：　新民，你工作找得怎麼樣？

金新民：　有三個地方接受了我的申請，一個是金融銀行，兩個是咨詢公司。這兩天我正在考慮接受哪一個呢。

周華信：　真的嗎？現在的經濟還沒完全恢復，就業市場還不太景氣，競爭非常厲害，可是卻有三家公司要你，你真了不起[1]！祝賀你。

金新民：　謝謝。不過我覺得主要是我的運氣比較好。

周華信：　別謙虛了[2]。要找好的工作非要有好的條件不可。誰的條件不好都不行！

金新民：　也不完全如此，我還是比較幸運的。

周華信：　那你到底考慮去哪家公司呢？

金新民：　可能是那家大的咨詢公司吧，他們給的工資比較高。

周華信：　我倒寧願去金融銀行！金飯碗，打不破。

金新民：　你說得倒也對。銀行的工作比較穩定，待遇也很好。

周華信：　不過還要看他們付給你多少年薪[3]呢。

金新民：　銀行給我的起薪是六萬，小的咨詢公司是五萬二，大的是五萬五，不過他們都是上市公司，可以給我公司的股份。

---

1. 了不起(了不起)

了不起(了不起) means "amazing, extraordinary." This expression is used to show amazement. It can be used to describe a person or a thing. The negative form is "沒什麼了不起(没什么了不起)."

---

2. 別謙虛了(别谦虚了)

別謙虛了(别谦虚了): don't be modest. This is an expression spoken tongue-in-cheek. Generally in China modesty is a virtue, but here it implies that the speaker does not appreciate the modesty expressed by the previous speaker. It may be said either as a joke or as a serious statement.

---

3. 薪(薪)

薪(薪) means "salary or wages." It is the abbreviated form of 薪水(薪水), e.g., 起薪(起薪) (beginning salary), 月薪(月薪) (monthly salary), and 年薪(年薪) (annual salary). 工資(工资) is also used. Today, 工資(工资) is commonly used in mainland China while 薪水(薪水) is used in Taiwan.

Continued on page 614

课文 Language in Use: "Have You Had Any Job Offers?"
(简体字 Simplified Character Version)

周华信： 新民，你工作找得怎么样？

金新民： 有三个地方接受了我的申请，一个是金融银行，两个是咨询公司。这两天我正在考虑接受哪一个呢。

周华信： 真的吗？现在的经济还没完全恢复，就业市场还不太景气，竞争非常厉害，可是却有三家公司要你，你真了不起[1]！祝贺你。

金新民： 谢谢。不过我觉得主要是我的运气比较好。

周华信： 别谦虚了[2]。要找好的工作非要有好的条件不可。谁的条件不好都不行！

金新民： 也不完全如此，我还是比较幸运的。

周华信： 那你到底考虑去哪家公司呢？

金新民： 可能是那家大的咨询公司吧，他们给的工资比较高。

周华信： 我倒宁愿去金融银行！金饭碗，打不破。

金新民： 你说得倒也对。银行的工作比较稳定，待遇也很好。

周华信： 不过还要看他们付给你多少年薪[3]呢。

金新民： 银行给我的起薪是六万，小的咨询公司是五万二，大的是五万五，不过他们都是上市公司，可以给我公司的股份。

Continued on page 615

課文 Language in Use: "Have You Had Any Job Offers?"
(繁體字 Traditional Character Version) —— 接第六百一十二頁

周華信： 看樣子都很不錯嘛！那就決定了吧。

金新民： 可他們提供的待遇還是有點兒不一樣。

周華信： 得了，得了[4]！你真是婆婆媽媽[5]的。好吧，說說看，究竟有什麼不一樣？

金新民： 他們的退休計畫和醫療保險都差不多，出差的補貼也很高。但是，如果以後我想再去修一些研究生的課，銀行可以提供學費補貼，而咨詢公司卻沒有這方面的福利。所以我有點兒猶豫。

周華信： 要我說[6]，給的錢多就行。

金新民： 這我倒不太同意。對我來說，錢固然重要，可工作環境更重要。

周華信： 那倒也是。有時候，有一個好的工作環境確實比工資的多少更重要。

金新民： 其實我想去那家大的咨詢公司，聽說那兒的同事關係很融洽，上司也很好。

周華信： 這一點倒是非常重要的。

金新民： 我爸爸也說："你還年輕，錢以後總能賺得到，可是好的工作環境卻不是那麼容易得到的。"

周華信： 你爸爸說得有道理，聽他的沒錯。

---

4. 得了，得了(得了，得了)

得了，得了(得了，得了): all right, all right, just go ahead. This is an idiomatic expression used mostly in spoken Chinese. You may use one or two or even three 得了 (得了) in succession.

---

5. 婆婆媽媽(婆婆妈妈)

婆婆媽媽(婆婆妈妈) means "like an old woman." It implies "indecisiveness" and "hesitation" and is generally used in a negative way.

---

6. 要我說(要我说)

要我說(要我说) means "if you ask me . . . ." It is a very idiomatic expression used to introduce what the speaker's opinion is. It is a colloquial expression used mainly in spoken Chinese.

课文 Language in Use: "Have You Had Any Job Offers?"
(简体字 Simplified Character Version) —— 接第六百一十三页

周华信：看样子都很不错嘛！那就决定了吧。

金新民：可他们提供的待遇还是有点儿不一样。

周华信：得了，得了4！你真是婆婆妈妈5的。好吧，说说看，究竟有什么不一样？

金新民：他们的退休计划和医疗保险都差不多，出差的补贴也很高。但是，如果以后我想再去修一些研究生的课，银行可以提供学费补贴，而咨询公司却没有这方面的福利。所以我有点儿犹豫。

周华信：要我说6，给的钱多就行。

金新民：这我倒不太同意。对我来说，钱固然重要，可工作环境更重要。

周华信：那倒也是。有时候，有一个好的工作环境确实比工资的多少更重要。

金新民：其实我想去那家大的咨询公司，听说那儿的同事关系很融洽，上司也很好。

周华信：这一点倒是非常重要的。

金新民：我爸爸也说："你还年轻，钱以后总能赚得到，可是好的工作环境却不是那么容易得到的。"

周华信：你爸爸说得有道理，听他的没错。

語法 (语法) GRAMMAR

I. Adverbs Expressing Tone of Voice/Mood

Tone of voice is always very hard to express in any language. In Chinese, tone of voice is sometimes expressed through the use of adverbs. The most commonly used adverbs for this purpose are 卻(却), 倒, 到底, and 究竟. As they are all adverbs, they are placed before the verb.

A. 卻(却): an adverb used to mean "but."

Examples:

競爭這麼厲害，卻有三家公司要你！
竞争这么厉害，却有三家公司要你！
The competition is so intense, but three companies want to hire you!

我有好多事要做，卻不知道從哪兒開始。
我有好多事要做，却不知道从哪儿开始。
I have lots of work to do, but don't know where to start.

他說找到了工作，卻不告訴我是什麼工作。
他说找到了工作，却不告诉我是什么工作。
He said he had found a job, but would not tell me what.

我最近忙得要死，他卻說不知道我在幹什麼。
我最近忙得要死，他却说不知道我在干什么。
I've been extremely busy lately, but he said he did not know what I was doing.

Note: If the subject in the 卻(却) clause is the same as the one in the previous clause, it is usually omitted. However, if the subject is different it must be included.

B. 倒: an adverb that can be used in several ways:

a. As "but," "on the contrary," or "not as what was expected."

Examples:

你說大的咨詢公司不錯，我倒寧願去金融銀行。
你说大的咨询公司不错，我倒宁愿去金融银行。
You say the big consulting company is good, but I would prefer the financial bank.

我很擔心他找不到工作，(可是)他倒覺得沒什麼。
我很担心他找不到工作，(可是)他倒觉得没什么。
I am worried that he will not find a job, but (unexpectedly) he doesn't care.

我吃了他的藥，(不但沒有好)肚子倒更疼了。

我吃了他的药，(不但没有好)肚子倒更疼了。

After taking his medicine, (instead of getting better) my stomach ache got even worse.

你太客氣了，倒讓我覺得不好意思了。

你太客气了，倒让我觉得不好意思了。

You are too polite, which has made me feel embarrassed.

Notes:

- A comma "," must be used between the two clauses.
- 倒 generally has a stronger tone than 卻(却).
- 倒 must be used following a previous statement that provides the context for the unexpected result.
- In this usage, we may also use 反倒 which has exactly the same meaning.

b. To express concession.

Examples:

你說的倒也對，工作環境是很重要。

你说的倒也对，工作环境是很重要。

All right, what you said is right. The work environment is very important.

銀行的工作(穩定)倒是穩定，就是工資不太高。

银行的工作(稳定)倒是稳定，就是工资不太高。

Working at a bank is stable all right, but the pay is not very good.

這個名字我倒是聽說過，他在哪兒工作我就是記不得了。

这个名字我倒是听说过，他在哪儿工作我就是记不得了。

I have heard this name all right, but I just don't remember where he works.

我倒是已經畢業了，就是工作還沒有找到。

我倒是已经毕业了，就是工作还没有找到。

I have graduated all right, but have not found a job yet.

Notes:

When used to express concession,

- A comma "," must be used between the two clauses.
- 倒 is generally placed in the first clause.

c. To force somebody to do something right away. It is generally used when the speaker gets frustrated at somebody else's behavior.

Examples:

你倒是快來啊！
你倒是快来啊！
(Implies that it is already past the time for you to come)

你倒是快點決定呀！
你倒是快点决定呀！
(Implies that there is no time for us to delay the decision any longer)

Notes:
- When used in this way, 倒是 is generally used instead of only 倒.
- A particle indicating mood, such as 呀 or 啊, must be used at the end of the sentence.

C. 到底: when used in a statement, it means "eventually" or "at last" to express the idea that something has finally happened after many twists and turns. In a question, it means "after all" to indicate that the speaker wants to get to the bottom of a situation.

Examples:

他考慮了很久，到底還是去那家咨詢公司工作了！
他考虑了很久，到底还是去那家咨询公司工作了！
He has finally decided to take the job offer from the consulting company! (Implying that he had thought a lot before he finally decided to accept the job offer)

我勸他勸了那麼久，他到底還是同意我說的話了。
我劝他劝了那么久，他到底还是同意我说的话了。
He has eventually agreed with what I said. (Implying that it took quite a lot of effort to persuade him to agree)

(你說這家公司也好，那家公司也好，) 你到底決定去哪家公司呀?
(你说这家公司也好，那家公司也好，) 你到底决定去哪家公司呀?
(Implying "Come on, tell me, which company have you decided to go with after all?")

別猶豫了，告訴我，你到底還想不想考研究生院?
别犹豫了，告诉我，你到底还想不想考研究生院?
(Implying that you have been hesitating and I have become impatient, so just tell me whether you still want to take the entrance exam to a graduate school)

Notes:
- 到底 can be placed either immediately before the major verb of a sentence or before its subject.
- When used in a statement, 到底 can be replaced by 終究(终究) ([zhōngjiū]: eventually), while in a question it can be used interchangeably with 究竟 ([jiūjìng]: actually).

>>**Try it!** With a partner in the class, practice questions and answers using the expressions for tones of voice listed above. For example,

A: 你到底想不想買這台電腦? 我們這麼遠來這兒, 你卻不買了。
你到底想不想买这台电脑? 我们这么远来这儿, 你却不买了。

B: 這台電腦太貴了, 我買不起。我倒想買那台, 不太貴, 也很好。
这台电脑太贵了, 我买不起。我倒想买那台, 不太贵, 也很好。

II. Conjunction 固然

固然 is a conjunction generally used to acknowledge a certain existing fact and at the same time to introduce an adversative fact. Sometimes it may also be used to acknowledge the first fact, while at the same time not denying the truth of the second.

Examples:
錢<u>固然</u>重要, (但是)工作環境更重要。
钱<u>固然</u>重要, (但是)工作环境更重要。
Money is important all right, but the working environment is even more important.

公司大一些<u>固然</u>好, (可是)有時候小公司機會更多。
公司大一些<u>固然</u>好, (可是)有时候小公司机会更多。
It is true that a large company is good, but a small company may sometimes provide more opportunities.

Notes:
- 固然 can be used together with 但是 or 可是, but the latter may also be omitted.
- 固然 must be used before the main verb of the first clause. It is generally not placed before the subject.

>>**Try it!** With a partner, practice asking and answering questions using the expression 固然. For example,

A: 你為什麼不想去這個公司?
你为什么不想去这个公司?

B: 這個公司給我的工資固然不錯,但是我不太喜歡它的工作環境。
这个公司给我的工资固然不错,但是我不太喜欢它的工作环境。

III. Emphasis in Chinese Sentences (continued from Lesson 16) 非......不可 (must, have to)

非......不可 is commonly used for emphasis in Chinese.

Examples:

要找好工作<u>非</u>有好的條件<u>不可</u>! (你一定要有好的條件,否則你找不到好工作。)
要找好工作<u>非</u>有好的条件<u>不可</u>! (你一定要有好的条件,否则你找不到好工作。)

明天你<u>非</u>去聽講座<u>不可</u>。(明天的講座非常重要,你一定要去聽。)
明天你<u>非</u>去听讲座<u>不可</u>。(明天的讲座非常重要,你一定要去听。)

公司說我明天<u>非</u>出差<u>不可</u>。(我明天一定要出差去,不然公司老闆會不高興的。)
公司说我明天<u>非</u>出差<u>不可</u>。(我明天一定要出差去,不然公司老板会不高兴的。)

考研究生院<u>非</u>要教授的推薦信<u>不可</u>。(沒有教授的推薦信,很難考得上研究生院。)
考研究生院<u>非</u>要教授的推荐信<u>不可</u>。(没有教授的推荐信,很难考得上研究生院。)

>>**Try it!** | With a partner, construct a short dialogue using the pattern 非......不可.......
For example,

A: 你簡歷寄出去了嗎?
　　你简历寄出去了吗?

B: 還沒有呢。我明天非寄不可了。
　　还没有呢。我明天非寄不可了。

補充課文 (补充课文) SUPPLEMENTARY PRACTICE

Read the following passage. Then listen and repeat.

Choosing a Company (繁體字 Traditional Character Version)

四月五日　　　星期二　　　天氣：晴

　　昨天上午我接到了兩家公司打來的電話，他們已經決定接受我的申請了，我高興極了！要知道，現在的經濟情況還沒有完全恢復，就業市場還是不太景氣，找工作不容易。申請工作的時候，我也申請了研究生院，準備如果找不到工作，就先去讀書。

　　能有兩家公司要我是件好事，可是究竟去哪一家公司卻讓我很難決定。兩家公司都很好，工作的性質也差不多。他們給我提供的工資和福利待遇都很不錯，不但有醫療保險，還有很好的退休計畫。

　　我的父母一直希望我能去讀研究生院，我覺得繼續學習固然很重要，可是能夠先去工作、學點經驗，那也不錯。我在想，要是我能一邊工作，一邊學習，不用花錢就能拿到一個碩士學位，這難道不是一舉兩得的好事嗎？

　　不過爸爸倒提醒了我一件事：公司的工作環境怎麼樣？他說，不管在哪兒工作，同事之間的關係都很重要。

　　看來我還需要多了解一下兩家公司的情況，好好地比較比較，然後再做決定。

Notes:
晴(晴) [qíng]: sunny
性質(性质) [xìngzhì]: nature
花(花) [huā]: to spend (money or time)
一舉兩得(一举两得) [yìjǔliǎngdé]: to kill two birds with one stone
提醒(提醒) [tíxǐng]: to remind

補充課文 (补充课文) SUPPLEMENTARY PRACTICE

Read the following passage. Then listen and repeat.

Choosing a Company (简体字 Simplified Character Version)

四月五日   星期二   天气：晴

　　昨天上午我接到了两家公司打来的电话，他们已经决定接受我的申请了，我高兴极了！要知道，现在的经济情况还没有完全恢复，就业市场还是不太景气，找工作不容易。申请工作的时候，我也申请了研究生院，准备如果找不到工作，就先去读书。

　　能有两家公司要我是件好事，可是究竟去哪一家公司却让我很难决定。两家公司都很好，工作的性质也差不多。他们给我提供的工资和福利待遇都很不错，不但有医疗保险，还有很好的退休计划。

　　我的父母一直希望我能去读研究生院，我觉得继续学习固然很重要，可是能够先去工作、学点经验，那也不错。我在想，要是我能一边工作，一边学习，不用花钱就能拿到一个硕士学位，这难道不是一举两得的好事吗？

　　不过爸爸倒提醒了我一件事：公司的工作环境怎么样？他说，不管在哪儿工作，同事之间的关系都很重要。

　　看来我还需要多了解一下两家公司的情况，好好地比较比较，然后再做决定。

Exercises: work with a partner or in small groups

1. 有哪些這一課的生詞出現在這篇日記上？請把它們找出來。
   有哪些这一课的生词出现在这篇日记上？请把它们找出来。

2. 什麼事讓他非常高興？
   什么事让他非常高兴？

3. 兩家公司給了他什麼條件？
   两家公司给了他什么条件？

4. 他父母希望他上研究生院嗎？他自己呢？他說什麼是一舉兩得的好辦法呢？
   他父母希望他上研究生院吗？他自己呢？他说什么是一举两得的好办法呢？

5. 他爸爸給了他什麼建議？
   他爸爸给了他什么建议？

成語故事 (成语故事) IDIOM STORY

塞翁失馬 (塞翁失马) [sàiwēng shī mǎ]

Meaning: Saiweng lost his horse.

Usage: 塞翁失馬(塞翁失马) is often followed by 焉知非福(焉知非福) meaning "The old man on the frontier lost his horse. Who could have guessed it was a blessing in disguise?" It implies that a loss may turn out to be a gain.

Example: 他雖然沒拿到那家銀行的工作，可是 "塞翁失馬，焉知非福，" 他找到了更好的工作。

他虽然没拿到那家银行的工作，可是 "塞翁失马，焉知非福，" 他找到了更好的工作。

Pay special attention to adverbs used to express agreement or disagreement: 卻(却), 倒, 固然.

(繁體字 Traditional Character Version)

　　從前，在中國的北方住著一個老人，人們都叫他 "塞翁"。他養了很多馬。

　　有一天，有一匹馬不見了。找來找去都找不到。鄰居都感到很可惜，可是塞翁卻說："馬不見了不一定是壞事。說不定是好事呢。" 過了幾天，這匹馬真的回來了，還帶回來了一匹馬。鄰居們聽了都很高興地來祝賀他。可是塞翁倒沒有覺得很高興，他說："馬回來了倒是不錯，但也並不一定是好事，說不定是一件壞事呢。" 鄰居都覺得他很奇怪。

　　有一天，塞翁的兒子騎上了那匹新的馬去玩。沒想到那匹馬亂跑亂跳，把塞翁的兒子摔了下來，摔斷了腿。鄰居們都來安慰塞翁，可是塞翁卻說："腿摔斷了固然不好，可是說不定能帶來好事呢。" 鄰居們都很不理解。後來，那兒發生了戰爭，很多身體好的年輕人都非要當兵不可，結果都死在戰場上了。可是塞翁的兒子卻因為腿不好，所以沒有去當兵。這時，鄰居們到底才理解了塞翁的意思。

　　這個故事告訴我們，事情常常會有變化，壞事可能會變好事，好事也可能會變成壞事。

(简体字 Simplified Character Version)

从前，在中国的北方住着一个老人，人们都叫他"塞翁"。他养了很多马。

有一天，有一匹马不见了。找来找去都找不到。邻居都感到很可惜，可是塞翁却说："马不见了不一定是坏事。说不定是好事呢。"过了几天，这匹马真的回来了，还带回来了一匹马。邻居们听了都很高兴地来祝贺他。可是塞翁倒没有觉得很高兴，他说："马回来了倒是不错，但也并不一定是好事，说不定是一件坏事呢。"邻居都觉得他很奇怪。

有一天，塞翁的儿子骑上了那匹新的马去玩。没想到那匹马乱跑乱跳，把塞翁的儿子摔了下来，摔断了腿。邻居们都来安慰塞翁，可是塞翁却说："腿摔断了固然不好，可是说不定能带来好事呢。"邻居们都很不理解。后来，那儿发生了战争，很多身体好的年轻人都非要当兵不可，结果都死在战场上了。可是塞翁的儿子却因为腿不好，所以没有去当兵。这时，邻居们到底才理解了塞翁的意思。

这个故事告诉我们，事情常常会有变化，坏事可能会变好事，好事也可能会变成坏事。

Notes:

塞翁(塞翁) [sàiwēng]: an old man on the frontier

失(失) [shī]: to lose

從前(从前) [cóngqián]: once upon a time

養(养) [yǎng]: to raise

匹(匹) [pǐ]: measure word for horses

鄰居(邻居) [línjū]: neighbor

感到(感到) [gǎndào]: to feel

可惜(可惜) [kěxī]: it's a pity

說不定(说不定) [shuōbudìng]: maybe

並(并) [bìng]: and; besides; moreover

奇怪(奇怪) [qíguài]: strange

摔(摔) [shuāi]: to fall

斷(断) [duàn]: broken

腿(腿) [tuǐ]: leg

安慰(安慰) [ānwèi]: to console

戰爭(战争) [zhànzhēng]: war

當兵(当兵) [dāngbīng]: to join the army

死(死) [sǐ]: to die

戰場(战场) [zhànchǎng]: battlefield

Exercises: work with a partner or in small groups

1. 找出有下面語法的句子：卻，倒，到底，固然。
   找出有下面语法的句子：却，倒，到底，固然。

2. 用你自己的話說說"塞翁失馬"的故事。
   用你自己的话说说"塞翁失马"的故事。

3. 請用"塞翁失馬"造一個句子或者說一個"塞翁失馬"的例子。
   请用"塞翁失马"造一个句子或者说一个"塞翁失马"的例子。

4. "塞翁失馬"的故事，告訴了我們什麼?
   "塞翁失马"的故事，告诉了我们什么?

練習 (练习) ACTIVITIES

I. Listening Exercises

 19-1 新民 received two job offers. He is not sure which one to accept, so he is calling his father to ask his opinion. Listen to what he says and then complete the exercises below. Then check your answers with your partner.

Notes:
消息(消息) [xiāoxi]: news; information
芝加哥(芝加哥) [Zhījiāgē]: Chicago
友好(友好) [yǒuhǎo]: friendly
也許(也许) [yěxǔ]: maybe

1. Answer the following questions.

   a. 新民找到工作了嗎? 在哪兒? 是什麼工作?
      新民找到工作了吗? 在哪儿? 是什么工作?

   b. 兩家公司的工作有什麼不一樣?
      两家公司的工作有什么不一样?

   c. 哪家公司給的年薪比較高?
      哪家公司给的年薪比较高?

   d. 電腦公司的福利待遇是什麼?
      电脑公司的福利待遇是什么?

   e. 哪家公司的待遇更好?
      哪家公司的待遇更好?

   f. 兩家公司的工作環境怎麼樣?
      两家公司的工作环境怎么样?

   g. 你覺得新民應該去哪一家公司?
      你觉得新民应该去哪一家公司?

19-2 Based on what you have heard, work with your partner and fill in each blank with an appropriate word or expression to complete the sentence.

1. 兩家公司都 ＿＿＿＿ 新民去工作了。
   两家公司都 ＿＿＿＿ 新民去工作了。

2. 紐約公司的主要工作是 ＿＿＿＿ 軟件技術。
   纽约公司的主要工作是 ＿＿＿＿ 软件技术。

3. 芝加哥公司的 _____ 機會比較多。
   芝加哥公司的 _____ 机会比较多。

4. 紐約公司可以給我學費 _____。
   纽约公司可以给我学费 _____。

5. 兩家公司給我的 _____ 差不多，_____ 也差不多，
   都能給我 _____。
   两家公司给我的 _____ 差不多，_____ 也差不多，
   都能给我 _____。

II. Character Exercises

19-3 Work with a partner. Read the following words, phrases, and sentences.

穩 稳	福 福
穩定 稳定	福利 福利
比較穩定 比较稳定	福利待遇 福利待遇
工作比較穩定 工作比较稳定	這方面的福利待遇 这方面的福利待遇
銀行的工作比較穩定 银行的工作比较稳定	公司有這方面的福利待遇 公司有这方面的福利待遇
金融銀行的工作比較穩定 金融银行的工作比较稳定	咨詢公司有這方面的福利待遇 咨询公司有这方面的福利待遇

Now with your partner, try to use the following characters to make words, phrases, and then sentences.

1. 寧   2. 競   3. 謙   4. 薪   5. 股   6. 猶
   宁   竞   谦   薪   股   犹

7. 洽   8. 補   9. 環   10. 虛   11. 療   12. 固
   洽   补   环   虚   疗   固

19-4 Match the traditional characters with their simplified forms. Then check your answers with your partner.

慮	補	穩	猶	療	環	濟	複	卻	輕

疗	轻	济	犹	虑	复	稳	环	补	却

19-5 Each of the following pairs of characters looks somewhat similar. Work in small groups to write the Pinyin for each character, with tones, compose a phrase with each character, and then explain the phrase in English.

Example: 經(经) [jīng] 經濟(经济) economy
　　　　　 輕(轻) [qīng] 年輕(年轻) young

1. 慮(虑) [　] ＿＿＿＿＿＿＿ ＿＿＿＿＿＿＿
　 虛(虚) [　] ＿＿＿＿＿＿＿ ＿＿＿＿＿＿＿

2. 賀(贺) [　] ＿＿＿＿＿＿＿ ＿＿＿＿＿＿＿
　 資(资) [　] ＿＿＿＿＿＿＿ ＿＿＿＿＿＿＿

3. 謙(谦) [　] ＿＿＿＿＿＿＿ ＿＿＿＿＿＿＿
　 講(讲) [　] ＿＿＿＿＿＿＿ ＿＿＿＿＿＿＿

4. 遇(遇) [　] ＿＿＿＿＿＿＿ ＿＿＿＿＿＿＿
　 道(道) [　] ＿＿＿＿＿＿＿ ＿＿＿＿＿＿＿

19-6 Each of the following pairs of characters is a homophone. Work in groups and write the Pinyin for each character, with tones, compose a phrase with each character, and then explain the phrase in English.

Example: [xiū] 修(修): 修改(修改) to revise
　　　　　　　 休(休): 退休(退休) to retire

1. [　] 歷(历): ＿＿＿＿＿＿＿ ＿＿＿＿＿＿＿
　　　 屬(厉): ＿＿＿＿＿＿＿ ＿＿＿＿＿＿＿

2. [　] 境(境): ＿＿＿＿＿＿＿ ＿＿＿＿＿＿＿
　　　 競(竞): ＿＿＿＿＿＿＿ ＿＿＿＿＿＿＿

III. Grammar Exercises

19-7 You are discussing future job opportunities with your roommate. He/she has certain standards for the jobs he/she wants to apply for in the future. You agree with some of them but disagree with others. Now work with your partner and do the following.

Express your agreement or disagreement with the following statements he/she has made and also include your reasons. Remember, you must use 固然, 倒, 卻(却), or 到底 where appropriate in your responses.

1. 我想申請去一家大公司工作。
   我想申请去一家大公司工作。

   Your response: _____

2. 我覺得做開發軟件的工作很有意思。
   我觉得做开发软件的工作很有意思。

   Your response: _____

3. 最好經常有出差的機會。
   最好经常有出差的机会。

   Your response: _____

4. 同事之間的關係要融洽。
   同事之间的关系要融洽。

   Your response: _____

5. 工資一定要高。
   工资一定要高。

   Your response: _____

6. 福利待遇是最重要的。
   福利待遇是最重要的。

   Your response: _____

IV. Media Literacy

The short text below, written in the style of newspapers, magazines, or Internet news articles, will help you become familiar with the formal written expressions used in these genres.

講述你職場中的故事 (讲述你职场中的故事)
Narrating the Story of What You Encountered on the Job Market

繁體字：

講述你職場中的故事

在求職、工作時，你遇到過什麼煩惱嗎？請講述你職場中的故事，讓人力資源專家幫你解開心裡的困惑吧。

简体字：

讲述你职场中的故事

在求职、工作时，你遇到过什么烦恼吗？请讲述你职场中的故事，让人力资源专家帮你解开心里的困惑吧。

Notes:
講述(讲述) [jiǎngshù]: to narrate
職場(职场) [zhíchǎng]: job market
故事(故事) [gùshi]: story
煩惱(烦恼) [fánnǎo]: worry
人力資源(人力资源) [rénlì zīyuán]: human resources
專家(专家) [zhuānjiā]: expert, specialist
解開(解开) [jiěkāi]: to untie
困惑(困惑) [kùnhuò]: confusion, perplexity

Exercises for the article: work with a partner or a group to ask and answer the following questions.

1. What are the problems that people might encounter at work?

2. What does this article suggest that you do?

3. Can you find any written expressions? What are their spoken counterparts (e.g., 講述(讲述); 是否)?

V. Communicative Activities

19-8 You have heard about 新民's two job offers. Now work in pairs to discuss what suggestions you might make to him. Include the following vocabulary and grammar points from the lesson.

考慮，競爭，金融，穩定，起薪，股份，福利，待遇，
考虑，竞争，金融，稳定，起薪，股份，福利，待遇，

環境，關係，道理
环境，关系，道理

倒，卻，到底　　固然　　非……不可
倒，却，到底　　固然　　非……不可

19-9 Most of the students in your class are graduating soon. Some have received job offers and some are still searching for jobs. There are still others who are considering doing an internship. You are now having a discussion about job searches. You have also invited some students who have graduated and started to work at various places. Form small groups to carry on a discussion. The following is the list of tasks for each role.

1. Someone who has already worked at a consulting company for a year. Provide your work experience and thoughts on what are the most important features of the job.

2. Someone who has just received two job offers and is making decisions.
   Try to solicit information to help you make the decision.

3. Someone who is still searching for a job.
   Try to find out as much as you can about the job market.

4. Someone who is not graduating for two more years, but is considering doing an internship now.
   Try to find out what preparations are needed for your application.

文化知識 (文化知识) Culture Link

文化點滴 (文化点滴) CULTURE NOTES

中國的外資企業 (中国的外资企业) Foreign Businesses in China

China's economy has been developing rapidly since 1980, when the first 中外合資 (中外合资) [Zhōng wài hé zī] (Sino-foreign joint venture) company was established. Since then, the Chinese government has made it a policy to attract and use foreign capital. Sino-foreign joint ventures have expanded to cover almost all the basic industries and export-oriented enterprises, and provide numerous job opportunities for Chinese citizens. Indeed, employment with a foreign firm is coveted.

Numerous research and development centers have been set up by international consortia and transnational companies to bring about further development in the fields of communications, computer science, electronics, automobiles, and pharmaceuticals. China now ranks second worldwide in the use of 外資 (外资) [wàizī] (foreign capital), behind only the United States. Foreign investments have become an important source of capital for China's economic construction and development.

Foreign capital used directly by China totaled US$393.5 billion in the two decades

Do you know...

- how China has used foreign investment to develop its economy?
- how the Chinese government has attracted foreign investors?
- where most of the foreign-investment enterprises are located in China?

Read and find out!

since the mid-1980s, and after China's entry into the World Trade Organization in 2001, foreign investment increased even further. In order to continue to attract this high level of foreign investment, China has made great efforts to strengthen its infrastructure and create a suitable environment. More than 500 foreign-related economic laws and regulations have been revised and promulgated to provide a strong legal framework and adequate guarantees for foreign businesses. By the end of 2001, more than 170 countries and regions had invested in 390,000 foreign-investment enterprises in China. Of the 500 top transnational companies in the world, over 400 have invested in China. Most of these ventures are located in the coastal cities, but some have started to move to inland areas.

China's improvements in its trade and investment environment, made by boosting the confidence of foreign investors and attracting foreign businesses, have opened up new job opportunities for Chinese citizens and further enhanced the long-term development of China's economy.

Are there any foreign companies in your country? Name a few.

How do people in your country view the opportunity to work for a foreign company?

問題討論 (问题讨论) *Discuss the following with a partner or in small groups.*

1. 你知道中國有哪些外資企業嗎？請說出幾個。
   你知道中国有哪些外资企业吗？请说出几个。

   Do you know of any foreign businesses in China? Provide some examples.

2. 下面這些美國公司在中國都有企業，請說出它們的中文名字：
   下面这些美国公司在中国都有企业，请说出它们的中文名字：

   Below are some American companies that do business in China. Please provide their Chinese names.

Chase Manhattan	Citibank	Dell
Ford Motor Company	General Electric	General Motors
McDonald's (Fast Food)	Kentucky Fried Chicken	Microsoft
Morgan Stanley	Motorola	Whirlpool

趣味中文 (趣味中文) FUN WITH CHINESE

百尺竿頭，更進一步。
百尺竿头，更进一步。

To make further progress even if you've come a long way.

bǎi	chǐ	gān	tóu	gèng	jìn	yí	bù
百	尺	竿	頭	更	進	一	步
百	尺	竿	头	更	进	一	步
one hundred	foot	pole	head	further	advance	one	step

問題討論 (问题讨论) *Discuss the following with a partner or in small groups.*

1. This is a proverb that encourages people to make more progress. Can you find a similar expression in your own language?
2. Can you think of an occasion when you might need to use this proverb? Use it to make a sentence.

行動吧! (行动吧!) LET'S GO!

銀行廣告 (银行广告) Bank Advertisement

文華(文华) has found a job in a bank in China. He needs to know more about the services the bank provides. Take a look at this poster inside a Chinese bank and see whether you can answer the following questions with the help of the picture.

Notes:
理財(理财) [lǐcái]: to manage finance
金(金) [jīn]: gold, golden
享受(享受) [xiǎngshòu]: to enjoy
貴賓(贵宾) [guìbīn]: a distinguished guest
級(级) [jí]: rank, level
儲蓄(储蓄) [chǔxù]: deposit
集......為一體(集......为一体)
   [jí . . . wéi yìtǐ]: to put altogether
定期(定期) [dìngqī]: fixed term
   (certificate of deposit)
活期(活期) [huóqī]: current (e.g.,
   a savings account)
結算(结算) [jiésuàn]: to settle accounts
投資(投资) [tóuzī]: to invest
功能(功能) [gōngnéng]: function
齊全(齐全) [qíquán]: all available,
   complete
優先(优先) [yōuxiān]: priority
優惠(优惠) [yōuhuì]: preferential (service)

問題討論 (问题讨论) *Discuss the following with a partner or in small groups.*

1. What is the ad about?
2. Who is eligible to become a member of this club?
3. What special benefits are available to the members?
4. What services does this bank provide?
5. What bank is this?

20

畢業以後–復習
(毕业以后–复习)
After Graduation – Review

University graduates in China, who will face challenges finding jobs.

教學目標 (教学目标) OBJECTIVES

- Ask for advice
- Talk about the future
- Review conjunctions
- Review prepositions

CONNECTIONS AND COMMUNITIES PREVIEW

Discuss the following questions with a partner or your class. What similarities and differences do you think there might be between Chinese culture and your own culture?

1. Do many students in your country choose to go to graduate school after college?

2. What do you plan to do after you graduate from college, find a job or apply to graduate school? Why?

生詞 (生词) VOCABULARY

核心詞 (核心词) Core Vocabulary

	TRADITIONAL	SIMPLIFIED	PINYIN		
1.	與其⋯⋯ 不如⋯⋯	与其⋯⋯ 不如⋯⋯	yǔqí . . . bùrú	Conj.	rather than
2.	等待	等待	děngdài	V.	to wait
3.	跟⋯⋯有關	跟⋯⋯有关	gēn . . . yǒuguān		to be related to . . . , connected with . . .
4.	更別說	更别说	gèngbiéshuō		not to mention
5.	理想	理想	lǐxiǎng	N.	ideal
6.	緊張	紧张	jǐnzhāng	Adj.	nervous
7.	當時	当时	dāngshí	Adv.	then, at that time
8.	即使	即使	jíshǐ	Conj.	even if
9.	興奮	兴奋	xīngfèn	Adj.	excited
10.	既然	既然	jìrán	Conj.	now that
11.	挑選	挑选	tiāoxuǎn	V.	to choose
12.	體會	体会	tǐhuì	V. N.	to reflect upon reflections, things one has realized/learned
13.	想法	想法	xiǎngfǎ	N.	idea, thought
14.	參謀	参谋	cānmóu	V. N.	to give advice military advisor

	TRADITIONAL	SIMPLIFIED	PINYIN		
15.	以免	以免	yǐmiǎn	Conj.	lest, so that . . . not
16.	回想	回想	huíxiǎng	V.	to reflect on, recall
17.	收穫	收获	shōuhuò	N.	harvest, achievement
18.	今後	今后	jīnhòu	N.	from now on; in the future
19.	奮鬥	奋斗	fèndòu	V.	to fight for
20.	目標	目标	mùbiāo	N.	goal
21.	攻讀	攻读	gōngdú	V.	to pursue the study of

專名 (专名) Proper Nouns

	TRADITIONAL	SIMPLIFIED	PINYIN		
1.	健生	健生	Jiànshēng	N.	(given name) Jiansheng
2.	新民	新民	Xīnmín	N.	(given name) Xinmin

語文知識 (语文知识) LANGUAGE LINK

Read and listen to the following sentence patterns. These patterns use vocabulary, expressions, and grammar that you will study in more detail in this lesson. After reading the sentence patterns, read and listen to the Language in Use section that follows.

句型 (句型) Sentence Patterns

與其在家等待，不如申請
与其在家等待，不如申请
Yǔqí zài jiā děngdài, bùrú shēnqǐng

研究生院，再學習兩年。
研究生院，再学习两年。
yánjiūshēng yuàn, zài xuéxí liǎngnián.

現在要找一份工作很不容易，
现在要找一份工作很不容易，
Xiànzài yào zhǎo yífèn gōngzuò hěn bù róngyì,

更別說找一份理想的工作了。
更别说找一份理想的工作了。
gèng bié shuō zhǎo yífèn lǐxiǎng de gōngzuò le.

即使工資低一點兒，我也覺得很幸運了。
即使工资低一点儿，我也觉得很幸运了。
Jíshǐ gōngzī dī yìdiǎr, wǒ yě juéde hěn xìngyùn le.

既然三家公司都要我，我當然得
既然三家公司都要我，我当然得
Jìrán sānjiā gōngsī dōu yào wǒ, wǒ dāngrán děi

好好地挑選一下了。
好好地挑选一下了。
hǎohǎode tiāoxuǎn yíxià le.

我希望你能給我當當參謀，
我希望你能给我当当参谋，
Wǒ xīwàng nǐ néng gěi wǒ dāngdang cānmóu,

以免我說錯話。
以免我说错话。
yǐmiǎn wǒ shuō cuò huà.

課文 Language in Use: Which Job Offer Should I Accept?
(繁體字 Traditional Character Version)

健生：

你好！好久沒有跟你聯絡了。怎麼樣？好嗎？

我今年就要畢業了，一直在找工作，所以最近特別忙。我希望找一家既跟我的專業有關，又能提供好的福利待遇的公司。現在的經濟還沒有完全恢復，要找一份工作很不容易，更別說[1]是找到一份理想的工作了，所以我很緊張。我還準備如果找不到工作，與其在家等待，不如申請研究生院，再學習兩年，拿一個碩士學位，為以後在就業市場上競爭做準備。

1. 更別說(更别说)
更別說(更别说): "not to mention." An idiomatic expression used in spoken Chinese to emphasize that what follows is even less possible. The word "更(更)" can be omitted.

前些日子，我去一些公司參加面試，已經去了五家公司了。當時我想，只要其中一家要我，即使工資低一點，那我也很幸運了。想不到有三家公司接受了我，而且都是不錯的公司，這讓我興奮極了。

我還沒決定究竟去哪家公司。本來我想，不管是哪家公司要我，我都會去。現在既然有三家公司都要我，我當然得好好地挑選一下。

因為你工作了一年了，已經有一些經驗，所以我很想聽聽你的想法。我想知道，當我在跟公司談條件的時候，有哪些問題是我非提不可的。希望你能給我當當參謀[2]，以免我說錯話。

2. 當參謀(当参谋)
參謀(参谋) is a military term meaning "advisor." The meaning is borrowed here for use in everyday life to mean "to give advice."

四年的大學生活就要結束了，回想這四年的大學生活，覺得很有收穫。不但學了不少知識，而且也讓自己更了解今後的奮鬥目標。還有，我想先工作幾年，然後再回學校攻讀研究生院，多學一些東西。你呢？你不也是這麼想的嗎？

好了，不多寫了。祝

工作愉快

友　新民

四月二十五日

课文 Language in Use: Which Job Offer Should I Accept?
(简体字 Simplified Character Version)

健生：

你好！好久没有跟你联络了。怎么样？好吗？

我今年就要毕业了，一直在找工作，所以最近特别忙。我希望找一家既跟我的专业有关，又能提供好的福利待遇的公司。现在的经济还没有完全恢复，要找一份工作很不容易，更别说¹是找到一份理想的工作了，所以我很紧张。我还准备如果找不到工作，与其在家等待，不如申请研究生院，再学习两年，拿一个硕士学位，为以后在就业市场上竞争做准备。

前些日子，我去一些公司参加面试，已经去了五家公司了。当时我想，只要其中一家要我，即使工资低一点，那我也很幸运了。想不到有三家公司接受了我，而且都是不错的公司，这让我兴奋极了。

我还没决定究竟去哪家公司。本来我想，不管是哪家公司要我，我都会去。现在既然有三家公司都要我，我当然得好好地挑选一下。

因为你工作了一年了，已经有一些经验，所以我很想听听你的想法。我想知道，当我在跟公司谈条件的时候，有哪些问题是我非提不可的。希望你能给我当当参谋²，以免我说错话。

四年的大学生活就要结束了，回想这四年的大学生活，觉得很有收获。不但学了不少知识，而且也让自己更了解今后的奋斗目标。还有，我想先工作几年，然后再回学校攻读研究生院，多学一些东西。你呢？你不也是这么想的吗？

好了，不多写了。祝

工作愉快

友　新民

四月二十五日

語法 (语法) GRAMMAR

I. Review: Conjunctions (3) 與其......不如 (与其......不如), 即使......也......, 既然......就......, ..., 以免......

In Lessons 15 and 18, we summarized quite a few conjunctions. Here are some more.

Conjunctions	Features	Examples
1. 與其...... (倒)不如...... 与其...... (倒)不如...... rather than . . . , (I would prefer that) . . .	Used to connect two clauses to indicate preference. What follows 不如(不如) is usually the preferred option.	與其明天還要回來做，不如今天把它做完，(明天就可以休息了)。 与其明天还要回来做，不如今天把它做完，(明天就可以休息了)。 Rather than coming back to do it tomorrow, I would prefer to finish it today (so that we will be able to rest tomorrow).
2. 即使......也...... 即使......也...... even if/though . . . , . . . still	Used to connect two clauses to indicate supposition. What follows 即使(即使) indicates the supposition.	即使今天做不完，我也要做。 即使今天做不完，我也要做。 Even if I cannot finish it today, I will still do it. 即使中文再難，我也要學。 即使中文再难，我也要学。 Even if Chinese were harder (than this), I would still study it.
3. 既然......，就...... 既然......，就...... since . . . , then . . .	Used to connect two clauses to indicate a cause-and-effect relationship. What follows 既然(既然) is the cause/reason while the result comes after 就(就).	既然你喜歡出差，那就選那家咨詢公司吧。 既然你喜欢出差，那就选那家咨询公司吧。 Since you like to travel on business, then you'd better select that consulting company.

Conjunctions	Features	Examples
4. ......, 以免...... ......, 以免...... . . . lest . . . ; so that . . . not . . .	Used to connect two clauses to indicate a result that someone is trying to avoid.	請給我一些建議，<u>以免</u>我說錯話。 请给我一些建议，<u>以免</u>我说错话。 Please give me some suggestions so that I will not say anything wrong. 我昨天就把光碟放在包裡，<u>以免</u>今天忘記還給他。 我昨天就把光碟放在包里，<u>以免</u>今天忘记还给他。 I put the disk in my backpack yesterday so that I will not forget to return it to him today.

»Try it! With a partner, practice questions and answers using the conjunctions listed above. For example,

A: 你想去那個電腦公司嗎？
你想去那个电脑公司吗？

B: 那個電腦公司工作環境不太好，與其去那兒，不如去別的公司。
那个电脑公司工作环境不太好，与其去那儿，不如去别的公司。

II. Review: Prepositions 對 (对), 為 (为) and 給 (给)

In addition to other functions we have learned, these three words are also used as prepositions.

Prepositions	Features	Examples
1. 對(對於) 对(对于) for/to/toward regarding	Used to indicate the object.	他一直對我很關心。 他一直对我很关心。 He has been showing a lot of concern for me. 她對我說：“我們下星期就給你打電話。” 她对我说：“我们下星期就给你打电话。” She said to me: "We will call you next week." 對這件事，她沒有興趣。 对这件事，她没有兴趣。 Regarding this, she has no interest.
2. 為(为) for	Used to introduce the object.	他找到工作了，我們都為他高興。 他找到工作了，我们都为他高兴。 He's found a job. We are all happy for him. 我生病了，媽媽特別為我擔心。 我生病了，妈妈特别为我担心。 I've fallen ill and Mom is very worried about me.
3. 給(给) for/to (toward)/by	Used to introduce the object.	請給我修改一下簡歷。 请给我修改一下简历。 Please revise the résumé for me.
	Used in a passive sense sentence.	他把網址給我發過來了。 他把网址给我发过来了。 He sent the URL to me. 磁帶讓我給拉壞了。 磁带让我给拉坏了。 The tape was pulled apart by me.

>>Try it! With a partner, devise a short dialogue using the prepositions 對 (对), 為 (为) and 給 (给). For example,

A: 謝謝你們對我的關心和幫助，我已經找到工作了。
謝谢你们对我的关心和帮助，我已经找到工作了。

B: 你能這麼快地找到工作，我們都為你高興。
你能这么快地找到工作，我们都为你高兴。

補充課文 (补充课文) SUPPLEMENTARY PRACTICE

Read the following passage. Then listen and repeat.

An Alumni Workshop (繁體字 Traditional Character Version)

同學們，大家好！

我是去年從這所學校畢業的，現在已經工作了一年了。今天能回到母校，跟大家談談自己的工作體會，感到非常高興。

你們都問我當學生與去工作有什麼不同。既然你們問我，我就告訴你們實話：讀書跟工作真的很不一樣。在學校的時候，總是覺得太忙，功課太多，沒有時間睡覺。有時候真希望趕快畢業，離開學校，早點兒工作，以為工作會輕鬆得多。可是當自己真的離開了學校，才感到學生時代的生活是最快樂、最值得珍惜的。即使那些不眠之夜，也是值得留戀的。

工作了以後，我深深地感到，大學四年的學習對自己幫助很大。我不但學到了很多專業知識，而且懂得了怎麼生活。即使還有很多事我可能還不懂，但是大學的生活讓我知道了我今後的奮鬥目標。我很感謝學校和教授們對我的幫助。

希望你們珍惜在學校裡的時間，好好學習，為今後的生活和工作打一個很好的基礎。

謝謝大家。

Notes:

所(所) [suǒ]: (measure word for schools or institutions)
母校(母校) [mǔxiào]: school you graduated from, alma mater
感到(感到) [gǎndào]: to feel
與(与) [yǔ]: (written expression) and; with
實話(实话) [shíhuà]: honest words
以為(以为) [yǐwéi]: to understand as
時代(时代) [shídài]: times
珍惜(珍惜) [zhēnxī]: to treasure, cherish
不眠之夜(不眠之夜) [bùmiánzhīyè]: sleepless night
留戀(留恋) [liúliàn]: to be reluctant to leave
深深地(深深地) [shēnshēnde]: deeply
懂得(懂得) [dǒngde]: to understand
基礎(基础) [jīchǔ]: basis; foundation

補充課文 (补充课文) SUPPLEMENTARY PRACTICE

Read the following passage. Then listen and repeat.

An Alumni Workshop (简体字 Simplified Character Version)

同学们，大家好！

　　我是去年从这所学校毕业的，现在已经工作了一年了。今天能回到母校，跟大家谈谈自己的工作体会，感到非常高兴。

　　你们都问我当学生与去工作有什么不同。既然你们问我，我就告诉你们实话：读书跟工作真的很不一样。在学校的时候，总是觉得太忙，功课太多，没有时间睡觉。有时候真希望赶快毕业，离开学校，早点儿工作，以为工作会轻松得多。可是当自己真的离开了学校，才感到学生时代的生活是最快乐、最值得珍惜的。即使那些不眠之夜，也是值得留恋的。

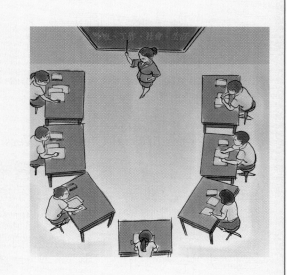

　　工作了以后，我深深地感到，大学四年的学习对自己帮助很大。我不但学到了很多专业知识，而且懂得了怎么生活。即使还有很多事我可能还不懂，但是大学的生活让我知道了我今后的奋斗目标。我很感谢学校和教授们对我的帮助。

　　希望你们珍惜在学校里的时间，好好学习，为今后的生活和工作打一个很好的基础。

　　谢谢大家。

Exercises: work with a partner or in small groups

1. 有哪些這一課的生詞和語法出現在這個演講上? 請把它們找出來。
   有哪些这一课的生词和语法出现在这个演讲上? 请把它们找出来。

2. 她說當學生跟工作有什麼不同?
   她说当学生跟工作有什么不同?

3. 她說大學四年的學習對她的工作有什麼幫助?
   她说大学四年的学习对她的工作有什么帮助?

成語故事（成语故事）IDIOM STORY

班門弄斧（班门弄斧）[bānmén nòng fǔ]

Meaning: To show off one's carpentry skills in front of Lu Ban (a master carpenter).

Usage: To display one's limited skill before an expert.

Example: 您是這方面的專家，經驗豐富，我怎麼敢在您面前 "班門弄斧" 呢？

您是这方面的专家，经验丰富，我怎么敢在您面前 "班门弄斧" 呢？

Pay special attention to conjunctions 即使……也……, 以免 and prepositions 對(对), 給(给), 為(为).

(繁體字 Traditional Character Version)

　　兩千五百年以前，中國有一個非常有名的木匠，他的名字叫魯班 [Lǔ Bān]。魯班是一個能工巧匠，即使是最沒有用的木頭，他也能做出非常漂亮的東西。人們對他非常尊敬，稱他為木匠的祖師。

　　一千二百多年前的唐朝，中國出了一個大詩人李白。李白是中國最有名的詩人之一。他死了以後，人們把他葬在長江邊。那兒風景非常美麗，人們都喜歡去那兒遊玩。除了看看那兒的風景以外，人們也去李白的墓地看看，其中有一些人還喜歡在李白的墓前寫幾句詩來紀念他。

　　後來有一個詩人到那兒玩，看到李白的墓前寫著很多詩，但是他發現那些詩都寫得不太好，就寫了幾句話，諷刺他們。他覺得，在大詩人李白的墓前寫詩就像是在魯班的門前玩斧一樣，不但太自不量力，而且也是對大師們的不敬。

　　從此以後，人們就不敢在李白的墓前隨便寫詩了，以免被人說是 "班門弄斧"。

(简体字 **Simplified Character Version**)

　　两千五百年以前，中国有一个非常有名的木匠，他的名字叫鲁班 [Lǔ Bān]。鲁班是一个能工巧匠，即使是最没有用的木头，他也能做出非常漂亮的东西。人们对他非常尊敬，称他为木匠的祖师。

　　一千二百多年前的唐朝，中国出了一个大诗人李白。李白是中国最有名的诗人之一。他死了以后，人们把他葬在长江边。那儿风景非常美丽，人们都喜欢去那儿游玩。除了看看那儿的风景以外，人们也去李白的墓地看看，其中有一些人还喜欢在李白的墓前写几句诗来纪念他。

　　后来有一个诗人到那儿玩，看到李白的墓前写着很多诗，但是他发现那些诗都写得不太好，就写了几句话，讽刺他们。他觉得，在大诗人李白的墓前写诗就像是在鲁班的门前玩斧一样，不但太自不量力，而且也是对大师们的不敬。

　　从此以后，人们就不敢在李白的墓前随便写诗了，以免被人说是 "班门弄斧"。

Notes:
弄(弄) [nòng]: to play with
斧(斧) [fǔ]: axe (a tool used by a carpenter)
木匠(木匠) [mùjiàng]: carpenter
能工巧匠(能工巧匠) [nénggōngqiǎojiàng]: a very skillful craftsman
木頭(木头) [mùtou]: wood
漂亮(漂亮) [piàoliang]: beautiful
尊敬(尊敬) [zūnjìng]: to respect
稱(称) [chēng]: to call
祖師(祖师) [zǔshī]: founding master
唐朝(唐朝) [Táng Cháo]: Tang Dynasty (618–907 A.D.)
詩人(诗人) [shīrén]: poet
葬(葬) [zàng]: to bury
長江(长江) [Chángjiāng]: the Yangtze River
墓地(墓地) [mùdì]: graveyard
句(句) [jù]: a sentence. 句 here is used as a measure word for poems.
紀念(纪念) [jìniàn]: to cherish the memory of
諷刺(讽刺) [fěngcì]: to mock
自不量力(自不量力) [zìbúliànglì]: to overrate one's own ability
對……不敬(对……不敬) [duì . . . bújìng]: not respectful toward . . .
從此以後(从此以后) [cóngcǐ yǐhòu]: from now on
敢(敢) [gǎn]: to dare
隨便(随便) [suíbiàn]: at will

Exercises: work with a partner or in small groups

1. 魯班和李白有什麼相同的地方?
   鲁班和李白有什么相同的地方?

2. 當那個詩人看見李白墓前的詩的時候,他是怎麼想的?
   当那个诗人看见李白墓前的诗的时候,他是怎么想的?

3. 這個故事告訴了我們什麼? 請用"班門弄斧"造一個句子。
   这个故事告诉了我们什么? 请用"班门弄斧"造一个句子。

練習 (练习) ACTIVITIES

I. Listening Exercises

 20-1 小業(小业) is graduating in a month and has already received a job offer. He is very grateful to his professors and university. At a meeting for graduating students, he expresses his gratitude. Listen to what he says, and answer the questions below. Then check your answers with your partner.

Notes:
知識(知识) [zhīshi]: knowledge
其次(其次) [qícì]: secondly
另外(另外) [lìngwài]: besides; moreover
社會(社会) [shèhuì]: society; community
付出(付出) [fùchū]: devotion
報答(报答) [bàodá]: to repay, pay back
貢獻(贡献) [gòngxiàn]: to contribute to; contribution

問題(问题):

1. 小業什麼時候畢業?
   小业什么时候毕业?

2. 小業首先想感謝誰? 為什麼?
   小业首先想感谢谁? 为什么?

3. 小業以後會記得誰?
   小业以后会记得谁?

4. 除了感謝老師以外，他還想感謝誰？為什麼？
   除了感谢老师以外，他还想感谢谁？为什么？

5. 小業覺得學校裡的活動怎麼樣？
   小业觉得学校里的活动怎么样？

6. 小業和同學們相處得怎麼樣？
   小业和同学们相处得怎么样？

7. 小業最想感謝的是誰？為什麼？
   小业最想感谢的是谁？为什么？

8. 小業畢業以後會做什麼？
   小业毕业以后会做什么？

Based on what you have heard, work with a partner and retell what 小業(小业) said in your own words.

II. Character Exercises

20-2 Work with a partner. Read the following words, phrases, and sentences.

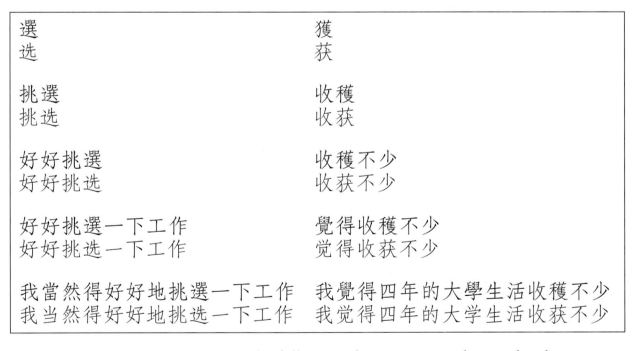

選	獲
选	获
挑選	收穫
挑选	收获
好好挑選	收穫不少
好好挑选	收获不少
好好挑選一下工作	覺得收穫不少
好好挑选一下工作	觉得收获不少
我當然得好好地挑選一下工作	我覺得四年的大學生活收穫不少
我当然得好好地挑选一下工作	我觉得四年的大学生活收获不少

Now with your partner, try to use the following characters to make words, phrases, and then sentences.

1. 免   2. 標   3. 奮   4. 攻   5. 與   6. 挑   7. 鬥   8. 謀
   免   标   奋   攻   与   挑   斗   谋

20-3 Read aloud the following words. Write them out using traditional characters. Then check your answers with a partner.

1. 联络 _____   2. 紧张 _____   3. 兴奋 _____

4. 体会 _____   5. 收获 _____   6. 目标 _____

7. 挑选 _____

20-4 Each of the following pairs of characters is a homophone. Work with your partner to write the Pinyin, with tones, for each character and make a phrase using each character.

Example: [lián] 聯：聯絡

　　　　　　联：联络

　　　　　　連：公司的福利真不錯，連出差都有補貼。

　　　　　　连：公司的福利真不错，连出差都有补贴。

1. [　　] 功：_____

　　　　功：_____

　　　　攻：_____

　　　　攻：_____

　　　　公：_____

　　　　公：_____

2. [　　] 封：_____

　　　　封：_____

　　　　風：_____

　　　　风：_____

3. [　　] 濟：_____

　　　　济：_____

　　　　技：_____

　　　　技：_____

　　　　計：_____

　　　　计：_____

　　　　記：_____

　　　　记：_____

　　　　績：_____

　　　　绩：_____

20-5 The following characters look similar, but have different pronunciations and meanings. Work in groups to write out the Pinyin, with tones, and make a phrase using each character.

Example:　使 [shǐ] 找工作不容易使我很緊張。
　　　　　使 [shǐ] 找工作不容易使我很紧张。

　　　　　便 [biàn] 這兒坐車去學校很方便。
　　　　　便 [biàn] 这儿坐车去学校很方便。

1. 既 [　] _____
   既 [　] _____
   即 [　] _____
   即 [　] _____

2. 選 [　] _____
   选 [　] _____
   造 [　] _____
   造 [　] _____

3. 驗 [　] _____
   验 [　] _____
   險 [　] _____
   险 [　] _____

4. 鬥 [　] _____
   斗 [　] _____
   門 [　] _____
   门 [　] _____

5. 獲 [　] _____
   获 [　] _____
   薦 [　] _____
   荐 [　] _____

III. Grammar Exercises

20-6 Work with your partner. Read aloud the following conjunctions. Select an appropriate one to complete the following sentences.

既然……就……，　與其……不如……，　即使……也……，　……，以免

既然……就……，　与其……不如……，　即使……也……，　……，以免

1. 這個公司的人都很好，_____ 年薪不太高，我 _____ 想去。

   这个公司的人都很好，_____ 年薪不太高，我 _____ 想去。

2. 現在就業市場不景氣，_____ 等工作，_____ 先去讀研究生院。

   现在就业市场不景气，_____ 等工作，_____ 先去读研究生院。

3. 我們再過幾個月就要放假了，我們得早點申請實習，_____ 機會都沒有了。

   我们再过几个月就要放假了，我们得早点申请实习，_____ 机会都没有了。

4. 我們就要離開學校了，_____ 我們學了不少的知識，_____ 應該好好地工作。

   我们就要离开学校了，_____ 我们学了不少的知识，_____ 应该好好地工作。

20-7 Form groups to read aloud the following sentences and select an appropriate preposition for each blank.

Prepositions: 對(对), 為(为), 給(给)

1. 四年的大學生活 _____ 我的幫助非常大，畢業以後我也要 _____ 學校做一些事。

   四年的大学生活 _____ 我的帮助非常大，毕业以后我也要 _____ 学校做一些事。

2. 請你 ＿＿＿ 我找幾個招聘網站，因為現在信息 ＿＿＿ 我來說是最重要的。

請你 ＿＿＿ 我找几个招聘网站，因为现在信息 ＿＿＿ 我来说是最重要的。

3. 學校 ＿＿＿ 我們提供了一流的設備，＿＿＿ 我們的學習幫助很大。

學校 ＿＿＿ 我们提供了一流的设备，＿＿＿ 我们的学习帮助很大。

4. 這些年來，爸爸媽媽 ＿＿＿ 我做了很多，我一定要努力學習。

这些年来，爸爸妈妈 ＿＿＿ 我做了很多，我一定要努力学习。

5. 我的好朋友 ＿＿＿ 我提了很多好的建議，＿＿＿ 我找工作很有幫助。

我的好朋友 ＿＿＿ 我提了很多好的建议，＿＿＿ 我找工作很有帮助。

IV. Media Literacy

The short text below, written in the style of newspapers, magazines, or Internet news articles, will help you become familiar with the formal written expressions used in these genres.

高校護理專業受到男生青睞 (高校护理专业受到男生青睐)
Nursing Major Favored by Male Students

繁體字：

高校護理專業受到男生青睞

今年的大學招生中出現一個少見的現象：一些男生踴躍填報護理專業。大學招生就業處負責人認為，主要原因是：世界上許多國家尤其在歐美國家男護士很受歡迎，男護士的就業前景看好。

简体字：

高校护理专业受到男生青睐

今年的大学招生中出现一个少见的现象：一些男生踊跃填报护理专业。大学招生就业处负责人认为，主要原因是：世界上许多国家尤其在欧美国家男护士很受欢迎，男护士的就业前景看好。

Notes:

高校(高校) [gāoxiào]: university, college
護理(护理) [hùlǐ]: to nurse
青睞(青睐) [qīnglài]: to be in favor of
招生(招生) [zhāoshēng]: to recruit students
現象(现象) [xiànxiàng]: phenomenon
踴躍(踊跃) [yǒngyuè]: actively
填報(填报) [tiánbào]: to apply
負責人(负责人) [fùzérén]: person in charge
認為(认为) [rènwéi]: to think
原因(原因) [yuányīn]: reason, cause
世界(世界) [shìjiè]: world
尤其(尤其) [yóuqí]: especially
歐美(欧美) [Ōuměi]: Europe and America
護士(护士) [hùshì]: a nurse
前景(前景) [qiánjǐng]: perspective
看好(看好) [kànhǎo]: promising

Exercises for the article: work with a partner or a group to ask and answer the following.

1. What is this story about?

2. Who is interested in this major?

3. Why is this major of interest to them?

4. Identify any expressions used solely in writing.

V. Communicative Activities

20-8 Form groups. Suppose you are having a meeting to discuss your thoughts about your studies and future career. Each of you takes one of the following roles and presents your thoughts to the group. You may use what you heard in the listening exercise as reference. Please use the following vocabulary and grammar points.

Vocabulary

就業(就业)，恢復(恢复)，景氣(景气)，競爭(竞争)，收穫(收获)，奮鬥(奋斗)，目標(目标)，當參謀(当参谋)，攻讀(攻读)

Grammar

Conjunctions:

與其......不如......(与其......不如......)
既然......就......(既然......就......)
即使......也......(即使......也......)
一面......一面......(一面......一面......)

Prepositions: 為(为), 對(对), 給(给)

Roles: 1. You are graduating in a month and have found a job.
2. You are graduating in a month but so far are still looking for a job.
3. You are a junior and in the process of deciding whether you want to look for a job or go to graduate school.

20-9 After each presentation, please ask each other questions. Your purpose is to elicit as much information as possible to get to know and learn from each other.

文化知識 (文化知识) Culture Link

文化點滴 (文化点滴) CULTURE NOTES

中國大學畢業生的就業情況 (中国大学毕业生的就业情况)
Employment of University Graduates in China

Before China began to implement reform policies in the early 1980s, university graduates were regarded as the "proud sons of Heaven." Upon graduation, every one of them was assigned to a job based on his/her performance at university. Since the early 1980s, however, when the Chinese government began to shift to a 市場經濟(市场经济) ([shìchǎng jīngjì]: market economy), job assignments were no longer a given for university graduates. And, with the rapid increase (over 20 percent annually since 1999) in university enrollment and Chinese students returning from overseas, millions of college and university graduates were joining the workforce every year, making it even more difficult to find jobs upon graduation. The current job shortage for university graduates makes for fierce competition in the 就業市場(就业市场) ([jiùyè shìchǎng]: job market).

This tight job market does not necessarily reflect a surplus of university graduates, however. Currently, college or university students account for only 7 percent of their age group and only 5 percent of the total population in China. This is much lower

> **Do you know...**
>
> - how university graduates were regarded before the 1980s?
> - why the job market in China is so competitive?
> - what kind of jobs Chinese students generally seek?
>
> **Read and find out!**

than the average level (18 to 20 percent) in developed nations. The employment dilemma for university graduates has more to do with job preferences relative to the imbalance of economic development in different areas of the country.

University graduates generally favor jobs at large 國營企業 (国营企业) ([guóyíng qǐyè]: state-owned enterprises), 外資公司(外资公司) ([wàizī gōngsī]: foreign-funded companies), or 政府機關 (政府机关) ([zhèngfǔ jīguān]: government organizations) in large metropolitan areas, such as Beijing, Shanghai, and Guangzhou. Such jobs offer a relatively high salary and good working conditions. These are the types of jobs for which there is strong competition. Although there is strong demand for college graduates in the western and central parts of China, these regions are not as economically advanced as the metropolitan areas, and therefore not as desirable.

Talented university graduates in certain fields, such as finance, computer science, business, and engineering are always in great demand. And in recent years, the need for a new group of professionals called 灰領(灰领) ([huīlǐng]: gray collar) workers has grown. This group includes occupations such as interior design, fashion design, and exhibition planning, and accounts for only 2 percent of the total workforce in China compared to 40 percent in developed countries.

More graduates have chosen to pursue graduate studies to enhance their competitiveness in the job market. The Chinese government has also taken measures to ease employment pressures encouraging government bureaux, state-owned enterprises, and private firms to hire university graduates, or to loan them money to start up their own businesses. Those who fail to find jobs within six months of graduation are eligible for free employment services. In addition, the government has a blueprint for the economic development of the central and western regions of China. Although these efforts will ease the employment pressures to some extent, the employment problem for university graduates in China will remain for the foreseeable future.

Students in China look for jobs or apply to graduate schools online. How about in your country?

Have you ever seen a job fair with this many people? Share your knowledge of job fairs.

問題討論 (问题讨论) *Discuss the following with a partner or in small groups.*

1. 你知道現在的大學生怎麼找工作嗎?
   你知道现在的大学生怎么找工作吗?

   Do you know how university graduates in China find jobs these days?

2. 以前，中國的大學生畢業以後不需要自己找工作，他們的工作是安排的、保證的。可是有時候他們不一定喜歡他們的工作。你覺得這樣好嗎? 你喜歡自己找工作還是接受安排的方式?

   以前，中国的大学生毕业以后不需要自己找工作，他们的工作是安排的、保证的。可是有时候他们不一定喜欢他们的工作。你觉得这样好吗? 你喜欢自己找工作还是接受安排的方式?

   In the past, university graduates in China did not need to find jobs on their own as jobs were assigned and guaranteed. Sometimes they did not like the jobs they were assigned to, however. What do you think? Which would you prefer—to find a job on your own or be assigned a job you don't like?

趣味中文 (趣味中文) FUN WITH CHINESE

吃得苦中苦，方為人上人。
吃得苦中苦，方为人上人。

Only after taking as much hardship as you can,
will you become successful in your career.

chī	de	kǔ	zhōng	kǔ	fāng	wéi	rén	shàng	rén
吃	得	苦	中	苦	方	為	人	上	人
吃	得	苦	中	苦	方	为	人	上	人
eat	(particle)	bitterness	inside	bitterness	can	to become	person	above	person

問題討論 (问题讨论) *Discuss the following with a partner or in small groups.*

1. This is a very popular Chinese saying. Parents use it to urge their children to study hard for their future. Do you have similar expressions in your language and culture to emphasize the value of education?

2. How do you view the importance of education in terms of your future career?

行動吧! (行动吧!) LET'S GO!

推薦信 (推荐信) Letter of Recommendation

In two months, 學中(学中) will graduate. He plans to pursue graduate studies. Please help him fill in this form he just downloaded from the Web.

报考攻读博士学位研究生专家推荐书						
考生姓名		性　别			年　龄	
专家姓名	职　称		工　作　单　位			职　务
推荐意见:						
推荐人 签名盖章			日　期			

Notes:

報考(报考) [bàokǎo]: to register to take the exam for
博士(博士) [bóshì]: doctoral degree
學位(学位) [xuéwèi]: academic degree
專家(专家) [zhuānjiā]: expert
考生(考生) [kǎoshēng]: examinee
職稱(职称) [zhíchēng]: academic title
職務(职务) [zhíwù]: work position/post
意見(意见) [yìjiàn]: comments
簽名(签名) [qiānmíng]: to sign, signature
蓋章(盖章) [gàizhāng]: to affix a seal

問題討論 (问题讨论) *Discuss the following with a partner or in small groups.*

1. Who should fill out this form?
2. Who is the form about?
3. What information is needed about the recommender?
4. On which areas should the recommender comment about the applicant?
5. Translate the following expressions into English:

推薦意見(推荐意见)

工作單位(工作单位)

簽名蓋章(签名盖章)

復習 (复习) Review

LESSON 19 TO LESSON 20

I. Conversation

You have just received two job offers. With a partner, make a phone call to your father to ask for his suggestions. Use at least 15 sentences. You must also include the following words, expressions, and major grammar points.

Notes:
景氣，競爭，厲害，非……不可，寧願，固然，待遇，起薪
景气，竞争，厉害，非……不可，宁愿，固然，待遇，起薪

福利，穩定，考慮，同事，融洽，環境，倒，卻，到底
福利，稳定，考虑，同事，融洽，环境，倒，却，到底

II. Speech

In a month you will graduate from university. When you look back at your four years at university, you feel you have much to say. Work in a small group to talk about your thoughts at this moment. Compose at least 15 sentences. Include the following in your talk.

Notes:
前景，更別說，老天爺，體會，回想，收穫，跟……有關，與其……不如，
前景，更别说，老天爷，体会，回想，收获，跟……有关，与其……不如，

即使……也……，既然……就……，以免……，既……又……
即使……也……，既然……就……，以免……，既……又……

III. Picture Description

Work in small groups and describe each of the following pictures. Please use the prepositions 對(对)，為(为)，and 給(给).

(1)　　　　　　(2)　　　　　　(3)　　　　　　(4)

IV. Traditional and Simplified Characters

Work with your partner to read each character aloud. Write its traditional form. Then make a phrase and a sentence using the character.

Example: 关 → 關 → 有關 → 這件事跟我的專業有關。

L19: 济 (　)　　竞 (　)　　云 (　)　　遇 (　)　　稳 (　)　　医 (　)
　　　补 (　)　　犹 (　)　　环 (　)　　轻 (　)

L20: 标 (　)　　获 (　)　　奋 (　)　　选 (　)　　阴 (　)

繁簡體字對照表 (繁简体字对照表)
TRADITIONAL/SIMPLIFIED CHARACTER TABLE

繁體字(繁体字)：[fán tǐ zì]　traditional character (or complex character)
簡體字(简体字)：[jiǎn tǐ zì]　simplified character

第十一課 (第十一课)　Lesson 11

| 繁： | 顧 | 厲 | 剛 | 況 | 護 | 診 | 腸 | 術 | 嚇 | 擔 | 順 | 養 | 結 |
| 简： | 顾 | 厉 | 刚 | 况 | 护 | 诊 | 肠 | 术 | 吓 | 担 | 顺 | 养 | 结 |

| 繁： | 緊 | 罵 | 頓 | 憐 |
| 简： | 紧 | 骂 | 顿 | 怜 |

第十二課 (第十二课)　Lesson 12

| 繁： | 亂 | 悶 | 檢 | 虧 | 設 | 煩 | 險 | 輔 | 補 | 楣 | 誼 |
| 简： | 乱 | 闷 | 检 | 亏 | 设 | 烦 | 险 | 辅 | 补 | 霉 | 谊 |

第十三課 (第十三课)　Lesson 13

| 繁： | 談 | 議 | 貨 | 專 | 禍 | 罰 | 遲 | 聲 | 諒 |
| 简： | 谈 | 议 | 货 | 专 | 祸 | 罚 | 迟 | 声 | 谅 |

第十四課 (第十四课)　Lesson 14

| 繁： | 撲 | 顯 | 瀝 | 溝 | 傷 | 淚 | 瞞 |
| 简： | 扑 | 显 | 沥 | 沟 | 伤 | 泪 | 瞒 |

第十五課 (第十五课)　Lesson 15

| 繁： | 聯 | 絡 | 卻 | 錄 | 絞 | 遍 | 購 |
| 简： | 联 | 络 | 却 | 录 | 绞 | 遍 | 购 |

第十六課 (第十六课)　Lesson 16

| 繁： | 級 | 噹 | 鈴 | 響 | 寶 | 齊 | 繼 | 續 | 讀 | 濟 | 碩 | 將 | 無 |
| 简： | 级 | 当 | 铃 | 响 | 宝 | 齐 | 继 | 续 | 读 | 济 | 硕 | 将 | 无 |

| 繁： | 獎 | 講 | 驗 | 擾 |
| 简： | 奖 | 讲 | 验 | 扰 |

第十七課 (第十七课) Lesson 17

| 繁： | 簡 | 複 | 雜 | 質 | 調 | 絕 | 細 | 薦 | 慮 | 聰 | 幹 | 願 |
| 简： | 简 | 复 | 杂 | 质 | 调 | 绝 | 细 | 荐 | 虑 | 聪 | 干 | 愿 |

第十八課 (第十八课) Lesson 18

| 繁： | 詢 | 軟 | 儘 | 績 | 組 | 織 | 項 | 論 |
| 简： | 询 | 软 | 尽 | 绩 | 组 | 织 | 项 | 论 |

第十九課 (第十九课) Lesson 19

| 繁： | 寧 | 競 | 爭 | 賀 | 謙 | 資 | 穩 | 萬 | 療 | 貼 | 猶 | 環 | 確 |
| 简： | 宁 | 竞 | 争 | 贺 | 谦 | 资 | 稳 | 万 | 疗 | 贴 | 犹 | 环 | 确 |

| 繁： | 賺 |
| 简： | 赚 |

第二十課 (第二十课) Lesson 20

| 繁： | 與 | 奮 | 選 | 謀 | 穫 | 鬥 | 標 |
| 简： | 与 | 奋 | 选 | 谋 | 获 | 斗 | 标 |

課文英文翻譯 (课文英文翻译)
ENGLISH TRANSLATIONS OF LANGUAGE IN USE

Lesson 11   My Unexpected Stay in Hospital

(Xiao Xie is hospitalized. His roommate Chang Tian is taking care of him. His classmate Mingxiu arrives.)

Mingxiu:	How are you? Are you feeling better?
Xiao Xie:	Much better. I'm fine. You are so busy but still found time to visit me. I feel bad (am so embarrassed) being such a bother to you.
Mingxiu:	Don't worry about it. As long as you are fine, that's what matters. What happened? Why are you in hospital?
Xiao Xie:	Oh! It was like this: a few days ago I had a stomach ache. I thought maybe it was something I ate and if I took some medicine I would be fine. So, I didn't pay attention to it. However, I still felt some pain every now and then. This went on for a couple of days. The morning of the day before yesterday it was so painful that I couldn't take it any more and was taken to the hospital.
Chang Tian:	Right! Zhongming and I just happened not to have class and were home. We saw that he was in severe pain and felt that things were not right, so we quickly called an ambulance to take him to the emergency room.
Xiao Xie:	The doctor said that it was acute appendicitis. He needed to operate immediately. As soon as I heard that I needed surgery I was scared to death. I was soon sent to the operating room.
Chang Tian:	Zhongming and I were waiting anxiously outside. However, it was not too bad. The operation went smoothly. When the operation was finished he was taken by a nurse to the ward to recuperate.
Mingxiu:	Oh (I see)! That's how it was. By the way, have you told your family yet? They must be very worried.
Xiao Xie:	Oh! Initially I was afraid that they would worry too much, so I didn't dare tell them. I waited until yesterday when the operation was over, and then I called my mom. I told her things are fine now, but she is still very worried. I was scolded by her on the phone, she asked why I didn't tell her earlier.
Chang Tian:	Your mom is concerned about you! Parents all over the world worry like this. They will hurry over to see you tomorrow.
Xiao Xie:	That's right. Oh! I will miss several weeks of classes. What am I going to do about my coursework?
Mingxiu:	Don't worry about school. I will help you ask for leave. When you are better we can help you review (the coursework).
Chang Tian:	Yes! Don't worry about it so much now. You should rest well so that you will recover sooner.
Xiao Xie:	Thank you very much.

Lesson 12   A Special Thanks for Your Help!

(Xiao Xie is recovering from his illness. In order to thank everyone for their help, his mom has specially cooked a feast to treat Mingxiu, Chang Tian, and Zhongming.)

Mingxiu: Congratulations to you, Xiao Xie, on being discharged from the hospital. You look fine and seem to be recovering well.

Xiao Xie: It's not bad. I hope I can be as active as before. However, at the moment I can't run around. I have no choice but to stay home. Most of the time, I just lie in bed. I'm in the house all day long and am extremely bored.

Mom: Don't think about it! If you had known it would come to this, you would have acted differently. If you had paid more attention to your health and went to check it out earlier, you wouldn't be in this condition.

Xiao Xie: Oh dear! I know I was wrong. I really regret it. I really won't dare to do it again.

Dad: Indeed, we were lucky to have your help. If it were not for your help things would have been even worse.

Mom: That's true. Thank goodness. There is great fortune amidst misfortune. Luckily you were both around, or the consequences would be unthinkable.

Xiao Xie: Sorry. This matter took up so much of your time. You had to go to the trouble of making several trips to the hospital. It was too much of a burden for you.

Chang Tian: It was nothing. No trouble at all. We didn't do much. You are all being too polite.

Zhongming: Right! It was no trouble at all. The hospital is close by and it was easy for me to come by after class to see you. It was really nothing.

Mingxiu: We did what we should have done. When you are away from home, it's hard to deal with these kinds of situations.

Mom: You are really kind. By the way, about school, are the matters of asking for leave and insurance resolved?

Mingxiu: They have all been taken care of. Xiao Xie has a note from the doctor, therefore his absence will be excused. When he comes back to school he can rejoin the class and make up the work. As for health insurance, Xiao Xie is covered so there's no problem there either.

Xiao Xie: Terrific! Due to your help, all the unlucky things have disappeared. I really appreciate it.

Dad: This has gone so smoothly because of your help. As the saying goes, "At home you have parents to count on; away from home you have to rely on friends." This is absolutely right!

Mom: Oh! Let's stop talking. You must all be hungry. Come on, please be seated. The food is getting cold.

Dad: Right! Come, please sit down. Let's have a toast to our health and friendship.

Dad, Mom, Xiao Xie, Zhongming, Chang Tian, and Mingxiu: OK. Cheers!

Lesson 13   I Need Some Advice

(Shi Wenchao has had a fight with his girlfriend. He is in a bad mood. He has come to find Shunqiang for a chat. Wenchao asks Shunqiang for some advice.)

Shi Wenchao: Shunqiang, may I come in to talk to you for a bit?

He Shunqiang (opens the door):   Hey! It's you, Wenchao! Please come in. What's up? Did you have a fight with your girlfriend again?

Shi Wenchao: Oh dear! You are so smart. You can read my mind immediately. Yes! I had a fight with Caiyi yesterday.

He Shunqiang: Oh! You two were fine yesterday. How could you have had another fight by today?

Shi Wenchao: Well, here's the story: she bought a digital camera and had some problems with it. She wanted to return it and wanted me to go with her. I accidentally overslept and she called me to tell me to hurry up. I hung up the phone and immediately drove over to pick her up.

He Sunqiang: That sounds fine. How did it end up with a fight?

Shi Wenchao: The problem came later. She told me to bring my cell phone. She also told me not to turn it on so I could concentrate on driving.

He Shunqiang: That doesn't seem to be a problem. She seems very cautious. Not bad.

Shi Wenchao: Let me finish the story, then you'll know. I drove onto the highway and there was a small accident in front of me so I ran into a traffic jam. I wanted to get off at the nearest exit, but the exit was closed. No cars were allowed through. I was totally stuck. At first I thought I could use my cell phone to call her, but I was in such a hurry when I headed out that I left my cell phone at home. I was worried that she had been waiting too long so I took a chance and drove on the shoulder, but I was caught by a policeman and got a ticket.

He Shunqiang: Uh oh. That's really bad luck.

Shi Wenchao: Yes! I really regretted it, but it was too late. When I arrived, I was two hours late. However, she was still there waiting for me. As soon as she saw me she gave me an angry "Humph!"and scolded me for always being late.

He Shunqiang: She was just angry. (She didn't really mean it.)

Shi Wenchao: True. However, I was already in a bad mood from getting a ticket and as soon as I heard her complaining I started to get angry. So we had a fight.

He Shunqiang: Oh, so it was like that. No problem. Listen to me, you need to remember that being on time is very important. Moreover, you have a quick temper and you should change that. As for Caiyi, a day has passed and she should feel better now. I suggest that first you apologize to her, then go with her to return the digital camera, then treat her to a movie or meal . . . something like that. I think she might forgive you then.

Shi Wenchao: OK. Let me think it over again. Thanks for the advice.

He Shunqiang: No need to thank me. Good luck!

Lesson 14   Please Accept My Apology

(After listening to Shunqiang's advice, Wenchao wanted to call Caiyi. However, he didn't know how to start talking to her. He thought he might send her an email, instead. It so happened that he saw that Caiyi was online. He suddenly had a good idea. He hoped to have an online chat with Caiyi to gain her understanding and forgiveness. Below is their online dialogue.)

Shi Wenchao writes: Caiyi, it's me, Wenchao. Are you all right? Are you still angry with me?

(Caiyi doesn't reply the first time.)

Shi Wenchao writes again: Dear Caiyi, how have you been? I know that you are online now. It is raining. The rain is pattering outside and my heart is going pitter-patter. I don't know what to say to you, but I do want to say the right thing. (Time is ticking by but Caiyi hasn't replied yet . . . . After a while Caiyi cannot help but reply . . . .)

Caiyi: I still feel bad. It seems that there is nothing for us to talk about. You left me feeling disappointed.

Shi Wenchao: Caiyi, it's you! I am so happy that you've finally started to talk. Oh dear! Actually, I also don't want to say too much. I just want to apologize. I would like to say "I'm sorry" to you. What happened yesterday was all my fault. It was a misunderstanding.

Caiyi: I am still very sad. At first, I thought I wouldn't pay attention to you but after I saw what you wrote, I just cannot help but start crying.

Shi Wenchao: You must feel wronged, so you feel bad and sad. Don't cry. The picture of you brimming with tears is hard for me to take.

Caiyi: Stop it! You never cared about my feelings at all!

Shi Wenchao: I am sorry. I really don't know what to say. I shouldn't have been late and made you wait so long for me. I was in a hurry and forgot my cell phone. On the way, I ran into a traffic jam and had no way to let you know. Then I drove on the shoulder and was caught by a policeman and got a ticket. At that time, I was in a very bad mood. I hope you can understand and accept my apology.

Caiyi: I didn't receive your call and thought that something might have happened to you. I was so worried. I was concerned about your safety!

Shi Wenchao: What you just said touches me and makes me happy. I am touched that you waited for me for so long and didn't leave. I am so happy to know that you still care about me.

Caiyi: To tell you the truth, I regretted our fight. I shouldn't have scolded you before I knew what had really happened.

Shi Wenchao: You were right to scold me. If I had left earlier, and if I were normally more punctual, you wouldn't have been so mad.

Caiyi:	Yes! I felt quite wronged. You should really change your bad habit.
Shi Wenchao:	I will definitely change it. By the way, I'm free tomorrow. How about I go with you to return the digital camera? What do you think?
Caiyi:	Hmm, OK. What time?
Shi Wenchao:	Is 3:00 P.M. fine with you?
Caiyi:	It should be fine.
Shi Wenchao:	You seem to have accepted my apology. Thank goodness! After returning the digital camera, let's go to eat and then go to a concert. How about that?
Caiyi:	It sounds good. OK, we have both agreed on it and you cannot be late again!
Shi Wenchao:	I guarantee it. I will definitely arrive there on time. See you tomorrow!
Caiyi:	See you tomorrow!

Lesson 15   Requesting a Favor

Sender: Shi, Wenchao <wenchao@zhongwen.edu>
Receiver: Gao, Xinyuan <xinyuan@hanyu.edu>
Subject: Please help me purchase tapes
Time of delivery: 4/21 3:45 P.M.

Xinyuan,

We haven't been in touch for quite a long time, and now that I am writing to you it is because I need to ask you a favor. I am a bit embarrassed, really. I've had a problem recently. If you can help me, please do.

Last week I got into an argument with my girlfriend Caiyi over some trivial thing and had just sorted it out when another unexpected problem came up.

Here is the story: Caiyi lent me an Elvis Presley tape. It is her favorite tape. When she handed it to me she emphasized to me repeatedly that I must take good care of it and I guaranteed her that nothing would happen to it. But when I was listening to it, it got tangled in my old tape recorder. When I quickly pulled it out from the tape recorder I used too much force. Not only did I fail to pull it out, I also broke it. I did not dare tell Caiyi. The moment I thought of her in tears, my heart was broken.

I was thinking of buying her another copy of the same tape and waiting until after I got the new tape to tell her about this and admit my carelessness. However, I have searched all the stores in the past two days and just cannot find the same tape. Therefore, I have no choice but to turn to you for help.

Can you look for me in the stores around your neighborhood? I hope I'll be able to find the Elvis Presley tape. Otherwise Caiyi will not forgive me!

Thanks for going to all this trouble for me.

Wenchao

Sender: Gao, Xinyuan <xinyuan@hanyu.edu>
Receiver: Shi, Wenchao <wenchao@zhongwen.edu>
Subject: I've got the CD
Time of delivery: 4/25 11:23 P.M.

Wenchao,

Don't worry. I've bought what you need. I was not able to get the Elvis Presley tape, but I found a CD.

Right after I received your email, I went to look in the nearby music stores. Although Elvis is still very famous here, I couldn't find it because his songs are not as popular as before. I searched online, but still no success. Finally I posted on e-store for tapes of Elvis and received an email this afternoon informing me that a CD was available. I thought a CD would be even better so I bought it for you.

Anyway, the problem is now solved and you should receive the CD very soon.

Xinyuan

Lesson 16   Visiting Teacher Xie

(It is spring break. Jianming Zhang and Ling Xia, two senior students, have come to visit Teacher Xie as they have in previous years. Jianming Zhang has also taken this opportunity to bring his girlfriend, Xiaoli Wu, to meet Teacher Xie.)

(Ring . . . The door bell rings. Teacher Xie comes to open the door.)

Zhang Jianming and Xia Ling: How are you, Teacher? Long time no see. We have come to visit you.
Teacher Xie: Oh, you are all here. Wonderful! Come on, step in please.
Zhang Jianming: Xiaoli, this is Teacher Xie whom I've mentioned to you many times. Teacher, this is my girlfriend, Xiaoli.
Wu Xiaoli: How do you do, Teacher Xie. I'm very glad to meet you. Jianming talks about you so often. He says you are his best teacher and that all the students like you.
Teacher Xie: It's not like that! They are all good students, hard-working and striving for the best. I find it very rewarding to teach them.
Zhang Jianming: You've taught us a lot, including, among other things, how to treat other people and to deal with things. This is very valuable.
Xia Ling: Yes. We've been thinking of you. No matter how busy we are, we have to come and visit you.
Teacher Xie: All of you are very thoughtful and caring. You never forget to come and visit. I cannot but feel touched. Come on, take a seat everyone. Don't stand on ceremony. Just make yourselves at home.

Zhang Jianming:	I hear that you are going to retire next year. What are you going to do after retirement?
Teacher Xie:	I am very much looking forward to retirement. I want to do more calligraphy and to study.
Xia Ling:	I remember that you like calligraphy. Whenever you were doing calligraphy, you were so focused. Sometimes you even forgot to eat. We really admire you for that.
Wu Xiaoli:	You are already so learned and knowledgeable. Why do you still want to study?
Teacher Xie:	It is never too late to learn more. You must remember, the more you study the more you feel you really know too little. Although I started to teach when I was only 20-something and have been teaching for more than 30 years, I still like to be a student. I can learn more and know more.
Zhang Jianming:	We really must learn from you. By the way, Ling Xia intends to continue her studies in graduate school.
Teacher Xie:	Is that so? Ling Xia, what graduate program are you interested in?
Xia Ling:	I want to study for a masters in economics. After two years, I want to continue on and am hoping to become a professor of economics.
Teacher Xie:	Good. You are going to have a very bright future.
Xia Ling:	You flatter me. Jianming says he's going to start his own company after graduation. Jianming, tell Teacher your plan.
Zhang Jianming:	OK. Teacher, you know I have interned at a computer company every summer and gained a lot of knowledge and experience. So after graduation I want to apply what I have learned. I am thinking of starting a computer network company. This will give me an opportunity to temper myself.
Wu Xiaoli:	He is determined to achieve success before the age of 30!
Teacher Xie:	Very good. You are all young and promising. I wish you success! I will be proud of you. Work hard. Hey, Xiaoli, are you also graduating this year?
Wu Xiaoli:	No. They are all graduating this year, but I'm not. My major is medicine. We have to study for six years.

(Teacher Xie continues to chat with his students. After two hours, the students prepare to leave.)

Zhang Jianming (looking at his watch):	Oh, it is late. We have bothered you for too long. We must be going.
Teacher Xie:	It's still early! No problem. Stay a bit longer.
Xia Ling:	No, thank you, Teacher. We really must go. We'll come to see you again when we have some time.
Teacher Xie:	All right, then. I'm very glad that you came to see me. Take your time.
Wu Xiaoli:	Take care, Teacher. Please don't bother to see us out. Goodbye.

Lesson 17   Let Me Help You Apply for an Internship

Shi Ruying: There was a lecture at the school career center yesterday. It explained how to write a résumé, and how to apply for jobs or to graduate schools. It was very helpful.

Zhang Huali: Come on, tell me . . . how do you write a résumé? I want to apply for an internship at a company this summer.

Shi Ruying: Didn't you apply last year?

Zhang Huali: Huh? Don't you remember I didn't get it last year? It was precisely because I didn't write my résumé well.

Shi Ruying: As a matter of fact, it's not very complicated to write a résumé. First of all, you need to be clear about what kind of job you want to apply for. Then adjust your résumé based on the requirements of the different jobs.

Zhang Huali: That is to say, if you apply for different jobs you need to write your résumé differently. Is that right?

Shi Ruying: Exactly. You must stress your strong points in your résumé. Didn't you write it like that last year?

Zhang Huali: No, I didn't. No wonder I was turned down last year. I've got to do a careful revision of my résumé. By the way, aren't you also going to do an internship this summer?

Shi Ruying: Yes, you're right. But I still don't know what companies have positions available.

Zhang Huali: There is a lot of information online. Didn't you know ? I'll send some to you tonight. Hey, didn't they give you any websites yesterday?

Shi Ruying: They did. They said we could download application forms directly from the Web, fill them in, and send them out. We can also apply online.

Zhang Huali: Right. I did my application online.

Shi Ruying: Next, I will need some recommendation letters.

Zhang Huali: Haven't you talked to your professors yet? You'd better hurry. Professors' time is limited.

Shi Ruying: I've thought about it. I am going to make a plan and talk to some professors in a few days. I hope they will agree to write recommendation letters for me.

Zhang Huali: I am sure they will be very willing to help you with the recommendation letters. You are so smart and capable, with such good qualifications. Don't worry.

Shi Ruying: I hope so (I hope what you said is right).

Lesson 18   "Why Are You Interested in This Job?"

Director Chen:	How do you do, Miss Wen. I am very happy that you are interested in our company.
Wen Ruhua:	How do you do, Director Chen. Thank you for giving me this opportunity.
Director Chen:	I read your résumé. You have double majors: e-commerce and computer science. You are graduating this year, right?
Wen Ruhua:	Yes, I am graduating this coming May, in about one month.
Director Chen:	Why are you interested in business?
Wen Ruhua:	Because my father is in business. Influenced by my father, I've had an interest in business since my childhood.
Director Chen:	Could you tell me why you want to come to work in our company?
Wen Ruhua:	I checked your company's website and learned that yours is a large computer consulting company. You not only develop your own software, but also provide a lot of consulting services.
Director Chen:	You're right. Although our company is only six years old, it has developed very fast. We now have around 300 employees.
Wen Ruhua:	I hear you've gone public, right?
Director Chen:	Exactly. Although we went public only at the beginning of last year, our business has been going very well. Can you tell me something about yourself?
Wen Ruhua:	I am a student at Zhonghua University. Besides majors in business and computer science, I also have a Chinese minor. My GPA is very high. I have received awards from the university several times and also worked as the SAC (Student Association Council) president of the business school. I have organized many activities. For all the important activities at our university, I was one of the organizers.
Director Chen:	Have you been involved in any research projects?
Wen Ruhua:	Yes, I have. Starting last year, I began doing some research with a professor. Now I am writing my graduation thesis.
Director Chen:	What else do you like to do besides study?
Wen Ruhua:	I like many things, but I like traveling the best.
Director Chen:	That's good. This job requires a lot of traveling.
Wen Ruhua:	That's exactly what I want! Even if I had to travel every day, I would love it.
Director Chen:	Do you have any other questions?
Wen Ruhua:	May I ask when you will make your decision?
Director Chen:	I would say next Monday. We will call you.
Wen Ruhua:	OK, I'll be waiting for your call. Thanks again for giving me this opportunity.

Lesson 19   "Have You Had Any Job Offers?"

Zhou Huaxin:	Xinmin, have you had any job offers?
Jin Xinmin:	I've had three offers: one financial bank and two consulting companies. In the past few days I have been trying to decide which one to accept.
Zhou Huaxin:	Really! At the moment the economy is not fully recovered. The job market is still weak and there is still very intense competition. But you have three job offers! How wonderful! Congratulations!
Jin Xinmin:	Thank you, but I think it's mainly because I have been lucky.
Zhou Huaxin:	Don't be so modest! Anybody who gets a good job must have good qualifications. No good qualifications, no good job!
Jin Xinmin:	Not really. I am just lucky.
Zhou Huaxin:	Then which company are you going to work for?
Jin Xinmin:	Maybe the big consulting company. Their pay is higher.
Zhou Huaxin:	I would take the bank offer. That's a "golden rice bowl" deal that can't be broken.
Jin Xinmin:	You may be right. Jobs at a large bank are more stable and the benefits are good too.
Zhou Huaxin:	But you still need to see what the salary will be.
Jin Xinmin:	The starting salary at the bank is $60K, the small consulting company $52K, and the large one $55K. But they are all public companies and they all offer stock options.
Zhou Huaxin:	That looks pretty good. Make a decision then!
Jin Xinmin:	But there are still some differences in the benefits they offer.
Zhou Huaxin:	OK, OK, you are just like an old woman! All right, tell me what the differences are.
Jin Xinmin:	Their retirement and health-insurance plans are basically the same, and they offer very good subsidies for business trips. However, if I want to take some graduate courses in the future, the bank offers some subsidies while the consulting companies do not have this benefit. That's why I am hesitating a bit.
Zhou Huaxin:	If you ask me, whichever pays well (is good).
Jin Xinmin:	I don't think I agree with you. To me, it is true that money is important, but the working environment is even more important.
Zhou Huaxin:	You are right there. Sometimes a good working environment is indeed more important than the salary.
Jin Xinmin:	As a matter of fact, I want to go to the large consulting company because I hear that the relationships among the people who work there are very good and the boss is nice as well.
Zhou Huaxin:	This is indeed an important issue.
Jin Xinmin:	My dad also said: "You are still young. You will be able to make money sooner or later, but a good working environment is not that easy to find."
Zhou Huaxin:	What your dad said is exactly right. Follow his words and you won't go wrong.

Lesson 20   Which Job Offer Should I Accept?

Jiansheng,

How are you? We haven't been in touch for quite a while. How have you been? Is everything all right?

I am graduating this year and have been job hunting, so I've been very busy recently. I had hoped to find a company that offered jobs in my field and good benefits as well. As the economy is not fully recovered yet, it is not very easy to find a job, not to mention an ideal job. Therefore, I was very nervous. I was also prepared, in case I could not find a job, to apply to graduate school to study for another two years and get a master's degree, rather than staying at home waiting.

Some time ago, I went to some companies for interviews. I went to five companies. I was thinking that as long as a company would hire me, I would accept even though the salary might be low. I had not expected that three companies, all of them good companies, would make offers. I am very pleased.

I have not decided which company's offer I will take. Originally, I was thinking I would go to whichever company would hire me. Now that I've got three offers, I certainly need to make a good choice.

Because you've been working for a year, and you must have some experiences, I would like to know your opinion. I very much want to know what kind of questions I should ask when I negotiate with them. I hope you can give me some advice so that I won't say the wrong thing.

Four years of university life will soon be over. Looking back on the four years, I feel I have achieved a great deal. I have not only gained a lot of knowledge, what's more important is that I have gained a clearer picture of my goals for the future. What's more, I want to work for a few years, and then come back to school to pursue graduate studies so that I can learn more things. How about you? Isn't it true that you are thinking about the same thing?

All right, I'll stop here. I hope you are happy in your work.

Your friend,
Xinmin

課文拼音 (课文拼音)
LANGUAGE IN USE WITH PINYIN

Lesson 11   My Unexpected Stay in Hospital

(小謝住院了，他的室友常天在旁邊照顧他，
(小谢住院了，他的室友常天在旁边照顾他，
(Xiǎo Xiè zhùyuàn le, tāde shìyǒu Cháng Tiān zài pángbiān zhàogu tā,

他的同學明修來了。)
他的同学明修来了。)
tāde tóngxué Míngxiū láile.)

明修:	怎麼樣，好多了嗎?
明修:	怎么样，好多了吗?
Míngxiū:	Zěnmeyàng, hǎoduō le ma?

小謝:	好多了，沒事了。你那麼忙還過來看我，真不好意思。
小谢:	好多了，没事了。你那么忙还过来看我，真不好意思。
Xiǎo Xiè:	Hǎoduōle, méishì le. Nǐ nàme máng hái guòlái kàn wǒ, zhēn bùhǎoyìsi.

明修:	哪兒的話，平安就好。到底是怎麼回事? 你怎麼住院了呢?
明修:	哪儿的话，平安就好。到底是怎么回事? 你怎么住院了呢?
Míngxiū:	Nǎr de huà, píngān jiùhǎo. Dàodǐ shì zěnme huíshì? Nǐ zěnme zhùyuàn le ne?

小謝:	唉! 事情的經過是這樣的: 前幾天我就覺得肚子不舒服，
小谢:	唉! 事情的经过是这样的: 前几天我就觉得肚子不舒服，
Xiǎo Xiè:	Ài! Shìqing de jīngguò shì zhèyàngde: Qiánjǐtiān wǒ jiù juéde dùzi bùshūfu,

以為是吃壞肚子了，吃了藥就會好了，也就沒管它。但是
以为是吃坏肚子了，吃了药就会好了，也就没管它。但是
yǐwéi shì chīhuài dùzi le, chīleyào jiùhuì hǎole, yějiù méi guǎn tā. Dànshì

有時候還是會疼，拖了一兩天。前天早上疼得屬害，
有时候还是会疼，拖了一兩天。前天早上疼得厉害，
yǒushíhou háishì huì téng, tuōle yìliǎngtiān. Qiántiān zǎoshang téngde lìhai,

受不了了。就這樣，我被送進醫院了。
受不了了。就这样，我被送进医院了。
shòubuliǎo le. Jiùzhèyàng, wǒ bèi sòng jìn yīyuàn le.

常天：　　　是呀！中明和我剛好沒課在家，看他疼得厲害，
常天：　　　是呀！中明和我刚好没课在家，看他疼得厉害，
Cháng Tiān:　Shìyā! Zhōngmíng hé wǒ gānghǎo méikè zàijiā, kàn tā téngde lìhai,

　　　　　　覺得情況不對，就馬上打電話叫救護車，
　　　　　　觉得情况不对，就马上打电话叫救护车，
　　　　　　juéde qíngkuàng búduì, jiù mǎshàng dǎdiànhuà jiào jiùhùchē,

　　　　　　把他送進急診室去了。
　　　　　　把他送进急诊室去了。
　　　　　　bǎtā sòngjìn jízhěnshì qùle.

小謝：　　　醫生說是急性盲腸炎，要馬上開刀。
小谢：　　　医生说是急性盲肠炎，要马上开刀。
Xiǎo Xiè:　Yīshēng shuō shì jíxìng mángchángyán, yào mǎshàng kāidāo.

　　　　　　一聽要動手術，就把我嚇死了，很快我就被送進
　　　　　　一听要动手术，就把我吓死了，很快我就被送进
　　　　　　Yì tīng yào dòngshǒushù, jiùbǎ wǒ xiàsǐle, hěnkuài wǒjiù bèi sòngjìn

　　　　　　手術室了。
　　　　　　手术室了。
　　　　　　shǒushùshì le.

常天：　　　我和中明在外面挺擔心的，不過還好，
常天：　　　我和中明在外面挺担心的，不过还好，
Cháng Tiān:　Wǒ hé Zhōngmíng zài wàimiàn tǐng dānxīn de, búguò háihǎo,

　　　　　　手術進行得很順利。手術完了以後，他就讓護士給
　　　　　　手术进行得很顺利。手术完了以后，他就让护士给
　　　　　　shǒushù jìnxíngde hěn shùnlì. Shǒushù wánle yǐhòu, tā jiù ràng hùshì gěi

　　　　　　推進病房休養了。
　　　　　　推进病房休养了。
　　　　　　tuījìn bìngfáng xiūyǎng le.

明修：　　　喔！原來是這樣的。對了，你通知家人了嗎？他們一定急死了。
明修：　　　喔！原来是这样的。对了，你通知家人了吗？他们一定急死了。
Míngxiū:　Ō! Yuánlái shì zhèyàngde. Duìle, nǐ tōngzhī jiārén le ma? Tāmen yídìng jísǐ le.

小謝：   唉！本來我怕他們擔心，不敢告訴他們。昨天等手術
小谢：   唉！本来我怕他们担心，不敢告诉他们。昨天等手术
Xiǎo Xiè: Ài! Běnlái wǒ pà tāmen dānxīn, bùgǎn gàosu tāmen. Zuótiān děng shǒushù

結束以後，才給媽媽打電話，告訴她不要緊了，可是她還是
结束以后，才给妈妈打电话，告诉她不要紧了，可是她还是
jiéshù yǐhòu, cái gěi māma dǎdiànhuà, gàosù tā búyàojǐn le, kěshì tā háishì

擔心得很，還生氣呢。我還叫她在電話裡給罵了一頓，
担心得很，还生气呢。我还叫她在电话里给骂了一顿，
dānxīn de hěn, hái shēngqì ne. Wǒ hái jiào tā zài diànhuàlǐ gěi màle yídùn,

說我怎麼這麼晚才告訴她。
说我怎么这么晚才告诉她。
shuō wǒ zěnme zhèmewǎn cái gàosu tā.

常天：   你媽媽是關心你啊！可憐天下父母心！你看他們明天
常天：   你妈妈是关心你啊！可怜天下父母心！你看他们明天
Cháng Tiān: Nǐ māma shì guānxīn nǐ a! Kělián tiānxià fùmǔxīn! Nǐkàn tāmen míngtiān

就要趕過來看你了。
就要赶过来看你了。
jiùyào gǎnguòlái kàn nǐ le.

小謝：   說的也是。唉！我要好幾個星期都不能上課了，
小谢：   说的也是。唉！我要好几个星期都不能上课了，
Xiǎo Xiè: Shuōde yěshì. Ài! Wǒyào hǎojǐge xīngqī dōu bùnéng shàngkè le,

功課怎麼辦？
功课怎么办？
gōngkè zěnmebàn?

明修：   學校那邊，你不要擔心，我會幫你請假的。
明修：   学校那边，你不要担心，我会帮你请假的。
Míngxiū: Xuéxiào nàbiān, nǐ búyào dānxīn, wǒ huì bāngnǐ qǐngjiàde.

等你好了以後，我們再幫你復習。
等你好了以后，我们再帮你复习。
Děng nǐ hǎole yǐhòu, wǒmen zài bāng nǐ fùxí.

常天：　　　是呀，現在就別管那麼多了。你好好地休養，
常天：　　　是呀，现在就别管那么多了。你好好地休养，
Cháng Tiān:　Shìya, xiànzài jiù biéguǎn nàmeduō le. Nǐ hǎohǎode xiūyǎng,

才能早日康復。
才能早日康复。
cáinéng zǎorì kāngfù.

小謝：　　　那就太謝謝你們了。
小谢：　　　那就太谢谢你们了。
Xiǎo Xiè:　　Nà jiù tài xièxie nǐmen le.

Lesson 12   A Special Thanks for Your Help!

(小謝病好了，為了要答謝大家的幫助，媽媽特地煮了一桌菜
(小谢病好了，为了要答谢大家的帮助，妈妈特地煮了一桌菜
(Xiǎo Xiè bìnghǎole, wèile yào dáxiè dàjiā de bāngzhù, māma tèdì zhǔle yìzhuō cài

請明修、常天和中明來吃飯。)
请明修、常天和中明来吃饭。)
qǐng Míngxiū, Cháng Tiān hé Zhōngmíng lái chīfàn.)

明修：　　　小謝，恭喜你出院了。你看起來精神不錯，恢復得很好。
明修：　　　小谢，恭喜你出院了。你看起来精神不错，恢复得很好。
Míngxiū:　　Xiǎo Xiè, gōngxǐ nǐ chūyuàn le. Nǐ kànqǐlái jīngshén búcuò, huīfù de hěnhǎo.

小謝：　　　還可以啦！希望我能跟以前一樣靈活。但是這段
小谢：　　　还可以啦！希望我能跟以前一样灵活。但是这段
Xiǎo Xiè:　　Hái kěyǐ la! Xīwàng wǒ néng gēn yǐqián yíyàng línghuó. Dànshì zhèduàn

時間，我不能亂跑，只好待在家裡，差不多天天
时间，我不能乱跑，只好待在家里，差不多天天
shíjiān, wǒ bùnéng luànpǎo, zhǐhǎo dāizài jiālǐ, chàbùduō tiāntiān

都躺在床上。整天被關在家裡，快把我悶死了！
都躺在床上。整天被关在家里，快把我闷死了！
dōu tǎngzài chuángshàng. Zhěngtiān bèi guānzài jiālǐ, kuài bǎ wǒ mēnsǐle!

媽媽:	算了吧！早知如此，何必當初。你要是能多注意身體，
妈妈:	算了吧！早知如此，何必当初。你要是能多注意身体，
Māma:	Suànle ba! Zǎozhī rúcǐ, hébì dāngchū. Nǐ yàoshì néng duō zhùyì shēntǐ,

早點兒去檢查，就不會到這樣的地步了。
早点儿去检查，就不会到这样的地步了。
zǎodiǎr qù jiǎnchá, jiù búhuì dào zhèyàng de dìbù le.

小謝:	哎呀！我知道錯了，真後悔！下次真的不敢了！
小谢:	哎呀！我知道错了，真后悔！下次真的不敢了！
Xiǎo Xiè:	Āiya! Wǒ zhīdào cuòle, zhēn hòuhuǐ! Xiàcì zhēnde bùgǎn le!

爸爸:	說真的，這次真是多虧了你們。要不是你們的幫助，
爸爸:	说真的，这次真是多亏了你们。要不是你们的帮助，
Bàba:	Shuō zhēnde, zhècì zhēnshì duōkuī le nǐmen. Yàobúshì nǐmende bāngzhù,

事情可能會更糟呢。
事情可能会更糟呢。
shìqing kěnéng huì gèngzāo ne.

媽媽:	說的也是，真是謝天謝地，不幸中的大幸。
妈妈:	说的也是，真是谢天谢地，不幸中的大幸。
Māma:	Shuōde yěshì, zhēnshì xiètiānxièdì, búxìng zhōng de dàxìng.

還好有你們在，不然後果就不堪設想了。
还好有你们在，不然后果就不堪设想了。
Háihǎo yǒu nǐmen zài, bùrán hòuguǒ jiù bùkānshèxiǎng le.

小謝:	對不起，這次可把你們忙壞了，害你們跑了好幾趟醫院。
小谢:	对不起，这次可把你们忙坏了，害你们跑了好几趟医院。
Xiǎo Xiè:	Duìbuqǐ, zhècì kě bǎ nǐmen mánghuài le, hài nǐmen pǎole hǎo jǐtàng yīyuàn.

真是太麻煩你們了。
真是太麻烦你们了。
Zhēnshì tài máfan nǐmen le.

常天:	沒什麼，不麻煩。我們沒幫什麼忙，你們太客氣了。
常天:	没什么，不麻烦。我们没帮什么忙，你们太客气了。
Cháng Tiān:	Méi shénme, bù máfan. Wǒmen méi bāng shénme máng, nǐmen tài kèqi le.

中明： 是呀！一點都不麻煩，醫院就在附近，我也是下課以後就
中明： 是呀！一点都不麻烦，医院就在附近，我也是下课以后就
Zhōngmíng: Shìya! Yìdiǎn dōu bù máfan, yīyuàn jiùzài fùjìn, wǒ yěshì xiàkè yǐhòu jiù

順便過去看看。小事兒，沒什麼。
顺便过去看看。小事儿，没什么。
shùnbiàn guòqù kànkan. Xiǎoshèr, méi shénme.

明修： 這是我們應該做的。出門在外，總是會有不方便
明修： 这是我们应该做的。出门在外，总是会有不方便
Míngxiū: Zhèshì wǒmen yīnggāi zuòde. Chūmén zàiwài, zǒngshì huìyǒu bù fāngbiàn

的時候。
的时候。
de shíhou.

媽媽： 你們真好。對了，學校那邊，關於請假和保險的事情
妈妈： 你们真好。对了，学校那边，关于请假和保险的事情
Māma: Nǐmen zhēnhǎo. Duìle, xuéxiào nàbiān, guānyú qǐngjià hé bǎoxiǎn de shìqing

都解決了嗎？
都解决了吗？
dōu jiějué le ma?

明修： 都辦好了。小謝有醫生證明，因此不會被記缺席。
明修： 都办好了。小谢有医生证明，因此不会被记缺席。
Míngxiū: Dōu bànhǎo le. Xiǎo Xiè yǒu yīshēng zhèngmíng, yīncǐ búhuì bèi jì quēxí.

等他回來上課以後，也可以參加輔導、補考。至於保險
等他回来上课以后，也可以参加辅导、补考。至于保险
Děng tā huílái shàngkè yǐhòu, yě kěyǐ cānjiā fǔdǎo, bǔkǎo. Zhìyú bǎoxiǎn

方面，因為小謝有健康保險，所以也沒問題。
方面，因为小谢有健康保险，所以也没问题。
fāngmiàn, yīnwèi Xiǎo Xiè yǒu jiànkāng bǎoxiǎn, suǒyǐ yě méi wèntí.

小謝： 太好了！由於你們的幫助，這些倒楣事兒全沒了。
小谢： 太好了！由于你们的帮助，这些倒霉事儿全没了。
Xiǎo Xiè: Tàihǎo le! Yóuyú nǐmende bāngzhù, zhèxiē dǎoméi shèr quán méi le.

爸爸:	事情能進行得這麼順利，是由於你們的幫助。俗話
爸爸:	事情能进行得这么顺利，是由于你们的帮助。俗话
Bàba:	Shìqíng néng jìnxíng de zhème shùnlì, shì yóuyú nǐmende bāngzhù. Súhuà

說："在家靠父母，出外靠朋友"，真是一點兒也沒錯！
说："在家靠父母，出外靠朋友"，真是一点儿也没错！
shuō: "zàijiā kào fùmǔ, chūwài kào péngyǒu", zhēnshì yìdiǎr yě méicuò!

媽媽:	喔！不要只顧著說話，你們都餓了吧。來來來，請上座，
妈妈:	喔！不要只顾着说话，你们都饿了吧。来来来，请上座，
Māma:	Ō! Búyào zhǐ gùzhe shuōhuà, nǐmen dōu è le ba. Lái lái lái, qǐng shàngzuò,

菜可要涼了。
菜可要凉了。
cài kěyào liáng le.

爸爸:	是呀！來來來，請坐，請坐。我們一起為我們的健康和
爸爸:	是呀！来来来，请坐，请坐。我们一起为我们的健康和
Bàba:	Shìya! Lái lái lái, qǐngzuò, qǐngzuò. Wǒmen yìqǐ wèi wǒmende jiànkāng hé

友誼乾一杯吧。
友谊干一杯吧。
yǒuyì gān yì bēi ba.

爸爸、媽媽、小謝、中明、常天、明修：好，乾杯！
爸爸、妈妈、小谢、中明、常天、明修：好，干杯！
Bàba, Māma, Xiǎo Xiè, Zhōngmíng, Cháng Tiān, Míngxiū: Hǎo, gānbēi!

Lesson 13   I Need Some Advice

(史文超和女朋友吵架了，心情很不好，他來找順強談談，
(史文超和女朋友吵架了，心情很不好，他来找顺强谈谈，
(Shǐ Wénchāo hé nǚpéngyou chǎojià le, xīnqíng hěn bùhǎo, tā lái zhǎo Shùnqiáng tántan,

請他給一些建議。)
请他给一些建议。)
qǐng tā gěi yìxiē jiànyì.)

史文超:	順強，我能進來跟你談談嗎？
史文超:	顺强，我能进来跟你谈谈吗？
Shǐ Wénchāo:	Shùnqiáng, wǒ néng jìnlai gēn nǐ tántan ma?

何順強(開門):　　　　　嘿，文超是你呀！請進，怎麼搞的，是不是又跟
何顺强(开门):　　　　　嘿，文超是你呀！请进，怎么搞的，是不是又跟
Hé Shùnqiáng (kāimén):　Hèi, Wénchāo shì nǐ yā! Qǐngjìn, zěnme gǎo de, shìbushì yòu gēn

　　　　　　　　　　女朋友吵架啦？
　　　　　　　　　　女朋友吵架啦？
　　　　　　　　　　nǚpéngyou chǎojià la?

史文超:　　　　　哎呀！你真厲害，馬上就知道我的心事了。是啊！
史文超:　　　　　哎呀！你真厉害，马上就知道我的心事了。是啊！
Shǐ Wénchāo:　　Āiya! Nǐ zhēn lìhai, mǎshàng jiù zhīdào wǒde xīnshì le. Shì a!

　　　　　　　　　　昨天我和彩宜吵架了！
　　　　　　　　　　昨天我和彩宜吵架了！
　　　　　　　　　　Zuótiān wǒ hé Cǎiyí chǎojià le!

何順強:　　　　　喔！你們倆昨天還好好的，怎麼今天就吵架了！
何顺强:　　　　　喔！你们俩昨天还好好的，怎么今天就吵架了！
Hé Shùnqiáng:　　Ō! Nǐmen liǎ zuótiān hái hǎohǎode, zěnme jīntiān jiù chǎojià le!

史文超:　　　　　唉！事情是這樣的：她買了一部數碼相機，出了一些問題。
史文超:　　　　　唉！事情是这样的：她买了一部数码相机，出了一些问题。
Shǐ Wénchāo:　　Āi! Shìqíng shì zhèyàng de: tā mǎile yíbù shùmǎ xiàngjī, chūle yìxiē wèntí.

　　　　　　　　　　她想退貨，要我陪她去，我不小心睡過頭了。
　　　　　　　　　　她想退货，要我陪她去，我不小心睡过头了。
　　　　　　　　　　Tā xiǎng tuìhuò, yào wǒ péi tā qù, wǒ bùxiǎoxīn shuì guòtóu le.

　　　　　　　　　　她打電話來催我快一點兒，我掛了電話，馬上就
　　　　　　　　　　她打电话来催我快一点儿，我挂了电话，马上就
　　　　　　　　　　Tā dǎ diànhuà lái cuī wǒ kuài yìdiǎr, wǒ guàle diànhuà, mǎshàng jiù

　　　　　　　　　　開車去接她了。
　　　　　　　　　　开车去接她了。
　　　　　　　　　　kāichē qù jiē tā le.

何順強:　　　　　那很好啊！怎麼會到吵架的地步呢？
何顺强:　　　　　那很好啊！怎么会到吵架的地步呢？
Hé Shùnqiáng:　　Nà hěnhǎo a! Zěnme huì dào chǎojià de dìbù ne?

史文超：　問題就出在後面啦！她交代我要把手機帶著，
史文超：　问题就出在后面啦！她交代我要把手机带着，
Shǐ Wénchāo:　Wèntí jiù chū zài hòumiàn la! Tā jiāodài wǒ yào bǎ shǒujī dài zhe,

不可以讓手機開著，這樣才能專心開車。
不可以让手机开着，这样才能专心开车。
bù kěyǐ ràng shǒujī kāizhe, zhèyàng cáinéng zhuānxīn kāichē.

何順強：　聽上去好像沒什麼問題呀！她好像很小心，
何顺强：　听上去好像没什么问题呀！她好像很小心，
Hé Shùnqiáng:　Tīng shàngqu hǎoxiàng méi shénme wèntí yā! Tā hǎoxiàng hěn xiǎoxīn,

不錯嘛！
不错嘛！
búcuò ma!

史文超：　等我把故事說完你就知道了。我上高速公路以後，
史文超：　等我把故事说完你就知道了。我上高速公路以后，
Shǐ Wénchāo:　Děng wǒ bǎ gùshi shuōwán nǐ jiù zhīdào le. Wǒ shàng gāosù gōnglù yǐhòu,

前面有一個小車禍，碰到塞車了。我想要從
前面有一个小车祸，碰到塞车了。我想要从
qiánmiàn yǒu yíge xiǎo chēhuò, pèngdào sāichē le. Wǒ xiǎng yào cóng

出口下去，可是旁邊的出口又關起來了，禁止車子
出口下去，可是旁边的出口又关起来了，禁止车子
chūkǒu xiàqu, kěshì pángbiānde chūkǒu yòu guān qǐlái le, jìnzhǐ chēzi

通過，使我完全動不了了。原來想打手機通知她，
通过，使我完全动不了了。原来想打手机通知她，
tōngguò, shǐ wǒ wánquán dòngbuliǎo le. Yuánlái xiǎng dǎ shǒujī tōngzhī tā,

但是剛剛匆匆忙忙地跑了出來，手機叫我給
但是刚刚匆匆忙忙地跑了出来，手机叫我给
dànshì gānggāng cōngcōng mángmáng de pǎo le chūlái, shǒujī jiào wǒ gěi

忘在家裡了。我怕她會等太久，就逼自己走路肩，
忘在家里了。我怕她会等太久，就逼自己走路肩，
wàngzài jiālǐ le. Wǒ pà tā huì děng tàijiǔ, jiù bī zìjǐ zǒu lùjiān,

想碰碰運氣。結果被警察抓住了，吃了一張罰單。
想碰碰运气。结果被警察抓住了，吃了一张罚单。
xiǎng pèngpeng yùnqi. Jiéguǒ bèi jǐngchá zhuāzhù le, chī le yìzhāng fádān.

何順強：	喔！喔！真是的，吃虧了吧！
何顺强：	喔！喔！真是的，吃亏了吧！
Hé Shùnqiáng：	Ō! Ō! Zhēnshì de, chīkuī le ba!

史文超：	是啊！真後悔，可是已經來不及了。等我到的時候，已經
史文超：	是啊！真后悔，可是已经来不及了。等我到的时候，已经
Shǐ Wénchāo：	Shì a! Zhēn hòuhuǐ, kěshì yǐjīng láibují le. Děng wǒ dào de shíhòu, yǐjīng

遲到了兩個鐘頭。不過，她還在那兒等我。一見我就
迟到了两个钟头。不过，她还在那儿等我。一见我就
chídào le liǎngge zhōngtóu. Búguò, tā háizài nàr děng wǒ. Yíjiàn wǒ jiù

哼地一聲，把我罵了一頓，說我總是喜歡遲到。
哼地一声，把我骂了一顿，说我总是喜欢迟到。
hēng de yìshēng, bǎ wǒ mà le yídùn, shuō wǒ zǒngshì xǐhuān chídào.

何順強：	她是說氣話嘛！
何顺强：	她是说气话嘛！
Hé Shùnqiáng：	Tā shì shuō qìhuà ma!

史文超：	是啊！可是我剛剛叫警察給開了罰單，心情很不好。
史文超：	是啊！可是我刚刚叫警察给开了罚单，心情很不好。
Shǐ Wénchāo：	Shì a! Kěshì wǒ gānggāng jiào jǐngchá gěi kāi le fádān, xīnqíng hěn bùhǎo.

一聽她抱怨，我就生起氣來了。因此我們就吵架了。
一听她抱怨，我就生起气来了。因此我们就吵架了。
Yìtīng tā bàoyuàn, wǒ jiù shēng qǐ qì lái le. Yīncǐ wǒmen jiù chǎojià le.

何順強：	嗯！原來如此，不要緊的！聽我說，你要記住，守時是最
何顺强：	嗯！原来如此，不要紧的！听我说，你要记住，守时是最
Hé Shùnqiáng：	Ēn! Yuánlái rúcǐ, bú yàojǐn de! Tīng wǒ shuō, nǐ yào jìzhù, shǒushí shì zuì

重要的；還有，你的脾氣比較急，這樣是很容易吃虧的，
重要的；还有，你的脾气比较急，这样是很容易吃亏的，
zhòngyào de; háiyǒu, nǐde píqì bǐjiào jí, zhèyàng shì hěn róngyì chīkuī de,

應該改一改。至於彩宜呢，現在已經過了一天了，
应该改一改。至于彩宜呢，现在已经过了一天了，
yīnggāi gǎiyigǎi. Zhìyú Cǎiyí ne, xiànzài yǐjīng guòle yìtiān le,

她應該好多了。我建議你應該先向她道歉，
她应该好多了。我建议你应该先向她道歉，
tā yīnggāi hǎo duō le. Wǒ jiànyì nǐ yīnggāi xiān xiàng tā dàoqiàn,

陪她去把退貨的事情辦好，然後再請她去看個電影、
陪她去把退货的事情办好，然后再请她去看个电影、
péi tā qù bǎ tuìhuò de shìqing bànhǎo, ránhòu zài qǐng tā qù kàn ge diànyǐng,

吃頓飯什麼的。我想她大概就會原諒你了。
吃顿饭什么的。我想她大概就会原谅你了。
chīdùn fàn shénme de. Wǒ xiǎng tā dàgài jiùhuì yuánliàng nǐ le.

史文超：   好的，讓我再想想，謝謝你的建議。
史文超：   好的，让我再想想，谢谢你的建议。
Shǐ Wénchāo: Hǎode, ràng wǒ zài xiǎngxiang, xièxie nǐde jiànyì.

何順強：   不用謝啦！祝你好運！
何顺强：   不用谢啦！祝你好运！
Hé Shùnqiáng: Búyòng xiè la! Zhù nǐ hǎoyùn!

Lesson 14   Please Accept My Apology

(聽了順強的建議以後，文超想打電話給彩宜，可是又不知道
(听了顺强的建议以后，文超想打电话给彩宜，可是又不知道
(Tīng le Shùnqiáng de jiànyì yǐhòu, Wénchāo xiǎng dǎ diànhuà gěi Cǎiyí, kěshì yòu bù zhīdào

怎麼開口。他想寫一封電子郵件給她。剛好他的電腦顯示，
怎么开口。他想写一封电子邮件给她。刚好他的电脑显示，
zěnme kāikǒu. Tā xiǎng xiě yìfēng diànzǐ yóujiàn gěi tā. Gānghǎo tāde diànnǎo xiǎnshì,

彩宜也正在上網呢。他就靈機一動，希望能跟她在網上
彩宜也正在上网呢。他就灵机一动，希望能跟她在网上
Cǎiyí yě zhèngzài shàngwǎng ne. Tā jiù língjī yídòng, xīwàng néng gēn tā zài wǎngshàng

聊天室談談，得到她的諒解。以下是他們在網上的對話。)
聊天室谈谈，得到她的谅解。以下是他们在网上的对话。)
liáotiānshì tántan, dédào tāde liàngjiě. Yǐxià shì tāmen zài wǎngshàng de duìhuà.)

史文超寫道：   彩宜，是我，文超，你還好嗎？是否還在生我的氣呢？
史文超写道：   彩宜，是我，文超，你还好吗？是否还在生我的气呢？
Shǐ Wénchāo xiědào: Cǎiyí, shì wǒ, Wénchāo, nǐ háihǎo ma? Shìfǒu háizài shēng wǒde qì ne?

(彩宜第一次沒回)
(彩宜第一次没回)
(Cǎiyí dì yí cì méi huí)

史文超又寫道：　　　親愛的彩宜，你好嗎？我知道你正在上網。
史文超又写道：　　　亲爱的彩宜，你好吗？我知道你正在上网。
Shǐ Wénchāo yòu xiědào:　Qīn'ài de Cǎiyí, nǐ hǎo ma? Wǒ zhīdào nǐ zhèngzài shàngwǎng.

下雨了，外面的雨淅瀝淅瀝地下著，而我的心
下雨了，外面的雨淅沥淅沥地下着，而我的心
Xiàyǔ le, wàimiàn de yǔ xīlìxīlì de xiàzhe, ér wǒde xīn

撲通撲通地跳著。我不知道該對你說些
扑通扑通地跳着。我不知道该对你说些
pūtōngpūtōng de tiàozhe. Wǒ bùzhīdào gāi duìnǐ shuō xiē

什麼好，我想跟你好好地溝通溝通。
什么好，我想跟你好好地沟通沟通。
shénme hǎo, wǒ xiǎng gēn nǐ hǎohǎo de gōutōng gōutōng.

(時間滴答滴答地過去了，彩宜還沒有回信……過了有一會兒，
(时间滴答滴答地过去了，彩宜还没有回信……过了有一会儿，
(Shíjiān dīdādīdā de guòqù le, Cǎiyí hái méiyǒu huíxìn . . . Guòle yǒu yíhuèr,

彩宜才忍不住回信了……)
彩宜才忍不住回信了……)
Cǎiyí cái rěn búzhù huíxìn le . . .)

彩宜：　　　我還在傷心呢！我們之間好像沒什麼好說的，
彩宜：　　　我还在伤心呢！我们之间好像没什么好说的，
Cǎiyí:　　　Wǒ háizài shāngxīn ne! Wǒmen zhījiān hǎoxiàng méi shénme hǎoshuō de,

你讓我很失望。
你让我很失望。
nǐ ràng wǒ hěn shīwàng.

史文超：　　　彩宜，是你啊！真高興你終於開口了。唉！其實，我也
史文超：　　　彩宜，是你啊！真高兴你终于开口了。唉！其实，我也
Shǐ Wénchāo:　Cǎiyí, shì nǐ a! Zhēn gāoxìng nǐ zhōngyú kāikǒu le. Ài! Qíshí, wǒ yě

不想多說什麼，只想向你道歉，說聲"對不起！"
不想多说什么，只想向你道歉，说声"对不起！"
bùxiǎng duō shuō shénme, zhǐ xiǎng xiàng nǐ dàoqiàn, shuōshēng "Duìbuqǐ!"

昨天都是我的錯，是一場誤會呀！
昨天都是我的错，是一场误会呀！
Zuótiān dōushì wǒde cuò, shì yìchǎng wùhuì ya!

彩宜： 我現在還是很難過，本來是不想理你的，但是看了你
彩宜： 我现在还是很难过，本来是不想理你的，但是看了你
Căiyí: Wǒ xiànzài háishì hěn nánguò, běnlái shì bùxiǎng lǐnǐ de, dànshì kàn le nǐ

寫的話以後，我又忍不住哭起來了。
写的话以后，我又忍不住哭起来了。
xiě de huà yǐhòu, wǒ yòu rěnbuzhù kū qǐlái le.

史文超： 你一定是覺得很委屈才會傷心難過的。別哭，
史文超： 你一定是觉得很委屈才会伤心难过的。别哭，
Shǐ Wénchāo: Nǐ yídìng shì juéde hěn wěiqū cái huì shāngxīn nánguò de. Bié kū,

你淚眼汪汪的樣子，一定很可憐。
你泪眼汪汪的样子，一定很可怜。
nǐ lèiyǎnwāngwāng de yàngzi, yídìng hěn kělián.

彩宜： 少來，你一點兒都不在乎人家的感受！
彩宜： 少来，你一点儿都不在乎人家的感受！
Căiyí: Shǎo lái, nǐ yìdiǎr dōu bú zàihu rénjiā de gǎnshòu!

史文超： 對不起，我實在是不知道說什麼好。我不應該遲到，
史文超： 对不起，我实在是不知道说什么好。我不应该迟到，
Shǐ Wénchāo: Duìbuqǐ, wǒ shízài shì bùzhīdào shuō shénme hǎo. Wǒ bù yīnggāi chídào,

害你等那麼久。我急急忙忙地出去，把手機給忘在
害你等那么久。我急急忙忙地出去，把手机给忘在
hài nǐ děng nàme jiǔ. Wǒ jíjímángmáng de chūqù, bǎ shǒujī gěi wàngzài

家裡了。路上又碰到塞車，所以沒辦法通知你。
家里了。路上又碰到塞车，所以没办法通知你。
jiālǐ le. Lùshàng yòu pèngdào sāichē, suǒyǐ méi bànfǎ tōngzhī nǐ.

然後走路肩又給警察開了罰單。那時候心情挺糟的，
然后走路肩又给警察开了罚单。那时候心情挺糟的，
Ránhòu zǒu lùjiān yòu gěi jǐngchá kāi le fádān. Nàshíhou xīnqíng tǐng zāo de,

希望你能理解，接受我的道歉。
希望你能理解，接受我的道歉。
xīwàng nǐ néng lǐjiě, jiēshòu wǒde dàoqiàn.

彩宜： 我等不到你的電話，以為你出事了，非常著急。
彩宜： 我等不到你的电话，以为你出事了，非常着急。
Cǎiyí: Wǒ děng búdào nǐde diànhuà, yǐwéi nǐ chūshì le, fēicháng zhāojí.

人家是擔心你的安危呀！
人家是担心你的安危呀！
Rénjiā shì dānxīn nǐde ānwēi ya!

史文超： 聽你這麼說我是既感動又高興。
史文超： 听你这么说我是既感动又高兴。
Shǐ Wénchāo: Tīng nǐ zhème shuō wǒ shì jì gǎndòng yòu gāoxìng.

感動的是，你為我等了那麼久，都沒離開。
感动的是，你为我等了那么久，都没离开。
Gǎndòng de shì, nǐ wèi wǒ děng le nàme jiǔ, dōu méi líkāi.

高興的是，覺得你還是很在乎我的喔！
高兴的是，觉得你还是很在乎我的喔！
Gāoxìng de shì, juéde nǐ háishì hěn zàihu wǒ de ō!

彩宜： 不瞞你說，自從我們吵架以後，我也有一點兒後悔。
彩宜： 不瞒你说，自从我们吵架以后，我也有一点儿后悔。
Cǎiyí: Bùmán nǐ shuō, zìcóng wǒmen chǎojià yǐhòu, wǒ yě yǒu yìdiǎr hòuhuǐ.

我不應該沒問清楚就劈里啪啦地把你罵了一頓。
我不应该没问清楚就劈里啪啦地把你骂了一顿。
Wǒ bù yīnggāi méi wèn qīngchǔ jiù pīli pālā de bǎ nǐ mà le yídùn.

史文超： 你罵我是應該的。我要是早點兒出門，
史文超： 你骂我是应该的。我要是早点儿出门，
Shǐ Wénchāo: Nǐ mà wǒ shì yīnggāi de. Wǒ yàoshì zǎodiǎr chūmén,

平常準時一點兒，你也不會生這麼大的氣。
平常准时一点儿，你也不会生这么大的气。
píngcháng zhǔnshí yìdiǎr, nǐ yě búhuì shēng zhème dà de qì.

彩宜： 是啊！我覺得挺委屈的！你的老毛病真的要改一改呀！
彩宜： 是啊！我觉得挺委屈的！你的老毛病真的要改一改呀！
Cǎiyí: Shì a! Wǒ juéde tǐng wěiqū de! Nǐde lǎo máobìng zhēnde yào gǎiyigǎi ya!

史文超：	我一定會改的。對了，明天我沒事，我陪你去退貨，
史文超：	我一定会改的。对了，明天我没事，我陪你去退货，
Shǐ Wénchāo:	Wǒ yídìng huì gǎi de. Duìle, míngtiān wǒ méishì, wǒ péi nǐ qù tuìhuò,
	怎麼樣？
	怎么样？
	zěnmeyàng?

彩宜：	嗯！好呀！幾點？
彩宜：	嗯！好呀！几点？
Cǎiyí:	Ēn! Hǎoyā! Jǐdiǎn?

史文超：	下午三點，行嗎？
史文超：	下午三点，行吗？
Shǐ Wénchāo:	Xiàwǔ sāndiǎn, xíng ma?

彩宜：	應該可以。
彩宜：	应该可以。
Cǎiyí:	Yīnggāi kěyǐ.

史文超：	那你是接受我的道歉了！謝天謝地！退了貨以後，
史文超：	那你是接受我的道歉了！谢天谢地！退了货以后，
Shǐ Wénchāo:	Nà nǐ shì jiēshòu wǒde dàoqiàn le! Xiètiān xièdì! Tuìle huò yǐhòu,
	我們去吃飯，然後去聽音樂會，怎麼樣？
	我们去吃饭，然后去听音乐会，怎么样？
	wǒmen qù chīfàn, ránhòu qù tīng yīnyuè huì, zěnmeyàng?

彩宜：	聽上去好像很不錯，行！說好了，可不能再遲到喔！
彩宜：	听上去好像很不错，行！说好了，可不能再迟到喔！
Cǎiyí:	Tīng shàngqù hǎoxiàng hěn búcuò, xíng! Shuō hǎole, kě bùnéng zài chídào ō!

史文超：	我保證，我一定會準時到的。明天見！
史文超：	我保证，我一定会准时到的。明天见！
Shǐ Wénchāo:	Wǒ bǎozhèng, wǒ yídìng huì zhǔnshí dào de. Míngtiān jiàn!

彩宜：	明天見！
彩宜：	明天见！
Cǎiyí:	Míngtiān jiàn!

Lesson 15　Requesting a Favor

發件人: 史文超 <wenchao@zhongwen.edu>
发件人: 史文超 <wenchao@zhongwen.edu>
Fājiànrén: Shǐ Wénchāo

收件人: 高新遠 <xinyuan@hanyu.edu>
收件人: 高新远 <xinyuan@hanyu.edu>
Shōujiànrén: Gāo Xīnyuǎn

主題: 請幫我買磁帶
主题: 请帮我买磁带
Zhǔtí: Qǐng bāng wǒ mǎi cídài

發送時間: 4/21 3:45 P.M.
发送时间: 4/21 3:45 P.M.
Fāsòng shíjiān: 4/21

新遠:
新远:
Xīnyuǎn:

很久沒有跟你聯絡了，好不容易給你寫信卻是有事要找
很久没有跟你联络了，好不容易给你写信却是有事要找
Hěnjiǔ méiyou gēn nǐ liánluò le, hǎo bùróngyì gěi nǐ xiěxìn què shì yǒushì yào zhǎo

你幫忙，真不好意思。我最近遇到一件麻煩事，如果可以的話，
你帮忙，真不好意思。我最近遇到一件麻烦事，如果可以的话，
nǐ bāngmáng, zhēn bùhǎo yìsi. Wǒ zuìjìn yù dao yíjiàn máfan shì, rúguǒ kěyǐ de huà,

能不能請你幫個忙?
能不能请你帮个忙?
néngbunéng qǐng nǐ bāngge máng?

上個星期，我和女朋友彩宜為了一個小誤會而吵架了。
上个星期，我和女朋友彩宜为了一个小误会而吵架了。
Shàngge xīngqī, wǒ hé nǚpéngyou Cǎiyí wèi le yíge xiǎo wùhuì ér chǎojià le.

我們剛剛才和好，可是現在又出問題了。
我们刚刚才和好，可是现在又出问题了。
Wǒmen gānggāng cái héhǎo, kěshì xiànzài yòu chū wèntí le.

事情的經過是這樣的: 彩宜把一盤 "貓王" 的磁帶借給我聽，
事情的经过是这样的: 彩宜把一盘 "猫王" 的磁带借给我听，
Shìqíng de jīngguò shì zhèyàng de: Cǎiyí bǎ yìpán "Māowáng" de cídài jiè gěi wǒ tīng,

這是她最喜歡的一盤磁帶了。當她把磁帶給我的時候，還交代
这是她最喜欢的一盘磁带了。当她把磁带给我的时候，还交代
zhè shì tā zuì xǐhuān de yìpán cídài le. Dāng tā bǎ cídài gěi wǒ de shíhou, hái jiāodài

我一定要小心，我也向她保證沒問題。可是我在聽磁帶的時候，
我一定要小心，我也向她保证没问题。可是我在听磁带的时候，
wǒ yídìng yào xiǎoxīn, wǒ yě xiàng tā bǎozhèng méiwèntí. Kěshì wǒ zài tīng cídài de shíhou,

我的老錄音機把磁帶絞了。當我急急忙忙地想把磁帶從
我的老录音机把磁带绞了。当我急急忙忙地想把磁带从
wǒde lǎo lùyīnjī bǎ cídài jiǎo le. Dāng wǒ jíjímángmáng de xiǎng bǎ cídài cóng

錄音機裡拿出來的時候，又因為太用力，磁帶不但沒有被取出來，
录音机里拿出来的时候，又因为太用力，磁带不但没有被取出来，
lùyīnjī lǐ ná chūlái de shíhou, yòu yīnwèi tài yònglì, cídài búdàn méiyǒu bèi qǔ chūlai,

反而讓我給拉壞了。我不敢把這件事告訴彩宜，一想到她
反而让我给拉坏了。我不敢把这件事告诉彩宜，一想到她
fǎn'ér rang wǒ gěi lā huài le. Wǒ bùgǎn bǎ zhèjiàn shì gàosu Cǎiyí, yì xiǎngdào tā

淚眼汪汪的樣子，我就不知道該怎麼辦才好。
泪眼汪汪的样子，我就不知道该怎么办才好。
lèiyǎnwāngwāng de yàngzi, wǒ jiù bù zhīdào gāi zěnmebàn cái hǎo.

　　我想再買一盤同樣的磁帶還給她，等買到新磁帶以後再
　　我想再买一盘同样的磁带还给她，等买到新磁带以后再
　　Wǒ xiǎng zài mǎi yìpán tóngyàngde cídài huán gěi tā, děng mǎidào xīn cídài yǐhòu zài

把這件事告訴她，向她道歉。但是這兩天我找遍了我這兒的
把这件事告诉她，向她道歉。但是这两天我找遍了我这儿的
bǎ zhèjiàn shì gàosu tā, xiàng tā dàoqiàn. Dànshì zhè liǎngtiān wǒ zhǎobiàn le wǒ zhèr de

商店，就是找不到同樣的磁帶，所以我現在只好求你幫忙了。
商店，就是找不到同样的磁带，所以我现在只好求你帮忙了。
shāngdiàn, jiùshi zhǎobudào tóngyàngde cídài, suǒyǐ wǒ xiànzài zhǐhǎo qiú nǐ bāngmáng le.

　　你能不能幫我在你那兒的商店找找看？希望我能買到
　　你能不能帮我在你那儿的商店找找看？希望我能买到
　　Nǐ néngbunéng bāng wǒ zài nǐnàrde shāngdiàn zhǎozhǎokàn? Xīwàng wǒ néng mǎidào

貓王的磁帶，不然彩宜是不會原諒我的呀！
猫王的磁带，不然彩宜是不会原谅我的呀！
Māowáng de cídài, bùrán Cǎiyí shì búhuì yuánliàng wǒ de ya!

太麻煩你了，謝謝！
太麻烦你了，谢谢！
Tài máfan nǐ le, xièxie!

文超
文超
Wénchāo

發件人：高新遠 <xinyuan@hanyu.edu>　　收件人：史文超 <wenchao@zhongwen.edu>
发件人：高新远 <xinyuan@hanyu.edu>　　收件人：史文超 <wenchao@zhongwen.edu>
Fājiànrén: Gāo Xīnyuǎn　　　　　　　Shōujiànrén: Shǐ Wénchāo

主題：買到了光碟　　　　　　　　　發送時間：4/25 11:23 P.M.
主题：买到了光碟　　　　　　　　　发送时间：4/25 11:23 P.M.
Zhǔtí: Mǎidào le guāngdié　　　　　　Fāsòng shíjiān: 4/25

文超：
文超：
Wénchāo:

　　不用擔心，我已經買到你要的東西了。我雖然找不到
　　不用担心，我已经买到你要的东西了。我虽然找不到
　　Búyòng dānxīn, wǒ yǐjīng mǎidào nǐ yào de dōngxi le. Wǒ suīrán zhǎobudào

貓王的磁帶，然而卻買到了同樣的音樂光碟。
猫王的磁带，然而却买到了同样的音乐光碟。
Māowáng de cídài, rán'ér què mǎi dào le tóngyàng de yīnyuè guāngdié.

　　我一收到你的電子郵件就去附近的商店找。雖然貓王
　　我一收到你的电子邮件就去附近的商店找。虽然猫王
　　Wǒ yì shōudào nǐde diànzi yóujiàn jiù qù fùjìn de shāngdiàn zhǎo. Suīrán Māowáng

很有名，但是貓王的歌已經不像以前那麼流行了，所以我一直
很有名，但是猫王的歌已经不像以前那么流行了，所以我一直
hěn yǒumíng, dànshì Māowáng de gē yǐjīng búxiàng yǐqián nàme liúxíng le, suǒyǐ wǒ yìzhí

找不到。我上網搜索，還是找不到。最後我只好在網上發了
找不到。我上网搜索，还是找不到。最后我只好在网上发了
zhǎobudào. Wǒ shàngwǎng sōusuǒ, háishì zhǎobudào. Zuìhòu wǒ zhǐhǎo zài wǎngshàng fā le

求購貓王磁帶的帖子。今天下午我終於收到了一封電子郵件，
求购猫王磁带的帖子。今天下午我终于收到了一封电子邮件，
qiúgòu Māowáng cídài de tiězi. Jīntiān xiàwǔ wǒ zhōngyú shōu dào le yìfēng diànzǐ yóujiàn,

說有貓王的光碟。我想光碟更好，就幫你把它買下來了。
说有猫王的光碟。我想光碟更好，就帮你把它买下来了。
shuō yǒu Māowáng de guāngdié. Wǒ xiǎng guāngdié gèng hǎo, jiù bāng nǐ bǎ tā mǎi xiàlái le.

　　總之，事情解決了。你應該很快就能收到光碟了。
　　总之，事情解决了。你应该很快就能收到光碟了。
　　Zǒngzhī, shìqing jiějué le. Nǐ yīnggāi hěn kuài jiù néng shōu dào guāngdié le.

　　　　　　　　　　　　　　　　　　　　　　　新遠
　　　　　　　　　　　　　　　　　　　　　　　新远
　　　　　　　　　　　　　　　　　　　　　　　Xīnyuǎn

Lesson 16   Visiting Teacher Xie

(放春假了，大學四年級的張建明、夏玲跟往年一樣，
(放春假了，大学四年级的张建明、夏玲跟往年一样，
(Fàng chūnjià le, dàxué sì niánjí de Zhāng Jiànmíng, Xià Líng gēn wǎngnián yíyàng,

到謝老師家拜訪。張建明也趁這個機會，把女朋友吳小麗
到谢老师家拜访。张建明也趁这个机会，把女朋友吴小丽
dào Xiè Lǎoshī jiā bàifǎng. Zhāng Jiànmíng yě chèn zhège jīhuì, bǎ nǚpéngyou Wú Xiǎolì

帶過來認識認識謝老師。)
带过来认识认识谢老师。)
dài guòlái rènshi rènshi Xiè Lǎoshī.)

("叮噹"，門鈴響了。謝老師去開門。)
("叮当"，门铃响了。谢老师去开门。)
("Dīngdāng", mén líng xiǎng le. Xiè Lǎoshī qù kāi mén.)

張建明、夏玲：	老師，您好！好久不見，我們過來看您了！
张建明、夏玲：	老师，您好！好久不见，我们过来看您了！
Zhāng Jiànmíng, Xià Líng:	Lǎoshī, nínhǎo! Hǎojiǔbújiàn, wǒmen guòlái kàn nín le!
謝老師：	喔！你們都來了，太好了，來，來，快請進。
谢老师：	喔！你们都来了，太好了，来，来，快请进。
Xiè Lǎoshī:	Ō! Nǐmen dōu lái le, tài hǎo le, lái, lái, kuài qǐngjìn.
張建明：	小麗，這位就是我常跟你提起的謝老師。
张建明：	小丽，这位就是我常跟你提起的谢老师。
Zhāng Jiànmíng:	Xiǎolì, zhèwèi jiùshì wǒ cháng gēn nǐ tíqǐ de Xiè Lǎoshī.
	老師，這是我的女朋友小麗。
	老师，这是我的女朋友小丽。
	Lǎoshī, zhèshì wǒde nǚpéngyou Xiǎolì.
吳小麗：	謝老師，您好，很高興認識您。建明老說著您呢，
吴小丽：	谢老师，您好，很高兴认识您。建明老说着您呢，
Wú Xiǎolì:	Xiè Lǎoshī, nínhǎo, hěn gāoxìng rènshi nín. Jiànmíng lǎo shuō zhe nín ne,
	說您是他最好的老師。您的學生沒有不喜歡您的。
	说您是他最好的老师。您的学生没有不喜欢您的。
	shuō nín shì tā zuì hǎo de lǎoshī. Nínde xuésheng méiyou bù xǐhuān nín de.

謝老師：　　　　　沒有啦！他們都是好學生，既用功又上進。
谢老师：　　　　　没有啦！他们都是好学生，既用功又上进。
Xiè Lǎoshī:　　　Méiyou la! Tāmen dōu shì hǎo xuésheng, jì yònggōng yòu shàngjìn.

　　　　　　　　　我教他們教得很有成就感呢。
　　　　　　　　　我教他们教得很有成就感呢。
　　　　　　　　　Wǒ jiāo tāmen jiāo de hěn yǒu chéngjiùgǎn ne.

張建明：　　　　　老師您教了我們很多東西，其中還包括
张建明：　　　　　老师您教了我们很多东西，其中还包括
Zhāng Jiànmíng:　Lǎoshī nín jiāo le wǒmen hěn duō dōngxi, qízhōng hái bāokuò

　　　　　　　　　待人處世的道理，這些東西可真寶貴呀！
　　　　　　　　　待人处世的道理，这些东西可真宝贵呀！
　　　　　　　　　dàirénchǔshì de dàolǐ, zhèxiē dōngxi kě zhēn bǎoguì ya!

夏玲：　　　　　　是呀！我們老想著您，不管怎麼忙，
夏玲：　　　　　　是呀！我们老想着您，不管怎么忙，
Xià Líng:　　　　Shìya! Wǒmen lǎo xiǎng zhe nín, bùguǎn zěnme máng,

　　　　　　　　　我們非過來看您不可。
　　　　　　　　　我们非过来看您不可。
　　　　　　　　　wǒmen fēi guòlái kàn nín bùkě.

謝老師：　　　　　你們這些孩子們都很懂事，是很有心的，
谢老师：　　　　　你们这些孩子们都很懂事，是很有心的，
Xiè Lǎoshī:　　　Nǐmen zhèxiē háizimen dōu hěn dǒngshì, shì hěn yǒuxīn de,

　　　　　　　　　每年都不忘過來看我，不能不讓我感動。
　　　　　　　　　每年都不忘过来看我，不能不让我感动。
　　　　　　　　　měi nián dōu bú wàng guòlái kàn wǒ, bùnéngbú ràng wǒ gǎndòng.

　　　　　　　　　來，大家請坐，別客氣。就把這兒當成自己的家吧。
　　　　　　　　　来，大家请坐，别客气。就把这儿当成自己的家吧。
　　　　　　　　　Lái, dàjiā qǐng zuò, biékèqi. Jiù bǎ zhèr dàng chéng zìjǐ de jiā ba.

張建明：　　　　　老師，聽說您明年就要退休了。退休以後，
张建明：　　　　　老师，听说您明年就要退休了。退休以后，
Zhāng Jiànmíng:　Lǎoshī, tīngshōu nín míngnián jiùyào tuìxiū le. Tuìxiū yǐhòu,

　　　　　　　　　打算做什麼呢？
　　　　　　　　　打算做什么呢？
　　　　　　　　　dǎsuàn zuò shénme ne?

謝老師:	我是很期待退休以後的日子的。我想多寫寫書法，
谢老师:	我是很期待退休以后的日子的。我想多写写书法，
Xiè Lǎoshī:	Wǒ shì hěn qīdài tuìxiū yǐhòu de rìzi de. Wǒ xiǎng duō xiěxie shūfǎ,

多學習學習。
多学习学习。
duō xuéxí xuéxí.

夏玲:	我記得您很喜歡寫書法，每當您拿著毛筆寫書法
夏玲:	我记得您很喜欢写书法，每当您拿着毛笔写书法
Xià Líng:	Wǒ jì dé nín hěn xǐhuān xiě shūfǎ, měi dāng ní ná zhe máobǐ xiě shūfǎ

的時候，就非常專心。有時候專心得連飯都
的时候，就非常专心。有时候专心得连饭都
de shíhou, jiù fēicháng zhuānxīn. Yǒushíhòu zhuānxīn de lián fàn dōu

忘了吃，真讓人佩服。
忘了吃，真让人佩服。
wàng le chī, zhēn ràng rén pèifú.

吳小麗:	老師您已經很有學問了，為什麼還要學習呢?
吴小丽:	老师您已经很有学问了，为什么还要学习呢?
Wú Xiǎolì:	Lǎoshī nín yǐjīng hěn yǒu xuéwèn le, wèishénme háiyào xuéxí ne?

謝老師:	是活到老學到老! 你們要記住，當我們學得
谢老师:	是活到老学到老! 你们要记住，当我们学得
Xiè Lǎoshī:	Shì huó dào lǎo xué dào lǎo! Nǐmen yào jìzhu, dāng wǒmen xuéde

越多的時候，就會越覺得自己懂的實在太少了。
越多的时候，就会越觉得自己懂的实在太少了。
yuè duō de shíhou, jiù huì yuè juéde zìjǐ dǒng de shízài tài shǎo le.

我雖然二十多歲就開始教書，到現在已經當了
我虽然二十多岁就开始教书，到现在已经当了
Wǒ suīrán èrshí duōsuì jiù kāishǐ jiāoshū, dào xiànzài yǐjīng dāng le

三十幾年的老師了，但是我也很喜歡當學生，
三十几年的老师了，但是我也很喜欢当学生，
sānshí jǐ nián de lǎoshī le, dànshì wǒ yě hěn xǐhuān dāng xuésheng,

可以多學習、多長知識。
可以多学习、多长知识。
kěyǐ duō xuéxí, duō zhǎng zhīshi.

张建明：　　　　我們可要好好地向您看齊呀！對了，夏玲也打算
张建明：　　　　我们可要好好地向您看齐呀！对了，夏玲也打算
Zhāng Jiànmíng:　Wǒmen kě yào hǎohǎode xiàng nín kànqí ya! Duìle, Xià Líng yě dǎsuàn

　　　　　　　　上研究生院繼續學習呢！
　　　　　　　　上研究生院继续学习呢！
　　　　　　　　shàng yánjiūshēngyuàn jìxù xuéxí ne!

謝老師：　　　　是嗎？夏玲，你要上什麼研究生院？
谢老师：　　　　是吗？夏玲，你要上什么研究生院？
Xiè Lǎoshī:　　　Shìma? Xià Líng, nǐ yào shàng shénme yánjiūshēngyuàn?

夏玲：　　　　　我要去讀經濟學碩士，碩士以後我還要再繼續學習，
夏玲：　　　　　我要去读经济学硕士，硕士以后我还要再继续学习，
Xià Líng:　　　　Wǒ yào qù dú jīngjìxué shuòshì, shuòshì yǐhòu wǒ hái yào zài jìxù xuéxí,

　　　　　　　　希望以後能當個經濟學教授。
　　　　　　　　希望以后能当个经济学教授。
　　　　　　　　xīwàng yǐhòu néng dāng ge jīngjìxué jiàoshòu.

謝老師：　　　　不錯，將來一定是前途無量。
谢老师：　　　　不错，将来一定是前途无量。
Xiè Lǎoshī:　　　Búcuò, jiānglái yídìng shì qiántúwúliàng.

夏玲：　　　　　您過獎了。對了，建明說畢業後，要自己開公司呢！
夏玲：　　　　　您过奖了。对了，建明说毕业后，要自己开公司呢！
Xià Líng:　　　　Nín guòjiǎng le. Duìle, Jiànmíng shuō bìyè hòu, yào zìjǐ kāi gōngsī ne!

　　　　　　　　建明，你來講講你的計畫吧。
　　　　　　　　建明，你来讲讲你的计划吧。
　　　　　　　　Jiànmíng, nǐ lái jiǎngjiǎng nǐde jìhuà ba.

张建明：　　　　好的。老師您是知道的，我每年暑假都去
张建明：　　　　好的。老师您是知道的，我每年暑假都去
Zhāng Jiànmíng:　Hǎode. Lǎoshī nín shì zhīdào de, wǒ měinián shǔjià dōu qù

　　　　　　　　電腦公司實習，在那兒學了不少知識和經驗。
　　　　　　　　电脑公司实习，在那儿学了不少知识和经验。
　　　　　　　　diànnǎo gōngsī shíxí, zài nàr xué le bùshǎo zhīshi hé jīngyàn.

　　　　　　　　因此畢業以後，我想把我所學的，好好地應用一下。
　　　　　　　　因此毕业以后，我想把我所学的，好好地应用一下。
　　　　　　　　Yīncǐ bìyè yǐhòu, wǒ xiǎng bǎ wǒ suǒxuéde, hǎohǎo de yìngyòng yíxià.

　　　　　　　　　我想開個電腦網絡公司，給自己一個機會，磨練磨練。
　　　　　　　　　我想开个电脑网络公司，给自己一个机会，磨练磨练。
　　　　　　　　　Wǒ xiǎng kāi ge diànnǎo wǎngluò gōngsī, gěi zìjǐ yíge jīhuì, móliàn móliàn.

吳小麗：　　　　他還下定決心，非要在三十歲以前做出一番事業不可。
吴小丽：　　　　他还下定决心，非要在三十岁以前做出一番事业不可。
Wú Xiǎolì:　　　Tā hái xiàdìngjuéxīn, fēiyào zài sānshísuì yǐqián zuò chū yìfān shìyè bùkě.

謝老師：　　　　很好，你們都是年輕有為，祝你們成功！
谢老师：　　　　很好，你们都是年轻有为，祝你们成功！
Xiè Lǎoshī:　　　Hěn hǎo, nǐmen dōu shì niánqīngyǒuwéi, zhù nǐmen chénggōng!

　　　　　　　　　我會以你們為榮的，好好加油。對了，小麗呢，
　　　　　　　　　我会以你们为荣的，好好加油。对了，小丽呢，
　　　　　　　　　Wǒ huì yǐ nǐmen wéi róng de, hǎohǎo jiāyóu. Duìle, Xiǎolì ne,

　　　　　　　　　你也是今年畢業嗎？
　　　　　　　　　你也是今年毕业吗？
　　　　　　　　　nǐ yě shì jīnnián bìyè ma?

吳小麗：　　　　不，他們都要畢業了，只有我今年還不能畢業。
吴小丽：　　　　不，他们都要毕业了，只有我今年还不能毕业。
Wú Xiǎolì:　　　Bù, tāmen dōuyào bìyè le, zhǐyǒu wǒ jīnnián hái bùnéng bìyè.

　　　　　　　　　我是學醫的，我們學醫的非得學六年不可！
　　　　　　　　　我是学医的，我们学医的非得学六年不可！
　　　　　　　　　Wǒ shì xuéyīde, wǒmen xuéyīde fēi děi xué liùnián bùkě!

(謝老師和學生們繼續聊天。兩個小時以後，學生們要走了。)
(谢老师和学生们继续聊天。两个小时以后，学生们要走了。)
(Xiè Lǎoshī hé xuéshengmen jìxù liáotiān. Liǎngge xiǎoshí yǐhòu, xuéshengmen yào zǒu le.)

張建明(看了看時間)：　　　喔！時間不早了，我們打擾您太久了，
张建明(看了看时间)：　　　喔！时间不早了，我们打扰您太久了，
Zhāng Jiànmíng (kànlekàn shíjiān):　Ō! Shíjiān bù zǎo le, wǒmen dǎrǎo nín tài jiǔ le,

　　　　　　　　　該走了。
　　　　　　　　　该走了。
　　　　　　　　　gāizǒu le.

謝老師：　　　　還早呢！沒關係，再待一會兒吧。
谢老师：　　　　还早呢！没关系，再待一会儿吧。
Xiè Lǎoshī:　　　Háizǎo ne! Méiguānxi, zài dāi yíhuèr ba.

夏玲：　　　　不了，老師，我們是真的該走了。下次有空再來看您。
夏玲：　　　　不了，老师，我们是真的该走了。下次有空再来看您。
Xià Líng:　　 Bùle, Lǎoshī, wǒmen shì zhēnde gāi zǒu le. Xiàcì yǒukòng zài lái kàn nín.

謝老師：　　　那，好吧! 很高興你們來看我。請慢走!
谢老师：　　　那，好吧! 很高兴你们来看我。请慢走!
Xiè Lǎoshī:　 Nà, hǎo ba! Hěn gāoxìng nǐmen lái kàn wǒ. Qǐng màn zǒu!

吳小麗：　　　您多保重，請留步。再見!
吴小丽：　　　您多保重，请留步。再见!
Wú Xiǎolì:　　 Nín duō bǎozhòng, qǐngliúbù. Zàijiàn!

Lesson 17　Let Me Help You Apply for an Internship

史如影：　　　昨天學校的就業中心有一個講座，介紹了如何寫
史如影：　　　昨天学校的就业中心有一个讲座，介绍了如何写
Shǐ Rúyǐng:　 Zuótiān xuéxiào de jiùyè zhōngxīn yǒu yíge jiǎngzuò, jièshào le rúhé xiě

　　　　　　　簡歷，如何申請工作或者研究生院，很有幫助。
　　　　　　　简历，如何申请工作或者研究生院，很有帮助。
　　　　　　　jiǎnlì, rúhé shēnqǐng gōngzuò huòzhě yánjiūshēngyuàn, hěn yǒu bāngzhù.

張華利：　　　來，說說看，簡歷該怎麼寫? 今年暑假我想申請去
张华利：　　　来，说说看，简历该怎么写? 今年暑假我想申请去
Zhāng Huálì:　Lái, shuōshuokàn, jiǎnlì gāi zěnme xiě? Jīnnián shǔjià wǒ xiǎng shēnqǐng qù

　　　　　　　公司實習。
　　　　　　　公司实习。
　　　　　　　gōngsī shíxí.

史如影：　　　你不是去年申請了嗎?
史如影：　　　你不是去年申请了吗?
Shǐ Rúyǐng:　 Nǐ búshì qùnián shēnqǐng le ma?

張華利：　　　哪兒啊? 你難道忘記了去年我沒有去成嗎?
张华利：　　　哪儿啊? 你难道忘记了去年我没有去成吗?
Zhāng, Huálì:　Nǎr ā? Nǐ nándào wàngjile qùnián wǒ méiyǒu qùchéng ma?

　　　　　　　就是因為我沒有把簡歷寫好。
　　　　　　　就是因为我没有把简历写好。
　　　　　　　Jiùshì yīnwèi wǒ méiyou bǎ jiǎnlì xiě hǎo.

史如影:　　　其實寫簡歷不複雜。首先，你要清楚自己想申請
史如影:　　　其实写简历不复杂。首先，你要清楚自己想申请
Shǐ Rúyǐng:　Qíshí xiě jiǎnlì bú fùzá. Shǒuxiān, nǐ yào qīngchǔ zìjǐ xiǎng shēnqǐng

什麼性質的工作。然後，根據不同的工作要求
什么性质的工作。然后，根据不同的工作要求
shénme xìngzhì de gōngzuò. Ránhòu, gēnjù bùtóng de gōngzuò yāoqiú

調整自己的簡歷。
调整自己的简历。
tiáozhěng zìjǐ de jiǎnlì.

張華利:　　　那就是說申請的工作不同，簡歷的寫法也要不同，
张华利:　　　那就是说申请的工作不同，简历的写法也要不同，
Zhāng Huálì:　Nà jiùshi shuō shēnqǐng de gōngzuò bùtóng, jiǎnlì de xiěfǎ yěyào bùtóng,

是嗎?
是吗?
shìma?

史如影:　　　正是如此。寫簡歷一定要突出重點。你去年不是
史如影:　　　正是如此。写简历一定要突出重点。你去年不是
Shǐ Rúyǐng:　Zhèng shì rúcǐ. Xiě jiǎnlì yídìng yào tūchū zhòngdiǎn. Nǐ qùnián búshì

這樣寫的嗎?
这样写的吗?
zhèyàng xiě de ma?

張華利:　　　沒有! 怪不得去年我被拒絕了! 我一定要仔仔細細地把簡歷
张华利:　　　没有! 怪不得去年我被拒绝了! 我一定要仔仔细细地把简历
Zhāng Huálì:　Méiyou! Guàibudé qùnián wǒ bèi jùjué le! Wǒ yídìng yào zǐzǐxìxì de bǎ jiǎnlì

修改一下。對了，你不是今年夏天也打算去實習的嗎?
修改一下。对了，你不是今年夏天也打算去实习的吗?
xiūgǎi yíxià. Duìle, nǐ búshì jīnnián xiàtiān yě dǎsuàn qù shíxí de ma?

史如影:　　　是的，可是我還不知道哪些公司在招聘。
史如影:　　　是的，可是我还不知道哪些公司在招聘。
Shǐ Rúyǐng:　Shìde, kěshì wǒ hái bù zhīdào nǎxiē gōngsī zài zhāopìn.

張華利:　　網上有很多信息，你不知道嗎？我今晚就給你發一些
张华利:　　网上有很多信息，你不知道吗？我今晚就给你发一些
Zhāng Huálì:　Wǎngshàng yǒu hěnduō xìnxī, nǐ bù zhīdào ma? Wǒ jīnwǎn jiù gěi nǐ fā yìxiē

過去。唉，難道昨天他們沒有給你們介紹網站嗎？
过去。唉，难道昨天他们没有给你们介绍网站吗？
guòqù. Ài, nándào zuótiān tāmen méiyou gěi nǐmen jièshào wǎngzhàn ma?

史如影:　　介紹了。他們說我們可以直接從網上下載申請
史如影:　　介绍了。他们说我们可以直接从网上下载申请
Shǐ Rúyǐng:　Jièshào le. Tāmen shuō wǒmen kěyǐ zhíjiē cóng wǎngshàng xiàzǎi shēnqǐng

表格，填好以後把表格寄出去，也可以就在網上填表
表格，填好以后把表格寄出去，也可以就在网上填表
biǎogé, tián hǎo yǐhòu bǎ biǎogé jì chūqù, yě kěyi jiù zài wǎngshàng tiánbiǎo

申請。
申请。
shēnqǐng.

張華利:　　對，我就是在網上申請的。
张华利:　　对，我就是在网上申请的。
Zhāng Huálì:　Duì, wǒ jiùshì zài wǎngshàng shēnqǐng de.

史如影:　　下一步我還需要幾封推薦信。
史如影:　　下一步我还需要几封推荐信。
Shǐ Rúyǐng:　Xiàyibù wǒ hái xūyào jǐfēng tuījiànxìn.

張華利:　　你還沒有找教授談過嗎？恐怕要趕快了，
张华利:　　你还没有找教授谈过吗？恐怕要赶快了，
Zhāng Huálì:　Nǐ hái méiyou zhǎo jiàoshòu tán guo ma? Kǒngpà yào gǎnkuài le,

教授們的時間是有限的。
教授们的时间是有限的。
jiàoshòumen de shíjiān shì yǒuxiàn de.

史如影:　　我已經考慮好了，準備安排一下兒，過幾天就去找一些
史如影:　　我已经考虑好了，准备安排一下儿，过几天就去找一些
Shǐ Rúyǐng:　Wǒ yǐjīng kǎolǜ hǎo le, zhǔnbèi ānpái yíxiàr, guò jǐtiān jiù qù zhǎo yìxiē

教授談一談。希望他們能同意為我寫推薦信。
教授谈一谈。希望他们能同意为我写推荐信。
jiàoshòu tányitán. Xīwàng tāmen néng tóngyì wèi wǒ xiě tuījiànxìn.

張華利：　我相信他們一定會很樂意幫你寫推薦信的。
张华利：　我相信他们一定会很乐意帮你写推荐信的。
Zhāng Huálì:　Wǒ xiāngxìn tāmen yídìng huì hěn lèyì bāng nǐ xiě tuījiànxìn de.

你那麼聰明、能幹，條件那麼好。不用擔心。
你那么聪明、能干，条件那么好。不用担心。
Nǐ nàme cōngmíng, nénggàn, tiáojiàn nàme hǎo. Búyòng dānxīn.

史如影：　但願如此。
史如影：　但愿如此。
Shǐ Rúyǐng:　Dànyuàn rúcǐ.

Lesson 18   "Why Are You Interested in This Job?"

陳主任：　文小姐，你好。很高興你對我們公司感興趣。
陈主任：　文小姐，你好。很高兴你对我们公司感兴趣。
Chén Zhǔrèn:　Wén xiǎojiě, nǐ hǎo. Hěn gāoxìng nǐ duì wǒmen gōngsī gǎn xìngqù.

文如華：　您好，陳主任。謝謝您給我這個機會。
文如华：　您好，陈主任。谢谢您给我这个机会。
Wén Rúhuá:　Nín hǎo, Chén Zhǔrèn. Xièxie nín gěi wǒ zhège jīhuì.

陳主任：　我看了你的簡歷，你有雙學位，電子商務和計算機
陈主任：　我看了你的简历，你有双学位，电子商务和计算机
Chén Zhǔrèn:　Wǒ kànle nǐ de jiǎnlì, nǐ yǒu shuāng xuéwèi, diànzǐ shāngwù hé jìsuànjī

科學，今年畢業，是嗎?
科学，今年毕业，是吗?
kēxué, jīnnián bìyè, shìma?

文如華：　是的。我今年五月份畢業，還有差不多一個月左右。
文如华：　是的。我今年五月份毕业，还有差不多一个月左右。
Wén Rúhuá:　Shìde. Wǒ jīnnián wǔ yuèfèn bìyè, háiyǒu chàbuduō yíge yuè zuǒyòu.

陳主任：　你為什麼對商學感興趣呢?
陈主任：　你为什么对商学感兴趣呢?
Chén Zhǔrèn:　Nǐ wèishénme duì shāngxué gǎn xìngqù ne?

文如華:　因為我爸爸是從商的，受爸爸的影響，所以我從
文如华:　因为我爸爸是从商的，受爸爸的影响，所以我从
Wén Rúhuá:　Yīnwèi wǒ bàba shì cóngshāng de, shòu bàba de yǐngxiǎng, suǒyǐ wǒ cóng

小就對商業感興趣。
小就对商业感兴趣。
xiǎo jiù duì shāngyè gǎn xìngqù.

陳主任:　能不能說一說你為什麼想來我們公司工作？
陈主任:　能不能说一说你为什么想来我们公司工作？
Chén Zhǔrèn:　Néngbunéng shuōyishuō nǐ wèishénme xiǎng lái wǒmen gōngsī gōngzuò?

文如華:　我查了一下你們公司的網站，了解到你們是
文如华:　我查了一下你们公司的网站，了解到你们是
Wén Rúhuá:　Wǒ chále yíxià nǐmen gōngsī de wǎngzhàn, liǎojiědào nǐmen shì

一家電腦咨詢公司。你們不但自己開發軟件技術，
一家电脑咨询公司。你们不但自己开发软件技术，
yìjiā diànnǎo zīxún gōngsī. Nǐmen búdàn zìjǐ kāifā ruǎnjiàn jìshù,

而且還提供大量的咨詢服務。
而且还提供大量的咨询服务。
érqiě hái tígōng dàliàng de zīxún fúwù.

陳主任:　是的。我們公司儘管只有六年的歷史，可是發展得
陈主任:　是的。我们公司尽管只有六年的历史，可是发展得
Chén Zhǔrèn:　Shìde. Wǒmen gōngsī jǐnguǎn zhǐyǒu liùnián de lìshǐ, kěshì fāzhǎn de

很快。現在公司的員工有三百個左右。
很快。现在公司的员工有三百个左右。
hěnkuài. Xiànzài gōngsī de yuángōng yǒu sānbǎige zuǒyòu.

文如華:　聽說你們是上市公司，是嗎？
文如华:　听说你们是上市公司，是吗？
Wén Rúhuá:　Tīngshuō nǐmen shì shàngshì gōngsī, shìma?

陳主任:　一點兒也沒錯。我們雖然去年年初才開始上市，不過
陈主任:　一点儿也没错。我们虽然去年年初才开始上市，不过
Chén Zhǔrèn:　Yìdiǎr yě méicuò. Wǒmen suīrán qùnián niánchū cái kāishǐ shàngshì, búguò

業務開展得很好。對了，能不能談談你自己的情況？
业务开展得很好。对了，能不能谈谈你自己的情况？
yèwù kāizhǎn de hěn hǎo. Duìle, néngbunéng tántan nǐ zìjǐ de qíngkuàng?

文如華：　　好的。我是中華大學的學生，除了商學和
文如华：　　好的。我是中华大学的学生，除了商学和
Wén Rúhuá:　Hǎode. Wǒ shì Zhōnghuá Dàxué de xuésheng, chúle shāngxué hé

計算機兩個主修專業以外，我還有一個中文副修。
计算机两个主修专业以外，我还有一个中文副修。
jìsuànjī liǎnggè zhǔxiū zhuānyè yǐwài, wǒ háiyou yíge Zhōngwén fùxiū.

我的平均成績很高，曾經多次得到過學校的嘉獎，
我的平均成绩很高，曾经多次得到过学校的嘉奖，
Wǒde píngjūn chéngjì hěngāo, céngjīng duōcì dédào guo xuéxiào de jiājiǎng,

還擔任過商學院的學生會主席，組織過很多
还担任过商学院的学生会主席，组织过很多
hái dānrèn guo shāngxuéyuàn de xuéshēnghuì zhǔxí, zǔzhī guo hěnduō

活動。凡是學校的重要活動，我都是組織人之一。
活动。凡是学校的重要活动，我都是组织人之一。
huódòng. Fánshì xuéxiào de zhòngyào huódòng, wǒ dōu shì zǔzhīrén zhī yī.

陳主任：　　你參加過研究項目嗎?
陈主任：　　你参加过研究项目吗?
Chén Zhǔrèn:　Nǐ cānjiā guo yánjiū xiàngmù ma?

文如華：　　參加過。從去年開始，我一直在跟教授做研究，
文如华：　　参加过。从去年开始，我一直在跟教授做研究，
Wén Rúhuá:　Cānjiā guo. Cóng qùnián kāishǐ, wǒ yìzhí zài gēn jiàoshòu zuò yánjiū,

現在正在寫畢業論文。
现在正在写毕业论文。
xiànzài zhèngzài xiě bìyè lùnwén.

陳主任：　　除了學習以外，你還喜歡做什麼呢?
陈主任：　　除了学习以外，你还喜欢做什么呢?
Chén Zhǔrèn:　Chúle xuéxí yǐwài, nǐ hái xǐhuān zuò shénme ne?

文如華：　　我喜歡很多東西。不過，我最喜歡旅行。
文如华：　　我喜欢很多东西。不过，我最喜欢旅行。
Wén Rúhuá:　Wǒ xǐhuān hěnduō dōngxi. Búguò, wǒ zuì xǐhuān lǚxíng.

陳主任：　　那好，我們這份工作就是要常常出差。
陈主任：　　那好，我们这份工作就是要常常出差。
Chén Zhǔrèn:　Nà hǎo, wǒmen zhèfèn gōngzuò jiùshì yào chángcháng chūchāi.

文如華:	那我是求之不得呀！哪怕天天在外面走，
文如华:	那我是求之不得呀！哪怕天天在外面走，
Wén Rúhuá:	Nà wǒ shì qiúzhībùdé ya! Nǎpà tiāntiān zài wàimiàn zǒu,

	我也會很高興。
	我也会很高兴。
	wǒ yě huì hěn gāoxìng.

陳主任:	你還有什麼問題嗎？
陈主任:	你还有什么问题吗？
Chén Zhǔrèn:	Nǐ háiyǒu shénme wèntí ma?

文如華:	請問，你們什麼時候能做決定呢？
文如华:	请问，你们什么时候能做决定呢？
Wén Rúhuá:	Qǐngwèn, nǐmen shénme shíhou néng zuò juédìng ne?

陳主任:	下個星期一吧。我們會給你打電話的。
陈主任:	下个星期一吧。我们会给你打电话的。
Chén Zhǔrèn:	Xiàge xīngqī yī ba. Wǒmen huì gěi nǐ dǎ diànhuà de.

文如華:	好，我等你們的電話。再次感謝您給我這個機會。
文如华:	好，我等你们的电话。再次感谢您给我这个机会。
Wén Rúhuá:	Hǎo, wǒ děng nǐmende diànhuà. Zàicì gǎnxiè nín gěi wǒ zhège jīhuì.

Lesson 19　"Have You Had Any Job Offers?"

周華信:	新民，你工作找得怎麼樣？
周华信:	新民，你工作找得怎么样？
Zhōu Huáxìn:	Xīnmín, nǐ gōngzuò zhǎode zěnmeyàng?

金新民:	有三個地方接受了我的申請，一個是金融銀行，
金新民:	有三个地方接受了我的申请，一个是金融银行，
Jīn Xīnmín:	Yǒu sānge dìfang jiēshòu le wǒde shēnqǐng, yíge shì jīnróng yínháng,

	兩個是咨詢公司。這兩天我正在考慮接受哪一個呢。
	两个是咨询公司。这两天我正在考虑接受哪一个呢。
	liǎngge shì zīxún gōngsī. Zhè liǎngtiān wǒ zhèngzài kǎolǜ jiēshòu nǎyíge ne.

周華信：　　　真的嗎？現在的經濟還沒完全恢復，就業市場還
周华信：　　　真的吗？现在的经济还没完全恢复，就业市场还
Zhōu Huáxìn:　Zhēnde ma? Xiànzài de jīngjì hái méi wánquán huīfù, jiùyè shìchǎng hái

不太景氣，競爭非常厲害，可是卻有三家公司要你，
不太景气，竞争非常厉害，可是却有三家公司要你，
bú tài jǐngqì, jìngzhēng fēicháng lìhai, kěshì què yǒu sānjiā gōngsī yào nǐ,

你真了不起！祝賀你。
你真了不起！祝贺你。
nǐ zhēn liǎobuqǐ! Zhùhè nǐ.

金新民：　　　謝謝。不過我覺得主要是我的運氣比較好。
金新民：　　　谢谢。不过我觉得主要是我的运气比较好。
Jīn Xīnmín:　Xièxie. Búguò wǒ juéde zhǔyào shì wǒde yùnqi bǐjiào hǎo.

周華信：　　　別謙虛了。要找好的工作非要有好的條件不可。
周华信：　　　别谦虚了。要找好的工作非要有好的条件不可。
Zhōu Huáxìn:　Bié qiānxū le. Yào zhǎo hǎode gōngzuò fēi yào yǒu hǎode tiáojiàn bùkě.

誰的條件不好都不行！
谁的条件不好都不行！
Shéide tiáojiàn bùhǎo dōu bùxíng!

金新民：　　　也不完全如此，我還是比較幸運的。
金新民：　　　也不完全如此，我还是比较幸运的。
Jīn Xīnmín:　Yě bù wánquán rúcǐ, wǒ háishì bǐjiào xìngyùn de.

周華信：　　　那你到底考慮去哪家公司呢？
周华信：　　　那你到底考虑去哪家公司呢？
Zhōu Huáxìn:　Nà nǐ dàodǐ kǎolǜ qù nǎjiā gōngsī ne?

金新民：　　　可能是那家大的咨詢公司吧，他們給的工資比較高。
金新民：　　　可能是那家大的咨询公司吧，他们给的工资比较高。
Jīn Xīnmín:　Kěnéng shì nàjiā dàde zīxún gōngsī ba, tāmen gěi de gōngzī bǐjiào gāo.

周華信：　　　我倒寧願去金融銀行！金飯碗，打不破。
周华信：　　　我倒宁愿去金融银行！金饭碗，打不破。
Zhōu Huáxìn:　Wǒ dào nìngyuàn qù jīnróng yínháng! Jīn fànwǎn, dǎbúpò.

金新民： 你說得倒也對。銀行的工作比較穩定，待遇也很好。
金新民： 你说得倒也对。银行的工作比较稳定，待遇也很好。
Jīn Xīnmín: Nǐ shuōde dào yě duì. Yínháng de gōngzuò bǐjiào wěndìng, dàiyù yě hěnhǎo.

周華信： 不過還要看他們付給你多少年薪呢。
周华信： 不过还要看他们付给你多少年薪呢。
Zhōu Huáxìn: Búguò hái yào kàn tāmen fù gěi nǐ duōshǎo nián xīn ne.

金新民： 銀行給我的起薪是六萬，小的咨詢公司是五萬二，
金新民： 银行给我的起薪是六万，小的咨询公司是五万二，
Jīn Xīnmín: Yínháng gěi wǒde qǐxīn shì liùwàn, xiǎode zīxún gōngsī shì wǔwàn èr,

大的是五萬五，不過他們都是上市公司，可以給我
大的是五万五，不过他们都是上市公司，可以给我
dàde shì wǔwàn wǔ, búguò tāmen dōu shì shàngshì gōngsī, kěyi gěi wǒ

公司的股份。
公司的股份。
gōngsīde gǔfèn.

周華信： 看樣子都很不錯嘛！那就決定了吧。
周华信： 看样子都很不错嘛！那就决定了吧。
Zhōu Huáxìn: Kànyàngzi dōu hěn búcuò ma! Nà jiù juédìng le ba.

金新民： 可他們提供的待遇還是有點兒不一樣。
金新民： 可他们提供的待遇还是有点儿不一样。
Jīn Xīnmín: Kě tāmen tígōng de dàiyù háishi yǒudiǎr bù yíyàng.

周華信： 得了，得了！你真是婆婆媽媽的。好吧，說說看，
周华信： 得了，得了！你真是婆婆妈妈的。好吧，说说看，
Zhōu Huáxìn: Déle, déle! Nǐ zhēnshì pópomāma de. Hǎoba, shuōshuokàn,

究竟有什麼不一樣？
究竟有什么不一样？
jiūjìng yǒu shénme bù yíyàng?

金新民：   他們的退休計畫和醫療保險都差不多，出差的補貼也
金新民：   他们的退休计划和医疗保险都差不多，出差的补贴也
Jīn Xīnmín: Tāmende tuìxiū jìhuà hé yīliáo bǎoxiǎn dōu chàbuduō, chūchāi de bǔtiē yě

很高。但是，如果以後我想再去修一些研究生的課，
很高。但是，如果以后我想再去修一些研究生的课，
hěngāo. Dànshì, rúguǒ yǐhòu wǒ xiǎng zài qù xiū yìxiē yánjiūshēngde kè,

銀行可以提供學費補貼，而咨詢公司卻沒有這方面
银行可以提供学费补贴，而咨询公司却没有这方面
yínháng kěyǐ tígōng xuéfèi bǔtiē, ér zīxún gōngsī què méiyou zhè fāngmiàn

的福利。所以我有點兒猶豫。
的福利。所以我有点儿犹豫。
de fúlì. Suǒyǐ wǒ yǒudiǎr yóuyù.

周華信：   要我說，給的錢多就行。
周华信：   要我说，给的钱多就行。
Zhōu Huáxìn: Yào wǒ shuō, gěide qián duō jiù xíng.

金新民：   這我倒不太同意。對我來說，錢固然重要，
金新民：   这我倒不太同意。对我来说，钱固然重要，
Jīn Xīnmín: Zhè wǒ dào bú tài tóngyì. Duì wǒ lái shuō, qián gùrán zhòngyào,

可工作環境更重要。
可工作环境更重要。
kě gōngzuò huánjìng gèng zhòngyào.

周華信：   那倒也是。有時候，有一個好的工作環境確實比
周华信：   那倒也是。有时候，有一个好的工作环境确实比
Zhōu Huáxìn: Nà dào yě shì. Yǒushíhou, yǒu yíge hǎode gōngzuò huánjìng quèshí bǐ

工資的多少更重要。
工资的多少更重要。
gōngzī de duōshǎo gèng zhòngyào.

金新民：   其實我想去那家大的咨詢公司，聽說那兒的同事關係
金新民：   其实我想去那家大的咨询公司，听说那儿的同事关系
Jīn Xīnmín: Qíshí wǒ xiǎng qù nàjiā dàde zīxún gōngsī, tīngshuō nàr de tóngshì guānxi

很融洽，上司也很好。
很融洽，上司也很好。
hěn róngqià, shàngsī yě hěn hǎo.

周華信:	這一點倒是非常重要的。
周华信:	这一点倒是非常重要的。
Zhōu Huáxìn:	Zhè yìdiǎn dào shì fēicháng zhòngyào de.

金新民:	我爸爸也說:"你還年輕,錢以後總能賺得到,
金新民:	我爸爸也说:"你还年轻,钱以后总能赚得到,
Jīn Xīnmín:	Wǒ bàba yě shuō: "Nǐ hái niánqīng, qián yǐhòu zǒng néng zhuàndedào,

	可是好的工作環境卻不是那麼容易得到的。"
	可是好的工作环境却不是那么容易得到的。"
	kěshì hǎode gōngzuò huánjìng què búshì nàme róngyì dédào de."

周華信:	你爸爸說得有道理,聽他的沒錯。
周华信:	你爸爸说得有道理,听他的没错。
Zhōu Huáxìn:	Nǐ bàba shuōde yǒu dàoli, tīng tāde méicuò.

Lesson 20   Which Job Offer Should I Accept?

健生:	
健生:	
Jiànshēng:	

	你好!好久沒有跟你聯絡了。怎麼樣?好嗎?
	你好!好久没有跟你联络了。怎么样?好吗?
	Nǐhǎo! Hǎojiǔ méiyou gēn nǐ liánluò le. Zěnmeyàng? Hǎo ma?

	我今年就要畢業了,一直在找工作,所以最近特別忙。
	我今年就要毕业了,一直在找工作,所以最近特别忙。
	Wǒ jīnnián jiùyào bìyè le, yìzhí zài zhǎo gōngzuò, suǒyǐ zuìjìn tèbié máng.

我希望找一家既跟我的專業有關,又能提供好的福利待遇的
我希望找一家既跟我的专业有关,又能提供好的福利待遇的
Wǒ xīwàng zhǎo yìjiā jì gēn wǒde zhuānyè yǒuguān, yòu néng tígōng hǎode fúlì dàiyù de

公司。現在的經濟還沒有完全恢復,要找一份工作很不容易,
公司。现在的经济还没有完全恢复,要找一份工作很不容易,
gōngsī. Xiànzàide jīngjì hái méiyou wánquán huīfù, yào zhǎo yífèn gōngzuò hěn bù róngyì,

更別說是找到一份理想的工作了，所以我很緊張。我還準備
更别说是找到一份理想的工作了，所以我很紧张。我还准备
gèng biéshuō shì zhǎodào yífèn lǐxiǎngde gōngzuò le, suǒyǐ wǒ hěnjǐnzhāng. Wǒ hái zhǔnbèi

如果找不到工作，與其在家等待，不如申請研究生院，再學習
如果找不到工作，与其在家等待，不如申请研究生院，再学习
rúguǒ zhǎobudào gōngzuò, yǔqí zài jiā děngdài, bùrú shēnqǐng yánjiūshēngyuàn, zài xuéxí

兩年，拿一個碩士學位，為以後在就業市場上競爭做準備。
两年，拿一个硕士学位，为以后在就业市场上竞争做准备。
liǎngnián, ná yíge shuòshì xuéwèi, wèi yǐhòu zài jiùyè shìchǎng shàng jìngzhēng zuò zhǔnbèi.

前些日子，我去一些公司參加面試，已經去了五家公司了。當時
前些日子，我去一些公司参加面试，已经去了五家公司了。当时
Qiánxiē rìzi, wǒ qù yìxiē gōngsī cānjiā miànshì, yǐjīng qùle wǔjiā gōngsī le. Dāngshí

我想，只要其中一家要我，即使工資低一點，那我也很幸運了。
我想，只要其中一家要我，即使工资低一点，那我也很幸运了。
wǒ xiǎng, zhǐyào qízhōng yìjiā yào wǒ, jíshǐ gōngzī dī yìdiǎn, nà wǒ yě hěn xìngyùn le.

想不到有三家公司接受了我，而且都是不錯的公司，這讓我
想不到有三家公司接受了我，而且都是不错的公司，这让我
Xiǎngbudào yǒu sānjiā gōngsī jiēshòu le wǒ, érqiě dōushì búcuò de gōngsī, zhè ràng wǒ

興奮極了。
兴奋极了。
xīngfèn jí le.

我還沒決定究竟去哪家公司。本來我想，不管是哪家公司
我还没决定究竟去哪家公司。本来我想，不管是哪家公司
Wǒ hái méi juédìng jiūjìng qù nǎjiā gōngsī. Běnlái wǒ xiǎng, bùguǎn shì nǎjiā gōngsī

要我，我都會去。現在既然有三家公司都要我，我當然得
要我，我都会去。现在既然有三家公司都要我，我当然得
yào wǒ, wǒ dōu huì qù. Xiànzài jìrán yǒu sānjiā gōngsī dōu yào wǒ, wǒ dāngrán děi

好好地挑選一下。
好好地挑选一下。
hǎohǎode tiāoxuǎn yíxià.

因為你工作了一年了，已經有一些經驗，所以我很想聽聽你的
因为你工作了一年了，已经有一些经验，所以我很想听听你的
Yīnwèi nǐ gōngzuò le yìnián le, yǐjīng yǒu yìxiē jīngyàn, suǒyǐ wǒ hěnxiǎng tīngting nǐde

想法。我想知道，當我在跟公司談條件的時候，有哪些問題
想法。我想知道，当我在跟公司谈条件的时候，有哪些问题
xiǎngfǎ. Wǒ xiǎng zhīdào, dāng wǒ zài gēn gōngsī tán tiáojiàn de shíhou, yǒu nǎxiē wèntí

是我非提不可的。希望你能給我當當參謀，以免我說錯話。
是我非提不可的。希望你能给我当当参谋，以免我说错话。
shì wǒ fēi tí bùkě de. Xīwàng nǐ néng gěi wǒ dāng dang cānmóu, yǐmiǎn wǒ shuō cuò huà.

四年的大學生活就要結束了，回想這四年的大學生活，
四年的大学生活就要结束了，回想这四年的大学生活，
Sìnián de dàxué shēnghuó jiùyào jiéshù le, huí xiǎng zhè sìnián de dàxué shēnghuó,

覺得很有收穫。不但學了不少知識，而且也讓自己更了解今後的
觉得很有收获。不但学了不少知识，而且也让自己更了解今后的
juéde hěn yǒu shōuhuò. Búdàn xuéle bùshǎo zhīshi, érqiě yě ràng zìjǐ gèng liǎojiě jīnhòu de

奮鬥目標。還有，我想先工作幾年，然後再回學校攻讀
奋斗目标。还有，我想先工作几年，然后再回学校攻读
fèndòu mùbiāo. Háiyǒu, wǒ xiǎng xiān gōngzuò jǐnián, ránhòu zài huí xuéxiào gōngdú

研究生院，多學一些東西。你呢？你不也是這麼想的嗎？
研究生院，多学一些东西。你呢？你不也是这么想的吗？
yánjiūshēngyuàn, duōxué yìxiē dōngxi. Nǐ ne? Nǐ bù yě shì zhème xiǎng de ma?

好了，不多寫了。祝
好了，不多写了。祝
Hǎo le, bù duō xiě le. Zhù

工作愉快
工作愉快
Gōngzuò yúkuài

友　新民
友　新民
Yǒu　Xīnmín

四月二十五日
四月二十五日
Sì yuè èrshíwǔ rì

拼音索引 (拼音索引)　PINYIN GLOSSARY

Each entry lists the Pinyin, traditional character, simplified character, part of speech, English meaning, and lesson number.

A

ài	唉	唉	*Int.*	(a sigh of sadness or regret)	11
àihàozhě	愛好者	爱好者	*N.*	amateur, enthusiast, fan	15
āiya	哎呀	哎呀	*Int.*	ah!, gosh!, oh dear!	12
ānpái	安排	安排	*V.*	to arrange	17
			N.	arrangement	
ānwēi	安危	安危	*N.*	safety and danger, safety	14

B

bāngzhù	幫助	帮助	*N.*	help	12
			V.	to help	
bǎoguì	寶貴	宝贵	*Adj.*	precious	16
bāokuò	包括	包括	*V.*	to include, comprise	16
bǎoxiǎn	保險	保险	*N.*	insurance	12
bàoyuàn	抱怨	抱怨	*V.*	to complain	13
bǎozhèng	保證	保证	*V.*	to pledge, guarantee, assure	14
bèi	被	被	*Prep.*	(introduces the agent in a passive sentence)	11
			N.	quilt	
bī	逼	逼	*V.*	to force	13
biàn	遍	遍	*Adj.*	all over	15
biǎogé	表格	表格	*N.*	form	17
bìngfáng	病房	病房	*N.*	ward (of a hospital)	11
bùkānshèxiǎng	不堪設想	不堪设想		cannot bear to think about it	12
bǔkǎo	補考	补考	*N.*	make-up test	12
bùmánnǐshuō	不瞞你說	不瞒你说		to tell you the truth 瞞 (to hide the truth from)	14
bùrán	不然	不然	*Conj.*	or else, otherwise, if not	12
bǔtiē	補貼	补贴	*V.*	to compensate	19
			N.	allowance	
búxìng	不幸	不幸	*N.*	adversity, misfortune	12
búyàojǐn	不要緊	不要紧		it doesn't matter, it's not serious	11

C

cānmóu	參謀	参谋	*V.*	to give advice	20
			N.	military advisor	
céngjīng	曾經	曾经	*Adv.*	once	18
chǎojià	吵架	吵架	*V.O.*	to quarrel	13
chēhuò	車禍	车祸	*N.*	car accident	13
chèn	趁	趁	*Prep.*	avail oneself of	16
chéngjì/chéngjī	成績	成绩	*N.*	grade, score, result, success	18
chéngjiùgǎn	成就感	成就感	*N.*	sense of achievement	16
chídào	遲到	迟到	*V.*	to be late	13
chīkuī	吃虧	吃亏	*V.O.*	to suffer losses, come to grief	13
chūchāi	出差	出差	*V.O.*	to go on a business trip	18
chūkǒu	出口	出口	*N.*	exit	13
chúle . . . yǐwài	除了……以外	除了……以外	*Conj.*	besides, except (for)	18
chūménzàiwài	出門在外	出门在外		to be away from home	12
chūshì	出事	出事	*V.O.*	to meet with a mishap, have an accident	14
chūyuàn	出院	出院	*V.O.*	to be discharged from the hospital	12
cídài	磁帶	磁带	*N.*	(magnetic) tape	15
cōngcōng mángmáng	匆匆忙忙	匆匆忙忙	*Adv.*	in a hurry	13
cōngmíng	聰明	聪明	*Adj.*	smart	17
cóngshāng	從商	从商	*V.*	to engage in business	18
cuī	催	催	*V.*	to urge	13

D

dāi	待	待	*V.*	to stay	12
dàirénchǔshì	待人處世	待人处世		the way one acts with others and conducts oneself in public	16
dàiyù	待遇	待遇	*N.*	salary and benefits	19
dàliàng	大量	大量	*N.*	large quantity	18
dàng	當	当	*V.*	to regard as, treat as	16
dāngchū	當初	当初		in the first place, originally	12
dāngshí	當時	当时	*Adv.*	then, at that time	20
dānrèn	擔任	担任	*V.*	to take the position of	18
dānxīn	擔心	担心	*V.*	to worry, feel anxious	11
dànyuàn	但願	但愿	*V.*	to wish	17
dàodǐ	到底	到底	*Adv.*	at last, finally, after all (used in an interrogative sentence to indicate an attempt to get to the bottom of the matter)	11

dàolǐ	道理	道理	N.	principle, argument	16
dǎoméi	倒楣	倒霉	Adj.	unlucky	12
dàoqiàn	道歉	道歉	V.O.	to apologize	13
dǎrǎo	打擾	打扰	V.	to disturb	16
dáxiè	答謝	答谢	V.	to thank	12
děngdài	等待	等待	V.	to wait	20
dìbù	地步	地步	N.	condition	12
dīdādīdā	滴答滴答	滴答滴答		onomatopoeia (e.g. tick, tick-tock)	14
dīngdāng	叮噹	叮当		onomatopoeia (e.g. jingle (of a bell))	16
dǒng	懂	懂	V.	to understand, grasp	16
dòng shǒushù	動手術	动手术	V.O.	to have a surgical operation	11
dòngbuliǎo	動不了	动不了		cannot move	13
dǒngshì	懂事	懂事	Adj.	intelligent, sensible	16
dú	讀	读	V.	to read, attend school	16
duàn	段	段	M.W.	(measure word for section, segment)	12
duìhuà	對話	对话	N.	dialogue	14
dùn	頓	顿	M.W.	(measure word for meals or scolds)	11
duōkuī	多虧	多亏		thanks to, luckily	12
dùzi	肚子	肚子	N.	belly	11

F

fádān	罰單	罚单	N.	ticket, citation	13
fājiàn	發件	发件	V.O.	to send mail	15
fān	番	番	M.W.	(measure word for cause)	16
fǎn'ér	反而	反而	Adv.	instead, on the contrary	15
fánshì	凡是	凡是	Adv.	all, every	18
fànwǎn	飯碗	饭碗	N.	rice bowl	19
fāsòng	發送	发送	V.	to dispatch (letters, etc.)	15
fēi . . . bùkě	非……不可	非……不可		have to, must	16
fèndòu	奮鬥	奋斗	V.	to fight for	20
fēng	封	封	M.W.	(measure word for mailing letters)	14
fǔdǎo	輔導	辅导	V.	to give guidance in studying, coach	12
fúlì	福利	福利	N.	welfare, benefit	19
fùmǔ	父母	父母	N.	father and mother	11
fùxiū	副修	副修	N.	minor	18
fùzá	複雜	复杂	Adj.	complicated, complex	17

G

gǎi	改	改	V.	to change, revise	13
gǎn	敢	敢	V.	to dare	11
gǎndòng	感動	感动	V.	to move, touch (emotions)	14
gānggāng	剛剛	刚刚	Adv.	a moment ago, just now	13
gānghǎo	剛好	刚好	Adv.	it so happened that, just	11
gǎnkuài	趕快	赶快	Adv.	speedily	17
gǎnshòu	感受	感受	V.	to be affected by, experience	14
			N.	emotional feeling	
gāosù gōnglù	高速公路	高速公路	N.	highway	13
gē	歌	歌	N.	song	15
gēn . . . yǒuguān	跟......有關	跟......有关		to be related to . . . , connected with . . .	20
gèngbiéshuō	更別說	更别说		not to mention	20
gōngdú	攻讀	攻读	V.	to pursue the study of	20
gōngxǐ	恭喜	恭喜	V.	to congratulate	12
gōngzī	工資	工资	N.	salary	19
gòu	購	购	V.	to purchase	15
gōutōng	溝通	沟通	V.	to communicate	14
			N.	communication	
guà	掛	挂	V.	to hang, hang up (telephone)	13
guǎn	管	管	V.	to mind, control	11
guāngdié	光碟	光碟	N.	compact disc	15
guānxīn	關心	关心	V.	to be concerned about	11
			N.	concern	
gǔfèn	股份	股份	N.	stock	19
guòjiǎng	過獎	过奖	V.	to give undeserved compliment	16
gùrán	固然	固然	Conj.	admittedly, though of course	19

H

hài	害	害	V.	to harm, cause trouble for	12
hébì	何必	何必		there is no need	12
héhǎo	和好	和好	V.	to make up (after a fight)	15
hòuguǒ	後果	后果	N.	consequence, aftermath	12
hòuhuǐ	後悔	后悔	V.	to regret	12
huán	還	还	V.	to return	15
huánjìng	環境	环境	N.	environment, surroundings	19
huí	回	回	V.	to return, reply	11
			M.W.	(measure word for indicating the frequency of action), (measure word [spoken form] for matters)	

huīfù	恢復	恢复	V.	to recover	12
huíxiǎng	回想	回想	V.	to reflect on, recall	20
hùshì	護士	护士	N.	nurse	11

J

jì . . . yòu	既……又	既……又	Conj.	both . . . and, as well as	14
jiājiǎng	嘉獎	嘉奖	V.	to award	18
			N.	award	
jiǎnchá	檢查	检查	V.	to examine	12
			N.	checkup, examination	
jiǎng	講	讲	V.	to talk	16
jiānglái	將來	将来	N.	future	16
jiǎngzuò	講座	讲座	N.	lecture	17
jiǎnlì	簡歷	简历	N.	résumé, curriculum vitae (C.V.)	17
jiànyì	建議	建议	V.	to advise, recommend	13
			N.	advice, recommendation	
jiǎo	絞	绞	V.	to twist, entangle	15
jiāodài	交代	交代	V.	to tell, explain, make clear	13
jiàoshòu	教授	教授	N.	professor	16
jiāoshū	教書	教书	V.O.	to teach	16
jiārén	家人	家人	N.	family members	11
jiāyóu	加油	加油	V.O.	to make an extra effort, "Go! Go!"	16
jiéguǒ	結果	结果	N.	result	13
jiějué	解決	解决	V.	to solve	12
jiéshù	結束	结束	V.	to end, finish	11
jíjímángmáng	急急忙忙	急急忙忙	Adj.	in a hurry, hurriedly	14
jīn	金	金	N.	gold	19
jǐngchá	警察	警察	N.	police	13
jīngguò	經過	经过	N.	process	11
jīngjìxué	經濟學	经济学	N.	economics	16
jǐngqì	景氣	景气	Adj.	prosperous	19
jǐnguǎn	儘管	尽管	Conj.	although	18
jīngyàn	經驗	经验	N.	experience	16
jìngzhēng	競爭	竞争	V.	to compete	19
			N.	competition	
jīnhòu	今後	今后	N.	from now on; in the future	20
jīnróng	金融	金融	N.	finance	19
jìnxíng	進行	进行	V.	to be in progress	11
jǐnzhāng	緊張	紧张	Adj.	nervous	20
jìnzhǐ	禁止	禁止	V.	to prohibit, ban	13
jìrán	既然	既然	Conj.	now that	20
jíshǐ	即使	即使	Conj.	even if	20
jìshù	技術	技术	N.	technology	18

jiùhùchē	救護車	救护车	N.	ambulance	11
jiūjìng	究竟	究竟	Adv.	after all	19
jiùyè	就業	就业	N.	employment	17
jiùyè zhōngxīn	就業中心	就业中心	N.	career center	17
jíxìng	急性	急性	N.	acute	11
jìxù	繼續	继续	V.	to continue	16
jízhěnshì	急診室	急诊室	N.	emergency room	11
juéxīn	決心	决心	V.	to be determined to	16
			N.	determination, resolution	
jùjué	拒絕	拒绝	V.	to refuse, reject	17

K

kāidāo	開刀	开刀	V.O.	(spoken form) to perform or have an operation	11
kāifā	開發	开发	V.	to develop	18
kāikǒu	開口	开口	V.O.	to open one's mouth, start to talk	14
kāizhǎn	開展	开展	V.	to carry on	18
kànqí	看齊	看齐	V.	to keep up with, emulate	16
kào	靠	靠	V.	to lean against, depend on	12
kǎolǜ	考慮	考虑	V.	to consider	17, 19
			N.	consideration	19
kělián	可憐	可怜	Adj.	to be in a sorry situation	11
			V.	to feel sorry for, to take pity on	
kēxué	科學	科学	N.	science	18
kǒngpà	恐怕	恐怕	Adv.	I am afraid that . . .	17
kū	哭	哭	V.	to weep, cry	14

L

la	啦	啦	Int.	(used at the end of a sentence to indicate sighing, questioning, etc.)	12
lèiyǎnwāngwāng	淚眼汪汪	泪眼汪汪		(eyes) brimming with tears	14
lèyì	樂意	乐意	V.	to be willing to	17
lǐ	理	理	V.	to pay attention to, show interest in	14
liàngjiě	諒解	谅解	V.	to understand, make allowances for	14
liánluò	聯絡	联络	V.	to contact	15
liǎojiě	了解	了解	V.	to know, understand	18
liáotiānshì	聊天室	聊天室	N.	chat room	14
lìhai	厲害	厉害	Adj.	severe	11

lǐjiě	理解	理解	V.	to understand, comprehend	14
língjīyídòng	靈機一動	灵机一动	V.	to have a sudden inspiration	14
liúxíng	流行	流行	Adj.	prevalent, popular	15
lǐxiǎng	理想	理想	N.	ideal	20
luànpǎo	亂跑	乱跑	V.	to run around	12
lùjiān	路肩	路肩	N.	shoulder (of a road)	13
lùnwén	論文	论文	N.	research paper, thesis	18
lùyīnjī	錄音機	录音机	N.	tape recorder	15

M

mà	罵	骂	V.	to scold	11
máfan	麻煩	麻烦	Adj.	troublesome	12
			V.	to put somebody to trouble	
mángchángyán (lánwěiyán)	盲腸炎 (闌尾炎)	盲肠炎 (阑尾炎)	N.	appendicitis	11
máobǐ	毛筆	毛笔	N.	calligraphy brush	16
máobìng	毛病	毛病	N.	defect, shortcoming, trouble	14
ménlíng	門鈴	门铃	N.	doorbell	16
mēnsǐ	悶死	闷死	V.C.	to be extremely boring	12
móliàn	磨練	磨练	V.	to temper oneself	16
mùbiāo	目標	目标	N.	goal	20

N

nándào	難道	难道	Adv.	Isn't it true . . .	17
nánguò	難過	难过	Adj.	feel sorry, feel sad	14
nǎpà	哪怕	哪怕	Conj.	even if	18
nénggàn	能幹	能干	Adj.	capable	17
niánjí	年級	年级	N.	grade	16
niánxīn	年薪	年薪	N.	annual salary	19
nìngyuàn	寧願	宁愿	Conj.	would rather . . . than	19

P

pà	怕	怕	V.	to fear, be afraid of	11
pán	盤	盘	N.	tray, plate, dish	15
			M.W.	(measure word for tray-shaped items, e.g. cassette tapes)	
péi	陪	陪	V.	to accompany	13
pèifú	佩服	佩服	V.	to admire	16
pèngdào	碰到	碰到	V.C.	to run into	13
pèngyùnqi	碰運氣	碰运气		to try one's luck	13

pīli pālā	劈里啪啦	劈里啪啦	*Int.*	onomatopoeia (e.g. crackle of firecracker, burst of gunfire)	14
píngcháng	平常	平常	*Adv.*	generally, usually	14
píngjūn	平均	平均	*Adj.*	average	18
píqì	脾氣	脾气	*N.*	temperament	13
pópomāmā	婆婆媽媽	婆婆妈妈		wordy, over-elaborate	19
pūtōngpūtōng	撲通撲通	扑通扑通		onomatopoeia (e.g. flop, thump, splash, pit-a-pat)	14

Q

qiántúwúliàng	前途無量	前途无量		great expectations	16
qiānxū	謙虛	谦虚	*Adj.*	modest	19
qīdài	期待	期待	*V.*	to expect, await	16
qīngchǔ	清楚	清楚	*Adj.*	clear	14
qǐngjià	請假	请假	*V.O.*	to ask for leave	11
qíngkuàng	情況	情况	*N.*	situation	11
qiú	求	求	*V.*	to beg, seek	15
qǐxīn	起薪	起薪	*N.*	starting salary	19
què	卻	却	*Adv.*	but, yet, however	15
quèshí	確實	确实	*Adv.*	indeed, really	19
quēxí	缺席	缺席	*V.O.*	to be absent	12
			N.	absence	

R

rán'ér	然而	然而	*Conj.*	yet, but, however	15
rěnbuzhù	忍不住	忍不住	*V.*	to be unable to bear, cannot help (doing something)	14
róngqià	融洽	融洽	*Adj.*	harmonious	19
róngyì	容易	容易	*Adj.*	easy	13
ruǎnjiàn	軟件	软件	*N.*	software	18
rúcǐ	如此	如此		so, thus	12
rúhé	如何	如何	*Pron.*	how	17

S

sāichē	塞車	塞车	*N.*	traffic jam	13
shàngjìn	上進	上进	*Adj.*	to aspire to improve	16
shàngshì	上市	上市	*V.*	to go public, to list on the market	18
shàngsī	上司	上司	*N.*	boss, supervisor	19
shāngwù	商務	商务	*N.*	business	18
shāngxīn	傷心	伤心	*Adj.*	sad, aggrieved, broken-hearted	14

shǎolái	少來	少来		stop, quit it, cut it out	14
shēng	聲	声	N.	sound	13
shǐ	使	使	V.	to make, cause	13
shìchǎng	市場	市场	N.	market	19
shìfǒu	是否	是否	Conj.	whether or not, whether, if	14
shìqíng	事情	事情	N.	matter	11
shīwàng	失望	失望	Adj.	disappointed	14
shìyè	事業	事业	N.	cause, undertaking, enterprise	16
shízài	實在	实在	Adv.	indeed	14
shòubuliǎo	受不了	受不了	Adj.	not be able to bear	11
shōuhuò	收穫	收获	N.	harvest, achievement	20
shōujiàn	收件	收件	V.O.	to receive mail	15
shǒushí	守時	守时	V.	to be on time	13
shǒushùshì	手術室	手术室	N.	operating room	11
shǒuxiān	首先	首先	Adv.	first of all	17
shùmǎ xiàngjī	數碼相機	数码相机	N.	digital camera	13
(shùwèi xiàngjī)	(數位相機)	(数位相机)			
shùnbiàn	順便	顺便	Adv.	conveniently, in passing	12
shùnlì	順利	顺利	Adv.	smoothly	11
shuōshēng	說聲	说声	V.O.	to say one word	14
shuòshì	碩士	硕士	N.	master	16
sōusuǒ	搜索	搜索	V.	to search for	15
suànleba	算了吧	算了吧		let it be, just forget it	12
súhuà	俗話	俗话	N.	common saying, proverb	12
suǒxuéde	所學的	所学的	N.	what has been learned	16

T

tǎng	躺	躺	V.	to lie, recline	12
tàng	趟	趟	M.W.	(measure word for trips)	12
tántan	談談	谈谈	V.	to chat	13
tiào	跳	跳	V.	to jump, leap, bounce	14
tiáojiàn	條件	条件	N.	qualifications	17
tiāoxuǎn	挑選	挑选	V.	to choose	20
tiáozhěng	調整	调整	V.	to adjust	17
			N.	adjustment	
tiězi	帖子	帖子	N.	a brief note	15
tígōng	提供	提供	V.	to provide	18
tǐhuì	體會	体会	V.	to reflect upon	20
			N.	reflections, things one has realized/learned	
tíqǐ	提起	提起	V.	to mention	16
tōngguò	通過	通过	V.	to go through	13
tóngyàng	同樣	同样	Adj.	of the same	15
tōngzhī	通知	通知	V.	to notify, inform	11

tūchū	突出	突出	V.	to make conspicuous	17
			Adj.	outstanding	
tuī	推	推	N.	to push	11
tuìhuò	退貨	退货	V.O.	to return merchandise	13
tuījiànxìn	推薦信	推荐信	N.	recommendation letter	17
tuìxiū	退休	退休	V.	to retire	16
tuō	拖	拖	V.	to delay, pull, drag	11

W

wàn	萬	万	Num.	ten thousand	19
wàngjì	忘記	忘记	V.	to forget	17
wǎngluò	網絡	网络	N.	Internet, network	16
wǎngnián	往年	往年	N.	(in) former years	16
wánquán	完全	完全	Adv.	totally, entirely	13
wěiqū	委屈	委屈	V.	to put somebody to great inconvenience	14
			Adj.	feel wronged	
wěndìng	穩定	稳定	Adj.	stable	19
wùhuì	誤會	误会	V.	to misunderstand	14
			N.	misunderstanding	

X

xiǎng	響	响	V.	to make a sound, ring	16
xiǎngfǎ	想法	想法	N.	idea, thought	20
xiàngmù	項目	项目	N.	project (a project is called 計畫(计划) in Taiwan)	18
xiāngxìn	相信	相信	V.	to believe, to be sure	17
xiǎnshì	顯示	显示	V.	to show, display	14
xiàsǐ	嚇死	吓死	V.C.	to be scared to death	11
xiàzǎi	下載	下载	V.	to download	17
xiědào	寫道	写道	V.	to write	14
xiěfǎ	寫法	写法	N.	style of writing, format	17
xīlìxīlì	淅瀝淅瀝	淅沥淅沥		onomatopoeia (e.g. the patter of rain, water)	14
xīngfèn	興奮	兴奋	Adj.	excited	20
xìngyùn	幸運	幸运	Adj.	lucky	19
xìngzhì	性質	性质	N.	characteristic, quality, nature	17
xīnqíng	心情	心情	N.	mood	13
xīnshì	心事	心事	N.	something weighing on one's mind	13
xìnxī	信息	信息	N.	information, message	17

xiū (kè)	修(課)	修(课)	V.	to study, take (a class)	19
xiūgǎi	修改	修改	V.	to revise	17
			N.	revision	
xiūyǎng	休養	休养	V.	to recuperate	11
xuéfèi	學費	学费	N.	tuition	19
xuéshēnghuì	學生會	学生会	N.	student committee	18
xuéwèi	學位	学位	N.	academic degree	18
xuéwèn	學問	学问	N.	knowledge, scholarship	16

Y

yāoqiú	要求	要求	V.	to require	17
			N.	requirement	
yèwù	業務	业务	N.	business	18
yǐ . . . wéiróng	以……為榮	以……为荣		to be proud of	16
yīliáo	醫療	医疗	N.	medical treatment	19
yǐmiǎn	以免	以免	Conj.	lest, so that . . . not	20
yīncǐ	因此	因此	Conj.	therefore	12
yǐngxiǎng	影響	影响	V.	to influence	18
			N.	influence	
yìngyòng	應用	应用	V.	to apply	16
			N.	application	
yīnyuèhuì	音樂會	音乐会	N.	concert	14
yǐwéi	以為	以为	V.	to think, consider	11
yǐxià	以下	以下	N.	below, the following	14
yònggōng	用功	用功	Adj.	hard-working, studious	16
yònglì	用力	用力	V.O.	to exert one's strength	15
yòu	又	又	Adv.	again	13
yóuyú	由於	由于	Conj.	due to, because of	12
yóuyù	猶豫	犹豫	V.	to hesitate	19
yǒuxiàn	有限	有限	Adj.	limited	17
yǒuyì	友誼	友谊	N.	friendship	12
yù	遇	遇	V.	to meet with	15
yuángōng	員工	员工	N.	employee	18
yuánliàng	原諒	原谅	V.	to excuse, forgive	13
			N.	forgiveness	
yuèfèn	月份	月份	N.	(a certain) month	18
yǔqí . . . bùrú	與其……不如……	与其……不如……	Conj.	rather than	20

Z

zàihu	在乎	在乎	V.	to care about, mind	14
zāo	糟	糟	Adj.	in a terrible state, chaotic	12
zǎorìkāngfù	早日康復	早日康复		get well soon, speedy recovery	11

zěnmegǎode	怎麼搞的	怎么搞的		what's wrong, what's the matter	13
zhàogu	照顧	照顾	V.	to look after, give consideration to	11
zháojí	著急	着急	V.	to worry, feel anxious	14
zhāopìn	招聘	招聘	V.	to hire	17
zhèngmíng	證明	证明	V.	to prove, certify	12
			N.	proof, certificate	
zhěngtiān	整天	整天	N.	the whole day	12
zhǐhǎo	只好	只好	Adv.	have to (no choice)	12
zhíjiē	直接	直接	Adv.	directly	17
zhīyī	之一	之一		one of	18
zhìyú	至於	至于	Prep.	as for, as to	12
zhòngdiǎn	重點	重点	N.	focus, major point	17
zhōngxīn	中心	中心	N.	center	17
zhǔ	煮	煮	V.	to cook	12
zhuàn	賺	赚	V.	to earn or make (money)	19
zhuānxīn	專心	专心	V.	to concentrate on	13
zhuānyè	專業	专业	N.	major subject	18
zhuāzhù	抓住	抓住	V.C.	to catch	13
zhùhè	祝賀	祝贺	V.	to congratulate	19
			N.	congratulations	
zhǔnshí	準時	准时	Adj.	on time	14
zhǔrèn	主任	主任	N.	director	18
zhǔtí	主題	主题	N.	subject	15
zhǔxí	主席	主席	N.	chairman	18
zhǔxiū	主修	主修	N.	major	18
zhùyuàn	住院	住院	V.O.	to be hospitalized	11
zìcóng	自從	自从	Prep.	since	14
zīxún	咨詢	咨询	V.	to consult	18
			N.	consultation	
zǐzǐxìxì	仔仔細細	仔仔细细	Adj.	very carefully	17
zǒngzhī	總之	总之	Conj.	in a word, in short, in brief	15
zuǒyòu	左右	左右		more or less	18
zǔzhī	組織	组织	V.	to organize	18
			N.	organization	

英文索引 (英文索引) ENGLISH GLOSSARY

Each entry lists the English meaning, traditional character, simplified character, Pinyin, part of speech, and lesson number.

A

a moment ago, just now	剛剛	刚刚	gānggāng	*Adv.*	13
absence	缺席	缺席	quēxí	*N.*	12
absent	缺席	缺席	quēxí	*V.O.*	12
academic degree	學位	学位	xuéwèi	*N.*	18
accident (to have one), meet with a mishap	出事	出事	chūshì	*V.O.*	14
accompany	陪	陪	péi	*V.*	13
acute	急性	急性	jíxìng	*N.*	11
adjust	調整	调整	tiáozhěng	*V.*	17
adjustment	調整	调整	tiáozhěng	*N.*	17
admire	佩服	佩服	pèifú	*V.*	16
admittedly, though of course	固然	固然	gùrán	*Conj.*	19
adversity, misfortune	不幸	不幸	búxìng	*N.*	12
advice, recommendation	建議	建议	jiànyì	*N.*	13
advise, recommend	建議	建议	jiànyì	*V.*	13
affected by, experience	感受	感受	gǎnshòu	*V.*	14
after all	究竟	究竟	jiūjìng	*Adv.*	19
again	又	又	yòu	*Adv.*	13
ah!, gosh!, oh dear!	哎呀	哎呀	āiya	*Int.*	12
all, every	凡是	凡是	fánshì	*Adv.*	18
all over	遍	遍	biàn	*Adj.*	15
allowance	補貼	补贴	bǔtiē	*N.*	19
although	儘管	尽管	jǐnguǎn	*Conj.*	18
amateur, enthusiast, fan	愛好者	爱好者	àihàozhě	*N.*	15
ambulance	救護車	救护车	jiùhùchē	*N.*	11
annual salary	年薪	年薪	niánxīn	*N.*	19
apologize	道歉	道歉	dàoqiàn	*V.O.*	13
appendicitis	盲腸炎 (闌尾炎)	盲肠炎 (阑尾炎)	mángchángyán (lánwěiyán)	*N.*	11
application	應用	应用	yìngyòng	*N.*	16
apply	應用	应用	yìngyòng	*V.*	16
arrange	安排	安排	ānpái	*V.*	17
arrangement	安排	安排	ānpái	*N.*	17
as for, as to	至於	至于	zhìyú	*Prep.*	12
ask for leave	請假	请假	qǐngjià	*V.O.*	11
aspire, improve	上進	上进	shàngjìn	*Adj.*	16

at last, finally, after all (used in an interrogative sentence to indicate an attempt to get to the bottom of the matter)	到底	到底	dàodǐ	*Adv.*	11
attend school, read	讀	读	dú	*V.*	16
avail oneself of	趁	趁	chèn	*Prep.*	16
average	平均	平均	píngjūn	*Adj.*	18
award	嘉獎	嘉奖	jiājiǎng	*N.*	18
award	嘉獎	嘉奖	jiājiǎng	*V.*	18
away from home	出門在外	出门在外	chūménzàiwài		12

B

beg, seek	求	求	qiú	*V.*	15
believe, to be sure	相信	相信	xiāngxìn	*V.*	17
belly	肚子	肚子	dùzi	*N.*	11
below, the following	以下	以下	yǐxià	*N.*	14
besides, except (for)	除了……以外	除了……以外	chúle . . . yǐwài	*Conj.*	18
bored, extremely so	悶死	闷死	mēnsǐ	*V.C.*	12
boss, supervisor	上司	上司	shàngsī	*N.*	19
both . . . and, as well as	既……又……	既……又……	jì . . . yòu . . .	*Conj.*	14
brief note	帖子	帖子	tiězi	*N.*	15
business	商務	商务	shāngwù	*N.*	18
business	業務	业务	yèwù	*N.*	18
but, yet, however	卻	却	què	*Adv.*	15
but, yet, however	然而	然而	rán'ér	*Conj.*	15

C

calligraphy brush	毛筆	毛笔	máobǐ	*N.*	16
cannot bear to think about it	不堪設想	不堪设想	bùkānshèxiǎng		12
cannot move	動不了	动不了	dòngbuliǎo		13
capable	能幹	能干	nénggàn	*Adj.*	17
car accident	車禍	车祸	chēhuò	*N.*	13
care about, mind	在乎	在乎	zàihu	*V.*	14
career center	就業中心	就业中心	jiùyè zhōngxīn	*N.*	17
carry on	開展	开展	kāizhǎn	*V.*	18
catch	抓住	抓住	zhuāzhù	*V.C.*	13
cause (measure word)	番	番	fān	*M.W.*	16
cause, undertaking, enterprise	事業	事业	shìyè	*N.*	16
center	中心	中心	zhōngxīn	*N.*	17
chairman	主席	主席	zhǔxí	*N.*	18
change, revise	改	改	gǎi	*V.*	13

characteristic, quality, nature	性質	性质	xìngzhì	N.	17
chat	談談	谈谈	tántan	V.	13
chat room	聊天室	聊天室	liáotiānshì	N.	14
check, examine	檢查	检查	jiǎnchá	V.	12
choose	挑選	挑选	tiāoxuǎn	V.	20
clear	清楚	清楚	qīngchǔ	Adj.	14
common saying, proverb	俗話	俗话	súhuà	N.	12
communicate	溝通	沟通	gōutōng	V.	14
communication	溝通	沟通	gōutōng	N.	14
compact disc	光碟	光碟	guāngdié	N.	15
compensate	補貼	补贴	bǔtiē	V.	19
compete	競爭	竞争	jìngzhēng	V.	19
competition	競爭	竞争	jìngzhēng	N.	19
complain	抱怨	抱怨	bàoyuàn	V.	13
complicated, complex	複雜	复杂	fùzá	Adj.	17
concentrate on	專心	专心	zhuānxīn	V.	13
concern	關心	关心	guānxīn	N.	11
concerned about	關心	关心	guānxīn	V.	11
concert	音樂會	音乐会	yīnyuèhuì	N.	14
condition	地步	地步	dìbù	N.	12
congratulate	恭喜	恭喜	gōngxǐ	V.	12
congratulate	祝賀	祝贺	zhùhè	V.	19
congratulations	祝賀	祝贺	zhùhè	N.	19
consequence, aftermath	後果	后果	hòuguǒ	N.	12
consider	考慮	考虑	kǎolù	V.	17, 19
consideration	考慮	考虑	kǎolù	N.	19
consult	咨詢	咨询	zīxún	V.	18
consultation	咨詢	咨询	zīxún	N.	18
contact	聯絡	联络	liánluò	V.	15
continue	繼續	继续	jìxù	V.	16
control, mind	管	管	guǎn	V.	11
conveniently, in passing	順便	顺便	shùnbiàn	Adv.	12
cook	煮	煮	zhǔ	V.	12
crackle of firecracker, burst of gunfire (onomatopoeia word)	劈里啪啦	劈里啪啦	pīli pālā	Int.	14

D

dare	敢	敢	gǎn	V.	11
determined to	決心	决心	juéxīn	V.	16
defect, shortcoming, trouble	毛病	毛病	máobìng	N.	14
delay, pull, drag	拖	拖	tuō	V.	11
determination, resolution	決心	决心	juéxīn	N.	16
develop	開發	开发	kāifā	V.	18

dialogue	對話	对话	duìhuà	N.	14
digital camera	數碼相機 (數位相機)	数码相机 (数位相机)	shùmǎ xiàngjī (shùwèi xiàngjī)	N.	13
directly	直接	直接	zhíjiē	Adv.	17
director	主任	主任	zhǔrèn	N.	18
discharged from the hospital	出院	出院	chūyuàn	V.O.	12
dispatch (letters, etc.)	發送	发送	fāsòng	V.	15
disappointed	失望	失望	shīwàng	Adj.	14
disturb	打擾	打扰	dǎrǎo	V.	16
doorbell	門鈴	门铃	ménlíng	N.	16
download	下載	下载	xiàzǎi	V.	17
due to, because of	由於	由于	yóuyú	Conj.	12

E

earn or make (money)	賺	赚	zhuàn	V.	19
easy	容易	容易	róngyì	Adj.	13
economics	經濟學	经济学	jīngjìxué	N.	16
emergency room	急診室	急诊室	jízhěnshì	N.	11
emotional feeling	感受	感受	gǎnshòu	N.	14
employee	員工	员工	yuángōng	N.	18
employment	就業	就业	jiùyè	N.	17
end, finish	結束	结束	jiéshù	V.	11
engage in business	從商	从商	cóngshāng	V.	18
environment, surroundings	環境	环境	huánjìng	N.	19
even if	即使	即使	jíshǐ	Conj.	20
even if	哪怕	哪怕	nǎpà	Conj.	18
examine	檢查	检查	jiǎnchá	V.	12
examination, checkup	檢查	检查	jiǎnchá	N.	12
excited	興奮	兴奋	xīngfèn	Adj.	20
excuse, forgive	原諒	原谅	yuánliàng	V.	13
exert one's strength	用力	用力	yònglì	V.O.	15
exit	出口	出口	chūkǒu	N.	13
expect, await	期待	期待	qīdài	V.	16
experience	經驗	经验	jīngyàn	N.	16
(eyes) brimming with tears	淚眼汪汪	泪眼汪汪	lèiyǎnwāngwāng		14

F

family members	家人	家人	jiārén	N.	11
father and mother	父母	父母	fùmǔ	N.	11
fear, be afraid of	怕	怕	pà	V.	11
feel sorry, feel sad	難過	难过	nánguò	Adj.	14

feel wronged	委屈	委屈	wěiqū	*Adj.*	14
fight for	奮鬥	奋斗	fèndòu	*V.*	20
finance	金融	金融	jīnróng	*N.*	19
first of all	首先	首先	shǒuxiān	*Adv.*	17
flop, thump, splash, pit-a-pat (onomatopoeia word)	撲通撲通	扑通扑通	pūtōngpūtōng		14
focus, major point	重點	重点	zhòngdiǎn	*N.*	17
force	逼	逼	bī	*V.*	13
forget	忘記	忘记	wàngjì	*V.*	17
forgiveness	原諒	原谅	yuánliàng	*N.*	13
form	表格	表格	biǎogé	*N.*	17
frequency of action; matters (spoken form)	回	回	huí	*M.W.*	11
friendship	友誼	友谊	yǒuyì	*N.*	12
from now on; in the future	今後	今后	jīnhòu	*N.*	20
future	將來	将来	jiānglái	*N.*	16

G

generally, usually	平常	平常	píngcháng	*Adv.*	14
get well soon, speedy recovery	早日康復	早日康复	zǎorìkāngfù		11
give advice	參謀	参谋	cānmóu	*V.*	20
give guidance in studying, coach	輔導	辅导	fǔdǎo	*V.*	12
go on a business trip	出差	出差	chūchāi	*V.O.*	18
go public, to list on the market	上市	上市	shàngshì	*V.*	18
go through	通過	通过	tōngguò	*V.*	13
goal	目標	目标	mùbiāo	*N.*	20
gold	金	金	jīn	*N.*	19
grade	年級	年级	niánjí	*N.*	16
grade, score, result, success	成績	成绩	chéngjì/chéngjī	*N.*	18
great expectations	前途無量	前途无量	qiántúwúliàng		16

H

hard-working, studious	用功	用功	yònggōng	*Adj.*	16
harmonious	融洽	融洽	róngqià	*Adj.*	19
hang up (telephone)	掛	挂	guà	*V.*	13
harm, cause trouble for	害	害	hài	*V.*	12
harvest, achievement	收穫	收获	shōuhuò	*N.*	20
have a sudden inspiration	靈機一動	灵机一动	língjīyídòng	*V.*	14
have a surgical operation	動手術	动手术	dòng shǒushù	*V.O.*	11

have to (no choice)	只好	只好	zhǐhǎo	Adv.	12
have to, must	非……不可	非……不可	fēi … bùkě		16
help	幫助	帮助	bāngzhù	N.	12
help	幫助	帮助	bāngzhù	V.	12
hesitate	猶豫	犹豫	yóuyù	V.	19
highway	高速公路	高速公路	gāosù gōnglù	N.	13
hire	招聘	招聘	zhāopìn	V.	17
hospitalized	住院	住院	zhùyuàn	V.O.	11
how	如何	如何	rúhé	Pron.	17
however, yet, but	然而	然而	rán'ér	Conj.	15

I

I am afraid that . . .	恐怕	恐怕	kǒngpà	Adv.	17
idea, thought	想法	想法	xiǎngfǎ	N.	20
ideal	理想	理想	lǐxiǎng	N.	20
improve	上進	上进	shàngjìn	Adj.	16
in a hurry	匆匆忙忙	匆匆忙忙	cōngcōng mángmáng	Adv.	13
in a hurry, hurriedly	急急忙忙	急急忙忙	jíjímángmáng	Adj.	14
in a terrible state, chaotic	糟	糟	zāo	Adj.	12
in a word, in short, in brief	總之	总之	zǒngzhī	Conj.	15
(in) former years	往年	往年	wǎngnián	N.	16
in progress	進行	进行	jìnxíng	V.	11
in the first place, originally	當初	当初	dāngchū		12
include, comprise	包括	包括	bāokuò	V.	16
indeed	實在	实在	shízài	Adv.	14
indeed, really	確實	确实	quèshí	Adv.	19
influence	影響	影响	yǐngxiǎng	N.	18
influence	影響	影响	yǐngxiǎng	V.	18
information, message	信息	信息	xìnxī	N.	17
instead, on the contrary	反而	反而	fǎn'ér	Adv.	15
insurance	保險	保险	bǎoxiǎn	N.	12
intelligent, sensible	懂事	懂事	dǒngshì	Adj.	16
Internet, network	網絡	网络	wǎngluò	N.	16
Isn't it true . . .	難道	难道	nándào	Adv.	17
it doesn't matter, it's not serious	不要緊	不要紧	búyàojǐn		11
it so happened that, just	剛好	刚好	gānghǎo	Adv.	11

J

| jingle (of a bell) (onomatopoeia word) | 叮噹 | 叮当 | dīngdāng | | 16 |
| jump, leap, bounce | 跳 | 跳 | tiào | V. | 14 |

K

keep up with, emulate	看齊	看齐	kànqí	*V.*	16
know, understand	了解	了解	liǎojiě	*V.*	18
knowledge, scholarship	學問	学问	xuéwèn	*N.*	16

L

large quantity	大量	大量	dàliàng	*N.*	18
late	遲到	迟到	chídào	*V.*	13
lean against, depend on	靠	靠	kào	*V.*	12
lecture	講座	讲座	jiǎngzuò	*N.*	17
lest, so that . . . not	以免	以免	yǐmiǎn	*Conj.*	20
let it be, just forget it	算了吧	算了吧	suànleba		12
letters (measure word)	封	封	fēng	*M.W.*	14
lie, recline	躺	躺	tǎng	*V.*	12
limited	有限	有限	yǒuxiàn	*Adj.*	17
look after, give consideration to	照顧	照顾	zhàogu	*V.*	11
lucky	幸運	幸运	xìngyùn	*Adj.*	19

M

(magnetic) tape	磁帶	磁带	cídài	*N.*	15
major	主修	主修	zhǔxiū	*N.*	18
major subject	專業	专业	zhuānyè	*N.*	18
make a sound, ring	響	响	xiǎng	*V.*	16
make an extra effort, "Go! Go!"	加油	加油	jiāyóu	*V.O.*	16
make conspicuous	突出	突出	tūchū	*V.*	17
make, cause	使	使	shǐ	*V.*	13
make up (after a fight)	和好	和好	héhǎo	*V.*	15
make-up test	補考	补考	bǔkǎo	*N.*	12
market	市場	市场	shìchǎng	*N.*	19
master	碩士	硕士	shuòshì	*N.*	16
matter	事情	事情	shìqíng	*N.*	11
matters (spoken form); frequency of action (measure word)	回	回	huí	*M.W.*	11
meals or scolds (measure word)	頓	顿	dùn	*M.W.*	11
medical treatment	醫療	医疗	yīliáo	*N.*	19
meet with	遇	遇	yù	*V.*	15
meet with a mishap, have an accident	出事	出事	chūshì	*V.O.*	14

mention	提起	提起	tíqǐ	V.	16
military advisor	參謀	参谋	cānmóu	N.	20
mind, control	管	管	guǎn	V.	11
minor	副修	副修	fùxiū	N.	18
misunderstand	誤會	误会	wùhuì	V.	14
misunderstanding	誤會	误会	wùhuì	N.	14
modest	謙虛	谦虚	qiānxū	Adj.	19
month (a certain)	月份	月份	yuèfèn	N.	18
mood	心情	心情	xīnqíng	N.	13
more or less	左右	左右	zuǒyòu		18
move, touch (emotions)	感動	感动	gǎndòng	V.	14

N

nervous	緊張	紧张	jǐnzhāng	Adj.	20
not be able to bear	受不了	受不了	shòubuliǎo	Adj.	11
not to mention	更別説	更别说	gèngbiéshuō		20
notify, inform	通知	通知	tōngzhī	V.	11
now that	既然	既然	jìrán	Conj.	20
nurse	護士	护士	hùshì	N.	11

O

of the same	同樣	同样	tóngyàng	Adj.	15
on time	準時	准时	zhǔnshí	Adj.	14
on time	守時	守时	shǒushí	V.	13
once	曾經	曾经	céngjīng	Adv.	18
one of	之一	之一	zhīyī		18
open one's mouth, start to talk	開口	开口	kāikǒu	V.O.	14
operating room	手術室	手术室	shǒushùshì	N.	11
or else, otherwise, if not	不然	不然	bùrán	Conj.	12
organize	組織	组织	zǔzhī	V.	18
organization	組織	组织	zǔzhī	N.	18
outstanding	突出	突出	tūchū	Adj.	17

P

passive sentence preposition (introduces agent)	被	被	bèi	Prep.	11
patter of rain, water (onomatopoeia word)	淅瀝淅瀝	淅沥淅沥	xīlìxīlì		14
pay attention to, show interest in	理	理	lǐ	V.	14

perform or have an operation (spoken form)	開刀	开刀	kāidāo	V.O.	11
(take) pity on, feel sorry for	可憐	可怜	kělián	V.	11
pledge, guarantee, assure	保證	保证	bǎozhèng	V.	14
police	警察	警察	jǐngchá	N.	13
precious	寶貴	宝贵	bǎoguì	Adj.	16
prevalent, popular	流行	流行	liúxíng	Adj.	15
principle, argument	道理	道理	dàolǐ	N.	16
process	經過	经过	jīngguò	N.	11
professor	教授	教授	jiàoshòu	N.	16
prohibit, ban	禁止	禁止	jìnzhǐ	V.	13
project (a project is called 計畫(计划) in Taiwan)	項目	项目	xiàngmù	N.	18
proof, certificate	證明	证明	zhèngmíng	N.	12
prosperous	景氣	景气	jǐngqì	Adj.	19
proud of	以......為榮	以......为荣	yǐ . . . wéiróng		16
prove, certify	證明	证明	zhèngmíng	V.	12
provide	提供	提供	tígōng	V.	18
purchase	購	购	gòu	V.	15
pursue the study of	攻讀	攻读	gōngdú	V.	20
push	推	推	tuī	N.	11
put someone to great inconvenience	委屈	委屈	wěiqū	V.	14

Q

qualifications	條件	条件	tiáojiàn	N.	17
quarrel	吵架	吵架	chǎojià	V.O.	13
questioning (used at the end of a sentence)	啦	啦	la	Int.	12
quilt	被	被	bèi	N.	11

R

rather than	與其...... 不如......	与其...... 不如......	yúqí . . . bùrú	Conj.	20
read, attend school	讀	读	dú	V.	16
receive mail	收件	收件	shōujiàn	V.O.	15
recommendation letter	推薦信	推荐信	tuījiànxìn	N.	17
recover	恢復	恢复	huīfù	V.	12
recuperate	休養	休养	xiūyǎng	V.	11
reflect on, recall	回想	回想	huíxiǎng	V.	20
reflect upon	體會	体会	tǐhuì	V.	20

reflections, things one has realized/learned	體會	体会	tǐhuì	N.	20
refuse, reject	拒絕	拒绝	jùjué	V.	17
regard as, treat as	當	当	dàng	V.	16
regret	後悔	后悔	hòuhuǐ	V.	12
related to . . . , connected with . . .	跟……有關	跟……有关	gēn . . . yǒuguān		20
reply, return	回	回	huí	V.	11
require	要求	要求	yāoqiū	V.	17
requirement	要求	要求	yāoqiū	N.	17
research paper, thesis	論文	论文	lùnwén	N.	18
result	結果	结果	jiéguǒ	N.	13
résumé, curriculum vitae (C.V.)	簡歷	简历	jiǎnlì	N.	17
retire	退休	退休	tuìxiū	V.	16
return	還	还	huán	V.	15
return merchandise	退貨	退货	tuìhuò	V.O.	13
return, reply	回	回	huí	V.	11
revise	修改	修改	xiūgǎi	V.	17
revision	修改	修改	xiūgǎi	N.	17
rice bowl	飯碗	饭碗	fànwǎn	N.	19
ring, make a sound	響	响	xiǎng	V.	16
run around	亂跑	乱跑	luànpǎo	V.	12
run into	碰到	碰到	pèngdào	V.C.	13

S

sad, aggrieved, broken-hearted	傷心	伤心	shāngxīn	Adj.	14
safety and danger, safety	安危	安危	ānwēi	N.	14
salary	工資	工资	gōngzī	N.	19
salary and benefits	待遇	待遇	dàiyù	N.	19
say one word	說聲	说声	shuōshēng	V.O.	14
scared to death	嚇死	吓死	xiàsǐ	V.C.	11
science	科學	科学	kēxué	N.	18
scold	罵	骂	mà	V.	11
(a) scolding (measure word)	頓	顿	dùn	M.W.	11
search for	搜索	搜索	sōusuǒ	V.	15
section, segment (measure word)	段	段	duàn	M.W.	12
send mail	發件	发件	fājiàn	V.O.	15
sense of achievement	成就感	成就感	chéngjiùgǎn	N.	16
severe	厲害	厉害	lìhai	Adj.	11
shoulder (of a road)	路肩	路肩	lùjiān	N.	13
show, display	顯示	显示	xiǎnshì	V.	14
sigh of sadness or regret	唉	唉	ài	Int.	11

sighing (used at end of a sentence)	啦	啦	la	*Int.*	12
since	自從	自从	zìcóng	*Prep.*	14
situation	情況	情况	qíngkuàng	*N.*	11
smart	聰明	聪明	cōngmíng	*Adj.*	17
smoothly	順利	顺利	shùnlì	*Adv.*	11
so, thus	如此	如此	rúcǐ		12
software	軟件	软件	ruǎnjiàn	*N.*	18
solve	解決	解决	jiějué	*V.*	12
something weighing on one's mind	心事	心事	xīnshì	*N.*	13
song	歌	歌	gē	*N.*	15
(be in a) sorry situation	可憐	可怜	kělián	*Adj.*	11
sound	聲	声	shēng	*N.*	13
speedily	趕快	赶快	gǎnkuài	*Adv.*	17
stable	穩定	稳定	wěndìng	*Adj.*	19
starting salary	起薪	起薪	qǐxīn	*N.*	19
stay	待	待	dāi	*V.*	12
stock	股份	股份	gǔfèn	*N.*	19
stop, quit it, cut it out	少來	少来	shǎolái		14
student committee	學生會	学生会	xuéshēnghuì	*N.*	18
study, take (a class)	修(課)	修(课)	xiū (kè)	*V.*	19
subject	主題	主题	zhǔtí	*N.*	15
suffer losses, come to grief	吃虧	吃亏	chīkuī	*V.O.*	13

T

take the position of	擔任	担任	dānrèn	*V.*	18
talk	講	讲	jiǎng	*V.*	16
tape recorder	錄音機	录音机	lùyīnjī	*N.*	15
teach	教書	教书	jiāoshū	*V.O.*	16
technology	技術	技术	jìshù	*N.*	18
tell, explain, make clear	交代	交代	jiāodài	*V.*	13
tell you the truth, (瞞 to hide the truth from)	不瞞你說	不瞞你说	bùmánnǐshuō		14
temper oneself	磨練	磨练	móliàn	*V.*	16
temperament	脾氣	脾气	píqì	*N.*	13
ten thousand	萬	万	wàn	*Num.*	19
thank	答謝	答谢	dáxiè	*V.*	12
thanks to, luckily	多虧	多亏	duōkuī		12
then, at that time	當時	当时	dāngshí	*Adv.*	20
there is no need	何必	何必	hébì		12
therefore	因此	因此	yīncǐ	*Conj.*	12
think, consider	以為	以为	yǐwéi	*V.*	11

tick, ticktock (onomatopoeia word)	滴答滴答	滴答滴答	dīdādīdā		14
ticket, citation	罰單	罚单	fádān	N.	13
totally, entirely	完全	完全	wánquán	Adv.	13
traffic jam	塞車	塞车	sāichē	N.	13
tray, plate, dish	盤	盘	pán	N.	15
tray-shaped items, e.g., cassette tapes (measure word)	盤	盘	pán	M.W.	15
trips (measure word)	趟	趟	tàng	M.W.	12
trouble someone	麻煩	麻烦	máfan	V.	12
troublesome	麻煩	麻烦	máfan	Adj.	12
try one's luck	碰運氣	碰运气	pèngyùnqi		13
tuition	學費	学费	xuéfèi	N.	19
twist, entangle	絞	绞	jiǎo	V.	15

U

unable to bear, cannot help (doing something)	忍不住	忍不住	rěnbuzhù	V.	14
understand, comprehend	理解	理解	lǐjiě	V.	14
understand, grasp	懂	懂	dǒng	V.	16
understand, make allowances for	諒解	谅解	liàngjiě	V.	14
to give undeserved compliment	過獎	过奖	guòjiǎng	V.	16
unlucky	倒楣	倒霉	dǎoméi	Adj.	12
urge	催	催	cuī	V.	13

V

very carefully	仔仔細細	仔仔细细	zǐzǐxìxì	Adj.	17

W

wait	等待	等待	děngdài	V.	20
ward (of a hospital)	病房	病房	bìngfáng	N.	11
way one acts with others and conducts oneself in public	待人處世	待人处世	dàirénchǔshì		16
weep, cry	哭	哭	kū	V.	14
welfare, benefit	福利	福利	fúlì	N.	19
what has been learned	所學的	所学的	suǒxuéde	N.	16
what's wrong, what's the matter	怎麼搞的	怎么搞的	zěnmegǎode		13

whether or not, whether, if	是否	是否	shìfǒu	*Conj.*	14
whole day	整天	整天	zhěngtiān	*N.*	12
willing to	樂意	乐意	lèyì	*V.*	17
wish	但願	但愿	dànyuàn	*V.*	17
wordy, over-elaborate	婆婆媽媽	婆婆妈妈	pópomāmā		19
worry, feel anxious	著急	着急	zháojí	*V.*	14
worry, feel anxious	擔心	担心	dānxīn	*V.*	11
would rather . . . than	寧願	宁愿	nìngyuàn	*Conj.*	19
write	寫道	写道	xiědào	*V.*	14
writing, format	寫法	写法	xiěfǎ	*N.*	17

Y

| yet, but, however | 然而 | 然而 | rán'ér | *Conj.* | 15 |

寫字簿的生字 (写字簿的生字)
CHARACTERS IN THE CHARACTER BOOK

The following list shows the 263 characters that appear in the Character Book, grouped by the lesson in which they are first introduced. Students are required to memorize how to read and write these key characters to build up their literacy skills. The items and number of new characters introduced in each lesson are carefully selected and controlled, and are provided in the list.

繁體字版 Traditional Character Version

(11) 第十一課　關心他人 (36 characters)
被 顧 底 唉 肚 管 拖 厲 害 剛 況 救 護 急 診 性 盲 腸 炎 術 嚇 擔 順 士 推
養 通 怕 敢 結 束 緊 罵 頓 憐 父

(12) 第十二課　感謝和感激 (37 characters)
由 解 答 煮 恭 恢 啦 段 亂 跑 待 躺 悶 此 何 初 檢 哎 悔 廚 糟 幸 堪 設 趙
麻 煩 險 缺 席 輔 補 至 楣 俗 靠 誼

(13) 第十三課　生氣 (36 characters)
催 吵 架 談 建 議 搞 又 退 貨 陪 專 速 禍 塞 禁 止 使 匆 逼 肩 警 察 抓 罰
遲 聲 抱 怨 守 脾 容 易 改 歡 諒

(14) 第十四課　散文和詩情表達 (28 characters)
撲 跳 封 顯 示 聊 否 淅 瀝 溝 滴 忍 傷 失 哭 委 屈 淚 汪 危 既 瞞 清 楚 劈
啪 毛 音

(15) 第十五課　音樂一復習 (18 characters)
求 磁 聯 絡 卻 遇 錄 絞 力 反 遍 碟 歌 流 搜 索 購 帖

(16) 第十六課　讚美與客套 (30 characters)
級 趁 叮 噹 鈴 響 提 括 世 寶 懂 佩 齊 繼 續 讀 濟 碩 授 將 途 無 量 獎 講
驗 磨 番 油 擾

(17) 第十七課　申請工作 (22 characters)
簡 複 雜 首 質 調 突 拒 絕 仔 細 修 招 聘 格 薦 恐 限 慮 聰 幹 願

(18) 第十八課　面談 (20 characters)
任 科 份 咨 詢 軟 供 儘 除 副 均 績 曾 嘉 組 織 凡 項 目 論

(19) 第十九課　選擇工作 (25 characters)
寧 融 競 爭 賀 謙 虛 資 穩 薪 萬 股 婆 竟 療 貼 福 猶 豫 固 環 境 確 洽 賺

(20) 第二十課　畢業以後–復習 (11 characters)
與 即 奮 挑 選 謀 免 獲 鬥 標 攻

简体字版 Simplified Character Version

(11) 第十一课　关心他人 (36 characters)
被 顾 底 唉 肚 管 拖 厉 害 刚 况 救 护 急 诊 性 盲 肠 炎 术 吓 担 顺 士 推
养 通 怕 敢 结 束 紧 骂 顿 怜 父

(12) 第十二课　感谢和感激 (37 characters)
由 解 答 煮 恭 恢 啦 段 乱 跑 待 躺 闷 此 何 初 检 哎 悔 亏 糟 幸 堪 设 趟
麻 烦 险 缺 席 辅 补 至 霉 俗 靠 谊

(13) 第十三课　生气 (36 characters)
催 吵 架 谈 建 议 搞 又 退 货 陪 专 速 祸 塞 禁 止 使 匆 逼 肩 警 察 抓 罚
迟 声 抱 怨 守 脾 容 易 改 歉 谅

(14) 第十四课　散文和诗情表达 (28 characters)
扑 跳 封 显 示 聊 否 淅 沥 沟 滴 忍 伤 失 哭 委 屈 泪 汪 危 既 瞒 清 楚 劈
啪 毛 音

(15) 第十五课　音乐–复习 (18 characters)
求 磁 联 络 却 遇 录 绞 力 反 遍 碟 歌 流 搜 索 购 帖

(16) 第十六课　赞美与客套 (30 characters)
级 趁 叮 当 铃 响 提 括 世 宝 懂 佩 齐 继 续 读 济 硕 授 将 途 无 量 奖 讲
验 磨 番 油 扰

(17) 第十七课　申请工作 (22 characters)
简 复 杂 首 质 调 突 拒 绝 仔 细 修 招 聘 格 荐 恐 限 虑 聪 干 愿

(18) 第十八课　面谈 (20 characters)
任 科 份 咨 询 软 供 尽 除 副 均 绩 曾 嘉 组 织 凡 项 目 论

(19) 第十九课　选择工作 (25 characters)
宁 融 竞 争 贺 谦 虚 资 稳 薪 万 股 婆 竟 疗 贴 福 犹 豫 固 环 境 确 洽 赚

(20) 第二十课　毕业以后—复习 (11 characters)
与 即 奋 挑 选 谋 免 获 斗 标 攻